CACICAS

Retrato de Sebastiana Ynés Josefa de San Agustín. India cacique (1757), oil painting, New Spain (present-day Mexico). Franz Mayer Museum.

Cacicas

THE INDIGENOUS WOMEN LEADERS
OF SPANISH AMERICA, 1492–1825

Edited by

MARGARITA R. OCHOA AND
SARA VICUÑA GUENGERICH

UNIVERSITY OF OKLAHOMA PRESS : NORMAN

This book is published with the generous assistance of the McCasland Foundation, Duncan, Oklahoma.

Library of Congress Cataloging-in-Publication Data

Names: Ochoa, Margarita R., editor. | Guengerich, Sara V., 1975– editor.
Title: Cacicas : the indigenous women leaders of Spanish America, 1492–1825 / Edited by
    Margarita R. Ochoa and Sara V. Guengerich.
Description: Norman : University of Oklahoma Press, [2021] | Includes bibliographical references
    and index. | Summary: "This volume showcases colonial cacicas as historical subjects who
    constructed their consciousness around their place, whether symbolic or geographic, and
    articulated their own unique identities" —Provided by publisher.
Identifiers: LCCN 2020038252 | ISBN 978-0-8061-6862-3 (hardcover)
ISBN 978-0-8061-9111-9 (paper)
Subjects: LCSH: Stateswomen—Latin America—Biography. | Minority women—Latin America—
    Biography. | Women—Latin America—Biography. | Latin America—History—To 1830—Biography.
Classification: LCC F1407 .C225 2021 | DDC 920.72/098—dc23
LC record available at https://lccn.loc.gov/2020038252

The paper in this book meets the guidelines for permanence and durability of the Committee on
Production Guidelines for Book Longevity of the Council on Library Resources, Inc. ∞

Contents

Acknowledgments

This book has truly been a collective process as many people have been part of it from its inception, and even before. We express our thanks here to all those who have been part of it in big and small ways. Most of all, we thank the contributors whose names appear in the table of contents. Your excitement and original ideas along with your dutiful work to carry this through despite individual setbacks is inspiring. We would especially like to thank Kimberly Gauderman, who mentored both of us during our years in graduate school at the University of New Mexico. Her commitment to teaching and researching the colonial period has been a true inspiration. We recognize that this collaboration would not have been possible without her.

On behalf of the contributors, the editors would also like to thank the administrators and staff working at the several archives in Mexico, Guatemala, Peru, Bolivia, Ecuador, Nicaragua, Argentina, Spain, and the United States for facilitating our research. A special thanks goes to Ricardo A. Pérez Alvarez and Tania Vargas Díaz at the Franz Mayer Museum in Mexico City for granting us the use of the portrait of *Sebastiana Ynés Josefa de San Agustín, India cacique* to grace our cover.

This project would not have come to fruition without the financial support of our institutions. We acknowledge the Faculty Research Expense Account award from the Bellarmine College of Liberal Arts at Loyola Marymount University and the Texas Tech Humanities Center Publication Subvention Award which have generously funded this volume.

We appreciate the interest in this project by the senior acquisitions editor, Alessandra Tamulevich at the University of Oklahoma Press as well as the anonymous peer review readers of the first drafts of our chapters and their constructive criticism at the initial stage. Our gratitude also goes to the second round of reviewers whose keen eye and diligent comments have helped us immensely to polish each of the chapters.

The process of writing and editing the works included have benefited from the constructive comments and intellectual support of friends and colleagues such as Dana Velasco Murillo and Alcira Dueñas. Scott Johnson's meticulous copyediting has exponentially helped our texts to flow seamlessly, something our readers will definitely appreciate. Thanks are also due to Bill Nelson, the cartographer who produced the maps to help orient our readers. None of this would be so gratifying without the support of our families, particularly our spouses, who keep us sane through our writing and rewriting activities.

Note on Terms and Languages

Many of the historic terms—for customary and legal procedures, political institutions, economic systems, and titles of nobility and authority—glossed in this edited volume originate in Spanish, Nahuatl, Quechua, Aymara, and other languages besides English. Although we employ a standardized spelling for such terms across all chapters, except when we are directly citing from a source, their glosses can vary according to the historical reality of the diverse and dynamic cultural landscape of Spanish America from 1492 to 1825. Deeper discussions of terms can also be found in the endnotes when not explained in context. After all, as the chapters herein reveal, even the meaning, status, and function of *cacica* varied across place and time.

Prologue

CACICAS IN THE EARLY SPANISH CARIBBEAN

Ida Altman

Columbus and his party made landfall somewhere in the Bahamas on October 12, 1492, yet arguably the most important episode during the period that followed occurred in early December when Columbus reached the large island of Hayti, which on December 6 he named Isla Española. Known today as Hispaniola (see map 1), this island would become the main focus of Spanish settlement and the first arena in which Europeans came into close and sustained contact with indigenous people in the Americas.

Columbus had anticipated reaching Asia (hence the name Indies, which Spaniards used to refer to American territories) and contacting wealthy trading societies. Previously he had encountered diverse societies while participating in voyages to the eastern Mediterranean and along the African coast, and he described the people of the Caribbean (whom he labeled "Indians") in terms of what he knew from his earlier travels. Although archaeologists and ethnohistorians debate the exact nature of the sociopolitical organization of the islands of the northern Caribbean,[1] Columbus and his party would not have been surprised to find that island peoples lived in hierarchical societies with recognized rulers. Hispaniola was the first place where they spent enough time among the local residents to begin to discern sociopolitical rankings.

After about a week and a half, during which the Europeans touched on various parts of Hispaniola, the December 16 entry in Columbus's diary

1

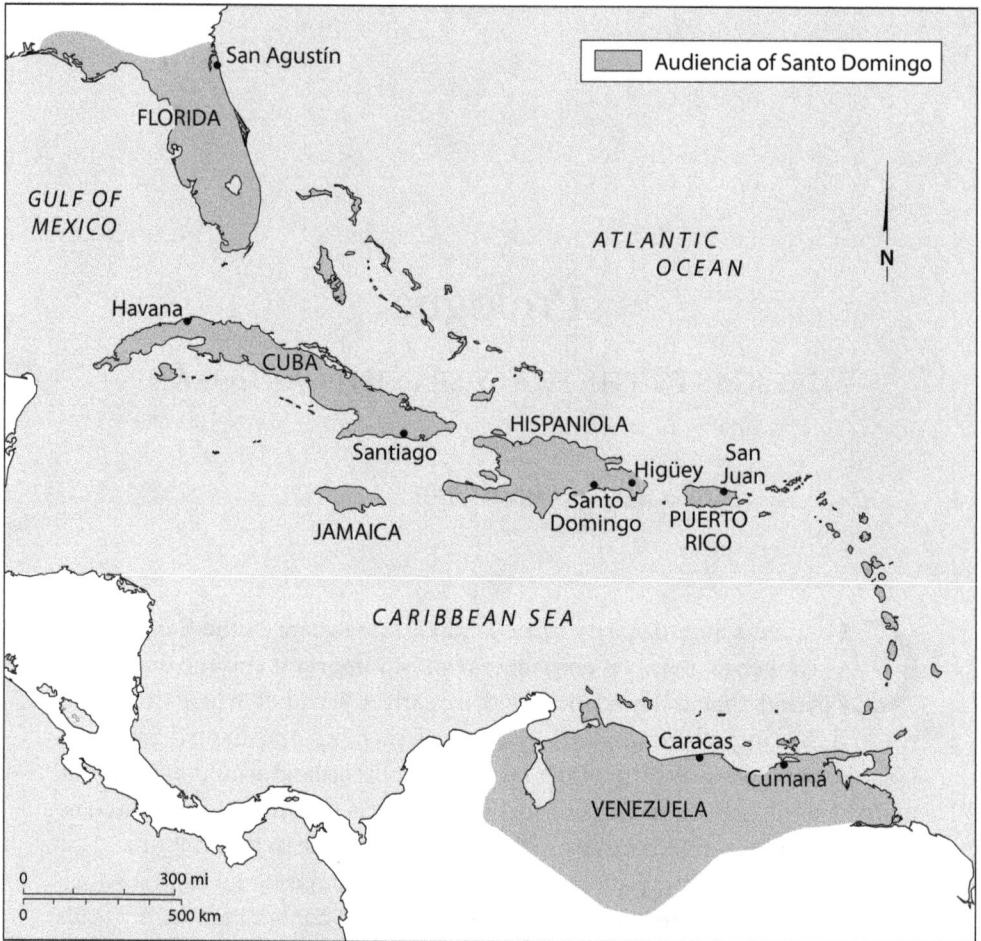

Map 1. Early Spanish Caribbean. Cartography by Bill Nelson.

records an encounter with a "king" (*rey*) to whom all paid respect (*acatamiento*). On the following day the diary includes a reference to someone whom "the admiral took to be the governor of that province, whom they called *cacique*."[2] Whether the word indeed meant governor or chief, Europeans thought that it did. Although they continued to refer at times to "kings" as they encountered other indigenous leaders, "cacique" became the preferred term, and Spaniards carried it to other parts of the Americas. During his initial stay on the island, Columbus developed a friendly relationship with one cacique in particular, Guacanagarí, near whose settlement Columbus's ship, the *Santa*

María, ran aground. Guacanagarí offered his assistance, and with wood salvaged from the incapacitated ship, Columbus had a fort built to house thirty-nine men who stayed behind when he left the Caribbean. Other caciques on the island might have seen Guacanagarí's apparent alliance with Columbus as a power grab, leading to conflict after Columbus's departure. All of the men left behind at La Navidad, as it was called, had died by the time Columbus returned to Hispaniola with a second and much larger expedition in late November 1493.[3]

Europeans produced all the historical records and chronicles of these events. None of them mention indigenous female rulers, nor does the archaeological literature. That absence in itself is not definitive proof that they did not exist but must be taken into account.[4] Only one woman, Anacaona, appears prominently in early sources. She clearly enjoyed high status and wealth and exercised influence. She was the principal wife of Caonabo, a leading cacique who was blamed for the deaths of the men who stayed behind at La Navidad. She was also sister to Behecchio, whom she possibly succeeded as ruler of the rich province of Xaraguá, or she may have succeeded her husband Caonabo as ruler of Maguana.[5] Notwithstanding the deference paid to her, not only by her own people but by Europeans as well (Bartolomé de Las Casas refers to her as queen), she became a victim of royal governor Nicolás de Ovando's 1503 campaign to break the power of the caciques of Xaraguá.[6] She escaped the fate of the caciques who possibly were trapped in a house and burned, but soon after that gruesome episode Spanish authorities hanged her.[7]

These early events and others signaled the end of any serious effort on the part of the Spanish colonizers to reconcile the cacique group or treat them as valued intermediaries. Ovando had formalized the practice that quickly took shape in Hispaniola by which Spanish men settled in indigenous communities, often marrying or cohabiting with local women, in order to gain access to native labor. Ovando started assigning rights to use indigenous labor in grants called *repartimientos* (later *encomiendas* [royal grant of indigenous tribute]). Initially he designated several indigenous men as *encomenderos* (encomienda holders) but soon abandoned the attempt when he became convinced that they were not suitable. Apart from some efforts that were made to create schools for their sons, there is little evidence that the caciques received much in the way of special treatment from the Spaniards. Enrique, or Enriquillo, was one of the boys who studied with the Franciscans at their monastery at Verapaz. He was the grandnephew of Anacaona. In 1519 he led some of his people into the mountains of the

Bahoruco and beyond the reach of Spanish control, agreeing finally in 1533 to a peace treaty with officials in Santo Domingo who recognized the autonomy of his community.[8]

In 1514 royal officials in Hispaniola undertook a complete reassignment of repartimientos on the island.[9] Although they were a minority among the chiefs, one of the novel elements of the Repartimiento of 1514 was the inclusion of nearly thirty cacicas.[10] "Cacica" was the feminized version of the term "cacique" that Spaniards invented. While some of these women seem to have headed small communities, in other cases the numbers were substantial. In Santo Domingo royal accountant Gil González was assigned the cacica Catalina de Ayabibix with 112 *personas de servicio* (laborers), the children who belonged to them, and 36 *viejos* (old men) who did not work. The cacica María Yamarez was assigned to the *veedor* (inspector) Cristóbal de Tapia with 72 people. The community headed by Catalina de Curjama included 138 personas de servicio divided among 4 *vecinos* (heads of household). In several towns (Puerto de Plata, Azua, San Juan de la Maguana, and others), however, no cacicas were recorded.

Perhaps most striking was the situation of Higüey in southeastern Hispaniola, which had been the scene of considerable violence, probably around 1502.[11] Early military campaigns, perhaps combined with flight or Juan Ponce de León's recruitment of native men from that area for his expedition to Puerto Rico, seem to have virtually eliminated the caciques in the region, although their disappearance also might have reflected Spaniards' success in imposing their own choices. Only one cacique, Juan Bravo, appears in the Repartimiento of 1514 for Higüey. In 1514 all the other chiefs were women: doña María de Higüey (one of the very few whose name appears with the honorific), Isabel de Iguanama, Carolina de Agara, and Catalina de Habacoa, while another cacica and her people apparently had been moved closer to Santo Domingo.[12] At least nominally under doña María de Higüey's authority were nearly four hundred people, while the laborers under Isabel de Iguanama numbered more than 280 (in one assignment the numbers were not specified). These assignments are interesting also in that they include some indication of the continued existence of hierarchical structures within the communities. One assignment of the people under cacica Isabel de Iguanama included the *nitaíno* Pedro Capitán.[13] The group of thirty-seven people under doña María assigned to encomendero Alonso de Trep included "el capitán del piloto [*sic*] y su gente" (the captain of the pilot [*sic*] and his people), while another included "la capitana Inés" (the [female] captain Inés). Perhaps the apparent increasing preference on the part of Spaniards for female rather than male rulers extended to lower levels of authority as well.[14]

Spaniards' possible bias in favor of female rulers might have reflected not just the dire impact of military campaigns on the cacique class, but also high mortality due to the harsh work regimen together with the effects of starvation and disease as well as native flight, recruitment for expeditions to other islands or the mainland, and marriage policies. Although in the early years both local officials and the crown hedged on the issue of Spanish-indigenous marriages, royal instructions to the three Jeronymites sent to implement reforms in the islands in late 1516 suggested that if a Spaniard married a cacica or the daughter of a cacique he thereby would assume the cacique's position.[15] Increasing the number of cacicas might have been seen as a way for Spaniards to gain more control over indigenous lands and people.

Another early source that mentions cacicas is a set of records from Puerto Rico for the years 1513–16 that lists the people who belonged to several groups working on the royal hacienda de Toa, some of which had been relocated there. It is not always clear whether the women labeled cacicas in these lists were considered chiefs in their own right or received the title because they were the wives or daughters of caciques.[16]

Doña María was a cacica who belonged to the hacienda de Toa community. As a young woman she succeeded her uncle Caguas as ruler even though at least one of her brothers was still alive in the 1520s. The bishop of Santo Domingo ordered Diego Muriel, the *mayordomo* (overseer) of the hacienda, to marry doña María, although possibly by the time they married she and Muriel already had formed an intimate relationship.[17] Existing records provide no insight into doña María's perspective, but contemporary testimony suggests that her partnership with Muriel might have provided some advantages for both of them and, in the short term, for her people.[18]

Doña María's situation points to the fundamental difficulty of reaching a firm conclusion regarding the prior existence of women rulers in Hispaniola and Puerto Rico.[19] The records consistently refer to her as cacica, yet she does not seem to have exercised any real authority over her people and possibly was forced into marriage with a Spaniard. The decision to pass over her brother Juan Comerio to serve as cacique suggests that Spaniards opted to deal with someone who essentially was powerless; the bishop instructed Muriel to marry doña María because she had no other source of protection. In contrast, her brother was sent to work in the mines, the most grueling and dangerous work associated with high mortality, suggesting he was seen as expendable.

The possibility that Spaniards' preference for dealing with female rulers contributed to the growing number of cacicas after contact may also be reflected in the names of chiefs. Although the evidence is ambiguous, with one possible exception all of the cacicas included in the Repartimiento of 1514 in Hispaniola and the lists of distributions of *cacona* in Puerto Rico have Spanish given names, whereas a number of the caciques kept their indigenous names (for example, Acanaorex, Maymotonex, and Anipana). This difference could mean that cacicas were more likely to have been baptized and received Christian names, suggesting that they were more closely tied to Spanish authorities than were the caciques. A number of both men and women rulers who had Christian first names, however, retained indigenous second names.

Scholars generally agree that chiefly succession among the Taíno peoples of the northern Caribbean usually was matrilineal, with preferred succession from a cacique to the son of his sister or possibly to a brother. This emphasis on the female line may in part underlie the conclusion of some scholars that prior to contact, women could have been rulers, not just mothers or sisters of rulers.[20] It may be argued that, given the clear indications that women of the chiefly caste like Anacaona were influential and wealthy in their own right and acted as respected counselors, their exercise of authority at the highest rank would not have been outside the norm. Before Enrique died in 1535, not long after negotiating a peace treaty, he designated his wife, doña Mencía, as his successor. Although an isolated and late example it nonetheless indicates that survivors among the cacique group accepted women as rulers. Yet the signs that Spaniards were choosing women over men as rulers to exert control are unmistakable. Barring the appearance of new archaeological evidence from the period before European contact, scholars are left with historical sources that do not clearly confirm the existence of female chiefs prior to the arrival of Europeans.

It is difficult to assess the significance of the Caribbean cacicas for Spanish attitudes toward, and interactions with, female rulers elsewhere in Spanish America. Having dealt with female rulers, perhaps mainly of their own creation, before they began to establish themselves in New Spain, Spaniards very likely were predisposed to accept and, perhaps in some circumstances, even favor them there. Evidence from the early Spanish Caribbean, together with the cases presented in this volume, suggests that almost from the outset, Spaniards in the Americas recognized the importance of female influence and authority in indigenous societies, helping to ensure the continuing prominence of cacicas throughout the colonial era.

NOTES

1. See William F. Keegan, Corinne L. Hofman, and Reniel Rodríguez Ramos, eds., *The Oxford Handbook of Caribbean Archaeology* (New York: Oxford University Press, 2013) for a recent compendium of archaeological studies.

2. Columbus's "diary" is a complex text; see David Henige, *In Search of Columbus: The Sources for the First Voyage* (Tucson: University of Arizona Press, 1991). The diary has been published many times in Spanish and English, all based on the text as written by Bartolomé de Las Casas, who had access to the original. Las Casas at times quotes Columbus's words directly and, at others, appears to paraphrase him. For an online version of the text in Spanish, see Bartolomé de Las Casas, "Cristóbal Colón: Los cuatro viajes del almirante y su testamento," Biblioteca Virtual Universal, accessed March 10, 2020, https://www.biblioteca.org.ar/libros/131757.pdf.

3. For a careful reconstruction of the first decade or so of European-indigenous interaction in the Caribbean, see Samuel M. Wilson, *Hispaniola: Caribbean Chiefdoms in the Age of Columbus* (Tuscaloosa: University of Alabama Press, 1990).

4. Wilson, *Hispaniola*, 119, refers to Ricardo E. Alegría's conclusion that "the presence of cacicas . . . was either illusory or the product of the collapsing sociopolitical structure under Spanish occupation." Francisco Moscoso, *Caguas en la conquista Española del siglo 16*, rev. ed. (Río Piedras: Publicaciones Gaviota, 2016), 34, writes of Puerto Rico that "igual que aconteció antes en La Española . . . la adjudicación de 'cacica' a madres, esposas, hermanas o descendientes femeninas de caciques fue el resultado de la intervención y cambios políticos en la jefatura taína introducidos por la conquista y colonización española" (just as had happened before in Hispaniola . . . the assignment of "cacica" to mothers, wives, sisters, or female descendants of caciques was the result of the intervention and political changes in the Taína leadership introduced by the Spanish conquest and colonization). See also Moscoso, *Caguas*, 89.

5. On Anacaona, see Wilson, *Hispaniola*, especially 120 and 129–34. See also Moscoso, *Caguas*, who devotes chap. 7 to her. Her life also has been fictionalized recently in a young adult novel by Edwidge Danticat, *Anacaona: Golden Flower, Haiti 1490* (New York: Scholastic, 2005). On cacicas more broadly, Moscoso, *Caguas*, 101, writes "las mujeres de linaje caciquil disfrutaban de alto prestigio y pudieron ejercer influencia, incluso de carácter político. . . . Una mujer de dicha condición social podía, en circunstancias muy particulares, ocupar interina y simbólicamente el sitial de jefatura" (the women of the chiefly lineage enjoyed prestige and could exercise influence, including of a political nature. . . . A woman of that social status could, in very specific circumstances, temporarily and symbolically occupy the position of leadership).

6. Moscoso, *Caguas*, 133, notes that while Las Casas used the terms *señora* (lady) and *reina* (queen) for Anacaona, Gonzalo Fernández de Oviedo was the first chronicler to call her "cacica."

7. Troy S. Floyd underscores the "ambiguity and obscurity" of these events and writes that "what seems certain is the Indians and their allies [in Xaraguá] were badly defeated and Anacaona was hanged," in *The Columbus Dynasty in the Caribbean, 1492–1526* (Albuquerque: University of New Mexico, 1973), 61–63.

8. Because of the importance of his revolt and the documentation it generated, Enrique is one of the few postcontact caciques about whom we know a fair amount; see Ida Altman, "The Revolt of Enriquillo and the Historiography of Early Spanish America," *Americas* 63, no. 4 (2007): 587–614. Records for the hacienda of Toa in Puerto Rico show that caciques, their wives, and other high-ranking individuals received more goods, or *cacona*, in compensation for their labor, often including items such as mirrors and beads along with basic clothing, than did commoners. Archivo General de la Nación (hereafter as cited as AGI) Contaduría leg. 1072.

9. The Repartimiento of 1514 has been transcribed and published in Emilio Rodríguez Demorizi, *Los dominicos y las encomiendas de indios de la Isla Española* (Santo Domingo: Editora del Caribe, 1971).

10. In some cases where more than one cacica bears the same name, it is not clear if they are the same individual.

11. See Wilson, *Hispaniola*, 123, and also Floyd, *Columbus Dynasty*, 56–58, especially 241n12.

12. La cacica de Catabano de Higüey (surely a place name rather than a proper name) and 281 persons were assigned to vecinos of Santo Domingo.

13. *Nitaíno* was an indigenous term for high-status people.

14. For the assignments in Salvaleón de Higüey, see Rodríguez Demorizi, *Los dominicos*, 170–76.

15. See Moscoco, *Caguas*, 143–44.

16. See AGI Contaduría, Legajo 1072. The lists are transcribed in Aurelio Tanodi, comp. and trans., *Documentos de la real hacienda de Puerto Rico, Vol. 1: 1510–1519* (San Juan, Universidad de Puerto Rico, 1971). On relocating people to Ribera de Toa see Moscoco, *Caguas*, 76, 84.

17. Diego Muriel's información is in AGI Santo Domingo, 10n4. See also AGI Patronato 175 Ramo 18.

18. For more on doña María and the hacienda de Toa see Ida Altman, "Failed Experiments: Negotiating Freedom in Early Puerto Rico and Cuba," *Colonial Latin American Review* 29, no. 1 (2020).

19. We have no information on female rulers in Cuba or Jamaica.

20. Jalil Sued Badillo argues that they were. He writes, "Nuestras cacicas, lejos de estar esperando a que los españoles les permitieran gobernar sobre sus propios pueblos, estaban en bastante control de su situación y parecen haber estado dictando las normas de aquellos primeros encuentros" (Our cacicas, far from waiting for Spaniards to allow them to govern their own communities, were well in control of their situation and appear to have been dictating the norms of our encounters), in *La mujer indígena y su sociedad*, 6th ed. (Rio Piedras: Editorial Cultural, 2010), 67–96, quotation from 83.

Introduction

Sara Vicuña Guengerich and Margarita R. Ochoa

The beautiful cover image of the lavishly clad doña Sebastiana Ynés Josepha de San Agustín is truly evocative. One can admire the jewels, dress, and rich colors of this 1757 portrait while also pondering the meaning and significance of a colonial woman depicted in this manner. The inscribed text offers a brief genealogy of her as the legitimate daughter of don Mathías Alexo Martínez and doña Thomasa de Dios y Mendiola. Further historical records indicate that Sebastiana Ynés entered the Convent of Corpus Christi in Mexico City, a convent dedicated to the daughters of indigenous elites ranked as *nobles* and *principales*.[1] A foundational document of this convent establishes the distinction between the two. *Nobles* were defined as the legitimate descendants of those who governed in pre-Hispanic times, the equivalent of the Spanish ranks of duke, marquis or count. *Principales* were the descendants of pre-Hispanic nobility, equated with *hidalgos* (lesser Spanish nobles).[2] The daughters of both, nonetheless, were fancied cacicas.

This frontispiece, as well as Ida Altman's prologue to this volume, introduces us, both visually and textually, to the central problems addressed by our contributors: Who could be a cacica? And what did it mean to be a cacica in a given time and place? The term *cacica* had a range of meanings in Spanish America, from the female relatives of ruling *caciques* (native leaders)—or their destitute widows—to female governors and tribute collectors who owned sizeable property from the first years after contact to the early republican era. This explains why, at some point or another, many of us have found records of cacicas while searching for other topics in colonial archives.

In spite of their ubiquity in colonial textual and visual sources, no previous book-length study has been devoted entirely to cacicas. Rather, most discussions of these women have been anecdotal. The purpose of this volume is thus to uncover the history of colonial cacicas, moving beyond anecdotal visions of individuals in Spanish America. We want to contribute to an understanding of the evolution of and changes to indigenous leadership as well as to our understanding of lineage and succession of these positions in different regions through the study of native women's political activism. By political activism, we are referring to actions that influence internal movements and events that are specifically visible to members of native communities, but which may also influence the actions of elected leaders. Though Spaniards were largely concerned with formal or official political authority in the public sphere, we consider political the intervention of cacicas in the economic, familial, and religious realms as well as their personal authority, which mattered enormously to native societies under colonial rule. The political influence of colonial cacicas was also rooted in indigenous kinship and communal decision making, which allowed both men and women to participate in governance. Aware that "cacica" was a Spanish linguistic invention, we assert that its meanings were adapted and manipulated by natives creating, even where it previously may not have existed, a new social stratum of indigenous elites. While previous scholarship has focused on elite cacica nuns in colonial Mexico, our collection further enhances the analysis of gender, race, and the engagements of cacicas with the legal system in Spanish America. Overall, the volume contributions showcase that colonial cacicas were purposeful historical subjects who constructed their consciousness around their place—symbolic or geographic—and articulated their identities from within, rather than from below.

Our vision of cacicas as purposeful historical subjects who have been neglected by the colonial historiography is inspired by scholarship that uncovers the silences surrounding other ignored colonial populations by considering multiple factors of their colonial experience. In her review of the scholarship on Afro-Latin American agency, Rachel O'Toole invites us to move from agency to subjectivity. Her discussion was particularly influenced by the work of Haitian anthropologist, Michel-Rolph Trouillot.[3] In *Silencing the Past: Power and the Production of History,* Trouillot conceives of purposeful historical subjects as individuals aware of their own voices and able to articulate an interior self, be that to contest an oppressive system or claim a position within it. He argues that the capacity of subjectivity, that is, the specific, articulated consciousness of one's condition, makes humans fully historical beings.[4] A continual discovery of cacicas as conscious political actors who shaped and influenced native hierarchies, mobilized rebellions, and pledged allegiance to colonial powers allows us to analyze their place within indigenous political structures, succession practices, and identity formation as native women who were cognizant of their colonial condition, but not subservient to it.

As we aim to expand the geographic range, chronological scope, and thematic content of studies on colonial cacicas, we would also like to state what this volume does not do. First, this volume does not answer the question of whether or not female indigenous leaders existed before conquest in some or all regions of Spanish America nor whether they were a purely Spanish invention. Second, we do not argue that the title of cacica meant the same everywhere; rather, local conditions influenced the presence, authority or disappearance of cacicas. Lastly, this volume does not claim that the status of cacica was elevated everywhere in Spanish America or always allowed this colonial stratum to leverage its supposed status within the Spanish legal system.

COLONIAL CACIQUES AND CACICAZGOS: A HISTORIOGRAPHY

We must begin with an overview of the scholarship of caciques as well as their *cacicazgos* (entailed estate of a cacique) to situate the current status of the studies of cacicas in Spanish America from 1492–1825. The task of reconstructing and understanding the chiefdoms that Europeans found in the Caribbean is challenging not only because the written records of this period are few in number but also because a handful of them cannot be considered either contemporary or firsthand accounts. Scholars who have worked on Caribbean cacicazgos since the 1990s have mainly taken anthropological and archaeological approaches, yet still used narrative histories to identify specific events as foci for their analyses.[5] Interest in the women identified as cacicas in European narratives such as Anacaona, the wife of a leading cacique in the age of Columbus and one that appears prominently in these sources, has been carried out by literary scholars.[6] Yet, as Ida Altman points out in the prologue of this volume, notwithstanding Anacaona's high status, it is not clear that she ever formally was recognized as ruler. Altman's piece also mentions numerous examples of women who were called cacicas. Nonetheless, it is hard to know to what extent, if any, they acted as rulers. Thus, without more detailed analysis of the content, objectives, and chronology of the extant written sources or the appearance of new archaeological evidence, the existence of precontact female chiefs in the Caribbean region cannot be clearly confirmed.

The majority of studies on caciques and cacicazgos in New Spain have been focused on the sixteenth century. Following the first wave of conquests, the sixteenth century was the period in which indigenous rulership among sedentary native populations of Spanish America was officially transformed from local systems to the Spanish-styled system led by caciques and cacicazgos. The significance of this era merits such a focus. With little debate, the scholarship on the establishment and function of the native *cabildo* (Spanish-style city council) in New Spain traced Spanish disruptions of precontact native ruling structures while also highlighting native adaptation of the cabildo to fit precontact forms of indigenous government and society. Charles Gibson, for example, meticulously uncovered how Hernán Cortés and Spanish *encomenderos* (holders of royal grants of tribute) "interfered with succession rules, approved or disallowed particular cacique inheritances, and at times assumed full powers of cacique appointment. Spaniards seized lands, goods, and retainers by force."[7] Nevertheless, Gibson adds, "Spaniards favored those Indian rulers who cooperated, assuring them of their positions, confirming their titles, and approving their possession of lands and vassals."[8]

Caciques and principales (or in Nahuatl, *pilli* [sing.] and *pipiltin* [pl.]) would learn to adapt to this Spanish system of force, cooperation, and reward. Adaptation in the sixteenth century allowed native nobles to maintain an elevated social status vis-à-vis indigenous commoners and strategically win the political favor of Spanish rulers, transforming them into an "intermediary authority" to subordinate their equals. In this same vein, James Lockhart's exhaustive study of the Nahuas of central Mexico revealed the accelerating decline of most cacical hereditary lineages and the entailed estates that were the basis of sixteenth-century cacicazgos.[9] By the eighteenth century, Lockhart notes, the term "cacique" "was not far from meaning what Nahuatl 'pilli' had meant earlier, though it was used more pragmatically than genealogically and had little or no legal standing."[10] Work by John Chance on the caciques of late colonial Tecali, near Puebla, also indicated that "cacique" (as well as "cacica") became a term more associated with ethnicity and applied generally to all indigenous nobles.[11] Additionally, Robert Haskett's research on indigenous rulers in Cuernavaca corroborated that only a few caciques with entailed cacicazgos remained by the eighteenth century.[12] Haskett's study on Cuernavaca—Cortés's Marquesado del Valle and a place of political and economic importance to Spanish rule—nonetheless was pioneering in demonstrating how the "power and authority of the jurisdiction's traditional ruling [native] elite was preserved rather than removed by the establishment of the cabildo system," in the sixteenth and seventeenth centuries.[13]

In southern Mexico, research on Oaxaca has demonstrated the ongoing presence of cacicazgo estates from the sixteenth to eighteenth centuries. Here, caciques also mediated between community and Spanish institutions and maintained political and personal relations with Spanish bureaucrats. Their intermediary roles had both individual and political benefits: permitting caciques to retain personal assets and allowing caciques to satisfy the needs of their communities.[14] Studies on Oaxaca also highlight changes to the political authority of caciques in the late colonial era, with legal and political challenges by commoner natives resulting in the loss of cacicazgo lands as well as fewer hereditary caciques serving as regional governors or in their local cabildos.[15] However, the caciques and cacicazgos of the sixteenth century matured, enduring through the end of the colonial era (with some continuing to function well into the post-Independence era of the nineteenth century).

In sharp contradistinction to the native populations of central and southern New Spain, distinctly local and indigenous systems of rule retained a viable presence among the colonial Maya. In her extensive social analysis of the Maya of colonial Yucatan, Nancy Farriss argued that the effects of Spanish conquest and colonization were minimal, comparatively speaking, in this region.[16] Rather than a history of dramatic decline of indigenous social institutions (i.e., family and kinship) and political governance (i.e., *batab(ob)* [local leader(s)] and *cahob* [indigenous communities]), the experience of the Yucatec Maya was instead largely characterized by Spanish "indirect rule."[17] As she put it, the Yucatan province "still resembled a mission territory well into the latter part of the eighteenth century, with the Spanish population for the most part huddled in the few urban centers and responsibility for the Indian hinterland shared by *encomenderos* and *doctrineros* [Spanish clergy]." And though the urban Spanish population was charged with governing the Maya, that responsibility was, in practice, "largely nominal, for the real job of governing the Indians was left in the hands of their own leaders."[18] Thus, the typical transformations of indigenous rule experienced in most other regions of sixteenth- and seventeenth-century New Spain are not as evident in Yucatan until the Bourbon Reforms. For the Yucatec Maya, "the second conquest" of the late colonial era had more devastating effects on their local autonomy than did the original conquest.[19]

Moreover, in Yucatan, caciques continued to govern semiautonomously well into the second half of the nineteenth century. In that same study by Nancy Farriss and in research by Matthew Restall, the archival record indicates that despite Bourbon Reforms and their attempts to undermine the *república de indios* (Republic of Indians) and local native authority through an increased Spanish bureaucratic presence in the region, caciques adapted to the new legal changes.[20] That is, even as the república was abolished, then reinstated, and finally abolished again during the "long" nineteenth century, caciques were still able to preside over their communities by adapting to political changes through strategic local alliances.[21]

More recent scholarship on colonial indigenous nobles has built on the histories of demographic collapse and political transformations to offer another layer of analysis of seventeenth- and eighteenth-century cacicazgos and the varied roles and institutional activities of the cacique class. Studies on the education of indigenous students at the University of Mexico, for example, highlight the end of precontact hereditary lineages while underscoring education as an avenue for the maintenance of cacique status as well as for social advancement.[22] An edited collection of essays on colonial cacicazgos in New Spain and the Philippines attempts to disentangle the varied local experiences of native rulership from the broad historical consensus on the general decline of native rule.[23] Despite increasing Spanish intervention in native politics, not all native cabildos succumbed to outside pressures, and thereby avoided devolving into bodies of chaos and endemic infighting. Rather, microhistorical studies of cacicazgos on multiple regions of the Kingdom of New Spain demonstrate that the history of caciques and cacicazgos was not linear. The historiography on the indigenous nobility of central Mexico, especially for the seventeenth and eighteenth centuries, is still growing. Research on native nobles in Tetzcoco and Tlaxcala, for example, underscores the important role of caciques in the creation of colonial society, as they fashioned and refashioned their relations with Spanish rule throughout the colonial era.[24]

Overall, the scholarship on native elites and rulership described so far is rich, varied, and continues to shed light on the colonial cacique, including increasingly nuanced social examinations of both male and female caciques within the diverse geographical contexts of New Spain. Work by William Connell and Yanna Yannakakis, for example, engaged in a concerted analysis of the spaces of indigenous autonomy carved out by caciques as they mediated the increasingly interventionist land and political policies by

Spanish institutions in the seventeenth and eighteenth centuries.[25] These studies demonstrate that in both peripheral and urban zones, including the administrative capital—Mexico City—indigenous local rule adapted to changing
conditions to stay the course. Indigenous leaders learned to maneuver within
New Spain's dominant legal culture. They honed their political and legal
expertise from their experiences in the sixteenth and seventeenth centuries.
And they strategized to better determine when and how Spanish officials
intervened in local native political and economic disputes.

Studies on female caciques in colonial Mexico by Josefina Muriel, Asunción Lavrin, and Mónica Díaz focused on cacica nuns currently dominate
this gendered approach—though more research is still underway.[26] Muriel,
Lavrin, and Díaz's research on the writings, portraits, and activities of the
daughters of native nobles in eighteenth-century convents reveal the wealth
expended by cacica nuns to express their identity and community through
religion. Their research, thus, adds another layer of complexity to our understanding of indigenous authority in Spanish America. As the daughters of
local caciques displayed their visages in baroque portraits (see the book's
frontispiece), their actions reaffirmed their families' and own native noble
status. Their families' strategic economic and political machinations to establish convents for their female relatives underscores another avenue by which
local native leaders adapted Spanish institutions to their own benefit and to
create spaces outside of direct Spanish control. Moreover, the charge, activities, and political intrigue of cacica nuns within the convent demonstrates the
purposeful maneuverings of cacicas. They behaved with an awareness of the
influence of their actions both within and beyond the walls of the convent.

Work on cacica nuns, however, is not the first historiographic foray into
the female cacique. While this collection is a dedicated examination of cacicas in Spanish America, it also engages with the presence of cacicas in the
rich historiography of caciques and cacicazgos. Research by Ronald Spores,
Kevin Terraciano, and John Chance on Mixtec (Ñudzahui) cacicas revealed
how these women figured in local politics, though they were not elected officials.[27] In Oaxaca, from the sixteenth through the early nineteenth century,
Spores described Mixtec cacicas as "active and influential in the social, economic, and political life of western Oaxaca," though they could not hold political office.[28] In her study of Spanish-Nahua relations in sixteenth- and
seventeenth-century Coyoacán, Rebecca Horn found that cacicas continued
to play important roles in establishing dynastic alliances.[29] Cacicas played
a central role in the pre- and postconquest practice of strategic marriage

alliances: maintaining an entailed estate, expanding landholdings, and reaffirming noble status. Robert Haskett's research on colonial Cuernavaca also discussed the role of cacicas. His work demonstrated that cacicas owned large estates and readily engaged in litigation to defend their property. A few exceptional cacicas even gained formal political power, such as the Tepoztlan cacica who led a political faction to challenge local ruling groups and the Taxco mine *repartimiento* (indigenous labor draft).[30] Lisa Sousa's recent historical examination of native women, commoner and elite, spanned the pre-Hispanic and first two centuries of the colonial period to unpack and expand our understanding of women's important and varied contributions to the survival of households and communities among the natives of highland Mexico (Nahuas of central Mexico, Mixtecs of the Mixteca Alta, and the Bènizàa [Zapotec] and Ayuuk [Mixe] of the Sierra Zapoteca).[31] An interesting omission in the historiography are the female batabob of Yucatan. Perhaps the markedly different trajectory of native rule in colonial Yucatan (discussed earlier) may be an important reason why the historiography on caciques and cacicazgos currently lacks entries for the female cacique or its equivalent among the Yucatec Maya.[32]

More research on indigenous women and native communal autonomy is needed in other regions of New Spain, such as colonial Central America. Catherine Komisaruk's chapter on late colonial Guatemala in this volume is a step toward representing this region, highlighting the macehualization of native hereditary authority.[33] Other research on colonial Guatemala has shed light on the racially diverse context of the economic and religious activities of women in Santiago de Guatemala.[34] Such studies span the entirety of the colonial era, also providing critical analyses of the transition from colony to nation-states. Beyond the Hispanized populations of Spanish urban centers lay the indigenous communities from which city migrants originated. For the early postconquest period, we have included a list of native women identified as cacicas in Spanish litigation from Nicaragua (see appendix). By including this list of cacicas of colonial Nicaragua we aim to encourage new research into the varied historical roles of indigenous women in this region. Also in Central America, research on the Mosquito Kingdom continues to expand our understanding of native and African-descent populations in the early-modern era, though more work on women's experiences needs to be done.[35]

In the north coast, highlands, and central Andes of South America, cacicazgos were referred to as *kurakazgos*, owing its name to the office of the *kuraka* (also spelled *curacazgos* and *curaca*), which the sixteenth-century linguist Diego Gonzales de Holguín defined as "he who speaks for all."[36] The scholarship on kurakas and kurakazgos is often part of studies on native nobilities, general studies on regional *señoríos* (native lordships), and the kurakas' relationship with the major restructuring of Andean societies under colonial rule. For this reason, the following assessment on the treatment of the kurakas and their kurakazgos (and related terms) highlights only the works directly related to this topic.

Works by Maria Rostworowski on the kurakazgos of the Peruvian north coast spearheaded the interest on the kurakas of this region and their succession practices since the 1960s. The variety of topics explored by Rostworowski in this and her subsequent works include discussions on dual authority, matrilineal descent, and gendered deities.[37] Nonetheless, it was perhaps the French scholar Nathan Wachtel, while adding new sources to George Kubler's celebrated article, "The Quechua in the Colonial World," who clarified the role played by the ethnic lords in the first decade after conquest.[38] Wachtel identified kurakas that enjoyed the new rights and privileges provided by the Spaniards but also those that organized armed resistance. Resistance, he claimed, took different forms, it was always present, and while some may interpret it as passive, the force of inertia behind it was deliberate, cultivated, and renewed by each generation. His work ends with a cunning question: Were the natives really vanquished? In considering an answer, one can say that the victories of the "vanquished" are still being uncovered as generations of scholars after him continue to find nuanced readings of natives' agency and historical subjectivity in the colonial era.

Karen Spalding and Susan Ramírez are scholars who added nuanced and innovative research to understanding the kurakazgos from the north coast to the central and highland regions in the pre- and postconquest eras. Both have shown that preconquest kurakas were not only their communities' representatives, they were also responsible for settling disputes among the members of their *ayllus* (kin groups), maintaining rituals, and enforcing the claims of the weaker or less prosperous members to goods and resources.[39] The rank and status of kurakas were correlated with the size of the population they controlled. These variables were also tied to their geographical location as coastal kurakas depended on the resources of highland ones and viceversa, in this vertical economic landscape. The changes in the kurakas' roles under the Inca Empire have been addressed by John Murra and Franklin Pease.[40] Their work suggests that at this stage, the kurakas were also responsible for enforcing the obligations of the community to the state, organizing work on state lands, making sacrifices to Inca deities, and so forth. The hierarchical differences among kurakas seem to have deepened as some were selected by the Incas as their *yanakuna* (roughly translated in this pre-Hispanic context as "personal dependents"), a relationship based on reciprocity.[41]

The changes to the kuraka office happened rapidly in the decades following the Spanish conquest. Kurakas became caciques, and as such, they also became part of the colonial order. Varón Gabai explores the fast changes that happened to kurakas in the Huaraz region (central Peruvian valley), a major transit route of Europeans into the heartland of the Inca Empire. While he highlights this "new generation of kurakas" as well versed in Spanish law and policy, he overlooks just how much these kurakas still interpreted basic native rights through Andean principles.[42] In the south-central Peruvian region of Huamanga prior to the 1640s, as examined by Steve Stern, "friendly Indians" became kurakas and established early alliances with Spaniards breaking traditional ties with their communities and searching for prosperity in the developing market economy. When messianic movements such as the Taki Onqoy (dancing sickness) hoped to throw off the Spanish order, few kurakas, particularly the wealthy ones, participated in it.[43] The work of Díaz Rementería examines how metropolitan officials and jurists perceived the caciques from the former Inca-dominated regions within the Spanish legal framework. After a period of vacillation (from the conquest to the late sixteenth century), the caciques emerged as important leaders who could be appointed by the Crown based on their *dignidad cacical* (cacical dignity), a reference to their noble native inheritance, Christianity, and ability to carry out the duties of collecting native tribute and maintaining order within their communities.[44] Not all the caciques, however, were fully supported by the Crown or Church. The prolific work of Luis Miguel Glave has shown many instances of the opposite. His assessment of a dynastic kuraka in the Titicaca basin (on the present-day borders of Peru and Bolivia), for instance, suggests the meddling of local priests in the successes or failures of kurakas.[45] In order to thrive, caciques had to cover all their bases, even the recreation of their pre-Hispanic past.

The work of Karen Powers, in her study of the Duchisela cacicazgo in Quito, for example, notes that to access privileged positions, native chiefs invented creative genealogies by manipulating ambivalent pre-Hispanic traditions.[46] These creative genealogies, often transformed into *probanzas de méritos* (merit inquests) ordered by caciques and other noble elites, are abundant in the colonial archives. Several scholars have also examined them to explore the creation of legal networks as much of the narratives about the pre-Hispanic past that justify cacicazgo appointments.[47] While Spaniards recognized caciques as cultural mediators and rewarded them with a legal status equivalent to *hidalguía* (Spanish nobility)—which granted them the right to hold personal estates, receive services from their native subjects, and tribute exemption—their communities' perception of their roles also changed dramatically. Susan Ramírez has also explored these changes, particularly in the Peruvian north coast. She calls attention to how the combined effects of population decline, disarticulation caused by the establishment of the *encomienda* (royal grant of tribute, typically paid in labor by natives), and *reducciones* (Spanish-style native settlements) destabilized the Andean ayllu structures causing the caciques to lose control of their native subjects.[48] Of particular attention among Ramírez's publications is her analysis of the relationship between kurakas and encomenderos in Chan Chan (on the Peruvian north coast) that involved the pillaging of ancient tombs in search of silver and gold when native labor was not enough to fulfill tribute obligations.[49] The abusive actions of many colonial kurakas, such as the appropriation of the community's income and labor in the central highlands, has been studied by Karen Spalding as avenues for opportunistic social climbing among this group.[50] In essence, the asymmetries of reciprocity between caciques and tributaries expanded as the caciques grew more dependent on colonial authorities, such as priests and *corregidores* (regional district magistrates), whose authority was increased during the administration of the viceroy Francisco de Toledo (1568–80).

The access to political power by appointed and hereditary kurakas destabilized Andean society in additional ways. Conflicts of power between savvy kurakas filled the colonial courts with myriad accusations. José Carlos de la Puente Luna examines accusations of witchcraft among kurakas in the seventeen century that were directly related to their political standing. The importance of this localized study (in Jauja) is the attention to ancient ethnic rivalries that continue throughout the colonial period.[51] A similar reading of ancient conflicts arising in the colonial context is provided in the analysis of discriminating language in legal disputes among caciques from the Lima valley.[52] The need of kurakas to distinguish themselves from others claiming aristocracy is seen in a positive light by Jeremy Mumford.[53] He argues that kurakas reinvented themselves in hybrid terms and that ultimately, the kurakas' pretensions to Castilian lordship, articulated ideas of race and indigenousness.

Studies on sixteenth- and seventeen-century kurakas and kurakazgos have barely covered the experience of cacicas. The condition of native women in general, rather than exclusively cacicas, has been explored by a generation of scholars combining history and ethnohistory. Initial interest in gender studies in the Andes began with the works of Peruvian scholars Ella Dunbar Temple and Maria Rostworowski, who focused on women in the social organization of pre-Columbian and colonial societies. In the United States, the controversial work of Irene Silverblatt placed gender at the center of pre-Hispanic social organization with the analysis of gender complementarity and parallelism, which became a common methodological framework for the next wave of researchers emphasizing the economic and sexual victimization of indigenous women.[54] As social historians shifted to examine specific regions, the study of native women in the Andes has provided a myriad of nuanced analyses. For example, studies by Kimberly Gauderman, Jane Mangan, and Karen Graubart provide complex visions of indigenous women in the economic and legal realms in the regions of Quito, Lima, Trujillo, and Potosí.[55] More recently, attention to noble native women has suggested that those that claimed direct descent from Inca rulers sought to emphasize historical continuity between the Inca Empire and the viceroyalty of Peru and engaged in the creation of historical and mythical narratives in order to do so.[56]

Andean scholars, however, have no certainty that a female version of the kurakas existed, even though references to preconquest female chiefs, particularly in the north coast and the central Andes, have been found.[57] Colonial chronicles are full of tales of female chiefs, from the gallant *capullanas* ("female chiefs" in unknown language of the north Peruvian coast) to the brave kuraka daughters that helped the Spaniards against other native factions. Karen Graubart has argued that the chroniclers' aim was to cast aspersions on the virility of indigenous men by suggesting that women ruled them, establishing an exoticism that also entailed an inverted hierarchy.[58] As cacicazgo authority became comparable to a *mayorazgo* (succession by right of blood that entitled an individual the rights of family property), it allowed female inheritance in the absence of male children. As Graubart notes, mayorazgo claims created power vacuums that were manipulated by local players.[59] The Spanish jurist, Juan de Solórzano y Pereira, for example, did not oppose female succession of cacicazgos where the custom was observed and proved to avoid contested succession.[60] Thus, Spanish inheritance laws opened the door for cacica heirs. Several scholars working on related topics have dedicated a few chapters to the analysis of some sixteenth- and seventeenth-century cacicas.

In a book devoted to the education of the Peruvian native elite, Monique Alaperrine-Bouyer brings our attention to several cacicas, daughters, sisters, or wives-to-be of the educated male caciques. Her assessment of these women, however, remains superficial since documents about these women are at best fragmentary.[61] A collection of essays on Peruvian women repeats some of the information provided by Alaperrine, adding only a few more descriptive entries of colonial cacicas through the late eighteenth century.[62]

The list of cacicas found in the archive grows by the late seventeenth century, yet no substantial research on the women of this period has been published. The chapters included in this volume, particularly those by Karen Graubart (chapter 5) and Chantall Caillavet (chapter 6) as well as Liliana Pérez and Renzo Honores (chapter 7), begin to fill this historiographical gap. Cacicas are more common and studied in the late colonial period. They tend to emerge as a result of the economic, political, and social convulsions of this era. If the structure of the colonial cacicazgo remained unchanged from the Toledan era, the Bourbon reform program under Charles III (r. 1759–88) catalyzed its changes. David Cahill argues that these reforms effected a governmental revolution in the Andes, hurting colonists' rights and privileges and restructuring the very foundations of the colonial system. These changes pressed especially hard upon the indigenous communities and paradoxically undermined the imperial control the reformists had sought to enhance.[63] The late colonial caciques and cacicas were more dependent on the colonial bureaucracy than their predecessors. Scarlett O'Phelan wrote a classic yet brief analysis of the status of kurakas and kurakazgos in the late colonial period, which examines the Cuzco-area hereditary caciques first rewarded by the Crown for their loyalty, then gradually substituted by appointed caciques after the Cuzco-based Great Andean Rebellion of Tupac Amaru II in the early 1780s.[64]

Scholarship on the Andean rebellions in general has provided great sources of information about late colonial caciques and cacicas. Sinclair Thomson, for example, provides a fresh look on the actions of peasant communities during the 1781 Tupac Katari rebellions in the Aymara regions of La Paz (present-day Bolivia), which were contemporary with those of Tupac Amaru II in Cuzco.[65] His work shows that when political tensions reached their apogee in these rebellions, local peasant communities (but not caciques) united behind a charismatic commoner, Julián Apaza (the later self-styled Tupac Katari) to achieve self-rule, racial equality, and even the elimination of the Spanish colonial order. This is truly a history from below that does not ignore the functioning of indigenous political mechanisms, which still responded to ancient traditional religious symbolism. While the Aymara regions of La Paz were close to Cuzco, the work of Nuria Sala i Vila shows that in other regions of Upper Peru (Bolivia), as well as central and southern Peru, the reality was different. Her work demonstrates the wide variation in local social arrangements that clarify domination, adaptation, and modes of resistance that were not universal.[66] She argues that the implementation of an overhauled tribute system in the late colonial period undermined the indigenous communities and the wider *campesinado* (rural native population) by permitting nonnatives to capture the network of a cacicazgo. In agreement with Sala i Vila, David Garrett's work adds gender nuance to the events happening in the late colonial period with his study on the cacicas from the Titicaca basin, from the 1750s through 1800s, and reaches several conclusions: (1) cacicas seem to have been more common in the Inca-dominated villages around the city of Cuzco than in the Aymara societies to the south; (2) cacical heiresses who inherited offices or whose husbands ruled either with them or in their names outnumbered cacicas who formally governed on their own; and (3) women who inherited or occupied cacicazgos did so through hereditary claim, continuing the authority of their families in the community.[67] Garrett, as well as several of these scholars, conclude that the great Andean uprisings of the 1780s radically transformed the colonial cacicazgo, showing the significant difference in social standings that separated nobles from the masses. They explore how the move toward the Hispanization of caciques and cacicas attracted the attention of intruders that eventually displaced any of their remaining authority. By the 1800s, the debilitation of the Andean cacicazgo was exacerbated by the Crown's policy to abolish hereditary cacicazgos and to appoint, at least on an interim basis, *criollos* (American-born Spaniards) and *mestizos* (people of mixed decent) in order to control native communities. The development, transformation, and demise of the Andean caciques, cacicas, and their cacicazgos is of fundamental importance to understanding the political foundation of the new republics in which native men and women have been enmeshed in the dynamics of gender and power to this day.

Up to this point, the rich historiography on caciques, their cacicazgos in Spanish America, and the changing dimensions of their status, authority, and wealth is still growing. This edited volume of essays aims to shed additional indirect light on the cacique by bringing the experiences of colonial cacicas to the forefront.

RACE, INDIGENOUSNESS, AND POLITICS

The young doña Sebastiana Ynés Josefa de San Agustín, whose portrait graces the cover, was one of the numerous cacicas who self-identified as *india pura* (pure Indian), so she could enter and profess at the Convent of Corpus Christi in late colonial Mexico.[68] While some scholars identify her as "probably not a pure india cacique, but rather a mestiza," others assert her indigenousness based on her skin color and her clothing.[69] Such studies claim that in spite of being made of exquisite materials—Chinese silk patterned with crowns and bicephalic eagles—her *huipil* (native blouse) would never have been worn by any but an indigenous woman in the eighteenth century.[70] These interpretations, for and against the "Indianness" of doña Sebastiana, encapsulate the problematic definitions of this term while also showcasing this woman's cultural and political choices to identify as "Indian."

In the early colonial era, Indianness was not tied to skin color or physical features but to the lack of Christian instruction and, in some cases, a perceived lack of a political organization. The native populations were considered *miserabiles* ("unfortunate persons," persons deserving of royal legal protection), a legal status that stemmed from Roman law and that applied to early modern Castilian laws. That legal status treated "Indians" as "legal minors" and required them to have *protectores* (legal advocates) for their juridical activities.[71] While in the legal arena natives often employed these labels (i.e., *indios miserables*, or "destitute Indians") to attain personal or communal goals,[72] or to have their cases moved to the high court of justice in first instance, as shown in the chapter by Pérez and Honores, it seems they embraced this category strategically, for it carried semantic implications of material or spiritual poverty, which also justified discriminatory practices.[73]

After all, the term "Indian" came to homogenize entire human groups that formerly thrived in their diversity. By using this term, the Spanish erased ethnic identities, and while they recognized the most visible native hierarchies, they essentialized the figure of the Indian, underlying their inability to culturally assimilate, and the impossibility of their true conversion. To overcome these perceptions and to emphasize their internal differences, as shown in the scholarship review above, natives turned to various strategies. While some sided with the Spaniards and offered them their loyalties, others accepted the Catholic religion, making public displays of their alleged new faith. The majority of natives, however, struggled daily to negotiate the impositions of colonial society.

In the first decades after contact, the surviving descendants of former rulers, particularly those who collaborated with the Spaniards, were classified as akin to hidalgos and were exempt from tribute and personal service so long as they also converted to Catholicism and displayed a superior conduct. Next in line were the caciques who rapidly made a place for themselves as the mediators between their communities and the new Spanish authorities. Under Spanish law, both noble natives and caciques came to share a similar status, and having been granted the right to hold personal estates and receive service from tributary natives, caciques would later claim distinct social and moral qualities.[74] Yet there was a catch. In order to be considered nobles or be appointed as caciques or cacicas, they also had to be "Indians" as it was their ancestral native heritage that granted them that status. In other words, they had to be "Indians," but not just "any Indians."

As the literature of this period has shown, savvy colonial natives adapted the Spanish ideology of *limpieza de sangre* (purity of blood or ancestry)—that is, a lineage free from any Semitic and heretical background—to claim the *pureza* (purity) of their pre-Hispanic dynasties.[75] Peter Villella has shown elsewhere that while limpieza preserved much of its rhetorical clout as a form of racial discourse, pureza implied honor. Thus, if natives could prove their honorable qualities, the king and his representatives were obliged to favor them and protect their noble status.[76] Throughout the colonial period, natives transformed their ancestral memories into lineage descriptions designed to prove their noble status or support of the Spanish conquest to Crown administrators in the format of Hispanic accounts of merits and genealogies, probanzas de méritos, or *servicios* (services to the Crown). These accounts facilitated their inclusion—some as ancestral nobles or ethnic rulers, others as "upstart" caciques whose authority derived from colonial-era changes—into a movable social category not based on their phenotype but social and moral qualities. While their privileged position depended heavily on the will of Spanish officials and the public opinion, we argue, especially in the case of cacicas, that their actions were articulated within the consciousness of their condition as political actors in colonial society.

The cases of early Hispaniola and Puerto Rico in the prologue demonstrate that notions of limpieza de sangre among the Spaniards did not prevent intermarriages with native cacicas. Ida Altman suggests that while Spaniards married these women to exert control over the native populations, we must not forget that these marriages were also advantageous for these women and their peoples. Yet alliances with Spaniards were not only marital, as the cases of the Otomí caciques showcase (see Villella, chapter 2). The female relatives of these "upstart" caciques of Querétaro gained their recognition not because of their ethnic origin but participation in the public life of the city. By the seventeenth century, the institution of cacicazgo recognized the female descendants of caciques as rightful successors. The cacicas of Teotihuacan (see Benton, chap. 1), for instance, maintained control of their cacicazgos for several generations in spite of their evident *mestizaje* (being of mixed races). In their case, the "purity" of their blood was not questioned by Spanish officials, but was policed by their native tributaries. A similar case about the adapted Spanish discourse of "bloodline inheritance" in the Peruvian north coast (see Graubart, chapter 5) shows the creative manipulations of ancient genealogies. These larger discourses of indigenous law and custom, however, were encouraged by the normalization of female succession laws created first for the *encomenderas* (female encomienda holders, usually inherited).

By the eighteenth century, when miscegenation altered the former meaning of "purity," colonial bodies became differently racialized. While the nineteenth-century scientific genetic concept of "race" was not yet defined as we know it today, racial thinking was already creating meaningful social categories. Racial thinking became contextualized in the physicality of individuals as well as in their inner traits. The alleged danger of mixed-blood individuals resulted in the intensification of the importance of genealogical antiquity among late colonial caciques and cacicas, many of whom continued identifying themselves as natives.

CACICAS LIVING IN A GENDERED WORLD

In January 2019, at a roundtable discussion on gender and women in colonial Mexico, Silvia Arrom described certain master narratives as "zombie theories" because they persistently mischaracterize the history of women.[77] Histories that generalize about Spanish American women as legal minors who lack marital choice and as passive individuals enclosed in a private or domestic space are, according to Arrom, narratives that will not die—despite the overwhelming archival evidence to the contrary.

Two decades after the publication of *Indian Women of Early Mexico*, we hope to continue building on the tradition begun by Susan Schroeder, Stephanie Wood, and Robert Haskett.[78] We aim to expand the historical knowledge of indigenous women, persons once considered to be "without history," to position them as purposeful historical subjects.

In the same vein that *Indian Women* evidenced the "capacity of native women for accommodation, cultural conservatism, and survival in the face of catastrophic change and seemingly insurmountable obstacles," so too this collection uncovers how native women engaged, adapted, and challenged both native and Iberian legal and political customs meant to exclude them. This collection covers the entirety of the colonial period and several regions in Spanish America. The broad scope of *Cacicas* permits a more nuanced understanding of native women, wherein we are able to amplify the history of elite native women and the changing nature of that elite status.

Though native women were not always successful, those labeled as cacicas in the colonial record labored to maintain their status and positions of power inherited from men and, in some instances, maneuvered to carve out novel positions of status and authority. The microhistorical studies herein describe the everyday lives and struggles of colonial native women who negotiated the extent of Spanish domination in their communities, details heretofore diluted in macrohistorical studies focused on the varying and complex roles of native men in examinations of Spanish-native relations. That rich history, as noted earlier, has nevertheless made repeated reference to the presence and actions of female caciques. Here we take a concerted and collaborative look at those native women—cacicas—who played important roles in the development of colonial society.

Studies of native women and gender have examined late pre-Hispanic gender systems, such as complementarity and parallelism. Ethnographic studies for the Nahuas, Mixtecs, and Andean peoples of Mesoamerica and the Andean world have demonstrated how the gendered activities—in the community, markets, religion, and government—of men and women were organized within a hierarchy that subordinated women to men, yet that hierarchy also recognized the mutual or parallel duties and responsibilities of both genders in order to maintain society.[79] Examinations of colonial practices of native authority and communal decision-making involving both men and women have also demonstrated that in some instances such practices were rooted in pre-Hispanic customs that were adapted to colonial rule. This study, however, is focused on the actions of women identified as cacicas in the historical record of Spanish America. This collection thus does not comment directly on the existence or continuance of pre-Hispanic gender norms, rather it questions their applicability in all regions as per the study of Chantal Caillavet (chapter 6). The overall collection is focused on unpacking colonial cacicas as women of varying degrees of status and authority within the vast geographical expanse of colonial Latin America.

In particular, this study examines cacicas as part of a gendered world characterized by the legal pluralism of the Spanish Empire. As the rule of law was flexible, so too were the power dynamics of that rule that were lived daily by the men and women of Spanish America. While this collection is not a legal history, several chapters examine civil and criminal litigation as well as early-modern Spanish legal codes to understand the actions of the cacicas and other native elite women who appear in those documents. In his study of the Tapia women who became the "founding mothers" of the largest community of nuns in seventeenth-century Queretaro, Peter Villella underscores the legal savvy of cacicas. So, too, the chapter by Sara Vicuña Guengerich demonstrates how doña Teresa, the cacica gobernadora of Azángaro Anansaya, deployed her familiarity with the Spanish legal system to petition for legal confirmation of her title. Yet she failed to meet the gender expectations from her community. The case studies of doña Juana Curilla and doña Magdalena Chimaca by Liliana Pérez and Renzo Honores further demonstrate how cacicas readily made use of all available legal concepts as strategies to battle to maintain their lands and to prosecute gender violence. Some cacicas copied the actions of Spanish women as evidenced by Karen Graubart's chapter. In the same manner by which the Spanish widows of encomenderos in northern Peru petitioned to keep their late husbands' encomiendas, so too did cacicas emphasize "both law and their personal histories," to develop and maintain female succession of cacicazgos.

Investigations into colonial families, including studies on marriage and marital violence, gender relations, and sexuality, have examined the rich archival record produced in Spanish and, where available, indigenous languages. Studies of women first revealed that colonial women actively and strategically inherited and bequeathed properties.[80] Subsequent studies, especially on Spanish families, further demonstrated that colonial women functioned as heads of households, ran family businesses, entered into their own business ventures, and managed their personal estates.[81] In her study of marital choice and disputes, Patricia Seed challenged the historical consensus on a father's absolute right to determine the marital partners of his children.[82] Significantly, Seed's work, which spanned nearly three centuries of colonial Mexican history, also uncovered how Spanish parental authority, especially that of the father over his children's marital choices, increased in the late colonial period. Family and marriage studies specifically focused on the *casta* (mixed-race) population depict the households of commoners as interethnic spaces. Those same commoner indigenous, Afro-descendant, and racially mixed women, moreover, labored as domestics in Spanish and elite households and provided remedies to sexual and familial conflicts through their sorcery and medicinal knowledge.[83]

Research on Spanish and indigenous women in convents has illustrated the independent and active roles of religious women within their religious spaces and in local economies.[84] Rich studies on honor, marriage, and the legitimacy and illegitimacy of children, spanning both sides of the Atlantic, have also reconstructed early-modern Iberian customs associated with the public and private reputations of colonial individuals. As Ann Twinam's multiple contributions have decidedly demonstrated, both men and women had honor, the meaning of which was negotiated daily through behavior—both their own and those connected to them—and their ability to, when necessary, defend that honor in the streets or in the courtrooms.[85] Though the historiography on women in colonial Latin America does not question the understanding of gender relations as male dominated, contributions to the field of women and gender, taken as a whole, call into question a traditional understanding of early Latin America as a patriarchal society. In this vein, works by Kimberly Gauderman and Chad Black on women in colonial Quito have directly challenged a classic iteration of the patriarchal paradigm, noting its historical origins in the early-modern North Atlantic. Instead, both Gauderman and Black propose an analytical framework—decentralization—that acknowledges the pluralistic and flexible nature of Spanish colonial rule and its influence on social relations.[86] Whether we label the dominant gender norms of Spanish America as decentralized or as a limited patriarchy, the rich and growing historiography underscores the many activities and abilities of women of all walks of life. This collection is a contribution to that literature, foregrounding the connections between gender and cacical status and authority in different regions of Spanish America, from the beginning of the colonial era to the end.

READING CACICAS IN WRITTEN AND VISUAL TEXTS

The bureaucratic landscape of Spanish America, characterized by a Habsburg legal culture, served as the context within which colonial authority, including gender authority, was performed.[87] But, by the late colonial period, the dominant social and legal practices that defined Spanish American society and its jurisprudence began to change. A central aim of the eighteenth-century Bourbon Reforms was to centralize power in the Spanish monarch. Achieving this goal would entail the systematic removal of power and status from local ruling bodies, including indigenous systems of rule created by the two-republic legal divisions of Spanish America.[88] Native elites did not passively receive late colonial reforms. The chapters by Catherine Komisaruk, Sara Vicuña Guengerich, and Margarita Ochoa depict how cacicas, like their male counterparts, engaged the courts in attempts—with varying degrees of success—to assert their titles and authority. In Mexico City, the legal cases of doña Marcela and other cacicas of the Bourbon era evidence the ways that cacicas exerted authority in domestic and communal realms without holding public office. In the case of the royalist cacica doña Teresa Choquehuanca from late colonial Peru, we witness the eighteenth-century phenomena of the rise of written documents—probanzas de méritos and *probanzas de hidalguía* (proofs of nobility) in particular.

The eighteenth-century boom in the production of texts, such as probanzas, was a direct result of the changing legal landscape of the later colonial era. This era ascribed increased importance to the visual and written word. As part of their reforms, the Bourbon government created laws allowing individuals born out of wedlock or those of mixed ancestry to petition the monarch for an edict of *gracias al sacar* (royal decree to remove [from birth or racial category]).[89] Whereas in the previous two centuries, wealthy individuals of mixed descent and with a good reputation could pass, even as Spanish, eighteenth-century legal changes began to influence the upper echelons of society, limiting the racial passing of mixed-race persons.[90] So, too, *hijos naturales*, persons born to individuals without legal impediment to marry, could also pass for legitimate prior to the enlightened legal and social changes increasingly restricting entrance into the elite levels of society. Women in particular were affected by the increasing social and legal importance placed on written texts. Where once verbal marriage promises would suffice to legally and socially pressure a man to rectify the honor of a woman through marriage, in the eighteenth century, only written evidence of marital promises would be legally sufficient to force a man to marry. Spanish women faced the particular conundrum of legally denouncing a man for failing to follow through on his marriage promise and through that process making her attendant deflowering public knowledge, on the one hand, or renouncing legal measures and instead maneuvering privately to maintain a public reputation of sexual virtue, on the other hand. Women of lower socioeconomic standing, however, readily used the legal system to demand economic retribution for their virginity when men did not follow through on their promises to marry.[91]

Among native populations, the late colonial period was also witness to a rise in the production of written texts, in particular the *títulos primordiales* (texts authenticating communal autonomy and corporate land holding). Like the earlier-mentioned probanzas, títulos primordiales were legal documents. However, these titles were manuscripts written in native languages to lay claims to lands and, in some cases, seek favor from local Spanish officials.[92] Many of these títulos were produced beginning in the late seventeenth century, in response to increasing Spanish demands for land title verifications through the *composiciones de tierras* (regularization of land titles) campaign. To do so, as Lisa Sousa and Kevin Terraciano's study of Nahuatl and Mixtec títulos primordiales from late-seventeenth-century Oaxaca demonstrates, some indigenous communities resorted to manufacturing these titles of possession.[93] In the process, the creators of the titles drew on existing written records, such as testaments, as well as on oral and written Mesoamerican traditions to reconstruct the history of their communities, create a written proof of land possession, and also treat Spanish conquests in local areas as major, even foundational, events in the history of their communities. Written almost two centuries after the "Original Conquest" of Mexico, títulos primordiales offer evidence of native familiarity and adaptation of Spanish systems and, in the words of Sousa and Terraciano, "a fascinating glimpse into the social memory of a community."[94] In the Andes, *memoriales* (written legal accounts of various sorts) were collective undertakings used at various moments in the colonial period and more visibly by late colonial Andean activists enmeshed in urban circuits to engage in discourses of justice, ethnic autonomy, and access to colonial power.[95]

Overall, the eighteenth century was an era of increased textual production, from memoriales to gracias al sacar and written marriage promises to probanzas and primordial titles. Of these written texts, the latter two hint at native adaptation and manipulation of Spanish legal instruments to secure their positions in society. The production of merit inquests in the Andean region became a legal tradition from the early years of Spanish rule, with native elites, such as Paullu Tupac Inca, the son of the last Inca emperor Huayna Capac, adapting the Spanish legal instrument to secure his status and that of his descendants.[96] But their rise in the late colonial era, including the production of ostensibly fake coats of arms, is a reflection of the changing status of native government under Bourbon rule.[97] What chapters in this collection demonstrate, however, is that cacicas in the late colonial period will also turn to the creation of probanzas to prove, maintain, and even create statuses where perhaps none existed before.

Finally, the eighteenth century also witnessed an explosion of visual texts among the sharp rise of tangible texts overall. Casta paintings provided colorful images of the wide spectrum of Spanish American categories of identity.[98] In the tradition of casta paintings, cacica nuns also sat for portraits.[99] Doña Josepha, our cover image, is depicted in the manner by which her contemporaries, other elite women, were portrayed. Artists adorned their bodies with fabrics, jewels, and other sumptuous materials and used richly colored backgrounds that depicted their subjects' high social status. Their bodies were thus controlled by the artist, for he manipulated her figure and told the viewer about the subject of his painting, not the subject herself. Yet, as a visual text, doña Josepha's painting tells us much more. Like the lay cacicas of this volume, doña Josepha could also be interpreted as a purposeful historical subject who adapted a Spanish instrument to her personal advantage. In sitting for her portrait, Josepha took part in the production of a Spanish text, a casta painting of a cacica nun, that like written texts served to inscribe her social status and, perhaps, that of her family and their descendants.

"CACICA": MORE THAN A TERM

The Spaniards first coined the term "cacique" from the Arawak language and applied it arbitrarily to male ethnic heads. It gradually substituted other indigenous titles reserved for local rulers, and in some cases for native elites. Terms such as *nitaino* (noble people among the Taíno society), *tlatoani* (dynastic rulers of an *altepetl*, a Nahua ethnic state; pl. *tlatoque*), batab, and kuraka (as discussed above for the Maya and Andean regions), are either used interchangeably or replaced altogether by "cacique" in colonial documentation from these regions. While terms for feminine native nobility, such as *coya, palla,* and *talla* (loosely translated as "queen," "princess," and "wife of a paramount lord," respectively) in Aymara- and Inca-dominated regions and *cihuapilli* (noblewoman) among the Nahuas, are widely accepted in the scholarship of this period, titles such as "capullana," in the northern Andes, raise questions for historical analysis as we cannot corroborate its actual meaning.

"Cacica," as the feminine term for cacique, was also invented by the Spaniards during their contact and conquest of island peoples in the early sixteenth century. As Ida Altman states in the prologue, Spaniards in Hispaniola interpreted "cacique" as governor or chief, and they took it to other parts of the conquered New World. They first assigned "cacica" to the female heads of indigenous communities when the male caciques were virtually eliminated from Higüey in eastern Hispaniola by 1514. The fact that the Spanish appointed these cacicas as the new heads of indigenous island communities is not proof of the existence of women rulers in the precontact period in this region, but as Altman suggests, these assignments indicate the continuation of hierarchies within these communities. Certainly, the societies that existed prior to the arrival of the Spanish conquerors functioned through a complex web of social relations that regulated social, economic, and political dealings among their members, and determined their access to the goods and resources produced by their fellows. As the example of Hispaniola, as well as the Nicaraguan cacicas listed in the appendix show, the long process of colonization that began in this early era fractured the social connections holding these societies together and replaced them with other relationships that implied negotiations with the conquerors.

"Cacique" and "cacica" ended up as umbrella terms used to distinguish native elites and rulers—ancestral or appointed—from those perceived as tributaries. Likewise, the native monikers for these tributaries are for the most part unknown. In colonial times, designations such as *naboría* (servant), *macehuales* (native commoners), and *hatunrunas* (native tributaries), were interpreted as people with a servile status. In addition, societies devoid of nobility, such as those in regions populated by a constellation of ethnic groups—as in the case of the pampas of the Río de la Plata and northern Andes (see chapters 6 and 9)—the term cacica is used to refer to the women related to male leaders, a title imposed by the colonizers.

We aim to disambiguate the term "cacica" by locating these women in the historical and regional contexts in which they appear. Following a chronological order of key moments in colonial history, we trace the evolution of cacicas and cacicazgos in the Caribbean islands, central valley of Mexico (containing Teotihuacan and Mexico City), and Bajío region of Querétaro. Examples from the territories that comprise the Kingdom of Guatemala (Chiapas, Guatemala, Honduras, Nicaragua, and Costa Rica) add to the nuances of the demise of colonial cacicas. The northern Andean regions populated by ethnic groups such as the Pasto, Otavalo, Panzaleo, and Latacunga of today's Ecuador and Colombia as well as the Peruvian north coast (Piura and Trujillo) and the central coastal valley of Chincha showcase the institution of cacica as a space of communal authority and litigation by elite native women. The Aymara- and Inca-dominated region of the Titicaca basin provides examples of cacicas from provincial elite lineages in full executive power. Finally, the women labeled as cacicas in the pampas of the Río de la Plata attest to their participation in the relations of colonial governance and diplomacy.

While not all regions that belonged to the Spanish American territories are included in this volume, we hope the examples, source materials, and focus we are using to fill the gap in the studies of colonial cacicas will encourage further research in the coming years.

NOTES

1. Josefina Muriel, *Las indias caciques de Corpus Christi*, 2nd ed. (Mexico City: Universidad Nacional Autónoma de México, Instituto de Investigaciones Históricas, 2001), http://www.historicas.unam.mx/publicaciones/publicadigital/libros/indias/caciques.html. We want to thank Jessica Criales for alerting us to the table in Muriel's work listing doña Josepha.

2. Dana Leibson and Barbara Mundy, "Portrait of an Indian Lady: Daughter of a Cacique, 1757," in *Vistas: Visual Culture in Spanish America*, accessed December 14, 2019, https://www.smith.edu/vistas/vistas_web/gallery/detail/portrait_cacica_det.htm; Mónica Díaz, *Indigenous Writings from the Convent: Negotiating Ethnic Autonomy in Colonial Mexico* (Tucson: University of Arizona Press, 2010), 26–27.

3. Rachel O'Toole, "As Historical Subjects: The African Diaspora in Colonial Latin American History," *History Compass* 11, no. 12 (December 2013). For O'Toole (1095), the difference between agency and subjectivity is subtle, but critical. If agency is any activity, action, or work within or in tangent to colonial structures, then subjectivity means a specific, articulated consciousness that is developed, historical, and shared regarding those same actions.

4. Michel-Rolph Trouillot, *Silencing the Past: Power and the Production of History* (Boston: Beacon Press, 1995), 23–25.

5. Samuel M. Wilson, *Hispaniola Caribbean Chiefdoms in the Age of Columbus* (Tuscaloosa: University of Alabama Press, 1990); José R. Oliver, *Caciques and Cemí Idols: The Web Spun by Taíno Rulers between Hispaniola and Puerto Rico* (Tuscaloosa: University of Alabama Press, 2009).

6. Jeanne Gillespie, "In the Shadow of Coatlicue's Smile: Reconstructing Indigenous Female Subjectivity in the Spanish Colonial Record," in *Women's Negotiations and Textual Agency in Latin America, 1500–1799*, ed. Mónica Díaz and Rocío Quispe-Agnoli (London: Routledge, 2017).

7. Charles Gibson, *The Aztecs under Spanish Rule: A History of the Indians of the Valley of Mexico, 1519–1810* (Stanford: Stanford University Press, 1964), 155, and see

especially chap. 6 for a detailed discussion. The encomienda system is generally described as a royal grant, in reward for meritorious service at arms, of the right to
enjoy the tribute of natives within a certain boundary, with the duty of protecting
them, and seeing to their religious welfare. An encomienda was not a grant in land.
For an ample study of encomienda and encomenderos in the Andes, see James
Lockhart, *Spanish Peru, 1532–1560. A Social History* (Madison: The University of
Wisconsin Press, 1994), 11. For the encomienda in Mexico as a "grant of Indian tribute and originally labor to a Spaniard," see James Lockhart, *The Nahuas after the
Conquest: A Social and Cultural History of the Indians of Central Mexico, Sixteenth
through Eighteenth Centuries* (Stanford: Stanford University Press, 1992), 4.

8. Gibson, *Aztecs under Spanish Rule*, 155.

9. James Lockhart, *Nahuas after the Conquest*, especially chap. 4.

10. Lockhart, *Nahuas after the Conquest*, 134.

11. John K. Chance, "The Caciques of Tecali: Class and Ethnic Identity in Late
Colonial Mexico," *Hispanic American Historical Review* 76, no. 3 (August 1996).

12. Robert Haskett, *Indigenous Rulers: An Ethnohistory of Town Government in
Colonial Cuernavaca* (Albuquerque: University of New Mexico Press, 1991).

13. Haskett, *Indigenous Rulers*, 5.

14. For a detailed discussion of cacicazgos and native intermediaries in colonial
Oaxaca, see Ronald Spores, *The Mixtec Kings and their People* (Norman: University
of Oklahoma Press, 1967); Kevin Terraciano, *The Mixtecs of Colonial Oaxaca: Ñudza-
hui History, Sixteenth through Eighteenth Centuries* (Stanford: Stanford University
Press, 2001); Yanna Yannakakis, *The Art of Being In-between: Native Intermediaries,
Indian Identity, and Local Rule in Colonial Oaxaca* (Durham: Duke University Press,
2008); John K. Chance, "Marriage Alliances among Colonial Mixtec Elites: The Villagómez Caciques of Acatlan-Petlalcingo," *Ethnohistory* 56, no. 1 (Winter 2009); and
John K. Chance, "From Lord to Landowner: The Predicament of the Late Colonial
Mixtec Cacique," *Ethnohistory* 57, no. 3 (Summer 2010).

15. In his study of late colonial Mixtec caciques, Chance reminds us that by law
in New Spain, *pueblos de indios* (Indian communities) that met certain political and
demographic criteria had the right to officially solicit a *fundo legal* (a grant of common lands) measuring 600 varas (1,645 ft [502 m]). In the Mixteca baja, many of
these common lands were carved out from cacicazgos. See Chance, "From Lord to
Landowner."

16. Nancy Farriss, *Maya Society under Colonial Rule: The Collective Enterprise of
Survival* (Princeton: Princeton University Press, 1984).

17. Farriss, *Maya Society*, 356.

18. Farriss, *Maya Society*, 356 (terms emphasized in original).

19. Farriss, *Maya Society*, chap. 12. This conquest wave of the Bourbon era is
likely a third wave. Dana Velasco Murillo has proposed a "second conquest wave" to
have occurred long before the Bourbon era. For more on the new concept and nascent literature on the "second wave," see Dana Velasco Murillo, "The Eighty-Year's
War of Indigenous Attrition," (paper presented at the 63rd Annual Meeting of the
American Society for Ethnohistory, Winnipeg, MB, October 12, 2017).

20. Farriss, *Maya Society*; Matthew Restall, *The Maya World: Yucatec Culture and Society, 1550–1850* (Stanford: Stanford University Press, 1999). The terms *república de indios* as well as *república de españoles* refer to the Spanish colonial two-republics administrative system established in America soon after conquest. Per this royal "policy of separation"—residential, social, and legal—native societies and their polities were "entitled to govern themselves under Spanish rule." See Brian P. Owensby, *Empire of Law and Indian Justice in Colonial Mexico* (Stanford: Standord University Press, 2008), 25. Moreover, though physical segregation between natives and Spaniards was difficult to maintain, over time the legal distinction between the republics provided "an institutional structure through which peninsular concepts of authority, governance, and justice could be translated into local cultural vernaculars." See Bianca Premo, *The Enlightenment on Trial: Ordinary Litigants and Colonialism in the Spanish Empire* (New York: Oxford University Press, 2017), 161.

21. For the nineteenth century, see Rajeshwari Dutt, *Maya Caciques in Early National Yucatán* (Norman: University of Oklahoma Press, 2017). For a study on nineteenth- and twentieth-century negotiated meanings of *pueblo*, or "community," among the Yucatec Maya, see Paul K. Eiss, *In the Name of the Pueblo: Place, Community, and the Politics of History in Yucatán* (Durham: Duke University Press, 2010).

22. A few generations of male indigenous students who attended the University of Mexico decades after the European conquest did not necessarily belong to precontact noble indigenous families. In fact, there were a handful of university students who belonged to commoner families without noble ties. The number of indigenous students who attended the university was low, though. This situation also occurred in other colleges such as San Gregorio or the Colegio de San Ildefonso, where commoner indigenous students attended classes, alongside students who belonged to native noble families, seeking to occupy positions of power in their local communities once they graduated. Eventually, having an education provided natives without noble lineages an opportunity for social advancement. See Margarita Menegus Bornemann and Rodolfo Aguirre Salvador, *Los indios, el sacerdocio y la Universidad en Nueva España, siglos XVI–XVIII* (Mexico City: Universidad Nacional Autónoma de México, Centro de Estudios Sobre la Universidad, Plaza y Valdés, 2006), especially chap. 2. We thank Argelia Segovia for sharing her expertise and providing this reference.

23. Margarita Menegus Bornemann and Rodolfo Aguirre Salvador, eds., *El cacicazgo en Nueva España y Filipinas* (Mexico City: Universidad Nacional Autónoma de México, Centro de Estudios Sobre la Universidad, Plaza y Valdés, 2005).

24. Bradley Benton, *The Lords of Tetzcoco: The Transformation of Indigenous Rule in Postconquest Central Mexico* (New York: Cambridge University Press, 2017); Peter Villella, *Indigenous Elites and Creole Identity in Colonial Mexico, 1500–1800* (New York: Cambridge University Press, 2016).

25. William F. Connell, *After Moctezuma: Indigenous Politics and Self-Government in Mexico City, 1524–1730* (Norman: University of Oklahoma Press, 2011); Yanna Yannakakis, *Art of Being In-Between.*

26. Josefina Muriel, *Las indias caciques*; Asunción Lavrin, *Brides of Christ: Conventual Life in Colonial Mexico* (Stanford: Stanford University Press, 2008); Mónica

Díaz, *Indigenous Writings*; and dissertation work in progress on cacica nuns in colonial Oaxaca and Mexico City by Jessica Criales at Rutgers University.

27. Ronald Spores, "Mixteca *Cacicas*: Status, Wealth, and the Political Accommodation of Native Elite Women in Early Colonial Oaxaca," in *Indian Women of Early Mexico*, ed. Susan Schroeder, Stephanie Wood, and Robert Haskett (Norman: University of Oklahoma Press, 1997); Kevin Terraciano, *The Mixtecs of Colonial Oaxaca*; John K. Chance, "Marriage Alliances" and "From Lord to Landowner."

28. Ronald Spores, "Mixteca *Cacicas*," 195.

29. Rebecca Horn, *Postconquest Coyoacan: Nahua-Spanish Relations in Central Mexico, 1519–1650* (Stanford: Stanford University Press, 1997).

30. Haskett, *Indigenous Rulers*; and Robert Haskett, "Activist or Adulteress? The Life and Struggle of Doña Josefa María of Tepoztlan," in *Indian Women of Early Mexico*, ed. Susan Schroeder, Stephanie Wood, and Robert Haskett (Norman: University of Oklahoma Press, 1997). The definition for repartimiento varies for each region. In the early Caribbean, following Columbus's encounter and occupation of Hispaniola, a repartimiento was an "allotment," or grant, of a village that entitled the recipient of said allotment to use the labor of the men of the village. The first governor of Hispaniola, Fray Nicolás de Ovando (r. 1502–9), would formalize these grants as encomiendas. See Ida Altman, Sarah Cline, and Juan Javier Pescador, *The Early History of Greater Mexico* (Upper Saddle River, NJ: Prentice Hall, 2003), 47. In colonial Mexico, however, the repartimiento was a draft labor system that required adult indigenous men to provide labor service on public and private Spanish enterprises; it resembled the preconquest Nahua *coatequitl* (public labor draft) and the colonial Andean *mita* ("cyclical corvée," reworked by the Spanish as a forced labor draft). See James Lockhart, *Nahuas After the Conquest*, 132 and 428–31. For more on the Mexican repartimiento as mita, see Matthew Restall and Kris Lane, *Latin America in Colonial Times*, 2nd ed. (New York: Cambridge University Press, 2018), 155–56. For the adapted uses of mita as a repartimiento, see Jeremy Ravi Mumford, *Vertical Empire: The General Resettlement of Indians in the Colonial Andes* (Durham: Duke University Press 2012).

31. Lisa Sousa, *The Woman Who Turned into a Jaguar and Other Narratives of Native Women in Archives of Colonial Mexico* (Stanford: Stanford University Press, 2017).

32. An earlier version of this volume included a chapter on Maya cacicas in colonial Yucatan. Per our communications with Matthew Restall, however, it is not clear that there were female batabob in the late pre-Hispanic period or in the colonial era of Yucatan. Restall added that we do have evidence of elite women, and women from native noble, or hidalgo, Maya dynasties, such as the Xiu, that enjoyed the doña title. This may hint at the presence of cacicas among the Yucatec Maya as the don title was restricted among Mayas to batabob, former batabob, and high-ranking natives. For studies related to this discussion on the Xiu dynasty and women in colonial Yucatan, see Matthew Restall, "The People of the Patio: Ethnohistorical Evidence of Yucatec Maya Royal Courts," in *Royal Courts of the Ancient Maya*, ed. Takeshi Inomata and Stephen D. Houston (New York: Westview Press, 2001); and

Marta Espejo-Ponce Hunt and Matthew Restall, "Work, Marriage, and Status: Maya Women of Colonial Yucatan," in *Indian Women of Early Mexico*, ed. Susan Schroeder, Stephanie Wood, and Robert Haskett (Norman: University of Oklahoma Press, 1997). We are grateful to Matthew Restall as well as graduate student Sami Davis, at Penn State, for graciously sharing their viewpoints on the historiography of elite Maya women of colonial Yucatan. Dissertation research underway may soon shed more light on these women. For example, Hannah Abrahamson (doctoral student at Emory University) examines encomenderas and their legal dependents, typically Maya servants and African-descended slaves. In a related project, Abrahamson is also examining doña Malintzin and her daughter, doña María, as encomenderas in colonial Yucatan.

33. Macehualization is understood as the process by which the rigid political division within the indigenous común broke down. Caciques lost power and became absorbed in larger bodies of principales; divisions within the community drove principales to ally themselves with macehuales, who, in turn, took advantage of this new flexibility to advance themselves politically and economically. See Greg Grandin, *The Blood of Guatemala: A History of Race and Nation* (Durham: Duke University Press, 2000); and Rodolfo Pastor, *Campesinos y reformas: la Mixteca, 1700–1856* (Mexico City: Colegio de México, 1987). We thank Catherine Komisaruk for providing these references.

34. Catherine Komisaruk, *Labor and Love in Guatemala: The Eve of Independence* (Stanford: Stanford University Press, 2013); Brianna Leavitt-Alcántara, *Alone at the Altar: Single Women and Devotion in Guatemala, 1670–1870* (Stanford: Stanford University Press, 2018); Christopher Lutz, *Santiago de Guatemala, 1541–1773: City, Caste, and the Colonial Experience* (Norman: University of Oklahoma Press, 1994).

35. For a discussion of "survivance" among the Masca native communities of colonial Honduras, see Russell N. Sheptak, "Moving Masca: Persistent Indigenous Communities in Spanish Colonial Honduras," in *Indigenous Persistence in the Colonized Americas: Material and Documentary Perspectives on Entanglement*, ed. Heather Law Pezzarossi and Russell N. Sheptak (Albuquerque: University of New Mexico Press, 2019). For a comprehensive overview of the literature on the Mosquito coast, see Daniel Mendiola, "The Rise of the Mosquito Kingdom in Central America's Caribbean Borderlands: Sources, Questions, and Enduring Myths," *History Compass* 16, no. 1 (December 2017).

36. Karen Spalding, "Kurakas and Commerce: A Chapter on the Evolution of Andean Society," *Hispanic American Historical Review* 53, no. 4 (November 1973), 583.

37. Maria Rostworowski, *Curacas y sucesiones. Costa norte* (Lima: Minerva, 1961); Maria Rostworowski, *Señoríos indígenas de Lima y Canta* (Lima: Instituto de Estudios Peruanos, 1978); Maria Rostworowski, *Estructuras andinas del poder: Ideología religiosa y política* (Lima: Instituto de Estudios Peruanos, 2007).

38. Nathan Wachtel, *The Vision of the Vanquished: The Spanish Conquest of Peru Through Indian Eyes, 1530–1570.* (Hassocks, Sussex: Harvester Press, 1977); George

Kubler, "The Quechua in the Colonial World," in *Handbook of South American Indians*, vol. 2, *The Andean Civilizations* (New York: Cooper Square, 1963).

39. Spalding, "Kurakas," 584; Susan Ramírez, "The 'Dueño de Indios': Thoughts on the Consequences of the Shifting Bases of Power of the 'Curaca de los Viejos Antiguos' Under the Spanish in Sixteenth-Century Peru," *Hispanic American Historical Review* 67, no. 4 (November 1987).

40. John V. Murra, "Social Structural and Economic Themes in Andean Ethnohistory," *Anthropological Quarterly* 34, no. 2 (April 1961): 51–54; Franklin Pease G. Y., *Inka y Kuraka: Relaciones de poder y representación histórica*, Working Papers 8 (College Park, MD: University of Maryland at College Park, 1992).

41. Pease, "Inka y Kuraka," 10. By reciprocity, the authors refer to the vital practice that infuse social relationships with a sense of mutuality. In the Andes, however, scholars have demonstrated that a culture of reciprocity may prove compatible with both asymmetry (imbalance) and symmetry (balance). See the work of Olivia Harris, "Complementarity and Conflict: An Andean View of Women and Men," in *Sex and Age of Principles of Social Differentiation*, ed. J. La Fontaine (London: Academic Press, 1978).

42. Rafael Varón Gabai, *Curacas y encomenderos. Acomodamiento native en Huaraz, siglos XVI y XVII* (Lima: P. L. Villanueva, 1980).

43. Steve Stern, *Peru's Indian Peoples and the Challenge of Spanish Conquest: Huamanga to 1640* (Madison: University of Wisconsin Press, 1982). Archaeological work on women's active role of the Taki Onqoy movement is currently underway by Scotti Norman at Vanderbilt University.

44. Carlos Díaz Rementería, *El cacique en el virreinato del Peru. Estudio histórico-jurídico* (Sevilla: Facultad de Filosofía y Letras de la Universidad de Sevilla, 1977).

45. Luis Miguel Glave, *Un curacazgo andino y la sociedad campesina del siglo XVII* (Lima: Insituto de Pastoral Andina, 1989).

46. Karen Powers, "A Battle of Wills: Inventing Chiefly Legitimacy in the Colonial North Andes," in *Dead Giveaways: Indigenous Testaments of Colonial Mesoamerica and the Andes*, ed. Susan Kellogg and Matthew Restall (Salt Lake City: University of Utah Press, 1998).

47. Carolina Jurado, "'Descendientes de los primeros': Las probanzas de méritos y servicios de la genealogía cacical. Audiencia de Charcas, 1574–1719," *Revista de Indias* 74, no. 261 (2014); Laura Escobari de Querejazú, *Caciques, yanaconas y extravagantes. Sociedad y educación colonial en Charcas, s. XVI–XVIII* (La Paz: Plural Editores, 2001); Bouysee-Cassagne Therese, Platt Tristan, and Harris Olivia, eds., *Qaraqara-Charca. Mallku, Inca y Rey en la provincia de Charcas (siglos XVI–XVII). Historia antropológica de una confederación Aymara* (La Paz: Plural, 2006); José Carlos de la Puente Luna, *Andean Cosmopolitans Seeking Justice and Reward at the Spanish Royal Court* (Austin: University of Texas, 2018).

48. Ramírez, "Dueño de Indios," 609.

49. Susan Ramírez, *The World Upside Down: Cross-Cultural Contact and Conflict in Sixteenth-Century Peru* (Stanford: Stanford University Press, 1998).

50. Karen Spalding, *Huarochirí: An Andean Society under Inca and Spanish Rule* (Stanford: Stanford University Press, 1984); Karen Spalding "Social Climbers: Changing Patterns of Mobility Among the Indians of Colonial Peru," *Hispanic American Historical Review* 50, no. 4 (November 1970).

51. José Carlos de la Puente Luna, *Los curacas hechiceros de Jauja: Batallas mágicas y legales en el Perú colonial* (Lima: Fondo Editorial de la Pontificia Universidad Católica del Perú, 2007).

52. Gabriela Ramos, "El rastro de la discriminación. Litigios y probanzas de caciques en el Perú colonial temprano," *Fronteras de la Historia* 21, no. 1 (June, 2016).

53. Jeremy Ravi Mumford, "Aristocracy in the Auction Block. Race, Lords, and the Perpetuity Controversy of Sixteenth-Century Peru," in *Imperial Subjects: Race and Identity in Colonial Latin America*, ed. Matthew O'Hara and Andrew Fisher (Durham: Duke University Press, 2009).

54. While Silverblatt convincingly argues that gender considerations were a normal part of Inca politics, she also underestimates the complexities of pre-Inca kingdoms and their degree of autonomy in Inca times. In addition, her analysis of the postconquest era gives excessive credit to partisan colonial accounts such as those of the seventeenth-century Andean chronicler Guaman Poma de Ayala. Irene Silverblatt, *Moon, Sun, and Witches: Gender Ideologies and Class in Inca and Colonial Peru* (Princeton: Princeton University Press, 1987).

55. Kimberly Gauderman, *Women's Lives in Colonial Quito: Gender, Law and Economy in Spanish America* (Austin: University of Texas Press, 2003); Jane Mangan, *Trading Roles: Gender, Ethnicity, and the Urban Economy in Colonial Potosí* (Durham: Duke University Press, 2005); Karen Graubart, *With Our Labor and Sweat: Indigenous Women and the Formation of Colonial Society in Peru, 1550–1700* (Stanford: Stanford University Press, 2007).

56. Sara Vicuña Guengerich is currently working on this topic for a book tentatively titled, *Daughters of the Inca Conquest: Indigenous Noblewomen in Colonial Peru.*

57. Fernández Oswaldo, "La huaca Narihuala: Un documento para la etnohistoria de la costa norte del Peru, 1000–1200 D.C.," *Boletín del Instituto Francés de Estudios Andinos* 19, no. 1 (1990).

58. Graubart, *With Our Labor*, 164.

59. Graubart, *With Our Labor*, 175.

60. Juan de Solórzano y Pereira, *Política Indiana*, vol. 2 (Madrid: Fundación Antonio de Castro, 1996), 564–65.

61. Monique Alaperrine-Bouyer, *La educación de las élites indígenas en el Perú colonial* (Lima: Instituto Francés de Estudios Andinos, 2007).

62. Elizabeth Puertas, "La mujer frente al poder en la sociedad colonial peruana (siglos XVI–XVIII)," in *La mujer en la historia del Perú (siglos XV al XX)*, ed. Carmen Meza and Teodoro Hampe (Lima: Fondo Editorial del Congreso, 2007).

63. David Cahill, "The Long Conquest: Collaboration by Native Andean Elites in the Colonial System, 1532–1825," in *Technology, Disease and Colonial Conquests, Sixteenth to Eighteenth Centuries*, ed. G. Raudzens (Leiden: Brill, 2003), 86.

64. Scarlett O'Phelan, *Kurakas sin sucesiones: Del cacique al alcalde de indios, Peru y Bolivia, 1750–1835* (Cusco: Centro de Estudios Bartolomé de las Casas, 1997).

65. Thomson Sinclair, *We Alone Will Rule: Native Andean Politics in the Age of Insurgency* (Madison: University of Wisconsin Press, 2002).

66. Nuria Sala i Vila, *Y se armó el tole tole. Tributo indígena y movimientos sociales en el virreinato del Perú, 1790–1814* (Arequipa: Instituto de Estudios Regionales José María Arguedas, 1996).

67. David Garrett, "'In Spite of Her Sex': The Cacica and the Politics of the Pueblo in the Late Colonial Cusco," *Americas* 64, no. 4 (April 2008); Ariel Morrone, "Mujeres cacicales en el tablero colonial. Familia, parentesco y poder étnico en el lago Titicaca, 1580–1750," *Andes Antropología e Historia* 1, no. 29 (2018).

68. See Muriel, *Las indias caciques*, 63.

69. Bernardette Butcher, *America Bride of the Sun: 500 Years Latin America and the Low Countries* (Leiden: Flemish Community Administration, 1991), 448.

70. Leibsohn and Mundy, "Indian Lady."

71. Paulino Castañeda Delgado, "La condición miserable del indio y sus privilegios," *Anuario de Estudios Americanos* 28 (1971).

72. Caroline Cunill, "El indio miserable: Nacimiento de la teoría legal en la América colonial del siglo XVI," *Cuadernos Intercambio* 8, no. 9 (2011).

73. Ramos, "Rastro de la discriminación," 65.

74. "Real Cédula que se considere a los descendientes de caciques como nobles en su raza," Madrid, March 26, 1697, in *Colección de documentos para la historia de la formación social de Hispanoamérica (1493–1810)*, vol. 3, ed. Richard Konetzke (Madrid: Consejo Superior de Investigaciones Científicas, 1953), 67; Carlos II, *Recopilación de leyes de los reinos de las Indias*, 5th ed. (Madrid: Boix, 1841), Lib. VI, tit. v, ley xviii; Lib. VI, tit. vii, ley iv.

75. María Elena Martínez, *Genealogical Fictions: Limpieza de Sangre, Religion, and Gender* (Stanford: Stanford University Press, 2011); Peter Villella, "'Pure and Noble Indians Untainted by Inferior or Idolatrous Races': Native Elites and the Discourse of Blood Purity in Late Colonial Mexico," *Hispanic American Historical Review* 91, no. 4 (2011).

76. Villella, "Pure and Noble Indians," 636.

77. Silvia M. Arrom, "Gender in Mexican History: How Are We Doing?" (discussion at the Mexican Studies Committee Roundtable, 133rd American Historical Association meeting, Chicago, IL, January 4, 2019).

78. Susan Schroeder, Stephanie Wood, and Robert Haskett, eds. *Indian Women of Early Mexico* (Norman: University of Oklahoma Press, 1997), 3.

79. For Mexico, see Susan Kellogg, *Law and the Transformation of Aztec Culture, 1500–1700* (Norman: University of Oklahoma Press, 1995), chap. 3; and Sousa, *Woman*, chap. 2. For the Andean region, see Karen Powers, *Women in the Crucible of Conquest: The Gendered Genesis of Spanish American Society, 1500–1600* (Albuquerque: University of New Mexico Press, 2005); and Irene Silverblatt, *Moon, Sun, and Witches*, chap 3.

80. For Mexico, see Asunción Lavrin, ed., *Latin American Women: Historical Perspectives* (Westport: Greenwood, 1978); Asunción Lavrin, ed., *Sexuality & Marriage in Colonial Latin America* (Lincoln: University of Nebraska Press, 1989); and Asunción Lavrin and Edith Couturier, "Dowries and Wills: A View of Women's Socioeconomic Role in Colonial Guadalajara and Puebla, 1640–1790," *Hispanic American Historical Review* 50, no. 2 (May 1979). For Brazil, see Muriel Nazzari, *Disappearance of the Dowry: Women, Families, and Social Change in São Paulo, Brazil, 1600–1900* (Stanford: Stanford University Press, 1991). For South America, see Karen Graubart, *With Our Labor*; and Eugene H. Korth and Della M. Flusche, "Dowry and Inheritance in Colonial Spanish America: Peninsular Law and Chilean Practice," *Americas* 43, no. 4 (April 1987).

81. For example, see Edith Couturier, "Women and the Family in Eighteenth-Century Mexico: Law and Practice," *Journal of Family History* 10 (September 1985).

82. Patricia Seed, *To Love, Honor, and Obey in Colonial Mexico: Conflicts Over Marriage Choice, 1574–1821* (Stanford: Stanford University Press, 1988).

83. Ruth Behar, "Sexual Witchcraft, Colonialism, and Women's Powers: Views from the Mexican Inquisition," in Lavrin, *Sexuality & Marriage*; Martha Few, *Women Who Live Evil Lives: Gender, Religion, and the Politics of Power in Colonial Guatemala, 1650–1750* (Austin: University of Texas Press, 2002).

84. Díaz, *Indigenous Writings*; Lavrin, *Brides of Christ*. For the Andean region, see Luis Martín, *Daughters of the Conquistadors: Women of the Viceroyalty of Peru* (University Park: Southern Methodist University Press, 1989); and Kathryn Burns, *Colonial Habits: Convents and the Spiritual Economy of Cuzco, Peru* (Durham: Duke University Press, 1999).

85. Ann Twinam, *Public Lives, Private Secrets: Gender, Honor, Sexuality, and Illegitimacy in Colonial Spanish America* (Stanford: Stanford University Press, 1999). See also, Lyman L. Johnson and Sonya Lipsett-Rivera, eds., *The Faces of Honor: Sex, Shame, and Violence in Colonial Latin America* (Albuquerque: University of New Mexico Press, 1998).

86. Gauderman, *Women's Lives*; Chad Thomas Black, *The Limits of Gender Domination: Women, the Law, and Political Crisis in Quito, 1765–1830* (Albuquerque: University of New Mexico Press, 2010).

87. For analyses of Habsburg legal culture in Iberia, see Richard Kagan, *Lawsuits and Litigants in Castile, 1500–1700* (Chapel Hill: University of North Carolina Press, 1981); Helen Nader, *Liberty in Absolutist Spain: The Sale of Habsburg Towns, 1516–1700* (Baltimore: Johns Hopkins University Press, 1993); and Tamar Herzog, *Frontiers of Possession: Spain and Portugal in Europe and the Americas* (Cambridge: Harvard University Press, 2015). For Spanish America, see John Leddy Phelan, *The Kingdom of Quito in the Seventeenth Century* (Madison: University of Wisconsin Press, 1967); Clarence H. Haring, *The Spanish Empire in America* (New York: Harcourt, 1975 [1947]); Charles R. Cutter, *The Legal Culture of Northern New Spain, 1700–1810* (Albuquerque: University of New Mexico Press, 1995); Alejandro Cañeque, *The King's Living Image: The Culture and Politics of Viceregal Power in Colonial Mexico* (New York: Routledge Press, 2002); and Brian P. Owensby, *Empire of Law*.

88. For more on the two-republic system (Republic of Indians and the Republic of Spaniards), see note 20, above.

89. See Twinam, *Public Lives, Private Secrets*, and especially the case in Ann Twinam's "Pedro de Ayarza: The Purchase of Whiteness," in *The Human Tradition in Colonial Latin America*, 2nd ed., ed. Kenneth J. Andrien (Lanham: Rowman & Littlefield, 2013).

90. For the sixteenth century, see Robert C. Schwaller, *Géneros de Gente in Early Colonial Mexico: Defining Racial Difference* (Norman: University of Oklahoma Press, 2016). For the later colonial era, see Ann Twinam, *Purchasing Whiteness: Pardos, Mulattos, and the Quest for Social Mobility in the Spanish Indies* (Stanford: Stanford University Press, 2015).

91. For women, sex, class, and honor, see Twinam, *Public Lives, Private Secrets*. For more on marriage promises, status, and honor, see Patricia Seed, "Marriage Promises and the Value of a Woman's Testimony in Colonial Mexico," *Signs* 13, no. 2 (Winter 1988).

92. For a study on primordial titles, see Robert Haskett, *Visions of Paradise: Primordial Titles and Mesoamerican History in Cuernavaca* (Norman: University of Oklahoma Press, 2005).

93. Lisa Sousa and Kevin Terraciano, "The 'Original Conquest' of Oaxaca: Nahua and Mixtec Accounts of the Spanish Conquest," *Ethnohistory* 50, no. 2 (Spring 2003).

94. Sousa and Terraciano, "Original Conquest," 3. Quote from Matthew Restall, Lisa Sousa, and Kevin Terraciano, eds., *Mesoamerican Voices: Native-Language Writings from Colonial Mexico, Oaxaca, Yucatan, and Guatemala* (Cambridge: Cambridge University Press, 2005), 48.

95. Alcira Dueñas, *Indians and Mestizos in the 'Lettered City': Reshaping Justice, Social Hierarchy and Political Culture in Colonial Peru* (Boulder: University of Colorado Press, 2010).

96. La Puente Luna, *Andean Cosmopolitans*, 21.

97. For a study of the rise of written documents and including fake documents, such as falsified coats of arms, see María Castañeda de la Paz, *Verdades y mentiras en torno a don Diego de Mendoza Austria Moctezuma* (Mexico City: Universidad Nacional Autónoma de México, Universidad Intercultural del Estado de Hidalgo, El Colegio Mexiquense, 2017).

98. Ilona Katzew, *Casta Painting: Images of Race in Eighteenth-Century Mexico* (New Haven: Yale University Press, 2004).

99. Magali M. Carrera, *Imagining Identity in New Spain: Race, Lineage, and the Colonial Body in Portraiture and Casta Paintings* (Austin: University of Texas Press, 2003), 22–43.

PART I

North and Central America

Map 2. North and Central America. Cartography by Bill Nelson.

CHAPTER 1

The Cacicas of Teotihuacan

EARLY COLONIAL FEMALE POWER AND WEALTH

Bradley Benton

In the period immediately preceding European contact, local Nahua (often also referred to as Aztec) rulers in central Mexico appear to have been exclusively male. Other highland Mesoamerican cultures such as the Mixtec farther south submitted to both male and female rule with some regularity, but Nahua women seem only to have held the local ruling title of *tlatoani* (pl. *tlatoque*) in rare circumstances and perhaps not at all by the late fifteenth century. As Lisa Sousa notes, "female rule [among the Nahuas] was an exception and may have occurred only as a result of disruption in dynastic descent."[1] Susan Schroeder has identified two *cihuatlatoque*, or "woman-rulers," in the precontact central Mexican kingdoms of Chalco from her studies of the early seventeenth-century work of Nahua historian Chimalpahin; these women held power in the fourteenth and early fifteenth centuries. And Rudolph van Zantwijk has suggested that Atotoztli, daughter of Moteucçoma Ilhuicamina and wife of Tezozomoc, may have ruled Tenochtitlan as tlatoani in her own right in the 1460s and '70s.[2] There is, though, hardly any other direct evidence of women rulers among the Nahuas.[3]

After nearly a century of colonial rule, however, in the late sixteenth century, the relationship between gender and power in local indigenous communities had experienced a great deal of change. To be sure, the Spaniards still insisted on having men occupy what they thought to be the most important local positions, but women nonetheless exercised power in new ways in the early colonial period that challenged aspects of both precontact Nahua and Spanish patriarchal gender norms.

One of the most striking examples of the ascendancy of female power is in the *altepetl*, or ethnic state, of Teotihuacan, located about thirty miles (fifty kilometers) to the northeast of Mexico Tenochtitlan. In Teotihuacan, the male tlatoani died ca. 1563 and power and property passed to his widow. More striking still, when his widow died in 1580, the estate passed to another woman, his daughter. Then when his daughter died in 1597, the estate again passed to a woman, his granddaughter, who held the estate until her death ca. 1639. These women were styled cacicas.[4] Collectively, Teotihuacan's three early colonial cacicas held Teotihuacan's *cacicazgo*—the entailed lordly estate roughly equivalent to an entailed *mayorazgo* in Spain—for more than seventy-five years. Their experiences point to dramatic changes afoot among the Nahua nobility. Not only did these women displace men as the most important native individuals in Teotihuacan, but they also contributed to larger changes in residency and ethnicity. And they were involved in the colonial courts to resolve property disputes both within Teotihuacan and in other altepetl. As the Teotihuacan cacicas demonstrate, native women were far from passive onlookers in the processes of colonial change and adaptation by the native aristocracy. They were active agents in the building of colonial society, challenging late Postclassic Nahua notions of rulership and female aristocratic life.

POSTCLASSIC AND EARLY COLONIAL TEOTIHUACAN

For most, the word Teotihuacan brings to mind the giant metropolis of the Classic Period (ca. 1–900 CE). Classic Period Teotihuacan was the largest urban center in the western hemisphere and the sixth largest city in the world at its height between 400 and 550 CE, with around one hundred thousand inhabitants occupying a site that was eight square miles (twenty-one square kilometers) in area.[5] Its two enormous pyramids are some of the most visited in Mexico today. But the Classic Period Teotihuacanos had already abandoned their pyramids and urban center by the time Nahuatl speakers arrived in central Mexico. And in the period just before conquest, the Teotihuacan community was a much more modest settlement, located just outside of the Classic Period site, and subject to the ruler of nearby Tetzcoco and the Triple Alliance.[6] The glamourous urban civilization of the Classic Period is not under discussion here. Instead, this chapter is focused on the smaller community of Teotihuacan during the late Postclassic and colonial periods, a community that in 1570 (after several decades of epidemics) numbered four thousand tribute-paying native people. This later Teotihuacan, though small in comparison with its Classic Period predecessor and with coeval Postclassic and early colonial centers like Mexico Tenochtitlan, was not insignificant. It was classified as a full altepetl by Nahuatl speakers, with its own tlatoani and dynastic ruling family. And while it rendered tribute to Tetzcoco, it collected income from the surrounding countryside and its *sujetos* (subject communities), which still numbered eighteen in 1580.[7]

The eighth tlatoani of Teotihuacan was a man named Quetzalmamalitzin, later baptized don Francisco Verdugo. He likely took his Christian name from a Spanish conquistador of the same name. This Spanish conquistador became Teotihuacan's first *encomendero* (holder of a royal grant of indigenous tribute), so we may assume that he served as Quetzalmamalitzin's baptismal sponsor.[8] Quetzalmamalitzin came to power just after the 1521 fall of Tenochtitlan, and his position as ruler of Teotihuacan was officially confirmed by the Spanish Crown in 1533. He lived in Teotihuacan, spoke Nahuatl, and never learned to read or write using the Latin alphabet.[9]

His father, grandfather, and great-grandfather had been both born in and served as tlatoani of Teotihuacan. Most of his female ancestors, however, had come from the nearby regional power, Tetzcoco, located about thirteen miles (twenty-one kilometers) south of Teotihuacan. His ancestry—the men from Teotihuacan and the women from Tetzcoco—was no accident. It was part of the way that Tetzcoco exerted its influence over Teotihuacan and other subordinate altepetl in the region. Pedro Carrasco has called this pattern interdynastic hypogamy, meaning that women from the ruling family of dominant altepetl married the rulers of subordinate altepetl. It was widespread among the Nahuas in the period before contact with Europeans. In this case, high-ranking Tetzcoca women—often the Tetzcoca tlatoani's sisters or daughters—married rulers of subordinate polities, including Teotihuacan. The sons of these unions—with Tetzcoco's help—would become the next generation of subordinate tlatoque in the region, thereby helping to cement loyalty to Tetzcoco among the ruling class of its subject polities and avoid rebellion.[10]

Quetzalmamalitzin's female ancestors, therefore, had been key figures in establishing and maintaining Tetzcoco's control over Teotihuacan. This pattern had prevailed for generations, and it was still very much in place around the time of contact with Spaniards. In fact, Quetzalmamalitzin's wife, too, was from Tetzcoco. It is not known what she was called before the Spaniards arrived, but her Christian name, given at her baptism, was doña Ana Cortés. Our story of Teotihuacan's cacicas begins with her.

DOÑA ANA CORTÉS

Doña Ana Cortés was born in Tetzcoco. She was the great-granddaughter of the legendary Tetzcoca tlatoani Nezahualcoyotl, granddaughter of Nezahualpilli, and daughter of Tetzcoco's conquest-era leader, Ixtlilxochitl, who was later baptized don Fernando Cortés. If we are to believe the accounts of doña Ana's great-grandson, the seventeenth-century chronicler don Fernando de Alva Ixtlilxochitl, her father had been extremely active in the conquest wars, fighting on the side of the Spaniards.[11] Ixtlilxochitl's alliance with the Spanish conquistador Hernando Cortés perhaps gave doña Ana's father the political and social boost needed to integrate himself and his children into Tetzcoco's regional power networks and marry doña Ana to the tlatoani of Teotihuacan.

If the marriage was arranged to meet political needs, it seems nonetheless to have been one in which personal respect and affection between the two developed. For as Quetzalmamalitzin lay dying in 1563, he declared in his will that much of his estate be left in the hands of doña Ana Cortés, "whom," he says, "I love dearly."[12] He left his wife all manner of things. First, he left her five specific properties that appear to be quite important, for he calls them *tecpantlalli* and *pillalli*.[13] Tecpantlalli (palace land) is land tied to palace buildings, while pillalli (noble's land) is land owned by the hereditary nobility, often contrasted with lands administered by the *calpolli* (constituent districts of the altepetl) and subject to redistribution.[14] The tecpantlalli and pillalli properties that Quetzalmamalitzin left his wife were called Atezcapan, Huitznahuac, Calpoltitlan, Cozotlan, and Atempan. In all of these places, Quetzalmamalitzin left doña Ana Cortés "both the land and fields as well as the vassals."[15] He also leaves her certain *tecpan* (palaces) themselves—apparently without any attendant land or vassals—in Mizquititlan, Xihuacan, and Aticpac. Doña Ana is also to receive all of his *tierras baldías* (land that is unoccupied and not under cultivation) and what appears to be a stone quarry. All of Quetzalmamalitzin's non–real estate property, his *bienes muebles* (movable property), was also to go to doña Ana Cortés, including his collection of featherwork, which was highly prized and likely quite valuable.[16]

Doña Ana Cortés, then, was clearly entrusted with a great deal—though not all—of the Teotihuacan lordly estate when Quetzalmamalitzin died. All of this property, together with other dowry lands that doña Ana brought to the marriage, constituted a sizable estate. And doña Ana, cacica of Teotihuacan, was in charge of it all until her death. She would have collected rents from the native commoners who worked the land and from any Spaniards, mestizos, or fellow nobles who may have lived on or made use of her properties. Even if she had remarried—and there is no indication that she did—Quetzalmamalitzin wanted her still to enjoy the use of half of this estate until the end of her life, when it would then pass to their children.[17]

In addition to this fortune, doña Ana was also given a fair amount of responsibility in her husband's will. For instance, Quetzalmamalitzin had been pursuing various claims to property in the courts, and he left her "in his place so that she might continue the said claim and not abandon it."[18] Moreover, near the end of the will, Quetzalmamalitzin reiterates and reinforces this idea that doña Ana Cortés will become functionally equivalent to himself after his death: "I give her all of my full authority. And so that she may have and possess my property and what was mine, as I have had and possessed it, I leave her in my place."[19]

This language of authority and place-taking strongly suggests that Quetzalmamalitzin intended his wife to become the local ruler when he died, to assume the role of tlatoani of Teotihuacan. He did not explicitly state that she was to become the tlatoani, but doña Ana Cortés was to control much of his property, continue his legal suits, and occupy his place in a general sense. He clearly did not envision his widow being sidelined in family and local affairs. Perhaps his great love for doña Ana—which he boldly proclaimed twice in his testament—led him to this decision. Perhaps it was her natural abilities and inclinations that convinced him that this was a prudent choice. Perhaps he wished to avoid angering doña Ana's relatives in Tetzcoco. Whatever the case, Quetzalmamalitzin flouted tradition. The leader after his death would be a woman.

Unfortunately, doña Ana Cortés did not leave us much of a record of what she did after her husband died. Her daughter explicitly states that she did not make a will and died intestate, thereby depriving us of a better understanding of her activities and circumstances.[20] The large collection of documents pertaining to the Teotihuacan cacicazgo preserved in Mexico's Archivo General de la Nación (AGN) as Vínculos, volume 232, expediente 1, does not include much information about doña Ana Cortés beyond that which is contained in Quetzalmamalitzin's will.

DOÑA FRANCISCA CHRISTINA VERDUGO

While doña Ana Cortés is an intriguing example of postconquest changes in native leadership practices, Quetzalmamalitzin's will further contradicts pre-Hispanic custom by ensuring that another woman would take possession of the Teotihuacan estate after doña Ana's death. Indeed, Quetzalmamalitzin's first order of business—after, of course, attending to the needs of his soul—was to name his daughter doña Francisca Christina Verdugo as his heir. He writes: "On the matter of my assets, I say, first, that I give this altepetl to my daughter doña Christina, that she may possess it as I have possessed it. And in the same way, my grandchildren are to inherit it because it is the tlatoani's property, along with all of the lands of the altepetl and its seven calpolli, through which the commoners pay tribute."[21] If Quetzalmamalitzin merely implied that his wife should become ruler after his death, he was more explicit about doña Francisca Cristina. His choice of words, in fact, suggest that he thought of her as the next tlatoani (or cihuatlatoani, perhaps). In the original Nahuatl, Quetzalmamalitzin states that the altepetl was *tlatocatlatqui* (tlatoani's property) and it should be possessed by doña Francisca. He further states that she also was to receive the tribute rendered by the altepetl commoners after he died. These two things, the altepetl and the tribute, were not Quetzalmamalitzin's personal property; they belonged to the office of the tlatoani. By assigning these things to his daughter, he clearly indicated that she should be tlatoani after him, to collect tribute and possess the altepetl as he had. His use of "tlatocatlatqui" leaves little room for doubt: he thought of doña Francisca as the next tlatoani. While doña Ana Cortés was to enjoy the use of the estate only, her daughter doña Francisca was to enjoy both the estate and the attendant political position.

One might assume that Teotihuacan rulership passed to women in the 1560s because there were no men. But this is not, in fact, the case. Two closely related men do appear in Quetzalmamalitzin's will. The first mentioned is Quetzalmamalitzin's son. This son was certainly an illegitimate child, born of a woman who was not doña Ana Cortés. "To a son of mine who is called Joseph," he wrote, "I leave two pairs of houses in Aticpac, where the community millstones turn." He also left Joseph a field in the place called Atezcapan that was a mere "twenty-eight *cuahuitl* long and nineteen *cuahuitl* wide."[22] Joseph's inheritance is a tiny fraction of Quetzalmamalitzin's many properties. Similarly, Quetzalmamalitzin mentions a brother in his will, but provides him with only a few properties: "Another large house with the door facing the hill they call Hueytepetl, I give to my brother Juan Marin. May he have it as his own. It is likewise in Aticpac. And that which I gave him in the past, the lands in the place called Nextlaleltitlan and another called Cacalo Milpan, I hereby confirm his right to them, for they belong to him and are his property."[23] So while these two men did inherit some property, their share was meager when compared to the wealth inherited by Quetzalmamalitzin's female heirs. The lion's share of Quetzalmamalitzin's large estate and the political power consciously and deliberately went to doña Ana Cortés and doña Francisca Verdugo, respectively.

Doña Francisca seems to have come into her full inheritance at the time of her mother's death around 1580. While her father's will was clear that she should be called tlatoani, Nahuatl-language documents concerning doña Francisca after his death have not come to light, making it impossible to know what she was called by native nobles or commoners in Teotihuacan. In Spanish-language documents she is called the cacica of Teotihuacan. Unlike her mother, however, who was also called cacica and who administered the estate after her husband's death, doña Francisca was not a cacica by virtue of marriage. She was cacica in her own right, a hereditary female cacique.

Doña Francisca's husband, in fact, was a Spaniard. His name was Juan Grande, and he was employed as an interpreter in the Real Audiencia (High Court) of Mexico. His father, Juan Grande Zarzabaraza, was a captain with Columbus on his third and fourth voyages.[24] It was not uncommmon for native noblewomen to marry Spaniards after the conquest. In Tetzcoco, for example, I have elsewhere detailed several examples. And Pedro Carrasco has identified many more from across New Spain. Native women, however, also continued to marry native noblemen.[25] Doña Francisca's decision to marry a Spaniard, then, was a conscious choice on her part. And this choice had implications for her children, place of residence, and social and economic opportunities. In fact, as seen below, her daughter, who was of mixed race, occupied a slightly different place in the minds of people in Teotihuacan, precisely because of her mixed parentage.

Somewhat surprisingly, the cacica of Teotihuacan and her husband did not live in Teotihuacan, but in Mexico City. This would have been inconceivable in the precontact period. There is evidence that the lords of Teotihuacan were required to be in Tetzcoco from time to time in the pre-Hispanic period to attend at the royal court and serve on tribunals there, but they certainly did not live in Tenochtitlan.[26] Doña Francisca and Juan Grande chose to live in the capital perhaps because of Grande's position there, but perhaps also because the capital offered greater access to status, prestige, and power. While doña Francisca owned many houses in Teotihuacan and undoubtedly spent time there, tiny Teotihuacan simply could not compete with Mexico City. The couple lived in the barrio of Santa Ana, which appears to be just a few blocks to the southwest of the plaza of Tlatelolco, just across Paseo de la Reforma today. A location near Tlatelolco is perhaps confirmed by the fact that doña Francisca wished to be buried in the monastery and church of Santiago Tlatelolco. Doña Francisca and her husband had had the buildings constructed specifically for their residence, thereby contributing to the phys-ical build-up of postcontact Mexico City and helping to transform it—both architecturally and socially—into the new viceregal capital.[27]

As cacica of Teotihuacan, doña Francisca likely enjoyed moderately high status in the capital. She spoke primarily Nahuatl, as her will attests, so it seems unlikely that she mingled with vicereines or other members of penin-sular high society, but she did have substantial contact and business dealings with Spaniards. For instance, she owed six pesos to a Spaniard named Diego Ruiz, and, in her will, she asked another Spaniard named Damián Pérez to take Diego the money she owed him.[28] Doña Francisca does not discuss how she came to owe this Spaniard money or why she trusted another Spaniard with the money to pay off the debt, but her connections to the Spaniards of Mexico City—connections of a fairly close nature—are nonetheless appar-ent. Moreover, she was a member of several Mexico City cofradías (Catholic lay organizations) including Nuestra Señora del Rosario, Nuestra Señora del Carmen, and the Augustinian Nombre de Jesús.[29] She appears, therefore, to have led a socially active life, funded in part no doubt by the income from her estate in Teotihuacan.

But while doña Francisca collected income in Teotihuacan, her role in local government was much diminished. Quetzalmamalitzin wanted her to be the tlatoani, which during his lifetime was a political office with attendant real estate wealth. The sixteenth century, however, brought radical changes to that office. Across the central valleys, tlatoque were either withdrawing or being forced out of local politics. They became known instead as caciques, wealthy individuals descended from the precontact rulers, but no longer participants in the day-to-day running of their communities. Daily operations were han-dled by individuals whom the Spaniards were calling gobernadores (gover-nors). These men—and they were all men—were, in the early years of the colony, often the tlatoque themselves. Or sometimes the Spanish office rotated among a group of high-ranking nobles from the old tlatoque dynasties.[30] As time passed, however, the new office of *juez gobernador* (judge-governor) came to dominate. These juez gobernadores were drawn from outside of the communities where they worked. They were still primarily native men, but they were not local natives. As outsiders they would, it was hoped, better represent the interests of the viceregal administration. By the late sixteenth and early seventeenth centuries, the viceroy had amassed a cadre of such outsiders, whom he appointed to the various communities around the capital.[31]

Doña Francisca, by virtue of her sex, would have been ineligible to serve as either gobernador or juez gobernador. And while the surviving documents do not speak to who occupied this position in Teotihuacan during doña Francisca's lifetime, it certainly would not have been her. Like her counterparts in many other central Mexican altepetl, she seems to have made the shift from tlatoani to cacica. Her absence from Teotihuacan and residence in Mexico City appears to confirm her role as a wealthy private individual removed from local government. She continued to enjoy the real estate wealth, the cacicazgo, which was bequeathed to her by her father, but she was no longer officially in charge in Teotihuacan.

This is not, of course, unique to doña Francisca. It is not even unique to women in this period. Across central Mexico, in fact, cacicazgos were being separated from the political offices to which they had once been attached. Most of the old pre-Hispanic ruling families were able to hold on to their real estate wealth, but local government fell into the hands of other people. In Teotihuacan, the fact that doña Francisca was a woman—and not eligible to serve as governor—probably helped to speed this separation process along. Those who wished to take political power away from doña Francisca's family no doubt found the restrictions placed on women convenient for their purposes. But, to be fair, the separation of the property from the political office might have occurred if Quetzalmamalitzin had bequeathed everything to a son instead of a daughter, as in fact happened in Tetzcoco in 1564.[32]

While doña Francisca was not the local political leader in Teotihuacan, she did not simply retire to her townhome in Tlatelolco. In fact, she was quite involved in politics in her mother's hometown of Tetzcoco. Tetzcoco had been one of the three capitals of the Aztec Triple Alliance in the pre-Hispanic period, and the wealth of its pre-Hispanic native rulers was apparently quite spectacular. In the 1570s and '80s, these riches were at the center of a court battle between rival factions of the Tetzcoco ruling family.

The Tetzcoco cacicazgo also attracted the attention of doña Francisca, who was related to all of the litigants through her Tetzcoca mother. In a document from 1576, doña Francisca and her husband officially aligned themselves with one of the warring factions, pledging to aid one set of cousins in their legal battles against another set. In return for her political and economic support, doña Francisca was promised a portion of the cacicazgo once it was won.[33] Her cousins' desire to have her as an ally confirms that she was a woman of substantial political clout in regional politics. Unfortunately for doña Francisca, it took twenty years for her cousins in Tetzcoco to settle their dispute. And even though doña Francisca had supported the side that eventually won, she never received any properties from the Tetzcoco cacicazgo. Doña Francisca would not drop the issue, though. And even as she lay dying, dictating her will, she still believed she was entitled to part of the Tetzcoco cacicazgo and left detailed instructions for her heirs to continue her fight for it.[34] Even though doña Francisca was officially excluded from Teotihuacan government, she remained involved in the machinations of the regional Nahua elite and worked diligently to expand her estate. Doña Francisca, the woman who would have been tlatoani, instead led the transition in Teotihuacan from a precontact-style native leader to a thoroughly colonial wealthy private individual.

DOÑA ANA CORTÉS IXTLILXOCHITL

One of the things that makes Teotihuacan an interesting case study of cacicas is that when doña Francisca died, the cacicazgo again passed to a woman. In 1596, in poor health, doña Francisca dictated to a notary the way she wanted her estate handled once she passed away. As her heirs, she named her two daughters, doña Ana Cortés Ixtlilxochitl and doña Juana Verdugo.[35] And while doña Francisca mentioned a son, Luis Grande, in her will, it seems that he was already dead at the time she was making her testament. She wished to use his estate, which she apparently controlled, to endow a chaplaincy. This chaplaincy was to be used to support one of her grandsons if any of them decided to become a priest.[36] So when doña Francisca died in 1597, the cacicazgo of Teotihuacan did not pass to her son Luis but rather her daughter. The Teotihuacan cacicazgo again passed to a female cacica. This new cacica was doña Ana Cortés Ixtlilxochitl. She held the position from her mother's death in 1597 until the end of her life around 1640.

Doña Ana was born and raised in Mexico City. Her will, drafted in 1639 near the end of her life, states that she was still living in the same Santa Ana neighborhood in Mexico City as her parents had. Like her mother before her, doña Ana married a Spaniard, Juan Pérez de Peraleda, whose family came from Seville. Like her father, Juan Grande, doña Ana's husband, Juan Pérez, also worked as an interpreter in the Real Audiencia of Mexico.[37] Her life in Mexico City must have been quite similar to the one her mother had led there.

Doña Ana was certainly preoccupied with many of the same concerns as doña Francisca. For instance, doña Ana's will mentions the cacicazgo of Tetzcoco. Doña Francisca had not been able to secure any portion of the Tetzcoco cacicazgo, but doña Ana was keen to keep this fight alive. Her will reminded everyone of her mother's alliance with her Tetzcoca cousins, an agreement that was, by then, more than sixty years old. Doña Ana had not given up hope, however, and urged her descendants and heirs to seek out and claim the parts of the Tetzcoco cacicazgo that rightfully belonged to them. Doña Ana also mentioned that she had inherited properties in the town of Tepepulco, located about twenty-five miles (forty kilometers) away from Teotihuacan. She had inherited these properties from her great-aunt, doña Luisa Cortés, her grandmother's sister, who had been married to the tlatoani of that community.[38] It is unclear if doña Ana actually had possession of these properties, but she did present documents that proved that her great-aunt had bequeathed them to her. Even if she did not actually possess them, though, it is clear that doña Ana was keenly interested, just like her mother, in her real estate wealth and in expanding her estate.

If there is one area where doña Ana and her mother diverged, it was in ethnicity. While doña Francisca's parents were both Nahuas, doña Ana had one indigenous parent and one Spanish parent. Whereas doña Francisca was unambiguously native, doña Ana was not. Later generations would have called doña Ana a *mestiza* (woman of mixed decent), but her rank and wealth make it difficult to determine how exactly she or her contemporaries would have understood her ethnicity. Some members of her family tended to emphasize the indigenous elements of their parentage, while others did not. Two of doña Ana's sons, for instance, approached their ethnicity in contrasting ways. Don Fernando de Alva Ixtlilxochitl went to great lengths to emphasize his native heritage, writing large volumes celebrating the pre-Hispanic past, while Bartolomé de Alva, a priest, may have found that heritage to be a liability in the church.[39]

Some degree of flexibility in ethnicity is expected in this period. But doña Ana's ethnicity was sufficiently ambiguous to cause her family some problems. In 1643, near the end of her life, four laborers from Teotihuacan accused doña Ana and her descendants of being Spaniards. They hoped, it would seem, to have the cacicazgo taken away from doña Ana and her family, because royal law prohibited Spaniards from holding these indigenous entailed estates.[40] It was an ingenious strategy on the part of the laborers, who would not have to pay rents to doña Ana if they had won the suit. But, in the end, it did not succeed; the audiencia confirmed doña Ana's possession of her cacicazgo. She kept it and passed it on to her children when she died. But while this suit came to naught, it is nonetheless important in that it shows us that the ethnic changes underway among the cacica class had not gone unnoticed by Teotihuacan's commoner population. The Teotihuacan cacicas, and noble native women across central Mexico, were reshaping ethnicity through their marriage choices.

EIGHTEENTH-CENTURY ECHOES

Almost a century and a half after doña Ana's death, one of her descendants—doña Josefa Antonia de Alva y Cortés—was still cognizant of the power and wealth commanded by these early colonial Teotihuacan cacicas. In a 1784 petition to the audiencia, doña Josefa demanded that she inherit the Teotihuacan cacicazgo and be named cacique.[41] Her claim rested on two points. First, her attorney noted that the cacicazgo of Teotihuacan's founding documents contained nothing that would bar women from holding the cacicazgo of Teotihuacan. In fact, the attorney declared that "there have been examples of several women possessing and enjoying [the cacicazgo]. Because doña Anna Fran[cisca] Berdugo possessed it. Also a certain doña Anna Cortés Ysquisuchil was its possessor."[42] Any attempt to deny doña Josefa the cacicazgo based on her sex, therefore, was completely baseless in his opinion. Her foremothers had, apparently, already established a clear precedent.

The second point her solicitor made was simple: doña Josefa was the eldest of her parents' children. This point is made straightforwardly and simply in the petition, as if it were noncontroversial. But the document reveals that doña Josefa had a least one brother. And if the Spanish legal system did in fact legally privilege the eldest son as rightful heir to entailed estates, then doña Josefa's petition would certainly have generated conflict. This brother would get nothing from the cacicazgo properties. Doña Josefa's claims seem to have been successful, however. In a subsequent document, a document in which doña Josefa gives her power of attorney to one of the lawyers of the audiencia, she is called "cacique."[43] She seems to have been able to convince the audiencia that she was the rightful heir based on birth order alone, with no consideration of her sex or the sex of her siblings.

Doña Josefa makes her claims to the cacicazgo by noting directly and explicitly the experiences of the early colonial cacicas of Teotihuacan, particularly doña Francisca Verdugo and doña Ana Cortés Ixtlilxochitl. These women were very much on the minds of upper-class women in Teotihuacan for centuries after their deaths. In fact, among some eighteenth-century legal documents related to the Teotihuacan cacicazgo is a portrait of doña Ana Cortés Ixtlilxochitl drawn, apparently, in 1648.[44] (See fig. 1.1.) This seventeenth-century drawing seems to have been submitted with court filings to support an eighteenth-century legal claim. The name of the eighteenth-century claimant is unknown; perhaps it was doña Josefa herself. In any case, it remains unclear what exact purpose this portrait was intended to serve. But what is clear is that the memory of doña Ana Cortés Ixtlilxochitl was important in

Fig. 1.1. *Doña Ana Cortés Ixtlilxochitl* (1648). Line drawing by unknown artist. (Archivo General de la Nación [México], Vínculos, vol. 233, fol. 10; photo courtesy of Amber Brian.)

making this particular legal claim. Her role as cacica and the property she controlled must have carried great weight in the eighteenth century for the litigant to include such a depiction, for portraits of this kind are exceedingly rare in the colonial land litigation documents of Mexico's AGN.

CONCLUSION

In the colonial period, native noble women were occupying positions of authority that they would not have occupied in the immediate precontact period. Quetzalmamalitzin appears to have intended for both his wife doña Ana Cortés and his daughter doña Francisca to act as tlatoque in Teotihuacan, passing over an illegitimate son and a brother for the job. Spanish practice, however, prevented them from acting as gobernadores of the town. The tlatoani's estate was divorced from the rulership and rebranded a cacicazgo, while the female tlatoque were rebranded as cacicas. The cacicas maintained control of the cacicazgo, however, while others vied for local political control. They themselves, and not their husbands, owned substantial wealth in the form of land and houses and collected rents from these properties from both native people and Spaniards. They disposed of it as they pleased. They bequeathed it to their children. And they were concerned with expanding their holdings, inserting themselves into their cousins' lawsuits in nearby Tetzcoco in an attempt to secure parts of the cacicazgo there.

These women also bucked tradition by leaving Teotihuacan and moving to Mexico City. Never before had the Teotihuacan tlatoque resided in Mexico. Doña Francisca and doña Ana lived a much more cosmopolitan life than their forebears. And doña Francisca actually helped to rebuild Mexico City after the destruction of the conquest, building her home in the parish of Santa Ana, leaving her architectural mark. As a result of their life in the metropolis, however, doña Francisca and doña Ana were even further removed from Teotihuacan's local government, though they remained connected to their cacicazgo lands there.

Moreover, these women were at the forefront of a revolution in ethnicity. Both doña Francisca and doña Ana married Spaniards, making their children and heirs ethnically different from themselves and somewhat ambiguous in the social hierarchy. At times, this served cacicas and their descendants well. Some of their male descendants eventually occupied positions that had once been held exclusively by Spaniards, such as court officials or even Catholic priests. At other times, however, these ethnic changes coupled with their geographical distance from Teotihuacan caused the family some trouble, as when commoners challenged doña Ana's claim to be cacica because she was not indigenous. The hereditary native nobility was experiencing a great deal of change in this period, and the cacicas of Teotihuacan were at the forefront of these changes.

As the eighteenth-century documents attest, the activities of these women did not go unnoticed. In their lifetimes and after their deaths, they were remembered for their pioneering pursuits, for their industriousness, and for their property. Their examples ensured that doña Ana Cortés Ixtlilxochitl would not be the last woman to hold the Teotihuacan cacicazgo. Women of native descent would continue to fight for and secure the estate even in the final decades of the colonial period. The early colonial cacicas of Teotihuacan helped to build a society that recognized and repeatedly confirmed female claims to wealth and power.

NOTES

1. Lisa Sousa, *The Woman Who Turned into a Jaguar and Other Narratives of Native Women in Archives of Colonial Mexico* (Stanford: Stanford University Press, 2017), 11. She notes that the Nahuas had a term for female ruler—*cihuatlatoani*—but that by the time the Spaniards arrived, the position of tlatoani was held by men. For the Mixtec, see Ronald Spores, *The Mixtec Kings and their People* (Norman: University of Oklahoma Press, 1967) and Kevin Terraciano, *The Mixtecs of Colonial Oaxaca: Ñudzahui History, Sixteenth through Eighteenth Centuries* (Stanford: Stanford University Press, 2001), 165–69.

2. Susan Schroeder, "The Noblewomen of Chalco," *Estudios de Cultura Nahuatl* 22 (1992): 48, 81–82; Rudoph van Zantwijk, *The Aztec Arrangement: The Social History of Pre-Spanish Mexico* (Norman: University of Oklahoma Press, 1985), 189–91. See also Susan D. Gillespie, *The Aztec Kings: The Construction of Rulership in Mexica History* (Tucson: University of Arizona Press, 1989).

3. Though the records contain few examples of direct female rulership, women nonetheless played important and powerful roles in local government. They often shared responsibilities with their tlatoque husbands in parallel and complementary positions of authority, were regents for their sons, and were crucial actors in regional alliance-building through their marriages. See especially Schroeder, "Noblewman of Chalco"; Susan Kellogg, *Weaving the Past: A History of Latin America's Indigenous Women from the Prehispanic Period to the Present* (New York: Oxford University Press, 2005), 26–27; and Pedro Carrasco, "Royal Marriages in Ancient Mexico," in *Explorations in Ethnohistory: Indians of Central Mexico in the Sixteenth Century*, ed. H. R. Harvey and Hanns J. Prem (Albuquerque: University of New Mexico Press, 1984).

4. For more on the origins of "cacica," see the prologue and introduction to this volume.

5. For the most recent discussion of Classic Period Teotihuacan's population, see Michael E. Smith, Abhishek Chatterjee, Angela C. Huster, Sierra Stewart, and Marion Forest, "Apartment Compounds, Households, and Population in the Ancient City of Teotihuacan, Mexico," *Ancient Mesoamerica* 30 (2019): 416.

6. The Triple Alliance refers to the ruling alliance among the Nahua altepetl of Tenochtitlan, Tetzcoco, and Tlacopan. The alliance is also often referred to as the Aztec Empire.

7. Peter Gerhard, *A Guide to the Historical Geography of New Spain*, rev. ed. (Norman: University of Oklahoma Press, 1993), 274.

8. Gerhard, *Guide to Historical Geography*, 273. The Catholic rite of baptism required—and continues to require today—that new Christians be presented to the clergy by a sponsor. It was socially advantageous to have a person of status serve as one's sponsor, and in sixteenth-century Mesoamerica, it was common for conquistadors and encomenderos to serve as sponsors for native people—especially for native nobles—in the regions under their control.

9. Quetzalmamalitzin's original will, which was submitted to the *audiencia* (high court of justice) by don Fernando de Alva Ixtlilxochitl in 1611 to be translated into Spanish, was written in Nahuatl. At the end of the will, fray Alonso Vera states that he was asked by the cacique to sign the will for him, "because he did not know how to write." Archivo General de la Nación (hereafter cited as AGN), Vínculos, vol. 232, expediente 1, fols. 10r and 20r.

10. Carrasco, "Royal Marriages," 47–49. See also Camilla Townsend "Polygyny and the Divided Altepetl: The Tetzcocan Key to Pre-conquest Nahua Politics," in *Texcoco: Prehispanic and Colonial Perspectives*, ed. Jongsoo Lee and Galen Brokaw (Boulder: University Press of Colorado, 2014).

11. See, for instance, Amber Brian, Bradley Benton, and Pablo García Loaeza, trans. and eds., *The Native Conquistador: Alva Ixtlilxochitl's Account of the Conquest of New Spain*, Latin American Originals 10 (University Park: Pennsylvania State University Press, 2015). See also Frederic Hicks, "Texcoco 1515–1519: The Ixtlilxochitl Affair," in *Chipping Away on Earth: Studies in Prehispanic and Colonial Mexico in Honor of Arthur J. O. Anderson and Charles E. Dibble*, ed. Eloise Quiñones Keber (Lancaster, CA: Labyrinthos, 1994) and Townsend, "Polygyny and the Divided Altepetl."

12. AGN, Vínculos, vol. 232, expediente 1, fol. 19r.

13. AGN, Vínculos, vol. 232, expediente 1, fol. 12r–v.

14. James Lockhart, *The Nahuas after the Conquest: A Social and Cultural History of the Indians of Central Mexico, Sixteenth Through Eighteenth Centuries* (Stanford: Stanford University Press, 1992), 156 and 161.

15. AGN, Vínculos, vol. 232, expediente 1, fol. 16r.

16. AGN, Vínculos, vol. 232, expediente 1, fols. 16v, 18v, and 19r.

17. AGN, Vínculos, vol. 232, expediente 1, fol. 17v.

18. AGN, Vínculos, vol. 232, expediente 1, fol. 16v.

19. AGN, Vínculos, vol. 232, expediente 1, fol. 18r.

20. AGN, Vínculos, vol. 232, expediente 1, fol. 22r.

21. The archival file includes early seventeenth-century copies of both the original Nahuatl document as well as a Spanish-language translation. Compare AGN, Vínculos, vol. 232, expediente 1, fols. 12r and 16r. Both have been transcribed (and the Nahuatl translated into Spanish) in Emma Pérez-Rocha and Rafael Tena, *La nobleza indígena de México después de la conquista* (Mexico City: Instituto Nacional de Antropología e Historia, 2000), 261–77. My English translation preserves the original Nahuatl political terms.

22. Cuahuitl, or quahuitl, which literally translates as "stick," was the primary Nahua unit of measure. It varied in length somewhat from place to place, though Spaniards often translated quahuitl as *braza* (fathom) which was about six feet (two meters). See Lockhart, *Nahuas after the Conquest*, 144–45. The field bequeathed to Joseph, therefore, would have been about 170 feet long by about 115 feet wide (52 by 35 meters).

23. AGN, Vínculos, vol. 232, expediente 1, fol. 16v.

24. Guido Munch, *El cacicazgo de San Juan Teotihuacan durante la colonia, 1521–1821* (Mexico City: Instituto Nacional de Antropología e Historia, Centro de Investigaciones Superiores, 1976), 62.

25. See Bradley Benton, *The Lords of Tetzcoco: The Transformation of Indigenous Rule in Postconquest Central Mexico* (New York: Cambridge University Press, 2017), chap. 4; and Pedro Carrasco, "Indian-Spanish Marriages in the First Century of the Colony," in *Indian Women of Early Mexico*, ed. Susan Schroeder, Stephanie Wood, and Robert Haskett (Norman: University of Oklahoma Press, 1997), 92–103.

26. Fernando de Alva Ixtlilxochitl, *Obras históricas*, vol. 2, ed. Edmundo O'Gorman (Mexico City: Universidad Nacional Autónoma de México, Instituto de Investigaciones Históricas, 1975), 94.

27. AGN, Vínculos, vol. 232, expediente 1, fols. 23r–v. For an extended discussion of this transformation, see Barbara E. Mundy, *The Death of Aztec Tenochtitlan, the Life of Mexico City* (Austin: University of Texas Press, 2015).

28. AGN, Vínculos, vol. 232, expediente 1, fol. 23r.

29. AGN, Vínculos, vol. 232, expediente 1, fol. 24v–25r. She was also *cofrada* (female member) of two cofradías in Teotihuacan: Nuestra Señora de la Concepción and the Hospital de San Juan Teotihuacan.

30. See Charles Gibson, "The Aztec Aristocracy in Colonial Mexico," *Comparative Studies in Society and History* 2 (1960): 167–72. See also Lockhart, *Nahuas after the Conquest*, 30–35; and Robert Haskett, *Indigenous Rulers: An Ethnohistory of Town Government in Colonial Cuernavaca* (Albuquerque: University of New Mexico Press, 1991).

31. See, for example, Benton, *Lords of Tetzcoco*, 129–31, 140–41, and 149–51; William F. Connell, *After Moctezuma: Indigenous Politics and Self-Government in Mexico City, 1524–1730* (Norman: University of Oklahoma Press, 2011), 35; María Castañeda de la Paz, *Conflictos y alianzas en tiempos de cambio: Azcapotzalco, Tlacopan, Tenochtitlan y Tlatelolco (siglos XII–XVI)* (Mexico City: Universidad Autónoma

de México, Instituto de Investigaciones Antropológicas, 2013), 298–99, 309; Rebecca Horn, *Postconquest Coyoacan: Nahua-Spanish Relations in Central Mexico, 1519–1650* (Stanford: Stanford University Press, 1997), 52; and Margarita Menegus Bornemann, *Del señorío a la república de indios: El caso de Toluca: 1500–1600* (Madrid: Ministerio de Agricultura, Pesca, y Alimentación, 1991) 96.

32. Benton, *Lords of Tetzcoco*, 134–56. After 1564 in Tetzcoco, the cacicazgo continued to pass from father to son within the old pre-Hispanic ruling family, but the highest political office did not. The governorship was instead held by people belonging to a variety of other groups: nobles from other native communities, nonnoble Tetzcoca, and even Spaniards.

33. AGN, Tierras, vol. 3594, expediente 2, fol. 12v.

34. AGN, Vínculos, vol. 232, expediente 1, fol. 22r–v.

35. AGN, Vínculos, vol. 232, expediente 1, fol. 24r.

36. AGN, Vínculos, vol. 232, expediente 1, fol. 25r.

37. Munch, *Cacicazgo de San Juan*, 61.

38. Munch, *Cacicazgo de San Juan*, 50.

39. See John Frederick Schwaller, "The Brothers Fernando de Alva Ixtlilxochitl and Bartolomé de Alva: Two 'Native' Intellectuals of Seventeenth-Century Mexico," in *Indigenous Intellectuals: Knowledge, Power, and Colonial Culture in Mexico and the Andes*, ed. Gabriela Ramos and Yanna Yannakakis (Durham, NC: Duke University Press, 2014), 53–55; Amber Brian, "The Alva Ixtlilxochitl Brothers and the Nahua Intellectual Community," in *Texcoco: Prehispanic and Colonial Perspectives*, ed. Jongsoo Lee and Galen Brokaw (Boulder: University Press of Colorado, 2014); and Barry D. Sell, Louise M. Burkhart, and Elizabeth R. Wright, *Nahuatl Theater, Vol. 3: Spanish Golden Age Drama in Mexican Translation* (Norman: University of Oklahoma Press, 2008), xv–xvi.

40. AGN, Vínculos, vol. 232, expediente 2, fols. 632–43. See also Alva Ixtlilxochitl, *Obras históricas*, 354–69.

41. She used the masculine form "cacique," instead of the feminine "cacica," in the document.

42. AGN, Vínculos, vol. 232, fol. 659r. Many thanks to Amber Brian for drawing my attention to these eighteenth-century documents and for providing her transcriptions of them.

43. AGN, Vínculos, vol. 232, fols. 666r–667r.

44. Amber Brian, *Alva Ixtlilxochitl's Native Archive and the Circulation of Knowledge in Colonial Mexico* (Nashville: Vanderbilt University Press, 2016), 45–48, 153n10. The image—found in AGN, Vínculos, vol. 233, fol. 10—is drawn on the reverse of a sheet of paper that bears a seal from 1648.

CHAPTER 2

Founding Mothers

THE TAPIAS OF QUERÉTARO, 1571–1663

Peter B. Villella

On September 23, 1663, the veiled women of the Convent of Santa Clara in Querétaro, New Spain, laid to rest one of their sisters in Christ, doña Luisa del Espíritu Santo. A former abbess, she had been one of the twelve founding members of the convent who, almost sixty years earlier, had settled in the growing colonial town. With due solemnity, they shrouded her body in black cloth and placed a palm branch in her hand and a crown on her head. After a mass in her honor, they interred her body in a special wooden tomb at a privileged location alongside the main altar.[1] The tomb already contained the remains of her father, don Diego de Tapia (d. 1615), and displayed his coat of arms. A wealthy landowner, mine operator, and former governor of Querétaro, in 1604 don Diego had committed the bulk of his estate to found and endow the convent that would house his daughter. Backed by the Tapia fortune, Santa Clara became the largest community of nuns in Querétaro, and one of the wealthiest religious institutions in all New Spain.[2] (See fig. 2.1.)

Religious communities like Santa Clara were integral to the lives of colonial Spanish American cities.[3] Beyond religious observance, they were property owners and economic producers; ran hospitals, charities, and schools; planned and realized festivals; enabled transgenerational asset management; and were repositories of the wealth and art that represented the sacred aspirations and civic-mindedness of the local population.[4] City leaders like the

Fig. 2.1. *Convent of Santa Clara de Querétaro.* Engraving by T. Balvanera. (In José María Zelaa e Hidalgo, *Las glorias de Querétaro; obra reimpresa por Mariano R. Velazquez, enriquecida con hermosas estampas litográficas* [Querétaro: Tip. del editor, 1859], 46.)

Tapias supported these communities with gifts and patronage; beyond pious motivations, this signaled wealth and status while also bringing honor to the donors.[5] But whereas the urban propertied elite elsewhere—and the conventual lives they underwrote—almost exclusively comprised Spaniards and their creole descendants, the Tapias were indigenous, of the local Hñähñu people, more commonly known as Otomís.[6] Indeed, doña Luisa del Espíritu Santo is the only known example of an indigenous nun in Mexico prior to the eighteenth century.[7]

Doña Luisa was not the first woman in her family to leave her mark in Querétaro. Her grandmother, mother, and four of her aunts, all of whom were Otomí-speaking cacicas, were influential in the region. Yet while the Tapia men are ubiquitous in city monuments, street names, and local lore, the Tapia cacicas remain largely overlooked in both popular history and professional historiography.[8] Records from the late sixteenth century, however, demonstrate that the women deserve recognition as city founders in their own right.

As frontier captains, the Tapias belonged to a category of "upstart" caciques whose authority derived from colonial-era changes rather than a historic lineage.[9] Thus, the Hispanic social concept that best captures the Tapias' particular role in the early development of Querétaro is *vecindad*. In medieval Castile, *vecinos* and *vecinas* were commoners with a defined set of obligations and privileges, yet in Spanish America the concept evolved to signify "a classification based on social reputation."[10] Colloquially, vecinos were core members of an urban community—often descended from a known town founder—who publicly performed that membership in word and deed. Their ownership of property, participation in (or support for) municipal governance, and overt patronage of religion afforded them a prestige that derived less from ancestral estates or the arcane alchemy of aristocratic bloodlines than from their command of economic resources and their practical stewardship of civic life. Although unable to exercise formal authority, vecinas were everywhere prominent in local commerce and religious activities. Within Spanish America's caste hierarchy, those considered vecinos were almost always of full or mostly full Spanish ancestry.[11] But while the Tapias were non-Spanish, they were also civic leaders and patrons in the manner of Spanish and creole vecinos.

This essay interprets the Tapia women as Otomí vecinas to illuminate both the particularities of sixteenth-century Querétaro as well as the broader colonial structures they navigated. All cacicas confronted at least three intersecting cultural presumptions and legal strictures regarding their participation in public life, the first two restrictive, and the last potentially empowering. They were *indios* ("Indians," and therefore legally constrained relative to Spaniards) and they were women (and therefore legally constrained relative to men), but they were also nobles—which, with sustained and active efforts, offered substantial economic and social possibilities, especially when the family maintained comity with the Spanish regime.[12] In the Tapias' case, they were monolingual Otomí-speakers, but they were also considered *indios amigos* (early indigenous partners of Spanish colonization).[13] Sixteenth-century Querétaro, meanwhile, was a *pueblo de indios* (Indian town) in a region where frontier dynamics and the emerging silver economy moderated the caste roles and quasi-feudal modes of production that defined central Mexico, giving rise to a more open and capitalistic set of social and economic relations.[14] This situation enabled native women along the old silver frontier, like the Tapias, to engage more freely in commerce as proprietors, producers, and even mine operators.[15] By accumulating and redirecting the wealth that ensued, the Tapias played a foundational role in Querétaro's emergence as the hub of religion and trade proudly described by later generations.[16]

THE TAPIA FORTUNE AND THE FOUNDATION OF QUERÉTARO, 1530–1570

The Tapias' success was, to a substantial degree, a product of the circumstances surrounding the origins of colonial Querétaro and the broader Bajío region—what, in the sixteenth century, had been known as the "Chichimeca Frontier."[17] (See map 3.) Fertile, pluriethnic, and strategically located, the pre-Hispanic Bajío was a culturally and economically dynamic area, the site of interaction between at least three discrete political communities, two or more settlement styles, and multiple linguistic groups. In the lowlands lived the city-dwelling and agriculturalist Nahuas, Otomís, and Purépecha-speaking Tarascans. In the hills, meanwhile, lived various semi-sedentary, hunter-gatherer groups that the Nahuas called "Chichimecas," including Pames, Jonaces, and Guachichiles.[18] In the fifteenth century, the people who lived near today's Querétaro were nominally tributaries of the Otomí lords of Xilotepec, themselves tributaries of the Tlacopaneca contingent within the Mexica (Aztec) Empire.[19] But given its remoteness from Xilotepec, status as a tributary of a tributary, and contested and multiethnic nature, the region enjoyed a large degree of de facto autonomy. This political complexity is evident within the name of Querétaro itself; while the contemporary toponym derives from Purépecha, early Nahua and Otomí accounts called its pre-Columbian settlement "Tlachco" and "Andamaxei" respectively, both meaning "place of the ball court."[20]

The Spanish conquest reconfigured, but did not entirely remake, the essential political geography of the Bajío. Indeed, autochthonous ethnic and political fault lines helped shape early colonial disputes over the right to extract wealth from Querétaro between two Spanish conquistadors, two evangelical jurisdictions, and the colonized indigenous polities attached to them.[21] Between the 1530s and 1570s, the disputed and semiautonomous nature of the region offered profit opportunities for those who could control irrigation and secure the trade with Mexico, Michoacan, and the emerging silver mines. The skills necessary for such a feat included the ability to forge alliances with very diverse groups—not only with encroaching Spaniards and the native agriculturalists in the river valleys, but also the hunters in the hills—as well as the bold willingness to use violence. One such man was

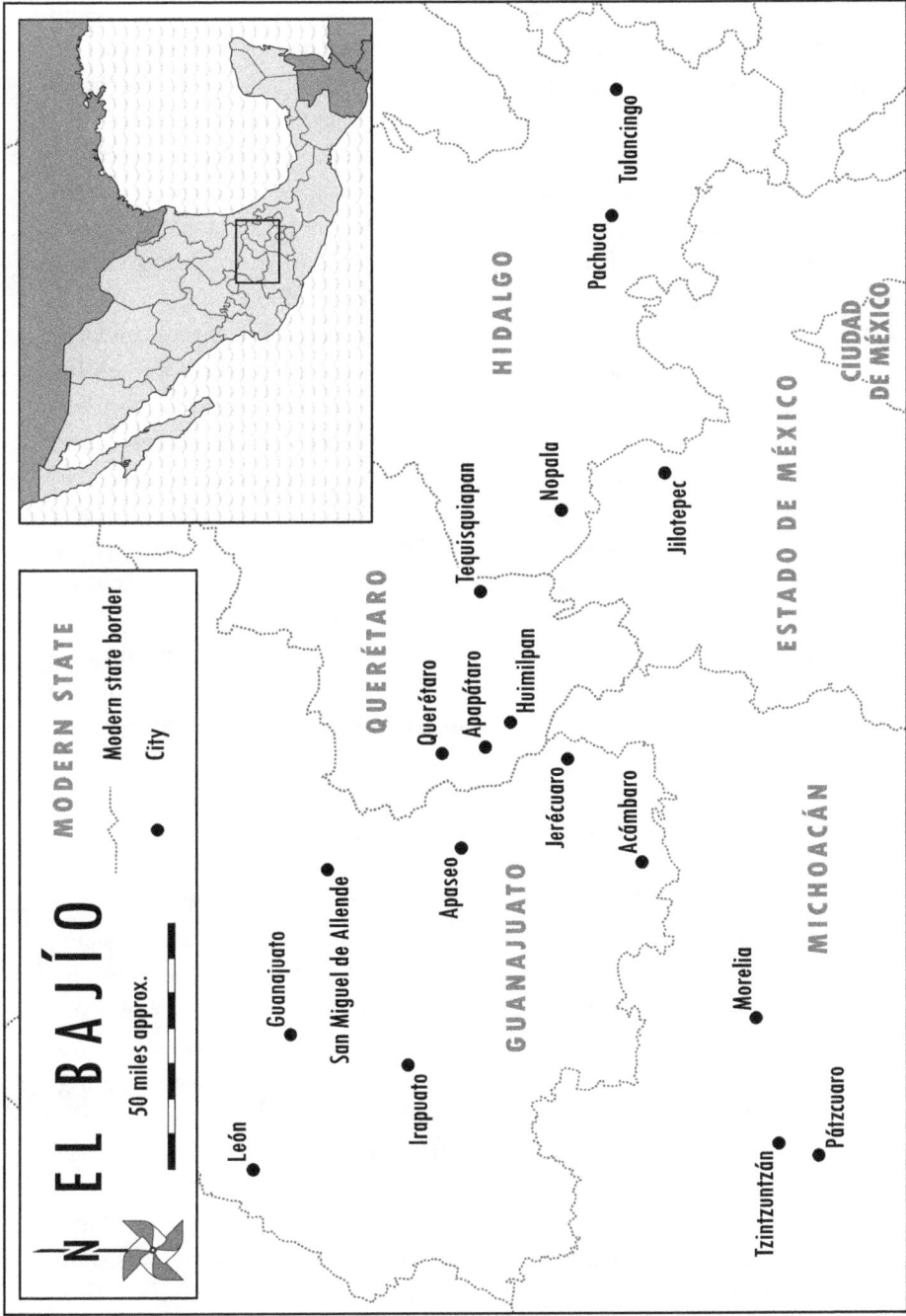

Map 3. Early colonial settlements of the Bajío. Cartography by Pablo García Loaeza.

Connin, an Otomí trader from Nopala who originally sold animal skins and cloth from the Bajío in the great markets of Tenochtitlan and Tlatelolco.[22] Amid the contests over religious and material spoils that followed the Spanish incursion, Connin became a critical power broker in the area.[23]

In the 1530s Connin formed an alliance with the Spanish conquistador Hernando Pérez de Bocanegra and his associate, the future priest Juan Sánchez de Alanís, headquartered at Acámbaro. The power and wealth of both Spaniards derived more from the Tarascan west than from Nahua central Mexico. The alliance between Connin—now baptized as don Fernando de Tapia—and Bocanegra became the basis for Querétaro's eventual independence from Xilotepec and the foundation of the Tapia fortune.[24] Fighting alongside Bocanegra and the Tarascan captains during the 1540s, don Fernando drove resident Chichimecas out of the best lands, expelled those loyal to Xilotepec, appropriated their farmlands, and declared himself cacique—not of Tlachco but of Querétaro, signaling his cultural and political alignment with Michoacan and the west.[25] This helped determine how Christian institutions entered the region, as it was the Franciscan province of Michoacan, not Mexico, that ultimately took root in Querétaro.[26] Actively aided by don Fernando de Tapia, the Michoacan Franciscans established communities in precisely those areas controlled by him.[27] In Querétaro proper, it was don Fernando himself who ordered the construction of their first church and dwellings.[28]

Spanish authorities were wary of don Fernando—semi-independent and uncontrollable—but they also relied on him to secure the area against unconquered peoples, especially after 1550, when silver began to remake the regional economy.[29] Accordingly, in the 1550s and '60s the viceroy confirmed don Fernando's landed spoils, including massive and highly profitable grazing and planting lands near the population centers of Querétaro, Acámbaro, Jurica, Huimilpan, and Tequisquiapan.[30] His violent gains were fiercely contested by both the Spanish encomenderos and caciques of Xilotepec, who resented the "theft" of Querétaro from their jurisdiction, as well as the indigenous commoners who bore the brunt of his ambitions.[31] In 1564, for example, a group of Chichimeca families reported that don Fernando had driven them off the land in Jurica where they had built houses. But all the viceroy could muster was a bland and inert statement in favor of the homeless families.[32] By the time of don Fernando's death in 1571, the Tapia estate was easily the largest in the region, described by a Spanish scribe as "very good, in a good area, with ample and well-made equipment, and very sufficient irrigation."[33]

Don Fernando's son, don Diego, continued to profit from frontier violence in subsequent years. Dubbed "Captain General of the Chichimecas, Conquistador of the San Francisco and Bledo Valleys, Discoverer of the Mines of Tangamanga, San Luis Potosí, and the Pozos" by a late-colonial chronicler, he expanded his mining interests into the north and acquired claims to indigenous draft labor.[34] In 1588, don Diego became governor of Querétaro and was officially granted its *cacicazgo* (the office of the cacique, including sometimes its political role, services, and property).[35] These were the origins of the Tapia fortune.

OTOMÍ VECINAS

The profitable lawlessness of the Chichimeca frontier subsided toward 1580 as epidemics diminished the native population, unconquered pagans became scarce, and Nahua, Spanish, and other nonnative immigrants arrived in greater numbers from central Mexico. In 1578, Querétaro was finally divided from the colonial jurisdiction of Xilotepec and given its own crown magistrate.[36] However, don Fernando's widow and children successfully adapted to the new conditions and continued to dominate the region for decades, not as conquerors and warlords, but as vecinos: as town founders, producers, and patrons.

In addition to don Diego, don Fernando de Tapia had four daughters with his wife, doña María Magdalena Ramírez (d. ~1588), all of whom spoke primarily Otomí and were regarded as cacicas in contemporary documentation: doña Catalina (d. <1578), doña Magdalena (d. 1598), doña Beatriz (d. 1602), and doña María (d. 1608).[37] (See fig. 2.2.) Don Fernando granted dowries to all his daughters and divided his estate equally between all five heirs when he died, making each of them independent property owners.[38] Yet his daughters also benefited from the emergence of an elite indigenous network in the Bajío, certain non-European conventions in gender relations, and most simply, the fact that they all outlived their husbands.

In sixteenth-century central Mexico, elite native women were often married to Spanish men, a practice which ultimately diminished the legitimacy and power of noble lineages.[39] In contrast, all four Tapia sisters married native leaders from families who had allied with Connin during the wars of the 1540s. Doña Beatriz married don Francisco de León, cacique and governor of the Otomí population of Acámbaro and Apaseo and the son of an old ally of Connin.[40] Doña Catalina married a Tarascan cacique from Taximaroa, don

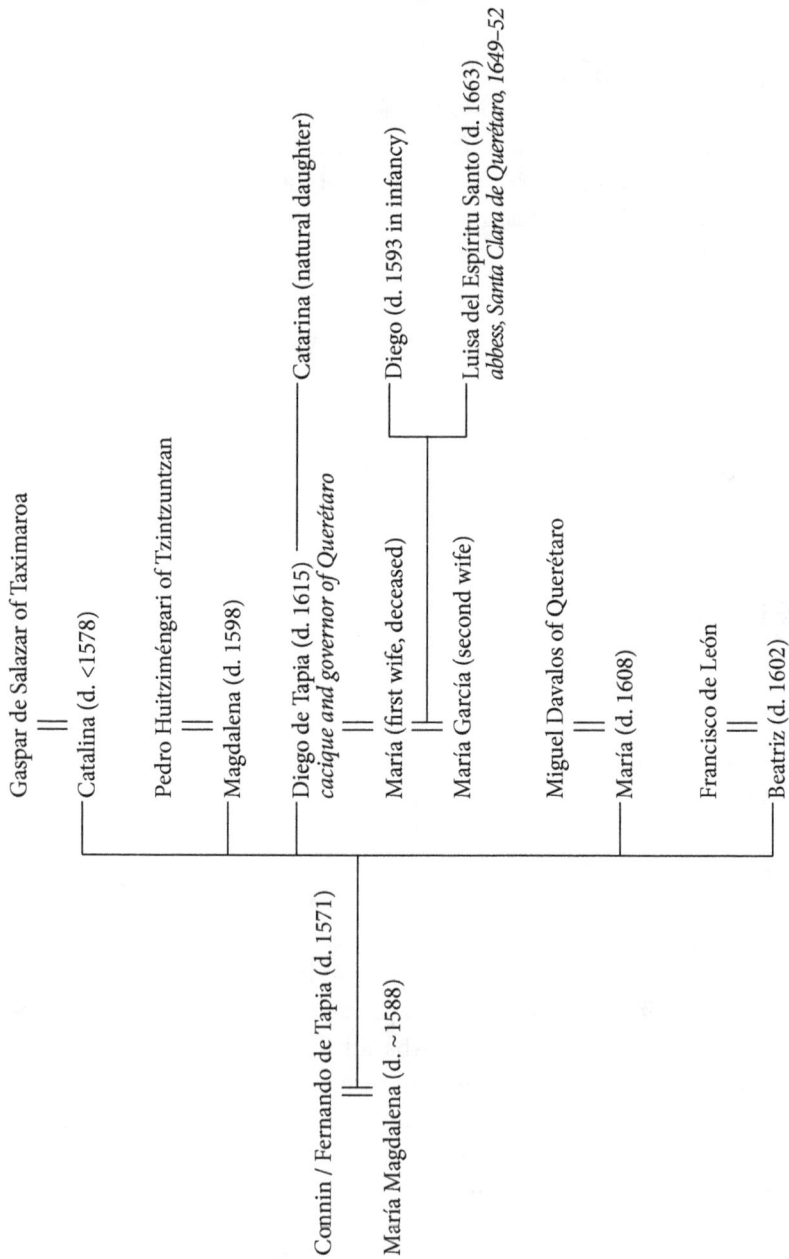

Fig. 2.2. Tapia genealogy

Gaspar de Salazar, while doña Magdalena married don Pedro Huitzimén-gari, of the most elite Tarascan lineage of Tzintzuntzan-Pátzcuaro.[41] Doña María de Tapia married don Miguel Dávalos, an Otomí ally of don Fernando who would also serve as governor of Querétaro.[42] These marriages indicate an elite indigenous network linking the Tapias to noble Tarascan and Otomí families from Querétaro all the way west and southwest to Pátzcuaro.

The Tapia cacicas also benefited from Otomí modes of gender relations, which seem to have been marginally less restrictive toward female author-ity and autonomy than those of the more patriarchal Nahuas and Span-iards.[43] This aligns with Lisa Sousa's finding that Hispano-Catholic ideals regarding female propriety were slower to take root outside of Nahua cen-tral Mexico.[44] Pedro Carrasco Pizana finds that the Otomís respected a relatively wide degree of female public authority and links this cultural characteristic to religious beliefs regarding their own origins. The authors of the *Codex Huamantla*, a sixteenth-century manuscript from an Otomí community in Tlaxcala, recorded themselves as descendants of the divine man-woman pair, Otonteuctli and Xochiquetzal.[45] The codex's depiction of this couple, face-to-face, recalls other Mesoamerican traditions outside of the Nahua core where aristocratic women commonly governed and dis-tributed wealth alongside their husbands within egalitarian marriage part-nerships.[46] And indeed, the Otomís practiced a matrilocal tradition in which suitors of highborn women offered services to their families; follow-ing the marriage, they would relocate to reside with the women's families.[47] Accordingly, rather than leave to become dependents of their husbands, all four of the Tapia sisters married in Querétaro and remained there.[48] With the sisters' local status thereby solidified, their husbands then served in various capacities in the municipal council of Querétaro during the 1570s and '80s.[49]

The Otomí acceptance of female autonomy also seems to have extended to sexual and marital choice. Xochiquetzal—sometimes revered by the Otomís as the "Old Mother"—was a goddess of love, fertility, and the moon who kept multiple lovers and spouses and in Mesoamerican representations was gen-erally identified with romantic freedom.[50] Indeed, in a colonial gender dis-course that routinely slurred all native people as sexually indiscreet, the Otomís were singled out for special disapproval.[51] For example, the Spanish scribe Francisco Ramos de Cárdenas, who was close with the Tapias, vehe-mently accused Otomí women of sexual licentiousness in 1582. They "give themselves up very easily," he reported, even to low-caste Black and *mulato* men, adding that "very few or none arrive at the marriage bed as virgins." He scornfully described a custom wherein Otomí women would have trial intercourse with their suitors; if the woman enjoyed the man, she told her parents that he would make a good husband, whereupon they would bless the union.[52] It seems, however, that Ramos was referring ignorantly to a female-friendly Otomí practice, identified by Carrasco, which simply allowed for marriage annulment in cases of incompatibility.[53]

Finally, three of the four Tapia sisters spent many years as widows and, as provided for in early modern Hispanic law, assumed independent control over their estates.[54] Doña María Magdalena, moreover, retained control over the Tapia cacicazgo until her death in the late 1580s. During her widowhood, she was the primary manager of the estate, not the young don Diego, and during those years she acted as his advocate and primary guarantor, despite speaking no Spanish.[55] But if widowhood helped enable the independence of the founding mothers of Querétaro, it cannot account for their success; they also relied on business acumen and legal savvy.

BUSINESSWOMEN OF THE BAJÍO, 1578–1608

In colonial Mexico—as elsewhere prior to the age of mechanization—the true value of landed property lay with the laborers who made them productive. Indeed, colonial documents describing lands listed the number of *indios gañanes* (male indigenous resident-workers) alongside pack animals, irrigation, farming implements, and other "features" that underlay the land's productive capacity.[56] The Tapias straddled colonial legal categories in an enormously beneficial way, one that afforded them multiple ways of exploiting this labor. That is, as the heirs of a conquistador, they controlled fertile lands and shares in mines, received draft labor to work them, and sold their products to indigenous and Spaniards alike in the years before such practices were officially forbidden.[57] Meanwhile, as caciques, they collected rents from native commoners who resided on cacicazgo lands and were entitled to a portion of their labor.[58] The Tapias' exercise of these rights persisted despite viceregal laws restricting them in the 1550s and '60s.[59] Meanwhile, as conquistadors rather than caciques of lineage, there is little evidence that the Tapias adhered to any obligations toward native commoners based on custom. It was not the Tapias' indigeneity but their status as landlords and mine operators that ultimately structured their economic relationships with their native and nonnative dependents, partners, and neighbors.

Provincial officials were well-acquainted with the Tapia women, who appeared frequently before the local notary as contractors of labor, creditors and debtors, and independent buyers and sellers of land and commodities. For example, doña María Magdalena maintained grazing lands and a farm just west of Querétaro in the nearby settlement of Santa María Magdalena. The farm had originally been part of doña Catalina's dowry, which by law remained her personal property; when the daughter died without children, she bequeathed the farm back to her mother.[60] That doña María Magdalena operated independently of her son is clear from a complaint she lodged against him in 1585. Don Diego tried to sell the land to a Spaniard, but his mother quickly and successfully had the sale nullified on the grounds that it was hers alone and not don Diego's to sell. During the proceedings, the commoners of Santa María Magdalena testified in support of their cacica, objecting to the sale of their land to a Spaniard.[61]

Doña Beatriz maintained the most active business profile of all the Tapia women, however. Although she could not speak Spanish—and her brother invariably served as her interpreter and male representative in legal and commercial proceedings—she nonetheless bought, sold, and litigated in her own name. When doña Beatriz married don Francisco de León of Acámbaro, her dowry consisted of 200 cattle, 1,500 sheep, 68 goats, 17 mares and a stud donkey, 7 asses, a bit of grape vine, 294 pesos, and a Black slave named Lucía.[62] When her husband died in 1590, doña Beatriz negotiated the repayment of the dowry with his surviving brother.[63] She received well-populated farmlands from the León family cacicazgo near Apaseo between the river and the main road to Mexico City, near the current town of San Bartolomé Aguacaliente, and sheep-grazing land to the south called Petemoro (near today's Jerécuaro).[64]

With these lands and her own inheritance, she became a critical node in the regional economy. Wheat, maize, chile, and vegetables from her farms went to every area where her family had local and regional connections, including her late husband's cacicazgo of Apaseo and Acámbaro, don Miguel Dávalos's home of San Juan del Río, and her brother's mining interests in Xichú (San Miguel de Allende).[65] Her produce went to the natives who labored on her own lands, in her family's mines, and her personal servants. Her accounts illustrate her central position within a local economy that was remarkably sophisticated despite a general scarcity of cash. Sometimes doña Beatriz accepted monetary payment, but more frequently she sold on credit or to satisfy her own estate's consumption of goods and services such as cloth, building materials, and repairs.[66] And her estate continued to grow; in

August of 1595, she and her sister doña Magdalena purchased a total of approximately 847 acres (343 hectares) of arable land along the Querétaro River from a Spaniard. When doña Magdalena died soon thereafter, she made doña Beatriz her universal heir.[67]

Like their mother, doña Beatriz and doña María frequently engaged colonial officials to defend their interests. At least twice during the 1590s, doña Beatriz successfully challenged Spaniards who were encroaching on her lands.[68] In another case, doña Beatriz sought restitution from a Spanish-speaker whose runaway mules had allegedly damaged her maize.[69] Doña María—also a widow and producer of wool, maize, wheat, and chile—ejected two native families she accused of squatting on land belonging to her dowry in Santa María Magdalena.[70] She seems to have lacked some of doña Beatriz's business sense, however; during the 1580s and '90s, merchants and wage laborers of all castes—Spanish, mestizo, and mulato—accused her of failing to repay debts, resulting in seizures of sheep and grain.[71]

Yet this is not to say that the Tapias' gender and indigeneity did not inflect their experiences. For all their wealth, they still found it necessary to defend themselves against Spaniards and other nonnatives who specifically or implicitly chafed against having to answer to indigenous women. Both doña Beatriz and doña María employed nonnative majordomos to oversee the native workers in exchange for a share of the harvests, a practice that seems to have led to conflict.[72] In 1594, a Spaniard who managed one of doña María's wheat fields allegedly stole from her; when she confronted him, he destroyed her *jacales* (huts) and threatened her life.[73] In 1597, doña Beatriz expelled her Spanish majordomo in Querétaro, accusing him of withholding produce for himself. Two years later, she brought complaints against another settler, described as a Greek foreigner, who rented rooms from her. She accused him of stealing chickens and flatware, mistreating her servants, and disrespecting her status as "an honorable noblewoman" with insults and evil words. Citing general laws against nonindigenous living among indigenous, the magistrate ejected the renter from doña Beatriz's house.[74] Furthermore, there was at least one magistrate who sought to dislodge the Tapias from their position of prominence. In 1590, Fernando de Mújica accused the Tapias' Spanish renters and majordomos of mistreating the native laborers, using violence to overwork and then underpay them. Citing royal provisions that prohibited Spaniards from entering indigenous dwellings, he announced restrictions and threatened penalties against all Spanish agents of the Tapias. Don Diego, doña Magdalena, doña María, and doña Beatriz all protested, arguing that such restrictions would damage their operations.[75] The Tapias were Otomí cacicas, but they were also landowners, and those economic interests shaped their relationships with native commoners and colonial authorities alike.

FOUNDING THE ORTHODOX SPIRITUAL WORLD OF QUERÉTARO

As vecinas, the Tapias played a key role in the establishment of a colonial religious culture in Querétaro. Their pious donations hint at their priorities and values. Their patronage built upon the close relationship between their family and the Franciscan province of Michoacan. Symbolizing the relationship, don Fernando, doña María Magdalena, doña Magdalena, and doña Beatriz were all laid to rest, wrapped in the habit of St. Francis, in the church they had built for the Franciscans in Querétaro.[76] Their priorities were typical of early modern Hispanic vecinas, yet they also expressed special concern for the native commoners of the region.

Doña Beatriz's account books from the 1590s reveal that her estate anchored the Franciscan province of Michoacan. Her wheat, for example, supported the friars as far to the southwest as Zinepécuaro, Guayangareo (Morelia), and Pátzcuaro. She also sustained the Franciscans of her husband's hometown of Acámbaro, the community of San Pedro Tolimán to the east and, of course, the friars of Querétaro itself. She provided wheat and maize to the local boys' school, supported Querétaro's feast day celebrations, and distributed food to individual clergymen.[77] Her accounts classify these latter distributions as voluntary *limosna* (alms) rather than *diezmos* (agricultural tithes) or sales. They are also distinct from her contributions to festivals in native communities, which always consisted of maize.[78]

In the mid-1590s, doña Beatriz and doña Magdalena jointly funded a *capellanía de misas* (chantry or religious endowment) to support regular masses in the Franciscans' church on behalf of the Tapia family. They stipulated that the chantry's lay patrons—those in charge of ensuring compliance and maintaining adequate supplies of wax, incense, wine, and oil—were to be the administrators of the multiethnic Confraternity of the Most Holy Sacrament, one of whom was their brother, don Diego. Doña Magdalena further stipulated that, should the confraternity relocate, the chantry was nonetheless to remain in the Franciscans' church in perpetuity.[79]

Historians know the value of testaments as intimate windows into civic, religious, and social priorities.[80] The detailed 1602 testament of doña Beatriz is a rich and intimate exemplar. Dictated in Otomí, it includes forty-six separate pious donations, ranging from the very small (such as candle wax and cloth for the church) to the very large.[81] It combines the hallmarks of vecindad, such as concern for the local poor and civic pride, with a distinctly Otomí sentimental inclination. That is, it reveals her as a shrewd property owner with economic ties to many parts of Queretano society, but who maintained a special noblesse oblige toward the indigenous commoners upon whom she relied in life. In her own words, she "had some obligations to the native Indians of this pueblo, dead and alive," and wished to care for them in her will.[82] This was a common way for dying caciques and cacicas in New Spain to express and realize their pious sentiments.[83]

For example, doña Beatriz left 140 pesos and paid for a total of eighteen masses in honor of her personal servants and their families, while leaving nothing to any secular Spaniards beyond debt settlement. She also sought to establish charitable institutions for native commoners, indicating that she had long planned these with her late sister, doña Magdalena. Most generously, she called for the establishment of a new hospital "where they care for poor local Indians" at the curative hot springs on the lands she inherited from her husband near San Bartolomé Aguacaliente. This hospital was to be sustained by incomes from her lands at Apaseo and Petemoro, sheep-grazing lands she inherited from her father near Tequisquiapan, and others that she had purchased for this explicit purpose.[84]

Doña Beatriz also gave generously to sustain Querétaro's confraternities and beautify its chapels. She founded a chantry in the Franciscans' church, naming don Diego de Tapia as its first patron. She directed one of her vineyards to support a chaplaincy dedicated to the Confraternity of Our Lady of the Assumption based in the indigenous church of San José de los Naturales.[85] At regular intervals throughout the year—and every Pentecost, to which doña Beatriz declared a special devotion—the chaplain and other clerics were to perform a full requiem mass for her soul and those of all her deceased family members, confraternity members, and all the natives of Querétaro. She stipulated, moreover, that the chaplaincy's administrators were to be exclusively indigenous.[86]

Of course, the Tapias' most famous religious legacy remains the Convent of Santa Clara, which colonial chroniclers attributed to the influence of the Franciscan fray Miguel López de Omasteguí of Navarre, who arrived from Michoacan in the 1590s and became the personal confessor of don Diego and doña Beatriz. They tell that don Diego wanted to provide for his only surviving heir and López convinced him to build a convent for her to live in.[87] Yet the records reveal that the 1604 Santa Clara donation was the end result of a longer process of wealth consolidation in which the Tapia sisters were central. In 1598, the Franciscan convent of San Juan de la Penitencia was chartered in the Moyotlan district of Mexico City, and doña Luisa traveled to join the community soon thereafter, accompanied by her aunt, doña María.[88] While in Mexico, doña María encountered the Jesuits, who at the time were aggressively learning Otomí and pursuing relationships with Christian caciques throughout New Spain to help expand their network of schools in native communities.[89] Likely seeking religious merit and cultural prestige for both herself and her city, the childless doña María pledged her entire estate to the Jesuits to entice them to settle in Querétaro.[90] Yet it would appear that the Tapias soon decided to prepare for a different donation, as doña María annulled her promise to the Jesuits in 1601, insisting that she had erred as "an ignorant woman unaware of what was best for [her]." In place of the Jesuits, she named her niece, doña Luisa, as her universal heir, and the guardian of the Franciscans of Querétaro as co-executor of her estate.[91] It is surely no coincidence that doña Beatriz—who had already inherited doña Magdalena's estate—also named doña Luisa as her universal heir at precisely the same time.[92]

Thus, when don Diego formally founded the convent in doña Luisa's name in 1604, his sisters' combined assets comprised a major portion of the donation. Furthermore, don Diego had also failed to execute doña Beatriz's plans for a native hospital in San Bartolomé; instead, he bundled her land there into the Santa Clara estate, and the hospital would not be built for another 170 years.[93] It is also the case that doña María cofounded the convent alongside her brother and niece. In fact, it was doña María, not don Diego, who provided the nuns with their earliest residence. She also assigned revenues from her other lands to pay for the construction of the permanent building, a great baroque edifice encompassing four city blocks, completed in 1633.[94] When she died in 1608, she committed the bulk of her estate to the fledgling convent. She endowed a novice to profess there on the condition that it institute a chantry on behalf of her own soul.[95] Thus did the Tapia women enable this rich and storied cloister, for centuries a cornerstone of Querétaro's religious, civic, and economic life. (See fig. 2.3.) Given its Otomí origins and doña Beatriz's overt concern for the welfare of Querétaro's indigenous inhabitants, it is darkly ironic that Santa Clara, at the express insistence of the viceroy, was established as an exclusively Spanish institution.[96]

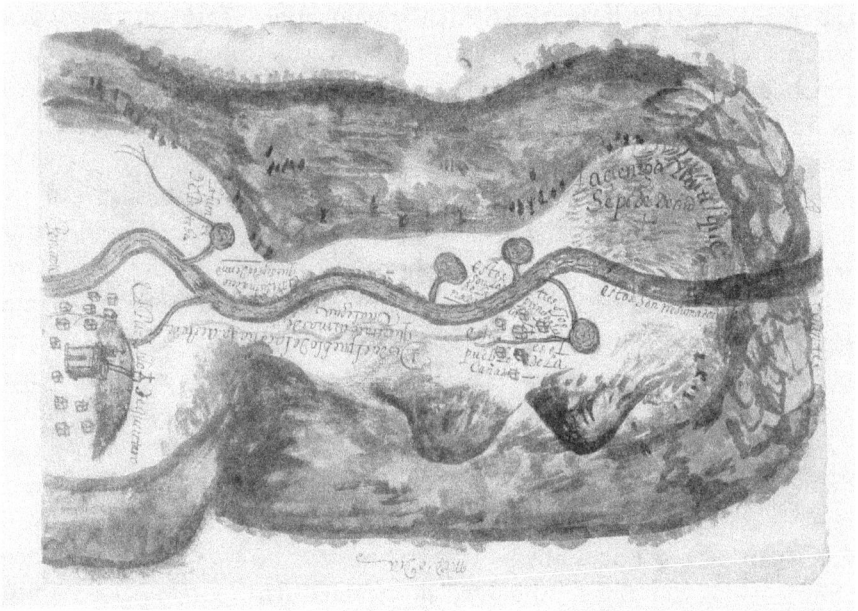

Fig. 2.3. Map of Querétaro and surroundings, commissioned circa 1620 by doña María García, indicating former Tapia properties bequeathed to the Convent of Santa Clara. ("Pintura presentada por parte de doña María García, mujer de don Diego de Tapia." Archivo Histórico de la Provincia Franciscana de Michoacán, in Dos planos para Querétaro [Querétaro: Archivo Histórico, Gobierno del Estado de Querétaro, 1999].)

CONCLUSION

The historical influence of the Tapia sisters was a result of many factors, including the Bajío's borderlands dynamic, Querétaro's founding as a pueblo de indios, the subtle legacy of Otomí gender relations, and their status as childless widows. Yet when doña Luisa took the veil at Santa Clara and don Diego died, the Tapia lineage and cacicazgo ended abruptly just as Querétaro was transitioning from an native pueblo to a Spanish town. In 1633, don Diego's and doña María's remains were transferred to the newly completed Convent of Santa Clara, where they were reburied beneath an equestrian portrait of don Diego in full armor.[97] In 1655, with doña Luisa ailing and deaf, the growing town was upgraded to an "imperial city," and its Otomí heritage became more symbolic than determinative, the stuff of civic identity and patriotic memory rather than its dominant social and cultural current.[98]

The great colonial-era chroniclers consistently hailed don Fernando and don Diego, but had essentially nothing to say of the Tapia women.[99] These omissions shaped how later generations of Queretanos learned of the foundations of their city and its cultural patrimony. Today, Querétaro maintains a proud sense of its own history and its central place in Mexican national history more generally. Visible homages to the Tapia men abound. A massive heroic statue of the fierce Otomí warrior Connin greets travelers entering the city, while a stoic and gentlemanly likeness of his Christian iteration, don Fernando de Tapia, presides over Founders' Plaza. The magnificent ex-Convent of Santa Clara, meanwhile, proclaims don Diego de Tapia as its founder and prominently displays his portrait. And while one of Querétaro's most famous and widely honored heroes is indeed a heroine—"La Corregidora" Josefa Ortíz de Domínguez—the Tapia sisters are not visibly represented among its monuments. Yet no assessment of Querétaro's history should ignore its founding mothers: three generations of cacicas who actively and extensively contributed to the economic and spiritual development of the colonial city.

NOTES

This essay was completed with the support of the National Humanities Center. I would like to thank John Tutino, Dana Velasco Murillo, Pablo Garcia Loaeza, and the volume's editors for their helpful criticisms of earlier drafts. I am also grateful to Jorge Marroquín Narváez at the Archivo General del Estado de Querétaro and Brooke Andrade and the Humanities Center library staff, all of whom provided important assistance at various stages of this project.

1. Burial of doña Luisa del Espíritu Santo, Querétaro, September 23, 1663, Archivo General de Indias, Seville, Spain (hereafter cited as AGI)-Escribanía de Cámara y Justicia (ECJ), 199B, Roll 8, fols. 97–98.

2. See Guillerma Ramírez Montes, *Niñas, doncellas, vírgenes eternas: Santa Clara de Querétaro (1607–1864)* (Mexico City: Universidad Nacional Autónoma de México, 2005), 52–62; Asunción Lavrin, "El convento de Santa Clara de Querétaro: La administración de sus propiedades en el siglo XVII," *Historia Mexicana* 25, no. 1 (1975); Asunción Lavrin, *Brides of Christ: Conventual Life in Colonial Mexico* (Stanford: Stanford University Press, 2008), 25; Celia Wu, "The Population of the City of Queretaro in 1791," *Journal of Latin American Studies* 16, no. 2 (November 1984): 289–91; and Myrna Lilí de las Mercedes Jiménez Jácome, "El Convento de Santa Clara de Jesús de Querétaro, mundo de privilegios y restricciones, 1607–1809" (PhD diss., Universidad Nacional Autónoma de Querétaro, 2012).

3. Karen Melvin, *Building Colonial Cities of God: Mendicant Orders and Urban Culture in New Spain* (Stanford: Stanford University Press, 2012).

4. Lavrin, *Brides of Christ*; Susan Migden Socolow, *The Women of Colonial Latin America*, 2nd ed. (New York: Cambridge University Press, 2015), 98–100; Ellen Gunnarsdóttir, "The Convent of Santa Clara, The Elite and Social Change in Eighteenth-Century Querétaro," *Journal of Latin American Studies* 33, no. 2 (May 2001).

5. Teofilo Ruiz, *From Heaven to Earth: The Reordering of Castillian Society, 1150–1350* (Princeton: Princeton University Press, 2004), 46–66; Gisela von Wobeser, "La función social y económica de las capellanías de misas en la Nueva España del siglo XVIII," *Estudios de Historia Novohispana* 16 (1996).

6. Socolow, *Women*, 112–13; Josefina Muriel, *Las indias caciques de Corpus Christi*, 2nd ed. (Mexico City: Unviersidad Nacional Autónoma de México, 2001); Ann Miriam M. S. M. Gallagher, "The Indian Nuns of Mexico City's *Monasterio* of Corpus Christi, 1724–1821," in *Latin American Women: Historical Perspectives*, ed. Asunción Lavrin (Westport, CT: Greenwood, 1978); Lavrin, *Brides of Christ*, 244–48; Mónica Díaz, "The Indigenous Nuns of Corpus Christi: Race and Spirituality," in *Religion in New Spain*, ed. Susan Schroeder and Stafford Poole (Albuquerque: University of New Mexico Press, 2007).

7. Socolow, *Women*, 112; Mónica Díaz, *Indigenous Writings from the Convent: Negotiating Ethnic Autonomy in Colonial Mexico* (Tucson: University of Arizona Press, 2010), 34–35.

8. A notable exception is John C. Super's doctoral dissertation of 1973. See John C. Super, "Querétaro: Society and Economy in Early Provincial Mexico, 1590–1630" (PhD diss., University of California, Los Angeles, 1973).

9. Margarita Menegus Bornemann, "El cacicazgo en la Nueva España," in *El cacicazgo en la Nueva España y Filipinas*, ed. Margarita Menegus Bornemann (Mexico City: Plaza y Valdés, 2005), 36–38.

10. Tamar Herzog, *Defining Nations: Immigrants and Citizens in Early Modern Spain and Spanish America* (New Haven: Yale University Press, 2003), 44. See also Teofilo Ruiz, *Spanish Society, 1400–1600* (Harlow, England: Pearson Education, 2001), 51–56.

11. On vecindad in Spanish America, see Herzog, *Defining Nations*, 6–8, 43–63; Ross Frank, *From Settler to Citizen: New Mexican Economic Development and the Creation of Vecino Society, 1750–1820* (Berkeley: University of California Press, 2000), 1; James Lockhart and Stuart Schwartz, *Early Latin America: A History of Colonial Spanish America and Brazil* (New York: Cambridge University Press, 1983), 96; John Tutino, *Making a New World: Founding Capitalism in the Bajío and Spanish North America* (Durham, NC: Duke University Press, 2011), 99–105.

12. On the legal status of Indians under Spanish rule, see Woodrow Borah, *Justice By Insurance: The General Indian Court of Colonial Mexico and the Legal Aides of the Half-Real* (Berkeley: University of California Press, 1983); Susan Kellogg, *Law and the Transformation of Aztec Culture, 1500–1700* (Norman: University of Oklahoma Press, 1995); and Brian Owensby, *Empire of Law and Indian Justice in Colonial Mexico* (Stanford: Stanford University Press, 2008). On the legal status of women, see Silvia M. Arrom, *The Women of Mexico City, 1790–1857* (Stanford: Stanford University Press, 1985), 53–97; Socolow, *Women*, 5–16, 120–39. On the legal status of

cacicas, see Lisa Sousa, *The Woman Who Turned into a Jaguar and Other Narratives of Native Women in Archives of Colonial Mexico* (Stanford: Stanford University Press, 2017), 207–08; Miriam Melton-Villanueva, "Cacicas, Escribanos, and Landholders: Indigenous Women's Late Colonial Mexican Texts, 1703–1832," *Ethnohistory* 65, no. 2 (April 2018); and Ronald Spores, "Mixteca *Cacicas:* Status, Wealth, and the Political Accommodation of Native Elite Women in Early Colonial Oaxaca," in *Indian Women of Early Mexico*, ed. Susan Schroeder, Stephanie Wood, and Robert Haskett (Norman: University of Oklahoma Press, 1997).

13. On indios amigos, see Michel R. Oudijk and Matthew Restall, "Mesoamerican Conquistadors in the Sixteenth Century," in *Indian Conquistadors: Indigenous Allies in the Conquest of Mesoamerica*, ed. Laura E. Matthew (Norman: University of Oklahoma Press, 2007). On the economic history of the Bajío, see Tutino, *Making a New World*, 65–115.

14. Tutino, *Making a New World*, 65–115.

15. See Dana Velasco Murillo, "Laboring Above Ground: Indigenous Women in New Spain's Silver Mining District, Zacatecas, Mexico, 1620–1770," *Hispanic American Historical Review* 93, no. 1 (February 2013): 11–15.

16. Patriotic homages to Querétaro are quite numerous. See Joseph María Zelaa e Hidalgo and Carlos de Sigüenza y Góngora, *Glorias de Querétaro, en la fundación y admirables progresos de la muy 1. y venerable congregación eclesiástica de presbíteros seculares de María Santísitma de Guadalupe de México* (Mexico City: Oficina de D. Mariano Joseph de Zúñiga y Ontiveros, 1803), esp. 42–43; and Francisco Antonio Navarrete, *Relación peregrina de la agua corriente que [. . .] goza la muy noble, leal, y florida ciudad de Santiago de Querétaro* (Mexico City: José Bernardo de Hogal, 1739), http://www.cervantesvirtual.com/nd/ark:/59851/bmc41780.

17. Philip Wayne Powell, "North America's First Frontier, 1546–1603," in *Essays on Frontiers in World History*, ed. George Wolfskill and Stanley Palmer (College Station, TX: Texas A&M University Press, 1983).

18. José Antonio Cruz Rangel, *Chichimecas, misioneros, soldados, y terratenientes: estrátegias de colonización, control, y poder en Querétaro y la Sierra Gorda, siglos XVI—XVIII* (Mexico: Archivo General de la Nación, 2003), 73–92; Yolanda Lastra, *Los otomíes: su lengua y su historia* (Mexico City: Universidad Nacional Autonoma de Mexico, 2006), 131–42; Sarah Albiez-Wieck, "Contactos exteriores del estado tarasco: influencias desde dentro y fuera de Mesoamérica" (PhD diss., Universität Bonn, 2011), 320–28, http://hss.ulb.uni-bonn.de/2011/2626/2626.htm.

19. Pedro Carrasco, *The Tenochca Empire of Ancient Mexico: The Triple Alliance of Tenochtitlán, Tetzcoco, and Tlacopan* (Norman: University of Oklahoma Press, 1999), 192–93.

20. Juan Ricardo Jiménez Gómez, "Estudio introductorio," in *Fundación y evangelización del pueblo de indios de Querétaro y sus sujetos, 1531–1585: Testimonios del cacique don Hernando de Tapia y otros indios españoles en el Pleito Grande, entre el Arzobispado de México y el Obispado de Michoacán*, ed. Juan Ricardo Jiménez Gómez (Mexico City: MA Porrúa, 2014), 25–27.

21. See Jiménez Gómez, "Estudio introductorio."

22. Jiménez Gómez, "Estudio introductorio," 15–21.

23. Cruz Rangel, *Chichimecas, misioneros, soldados*, 75; Tutino, *Making a New World*, 72–73.

24. Early records suggest that Connin initially called himself don Fernando Bocanegra. No scholars, to my knowledge, have satisfactorily accounted for when or why he eventually took the name "Tapia." See Cacique don Luis of Xilotepec v. Encomendero Hernán Pérez de Bocanegra, Mexico, 1533–41, AGI-Justicia 124, no. 1, unpaginated; and Manuel Septién y Septién, "Fundación y conquista de Querétaro," in *Obras de Manuel Septién y Septién* (Santiago de Querétaro: Gobierno del Estado de Querétaro, 1999), 4:45.

25. Albiez-Wieck, "Contactos exteriores," 522–25; Somohano Martínez, *La versión histórica*, 58–66; Jiménez Gómez, "Estudio introductorio," 27.

26. Jiménez Gómez, "Estudio introductorio."

27. On the Franciscan expansion into the Bajío and beyond, see David Charles Wright Carr, *La conquista del Bajío y los orígenes de San Miguel de Allende* (Mexico: Fondo de Cultura Económica, 1998) and Robert H. Jackson, *Frontiers of Evangelization: Indians in the Sierra Gorda and Chiquitos Missions* (Norman: University of Oklahoma Press, 2017), 35–44.

28. Francisco Ramos de Cárdenas, "Relación de Querétaro," in *Relaciones geográficas del siglo XVI*, ed. René Acuña (Mexico City: Universidad Nacional Autónoma de México, Instituto de Investigaciones Antropológicas, 1987), 9: 221–23, 247–48.

29. Somohano, *La versión histórica*, 79–102.

30. Grant of Viceroy Velasco to don Fernando de Tapia, Mexico, August 20, 1562, in *Documentos inéditos para la historia de Querétaro* (hereafter cited as DIHQ) (Querétaro: Universidad Autónoma de Querétaro, 1989), 7:164–67; Inventory of the Estate of don Diego de Tapia, Querétaro, 1614, AGI-ECJ 199A, fols. 243–251. See also Tutino, *Making a New World*, 83.

31. See José Antonio Cruz Rangel, *Chichimecas, misioneros, soldados*.

32. Amparo for the Indians of Jurica, Archivo General de la Nación: Mercedes 7:fol. 302v; and David Charles Wright Carr, *Conquistadores otomíes en la Guerra Chichimeca* (Querétaro: Gobierno del Estado de Querétaro, 1988), 370–76.

33. Inventory of the Possessions of don Diego de Tapia, Querétaro, December 30, 1604, AGI-ECJ 199B, rollo 8, fol. 109.

34. Zelaá e Hidalgo and Sigüenza y Góngora, *Glorias de Querétaro*, 100. See Juan Calderón de la Vega v. don Diego de Tapia, regarding the noncompliance of repartimiento Indians in the mines of Xichú and Palmar, Querétaro, June 27, 1599, in DIHQ l:1, 273–80. See also John C. Super, *La vida en Querétaro durante la colonia, 1531–1810* (Mexico City: Fondo de Cultura Económica, 1983), 239–48.

35. Possession of don Diego de Tapia of the Cacicazgo of Querétaro, Mexico, June 1, 1588, in Juan Ricardo Jiménez Gómez, ed., *Fundación y evangelización del pueblo de indios de Querétaro y sus sujetos, 1531–1585: Testimonios del cacique don Hernando de Tapia y otros indios españoles en el Pleito Grande, entre el Arzobispado de México y el Obispado de Michoacán* (Mexico City: MA Porrúa, 2014).

36. Peter Gerhard, *A Guide to the Historical Geography of New Spain*, rev. ed. (Norman: University of Oklahoma Press, 1993), 224.

37. The exact date of doña Catalina's death is unknown: she and her husband were named in don Fernando's will of 1571 but listed as deceased by 1578.

38. Testament of don Fernando de Tapia, Querétaro, February 6, 1571, in DIHQ 8:169.

39. Bradley Benton, *The Lords of Tetzcoco: The Transformation of Indigenous Rule in Postconquest Central Mexico* (New York: Cambridge University Press, 2017), 106–33.

40. Don Francisco's father was don Cristóbal de León; see Titles of don Christoval de León, Cacique of Acámbaro and Apaseo, Apaseo, November 1562, AGI-ECJ 200B, pieza 36, fols. 1017–1035.

41. The "Relación de Francisco Martín de la Puente," a seventeenth-century account of Otomí exploits during the Chichimeca wars, lists Petemoro and Taximaroa, whence came the husbands of doña Beatriz and doña Catalina, among the populations pacified. The Huitziméngaris were the descendants of the last *cazonci* (ruler) of Tzintzuntzan, some of whom fought alongside the Otomí captains during the 1540s. Wright, *Conquista del Bajío*, 119–27, esp. 20; Carlos Salvador Paredes Martinez, "La nobleza tarasca: poder político y conflictos en el Michoacán colonial," *Anuario de Estudios Americanos* 65, no. 1 (2008).

42. Estate of don Diego de Tapia, Querétaro, December 15, 1603, in "Información de los méritos y servicios presentados por don Fernando de Tapia, en la conquista y fundación de Querétaro y provanza del cacicazgo de don Diego de Tapia," *Boletín del Archivo General de la Nación* 5, no. 1 (1939): 47–49.

43. Yolanda Lastra warns against overly confident declarations regarding precontact Otomí religion and culture. Not only do few sources exist, those that do reflect the perspectives and biases of Christian Nahuas and Spaniards. Lastra, *Los otomíes*, 315.

44. Sousa, *Woman*, 176.

45. Pedro Carrasco Pizana, *Los otomíes: cultura e historia prehispánica de los pueblos mesoamericanos de habla otomiana* (Toluca: Gobierno del Estado de México, 1950), 98–100, 135–46; Lastra, *Los otomíes*, 315–18.

46. According to Spores, cacicas in the similarly semiautonomous Mixteca region maintained traditional property rights, noble exemptions, and socioeconomic distinctions until at least 1620. This was built atop the preexisting Mixteca tradition of *yuhuitayu* (union of two city-states by way of the marriage between hereditary male and female rulers). According to Terraciano, yuhuitayu recognized both male and female power without privileging one over the other, and this system influenced Mixteca political and economic relationships for several generations after the Spanish conquest; cacicas, for example, were barred from municipal government, but often controlled the community chests nonetheless. See Spores, "Mixteca *Cacicas*," and Kevin Terraciano, *The Mixtecs of Colonial Oaxaca: Ñudzahui History, Sixteenth through Eighteenth Centuries* (Stanford: Stanford University Press, 2001), 158–97. On Nahua and Mesoamerican gender ideologies, see Cecilia F. Klein, "None of the Above: Gender Ambiguity in Nahua Ideology," in *Gender in Pre-Hispanic America*, ed. Cecilia F. Klein (Washington, DC: Dumbarton Oaks Research Library and Collection, 2001).

47. Carrasco Pizana, *Los otomíes*, 312.

48. Probanza of doña Magdalena de Tapia, Querétaro, March 4, 1586, in Juan Ricardo Jiménez Gómez, *Autos civiles de indios ante el alcalde mayor del pueblo de Querétaro a finales del siglo XVI* (Mexico City: MA Porrúa, 2014), 186–89. See also the inheritance of don Diego de Tapia, in *Querétaro en el siglo XVI: Fuentes documentales primarias*, ed. David Charles Wright Carr (Querétaro: Gobierno del Estado de Querétaro, 1989), 323–55, quotation from 325.

49. Act of Possession of doña María de Tapia, Querétaro, November 24–December 5, 1576, in Jiménez Gómez, *Autos civiles de indios*, 154–55.

50. Sousa, *Woman*, 114–17

51. See Louise M. Burkhart, "Gender in Nahuatl Texts of the Early Colonial Period: Native 'Tradition' and the Dialogue with Christianity," in *Gender in Pre-Hispanic America*, ed. Cecilia F. Klein (Washington, DC: Dumbarton Oaks Research Library and Collection, 2001).

52. Ramos de Córdoba, "Relación geográfica de Querétaro," 9:228.

53. Carrasco Pizana, *Los otomíes*, 312; Lastra, *Los otomíes*, 319.

54. On the legal ramifications of widowhood, see Arrom, *Women of Mexico City*, 56–70; Susan Kellogg, "From Parallel and Equivalent to Separate but Unequal: Tenochca Mexica Women, 1500–1700," in *Indian Women of Early Mexico*, ed. Susan Schroeder, Stephanie Wood, and Robert Haskett (Norman: University of Oklahoma Press, 1997), 133–39; Socolow, *Women*, 94–96.

55. "Juan Rodríguez Galan v. don Diego de Tapia," Querétaro, 1578–84, in DIHQ, 1:8–26, esp. 11–12.

56. Inventory of the Estate of don Diego de Tapia, Querétaro, 30 Dec 1604, AGI-ECJ 199B, rollo 8, fols. 109–10.

57. See Marta Eugenia García Ugarte, *Breve historia de Querétaro* (Mexico City: Colegio de México, 1999), 74. On cacique-commoner relations and regulations in early colonial central Mexico, see James Lockhart, *The Nahuas after the Conquest: A Social and Cultural History of the Indians of Central Mexico, Sixteenth through Eighteenth Centuries* (Stanford: Stanford University Press, 1992), 102–13. On cacique privileges generally, see Charles Gibson, "The Aztec Aristocracy in Colonial Mexico," *Comparative Studies in Society and History* 2, no. 2 (1960); Delfina Esmeralda López Sarrelangue, *La nobleza indígena de Pátzcuaro en la época virreinal* (Mexico City: Universidad Nacional Autónoma de México, Instituto de Investigaciones Históricas, 1965), 111–14; Emma Pérez-Rocha and Rafael Tena, "Estudio preliminar," in *La nobleza indígena de México después de la conquista*, ed. Emma Pérez-Rocha and Rafael Tena (Mexico City: Instituto Nacional de Antropología e Historia, 2000); Margarita Menegus Bornemann and Rodolfo Aguirre Salvador, eds., *El cacicazgo en Nueva España y Filipinas* (Mexico City: Universidad Nacional Autónoma de México, Plaza y Valdés, 2005); Peter B. Villella, *Indigenous Elites and Creole Identity in Colonial Mexico, 1500–1800* (New York: Cambridge University Press, 2016), 39–48; and José-Juan López-Portillo, *"Another Jerusalem": Political Legitimacy and Courtly Government in the Kingdom of New Spain (1535–1568)* (Boston: Brill, 2017), 269–76.

58. See Pedro Carrasco and Johanna Broda, eds., *Estratificación social en la Mesoamérica prehispánica* (Mexico City: Centro de Investigaciones Superiores, Instituto Nacional de Antropología e Historia, 1976).

59. On regime constraints on cacique entitlements, see Luis Reyes García, *Cómo te confundes? Acaso no somos conquistadores?: Anales de Juan Bautista* (Mexico City: Centro de Investigaciones y Estudios Superiores en Antropología Social, 2001), 29–40; and Villella, *Indigenous Elites*, 39–48.

60. See Letter of Obligation between Diego de Tapia y Toribio de Escalante, Querétaro, November 9, 1583, in DIHQ, 1:33; and Information of doña María Magdalena de Tapia, Querétaro, November 26, 1585, in Jiménez Gómez, *Autos civiles de indios*, 163–65.

61. Doña María Magdalena de Tapia v. Diego Peguero, Querétaro, June 7, 1585–March 28, 1586, in Jiménez Gómez, *Autos civiles de indios*, 161–201.

62. Declaration of doña Beatriz de Tapia, Acámbaro, October 31, 1589, AGI-ECJ 200B, pieza 36, fols. 943–45.

63. Acts of Possession of don Cristóbal de Léon, Acámbaro, November 13–15, 1562, AGI-ECJ, pieza 36, fols. 1017–1040; Statement of the Province of San Hipólito Mártir of México Regarding the Ex-Estate of Cristóbal de Leon at Apaseo, México, December 23, 1721, AGI-ECJ 200B, pieza 36, fols. 1052–1070.

64. Accord between doña Beatriz de Tapia and don Cristóbal de León and Act of Possession, October 1589–June 1590, Celaya, AGI-ECJ 200B, pieza 36, fols. 947–53.

65. Doña Beatriz de Tapia v. Miguel de Saucedo, Querétaro, November 26, 1597–January 12, 1598, in DIHQ, 1:193–251.

66. Tutino, *Making a New World*, 102–12, esp. 107–8.

67. Inventory of the Estate of don Diego de Tapia, Querétaro, January 1615, AGI-ECJ 199A, fols. 247r–247v.

68. Inventory of doña Beatriz de Tapia, Querétaro, May 17, 1602, AGI-ECJ 200A, rollo 29, fols. 14–15.

69. Doña Beatriz de Tapia v. Gonzalo Gómez, Querétaro, December 11, 1596, in Jiménez Gómez, *Autos civiles de indios*, 415–24.

70. Act of Possession of doña María de Tapia, November 24–December 5, 1576, in Jiménez Gómez, *Autos civiles de indios*, 152–55.

71. See Debt of doña María de Tapia to Rodrigo Fernández, Querétaro, July 6, 1587, in DIHQ, 1:63–70; Debt of doña María de Tapia to Hernando Cardoso, Querétaro, February 26, 1589, in DIHQ, 1:113–20; Debt of doña María de Tapia to Francisco Hernández, Querétaro, December 4, 1593, in DIHQ, 1:153–56; and Collection of Debt Owed by doña María de Tapía to Melchor de Campos, Querétaro, January 28, 1595, in Jiménez Gómez, *Autos civiles de indios*, 370–83. Seizure of Wheat from doña María de Tapia on Behalf of María Thomas de Çamora, Querétaro, June 3, 1595, in Jiménez Gómez, *Autos civiles de indios*, 383–86.

72. Petition of Alonso Rodriguez de Alarcón on Behalf of Juan de León, Querétaro, October 29, 1590, in Jiménez Gómez, *Autos civiles de indios*, 307–8.

73. Doña María de Tapia v. Juan Bautista Treviño, Querétaro, November 9, 1594, in DIHQ, 1:159–70.

74. Doña Beatriz de Tapia v. Antonio de Mendoza, Querétaro, May 8, 1599, in DIHQ, 1:255–64, quotation from 255.

75. Appeal of don Diego de Tapia and His Sisters, Querétaro, August 27, 1590, in DIHQ, 1:121–26.

76. Testament of doña Beatriz de Tapia, Querétaro, October 17, 1601, in DIHQ, 3:167; Power of Attorney of doña Magdalena de Tapia, Querétaro, July 7, 1598, in DIHQ, 2:120.

77. Doña Beatriz de Tapia v. Miguel de Saucedo, Querétaro, November 26, 1597–January 12, 1598, in DIHQ, 1:239–45.

78. Wheat and Maize Distributions of doña Beatriz de Tapia between 1590–96, Querétaro, January 16, 1598, in DIHQ, 1:216–51.

79. Power of Attorney of doña Magdalena de Tapia, Querétaro, July 7, 1598, in DIHQ 2:118–23.

80. See Susan Kellogg and Matthew Restall, eds., *Dead Giveaways: Indigenous Testaments of Colonial Mesoamerica and the Andes* (Salt Lake City: University of Utah Press, 1998); Caterina Pizzigoni, ed. and trans., *Testaments of Toluca* (Stanford: Stanford University Press, 2007); and Mark Z. Christensen and Jonathan G. Truitt, eds., *Native Wills from the Colonial Americas: Dead Giveaways in a New World* (Salt Lake City: University of Utah Press, 2015). Regarding Querétaro specifically, see Juan Ricardo Jiménez Gómez, *Práctica notarial y judicial de los otomíes: manuscritos coloniales de Querétaro* (Mexico City: MA Porrúa, 2012), 58–76.

81. Testament of doña Beatriz de Tapia, Querétaro, October 17, 1601, AGI-ECJ 199B, rollo 15, fols. 1–15.

82. Testament of doña Beatriz de Tapia, Querétaro, October 17,1601, in DIHQ, 3:171.

83. Pizzigoni, *Testaments of Toluca*, 16–17.

84. Pizzigoni, *Testaments of Toluca*, 175.

85. On San José de los Naturales and the spiritual landscape of Otomí Querétaro, see Jiménez Gómez, *Práctica notarial y judicial*, 124–27.

86. Testament of doña Beatriz de Tapia, Querétaro, October 17, 1601, in DIHQ, 3:171–74.

87. See Alonso de la Rea, *Crónica de la orden de N. Seráfico P. S. Francisco, provincia de S. Pedro y S. Pablo de Mechoacán en la Nueva España* (Zamora, Michoacán: El Colegio de Michoacán, 1996), 177–78. Don Diego and doña María García had had a son, baptized Diego in 1593, but he did not survive; see Baptism of Diego, son of don Diego de Tapia and doña María García, Querétaro, November 18, 1593, in DIHQ, 4:17.

88. Lavrin, *Brides of Christ*, 359; Barbara E. Mundy, *The Death of Aztec Tenochtitlan, the Life of Mexico City* (Austin: University of Texas Press, 2015), 125–27.

89. See, for example, the correspondence between Jesuit authorities in Mexico and Rome and the Otomí cacique don Martín Maldonado of Tepotzotlan, who donated the lands and properties to establish the important Jesuit Colegio de San Martín for Otomí and Nahua Boys. Examples from Félix Zubillaga, ed., *Monumenta Mexicana* (Rome: Institutum Historicum Societate Iesu, 1956–91), include Estate of

the Colegio de Tepotzotlan, Mexico, 1582, 4:658–64; General Claudio Acquaviva to don Martín Maldonado of Tepotzotlan, Rome, May 15, 1589, 3:372–73; General Claudio Acquaviva to the Cabildo of Tepotzotlan, Rome, May 2, 1605, 8:489.

90. Testament of doña María de Tapia, Querétaro, December 1, 1608, in DIHQ, 8:79.

91. Power of Attorney of doña María de Tapia, Querétaro, August 3, 1601, in DIHQ, 3:145–47.

92. Survey of the Estate of don Diego de Tapia, in Ramírez Montes, *Niñas, doncellas, vírgenes eternas*, 54.

93. See Phelipe Fuertes, *Por el Real Convento de Religiosas de Santa Clara de Jesús de la Ciudad de Querétaro, en el pleyto con la Provincia de San Hypólito de esta Ciudad, de el Orden de la Charidad, sobre el cumplimiento y execución de un Legado de Hospital* [. . .] (Mexico City: Herederos de la Viuda de Miguel de Rivera, 1725); Zelaá e Hidalgo and Sigüenza y Góngora, *Glorias de Querétaro*, 40–41; Manuel Septién y Septién, "Breve crónica del pueblo de San Bartolomé Aguascalientes y apuntes históricos del hospital y baños de San Carlos Borromeo," in *Obras de Manuel Septién y Septién* (Santiago de Querétaro: Gobierno del Estado, 1999), 4:1–6. Not begun until 1771, the complex fell into disuse in the nineteenth century before being reestablished as a tourist destination by the Guanajuato state government in the 1930s. The baths were closed again in 2000, when nearby mining disrupted the springs. Brenda Cañada, "Agoniza San Bartolomé Aguas Calientes," *Periódico Correo*, December 21, 2015, https://periodicocorreo.com.mx/agoniza-san-bartolome-aguas-calientes.

94. Donation of doña María de Tapia to the Convent of Santa Clara de Querétaro, Querétaro, January 15, 1605, AGI-ECJ 199B, rollo 8, fols. 145–48.

95. Testament of doña María de Tapia, Querétaro, December 1, 1608, in DIHQ 8:71–80.

96. Donation of don Diego and doña Luisa de Tapia, Querétaro, December 29, 1604, AGI-ECJ 199B, rollo 8, fols. 123–62.

97. La Rea, *Crónica de la orden*, 184–85.

98. See Villella, *Indigenous Elites*, 210–18.

99. See Juan de Torquemada, *Monarquía indiana: Los veinte y un libros rituales y monarquía indiana* [. . .], 3rd ed. (Mexico City: Universidad Nacional Autónoma de México, Instituto de Investigaciones Históricas, 1978), 6:53; Rea, *Crónica de la orden*, 178–88; Balthasar de Medina, *Chrónica de la S. Provincia de S. Diego de México de Religiosos Descalços de N. S. P. S. Francisco en la Nueva España* (Mexico City: Juan de Ribera, 1682), 254r–54v; and Isidro Félix de Espinosa, *Crónica de la provincia franciscana de los apóstoles San Pedro y San Pablo de Michoacán* (Mexico City: Editorial Santiago, 1945), 356–61.

CHAPTER 3

Doña Marcela and the Cacicas of Bourbon Mexico City

FAMILY, COMMUNITY, AND INDIGENOUS RULE

Margarita R. Ochoa

Two centuries after the arrival of Europeans, native populations remained a dominant presence on the Mexican landscape. While their population numbers fluctuated—suffering tremendous losses at the end of the sixteenth century and experiencing significant growth at the end of the seventeenth century—their impact on the scope and manner by which Spanish domination of the Americas would transpire remained a constant. When it came to governing the growing and diverse populations of Mexico City, the administrative capital of the Viceroyalty of New Spain, indigenous presence was especially influential in the development of the Spanish social and political order. In the urban metropolis, the structures put in place to strengthen and disseminate Spanish dominion over native peoples negatively impacted native culture. Yet those same structures of domination, allowed native men and women to develop their own spaces of autonomy within which they negotiated and, at times, challenged the extent of Spanish rule in their urban *barrios* (neighborhoods).[1] By the late colonial era, the learned experiences of the previous centuries also provided deep familiarity and skilled ability in maneuvering within the legal culture of the viceregal capital. It is in this spatial and political context that this chapter examines the activities of eighteenth-century native leaders, specifically female caciques, or cacicas, from Mexico City.

The historiography on cacicas in central and southern Mexico indicates that these women owned, rented, and sold land and partook in litigation to protect their economic endeavors connected to that land.[2] They were also merchants engaged in the buying and selling of artisanal products. Additionally, some cacicas still held minor estates associated with *cacicazgos* (offices of the cacique, including sometimes their political roles, services, and properties) by the eighteenth century and managed the collection of native tribute from those lands. As wives and mothers, they headed households, commanded authority from members of their family, and were treated with deference by members of their communities. In Mexico City, despite a climate of imperial decline by the eighteenth century, which was followed by large-scale royal designs for bureaucratic change in the second half of that century, urban cacicas also engaged in a variety of cultural and political actions that set them apart from among city natives. Like their male counterparts, cacicas functioned as figures of respect and local authority in native barrios. Specifically, they resolved domestic disputes, ensured the peace and tranquility of native families and communities, and sought out the intervention of other indigenous leaders when necessary. In the process of their activities, cacicas complemented the role of caciques in negotiating the extent of direct Spanish intervention in the city's native communities. The efforts of city cacicas demonstrate that they were active agents in maintaining the systems of indigenous self-rule in Mexico City, and as women, their leadership was gendered and connected to community, family, and the home.

Eighteenth-century Mexico City was a locale replete with all the actors that helped shape and define colonial Latin America. From the very beginning, the native population of the city received, however reluctantly, Spaniards and their African slaves. Recent studies on the ethnoracial categories of the conquest era underscore the extent of racial mixture and how the resultant *géneros de gente* (types of people) were, at least initially, predominantly of a mixed indigenous and African descent.[3] As the *casta* (mixed-race) population of the city continued to grow, Asians also became a part of that population in the seventeenth century.[4] Spanish rule, however, intended for the administrative capital of its American kingdom to be organized according to a racial hierarchy that separated the indigenous of America from everyone else. In particular, the sixteenth-century official organization of Mexico City carved out a Spanish *traza* (central city district) and designated the vanquished *altepemeh* (indigenous ethnic states [sing. *altepetl*])—Tenochtitlan and Tlatelolco—as *parcialidades* (peripheral city districts) where natives were only to reside.[5] That division of the city's landscape and its population, between Indians and all others, represented more of a legal fiction than a lived reality. Yet the division of authority and the administration of justice was more real. For three centuries, the parallel Spanish and indigenous systems of rule in Mexico City governed the vast and diverse peoples within its jurisdictions. Each of the three major districts of the city—traza and two parcialidades—had their own *cabildo* (Spanish-style city council) and each of the parcialidades was governed also by a native *gobernador* (governor, often the indigenous leader responsible for collecting tribute and rousting labor). Despite classic interpretations of indigenous rule in eighteenth-century Mexico City as corrupt and decrepit, this chapter corroborates and adds to the findings of recent scholarship depicting a contrary view.[6] The native leadership of the eighteenth-century city had honed their political skills from their experiences with increased Spanish interventions, political infighting, and the changing status and make-up of the native elite in the previous two centuries. These processes are particularly evident in the archival record, especially in cases where native leaders are pitted against one another, and making strategic use of the Spanish legal system, when contesting the legitimacy of their own gubernatorial elections.[7] In doing so, natives evidenced both their political skill and their legal acuity in resorting to Spanish courts as another means to help advance their own political agendas within their parcialidades. The city's native leadership also worked to provide political order and resolutions to the everyday grievances of their community and family members. It is particularly here, within the politics of the communal realm, that cacicas exerted authority.

This chapter is based on the close reading of the details, patterns, and themes that emerge from the narratives contained in one of the most abundant genres of records from late-colonial Mexico City: litigation. The details of the accounts—denunciations, accusations, and witness testimonies—are read in their late-colonial context: a period of an expanding legal and policing bureaucracy in the city. A great example of this increased presence of Spanish officials in the daily lives of the diverse residents of the city was the rise in the quantity and activity of *rondas* (community policing units) seeking to arrest and prosecute men and women for an array of seemingly minor offenses, such as drunkenness and vagrancy, to more serious crimes, such as robbery, adultery, assault, prostitution, and homicide.[8] The concurrent expansion of the prosecution of crime in the city led to high rates of criminal litigation and punishment. Though complete counts of crimes and convictions for all districts of the city currently evade us, the records of criminal prosecutions demonstrate that the majority of the criminally accused were Spanish, though a per capita calculation reveals that natives were overrepresented.[9] The guilty were typically sentenced to fines, several months of jail time, and/or convict labor in textile and other factories. The effect of the increasing vigilance over the city was deliberate on the part of Bourbon magistrates. They sought to decrease crime and restore order by targeting the casta and poor, especially in the traza. After all, as the Viceroy Marqués de Croix put it in 1771, "the multitude is composed of many ethnic types and these are naturally vice-ridden. Their greatest inclination is towards drunkenness, gambling, lust and the love of luxury. There are many thieves among them, who are vulgarly known as *macutenos*. They are inclined to use knives, called *belduques*, which are used along with stones, to assault and maim."[10]

The textual sources from this era document the ubiquitous presence of natives in all city districts. Yet, in comparison to the Spanish and nonnative population, the extant record for persons identified as *indio* (Indian), cacique, or cacica and as belonging to either of the parcialidades of Mexico City is significantly smaller. One contributing factor for this is the late-eighteenth century reorganization of parishes in the city. By the late colonial era, when ethnic designations required in previous centuries were banned by royal decrees, the urban indigenous became less clearly designated in the paperwork produced daily by Spanish institutions.[11] Another important reason, indicated in the details of the cases examined in this chapter, is that native districts and neighborhoods were still governed by indigenous leaders. Coupled with the custom of local indigenous leaders to verbally adjudicate disputes, these are ample grounds for the comparably limited presence of male and female caciques in the written text; however, the details of extant litigation files comprise a record of the mundane cultural and political activities practiced by the city's native leadership, including that of cacicas.

DOÑA MARCELA ANTONIA DE REYNA

On the morning of March 21, 1785, doña María Loreto and María de los Santos García, two prominent native women from the parcialidad of Santiago Tlatelolco, were enjoying breakfast with their nephew don José de Arias, a *cacique y principal* (cacique and nobleman) of the same parcialidad, when their niece, María Manuela García approached and asked to speak in private with doña Loreto. According to don José, when his aunt rejoined the breakfast table, he could tell by the tears in her eyes that something terrible had occurred. María Manuela had come to inform doña Loreto that doña Marcela Antonia de Reyna, an *india cacique* (female Indian cacique) of the barrio of Santa Ana in Santiago Tlatelolco, had been stabbed by her own son-in-law.[12]

According to doña Marcela's own testimony, on the evening of March 20, at approximately nine o'clock, she, her two daughters, and her husband, the cacique don Antonio García, were settled in for the night when Pedro Leonardo appeared at her home. Catching his breath, the 15-year-old *indio libre* ("free Indian," a native minor free of tribute obligations) and gilding apprentice, notified the cacica that Antonio Adrean y Salas was *apporeando* (incessantly beating) doña Mónica García. In response to the boy's account, the cacica quickly gathered herself and headed out to remedy the situation.[13]

Once at Adrean and doña Mónica's home, the cacica began to "put [Adrean] in peace"[14] by publicaly admonishing him. Doña Marcela recalled that Adrean attempted to curtail her intervention by arguing that his wife had "offended him." But the cacica stayed firm and rebuked him anyway as she had on multiple other occasions during the seventeen-year marriage of Adrean and her daughter. She scolded him over his "pretense about being dishonored" and about his "pretending not to notice" that he habitually failed to meet his economic obligations to his wife and household. This evening, however, Adrean was angered by her actions. He charged at the cacica, stabbed her from behind with a *belduque* (large, pointed knife used in artisanal work), and realizing his "failure," he ran away.[15]

For almost two days, doña Marcela lay agonizing from her injury. According to the testimony of the *cirujano* (physician) that treated her on March 22, the cacica was suffering from a stab wound on the back of her right arm that was "two fingers wide" and "five fingers deep."[16] Moreover, the combination of depth of wound, inflammation, and "terrible pain" emanating from the sliced ligaments in her arm made the cacica's injury life threatening. In those two days, much had transpired. The details of the Sunday-night crime against doña Marcela were quickly transmitted across a barrio network of local caciques and cacicas, making their way to doña Loreto and don José by Monday morning. Later that day, don José would attempt to obtain medical care for the cacica, but the cirujano turned him away, insisting the cacique y principal first make a formal denunciation of the crime before the *alcalde del cuartel* (Spanish official). By Tuesday, the cacica's wounds were officially assessed and an investigation of the crime committed on her was underway. And, the result, a criminal case against Adrean—one of the many criminal files of the era, but in this case one in which an intricate network of male and female caciques and native community members served as witnesses—evidences the roles of cacicas as leading authority figures in resolving domestic disputes at the community level.

DOMESTIC MITIGATION

City cacicas served their communities as local leaders invested with the authority to mitigate and resolve domestic family problems. As the literature on marriage, adultery, and family has demonstrated, neighbors, parents, and family members of couples embroiled in violent and adulterous marriages readily appeared with them in court to bear witness to the histories of infidelities, scandalous behaviors (such as drunkenness), the failure of spouses to meet marital expectations (such as providing for the economic sustenance of the home), and domestic violence.[17] Their testimonies were often based on what they had seen, what they had heard, and their direct involvement in mitigating the violent behavior of a spouse.[18] Doña Marcela's actions corroborate that historiography. As doña Mónica's parent, the cacica was one of the first respondents to her daughter's violent quarrel with her husband. As the cacica, however, it was she who community locals expected to officially address the domestic scandal, and so they called directly on her.[19] According to the testimony of María de la O, a tributary native who was in doña Mónica's house and witnessed Adrean's attack, soon after Adrean struck doña Mónica and noticing that he was about to strike her a second time, she physically intervened to block his blows. While she interceded in the hopes of calming Adrean's ire, Pedro Leonardo, the young native apprentice, secretly escaped the house through a small window in order to call on the cacica. As María de la O declared, the cacica would know what to do. When she arrived, the cacica "promptly executed" her role to "put [Adrean] in peace" and "diffuse" the situation.[20] For these reasons, Pedro Leonardo sought the help of doña Marcela specifically, though, as the details of the document reveal, the cacica's husband (the cacique don Antonio) and don José de Arias, were nearby and also available that evening to execute their authority. Yet it was doña Marcela who was specifically called on to intercede in this marital dispute. On the night of March 20, 1785, the cacica promptly inserted herself in a domestic issue between her daughter and son-in-law to mitigate their altercation, reprimand the misbehavior of the abusive husband, and return peace and order to their home and barrio.

During the trial, the testimony of neighbors would also bear witness to the violent character of Adrean and their assessment of him as a husband based on direct and public knowledge of the history of his scandalous behavior. In his testimony, Balthasar de los Reyes Navarro, a mestizo resident of Santiago Tlatelolco, described the *muy mala vida* (very bad life) suffered by doña Mónica throughout her marriage. In fact, he added, her father don Antonio García so feared for her life that he once denounced Adrean to the *acordada* (eighteenth-century criminal tribunal). However, because Adrean was a soldier, the case against him did not move foreword.[21] Don Leonardo de San Pedro, a cacique of Santiago Tlatelolco and *maestro de capilla* (choirmaster) of the Santa Ana Parish, further corroborated the details of the mala vida endured by doña Mónica. As don Antonio's *consuegro* (father-in-law to a son or daughter of don Antonio), don Leonardo knew Adrean well, specifically his vice of excessive drinking and failure to maintain his household. In particular, don Leonardo declared, "far from fulfilling his marital obligations of providing [doña Mónica] with the basic necessities, instead it is she who provides them to him."[22] Moreover, María de la O, the tributary native who defended doña Mónica, also described Adrean's ire as unprovoked by his wife. According to her, minutes after Adrean arrived home, a *viejesito* (old man) came to the doorway of the house and asked if he could light his *cavito* (candle stub) and place it on doña Mónica's beautiful *oratorio* (oratory).[23] Hearing this interaction, Adrean became enraged, grabbed the candle stub away from Pedro Leonardo (who was lighting it), and tossed it. He then struck doña Mónica and accused her of an illicit relationship with the old man.[24] For his part, the viejesito Salvador Domingo de Rojas, a *castizo* (person of mixed native and Spanish ancestry) resident of Santiago Tlatelolco, declared that noticing the increasing tensions he "exercised his prudence and picked up his cavito and headed home."[25] Thus, according to relatives and neighbors, Adrean was a violent drunkard and bad husband. His long history of drinking and violence belied the accusations of adultery he hurled against his wife every time he became violent. The fact was, as the cacica had openly declared that fateful evening, his accusations were a tired ploy to create a scandal that would distract onlookers from the true problem plaguing his marriage: his failure as a husband, in particular his inability to economically maintain his household.

To minimize public shame or penalties resulting from a criminal investigation, some men could resort to counter-denouncing their wives for related crimes or highlighting extenuating circumstances, such as drunkenness.

During the colonial era, Spanish magistrates considered alcohol a "mitigating element in criminal prosecutions."[26] In their defense against accusations of domestic violence and adultery, husbands could blame their actions on their states of inebriation as a legal strategy to minimize their punishments. Husbands also often explained their violence as having been justified by their suspicions about the fidelity of their wives. Spanish law and custom provided that men could correct, through corporal punishment and even death, the sexual misbehavior of their wives and the resultant stain on the public reputation of husbands.[27] In this vein, accusing a married woman of adultery or lascivious behavior could prove as both a shrewd legal measure and a means by which to maintain a good public reputation. Adrean's claims, however, were not corroborated by those who knew or had heard of him.

As for the economics of the colonial household, though Spanish law did not define husbands as the sole breadwinners of the home, eighteenth-century moralists and popularly accepted customs made it so that the identity of men and their masculinities were tied to their occupations and ability to economically sustain their homes.[28] Among commoners and natives of the city, however, both husbands and wives worked to meet tribute obligations and economically support their households.[29] Yet the social expectation lay squarely on the husbands, including the husbands of women of elevated social status, such as cacicas.

SOCIAL STATUS AND HONOR

Doña Mónica, the cacica's daughter, was also identified in the criminal file as an "india cacique" of Santiago Tlatelolco and with the corresponding honorific (i.e., "doña"). More than likely, however, the identification of their titles as cacicas was of their own volition and a possible legal strategy to avoid being placed in depósito (deposited in a house of good reputation).[30] In recognition of the elevated status and authority of the cacicas and to underscore the gravity of Adrean's actions, the witnesses in this criminal case readily acknowledged doña Marcela, doña Mónica, and several more barrio neighbors as "caciques" and "cacicas" of Santiago Tlatelolco. Adrean was identified with neither a title nor an honorific but only as a "Spaniard" whose occupation was as a dorador (gilder). He worked in a low-skilled and poorly remunerated trade. Despite his Spanishness, per colonial Mexican conventions of status and honor, Adrean was a man of low socioeconomic status with a lower social standing than that of his wife and mother-in-law, especially while residing in the parcialidad.[31] His violent attack on doña Marcela thus violated local and colonial norms of status and honor. Assaulting his mother-in-law, however, was doubly egregious for he had insulted the honor of a social superior who was also an authority figure.

In light of the proximity of natives to Spanish governing institutions and bureaucrats, the roles of male and female caciques in Mexico City underwent changes different from those in other places, such as Yucatan, Oaxaca, and Cuernavaca. Whereas in these regions of Mexico, the presence of cacicazgos is evident well into the eighteenth century, studies on cacicazgos for late-colonial central Mexico depict a different trajectory.[32] In sum, by the end of the colonial era, the once-sizeable entailed estates connected to cacicazgos in central Mexico, particularly in Mexico City, were now mere vestiges of an earlier time. Eighteenth-century cacicazgo lands were disconnected *sitios* (land plots) that were rented to farmers or worked by a small tributary class of natives for male and female caciques. The cacique class of late-colonial Mexico City was thus no longer the hereditary *tlatoque* (native rulers [sing. *tlatoani*]) of the early colonial period who managed lucrative cacicazgos. Rather, many native leaders tended to have low-status occupations.[33] Yet deference by native commoners was expected and an attack on the cacica doña Marcela with such violence was both a strike against her status and a symbolic assault on the community she represented.[34]

Further evidence from criminal litigation also indicates the extent to which cacicas were willing to pursue legal avenues to maintain and defend their honor. The position of cacicas as persons of elevated social standing hinged on the status of their family members and on its recognition by the natives of their barrios. To defend that status, cacicas exerted their authority to mitigate domestic scandals in their communities. To advance that authority, cacicas could also make use of the Spanish legal system and reign in their misbehaving children and defend the public reputation and marriageability of their daughters. In 1806, for example, Gertrudis Gonzales, wife of Francisco Fernandez, the ex-governor of Santiago, denounced a member of the clergy for the rape of her daughter, Inés Fernandez.[35] In her declaration before the ecclesiastical tribunal, Inés described how this clergyman beat and subsequently raped her. Ultimately, the *provisor* (chief ecclesiastical judge) found the clergyman guilty by default, for failing to appear in court. In another example, in 1792, María Rafaela, an india principal, denounced her own daughter Thomasa Mora for adultery and indecorous behavior, requesting that she be reprimanded and placed in a *casa de honra* (house of honor).[36] Thomasa was reprimanded and held in public jail for several months, for which the india principal was economically responsible. María Rafaela was also asked to provide additional monies to cover her daughter's keep in the casa de honra following her release from jail. In yet another example, in February 1821, doña Ana Herrera complained to her parish priest that her husband, el Señor Capitan Comandante don José Gomes Escalante, gave her a *mala vida* ("bad life," including beatings and abandonment) and had had the audacity to "have carnal knowledge of her [own] daughter."[37] The husband was ultimately reprimanded and admonished not to continue in his bad behavior. Interestingly, both the husband and cacica mention, during separate interrogations, that the cacica had been unhappy from the beginning of their marriage, stating often that he was not the husband she had wanted to marry.[38] In these examples, cacicas turned to the courts to legally and publicly address the dishonorable behavior of family and community members and, in the process, uphold their own status and authority.

LEGAL SAVVY

The Spanish record of Mexico City cacicas as litigants is indicative of their legal savvy. They pursued legal avenues to defend their social status and honor and, by extension, that of their kin. From the Spanish perspective, these women were also of lower socioeconomic class standing, most possessing little wealth and occupied in poorly remunerated work. Yet the few cacicas who still owned and managed sitios—meager remnants of earlier entailed estates—could also turn to the Spanish legal system to defend what little they did possess and, in so doing, support the continuation of a uniquely indigenous system.

The sixteenth- and seventeenth-century predecessors of late-colonial cacicas enjoyed the social and economic benefits of acquiring and maintaining hereditary cacicazgos, but those entailments were challenged by political, economic, and demographic factors. By the latter half of the eighteenth century, cacicazgos, on the scale of those in southern Mexico (e.g., in Oaxaca and Yucatan), and even the few remaining in central Mexico (e.g., in Cuernavaca), were rare in Mexico City. The impact of population decreases at the end of the sixteenth century made tribute collection and the political intermediary role of Mexico City male caciques difficult, with tribute debts following some indigenous leaders beyond their terms as governors, and even beyond their deaths.[39] The demographic recovery of the late seventeenth century also strained relations between indigenous leaders and their barrios, especially over access to land and tribute obligations. The sale of cacicazgo lands to cover economic obligations meant that remnants of cacical land-holdings were going to be small and fiercely protected by indigenous rulers, including female caciques, in the late colonial period.

In 1809, doña María de Olalla Castro began a legal battle in the Juzgado General de Naturales (General Indian Court) that would pit her against the gobernador of San Juan Tenochtitlan, don Francisco Antonio Galicia, and her stepson, don José Santos, for over a decade.[40] Several years earlier, doña María had become the widow of don Gervacio Díaz, a cacique and former gobernador of San Juan. As the executor of her husband's will, she paid off some of his debts, distributed the items he left for his son, including a *lienzo* (painting on canvas) of Our Lady of Guadalupe, and took possession of her dowry, which comprised several sitios. By 1809, doña María had sold one of her sitios, was renting the others, and had invested in a *prensa* ("press," valued at 100 pesos) for the production of artisanal clothing. Her stepson had also come of age, and following his marriage, she gifted the prensa to don José and his wife for their economic sustenance. But in 1809 she also married a Spaniard and her troubles began.

Soon after her marriage, the gobernador don Francisco placed an embargo on doña María's lands. He claimed to be doing so in support of don José's inheritance claim against her property and because don Gervacio, her deceased husband, had an outstanding tribute balance from the years he had served as gobernador of San Juan. Doña María legally challenged the gobernador's embargo of her property. In an attempt to undermine her case, the gobernador argued that the embargo was part of an indigenous customary process for settling inheritance and land disputes. As part of that process, he explained, community elders and extended family members of don Gervacio were expected to come before him to share their "memories" of doña María's lands. The gobernador also stated that he feared doña María would sell the land to her Spanish husband or other Spaniards, to the detriment of her stepson and the parcialidad. Paradoxically, as the legal suit was still ongoing, it was the gobernador who sold a plot of doña María's lands for 121 pesos to Spaniards. He sold the land to the local Spanish military encampment, which they intended to use to expand their barracks.

Between 1809 and 1820, doña María received multiple judgments in her favor. With her parents' testaments and her dowry contract in tow, she easily demonstrated that her lands could not be used to pay the debts of her deceased husband and that the 121 pesos received by the gobernador for one of her sitios should be paid to her. Despite every legal win, don Francisco and a local intendant (Bourbon official) did not lift the embargo—the gobernador stood his ground arguing that his customary side of the legal process had yet to be completed. In June 1820, the legal battle finally reached the viceroy. He was briefed on the case and subsequently ordered the embargo on her lands lifted and any hold on the 121 pesos for the sale of one of her sitios removed. Doña María did not need to wait for the customary legal process in the parcialidad to be completed, the viceroy added, for her dowry was never subject to her deceased husband's debts and her stepson never had any rightful claim.[41]

In a separate case decades earlier, doña María de Villegas, cacica and widow of the former gobernador of Santiago Tlatelolco, don Lucas de Santiago y Rojas, was also embroiled in a legal battle over lands before the General Indian Court. In her 1724 case, she brought legal suit against her deceased husband's seven adult children from his first marriage.[42] As the executor of her husband's *memoria* (account) and testament, doña María distributed the multiple small religious *bultos* (statues) and lienzos (each of about 1–1.5 *varas* in size [ca. 0.8–1.3 m or 33–49 in]) among her stepchildren as well as multiple sitios and small houses (each of two or three rooms and an *oratorio* [oratory]). As for her own inheritance, when she attempted to take possession of her sitios and collect on the rents and tribute payments from those lands, she was violently threatened and prevented from doing so by her stepchildren. Together with their *compadre* ("friend and fictive kin," the godfather of the stepchildren's children), who was also the notary assigned to doña María's case, don Lucas's seven adult children maneuvered successfully to prevent the cacica from taking possession of her inheritance. Through her attorney, however, doña María would petition the court to have a different notary assigned to her case. A few months later, after presenting to the court both the memoria and testament of don Lucas, doña María and her fourteen-year-old daughter took possession of their rightful inheritance, which had included lands clearly stipulated in don Lucas's testament as having originally been part of doña María's dowry.

The cases of the San Juan Tenochtitlan and Santiago Tlatelolco cacicas in defense of their property evidence that some late colonial cacicas, in particular the widows of former parcialidad governors, owned cacicazgo lands, either inherited from their husbands or from their parents as part of their dowries. The details of those cases also reveal that such landowning cacicas relied on their ability to collect rent from those lands instead of *terrazgo* (tribute in kind and/or in native labor, typically on cacicazgo lands). By the eighteenth century, terrazgo does not appear to be a dependable source of income. Instead, most cacicas rented their land plots to both natives and nonnatives who could pay the rents they charged.

It is no surprise to find cacicas in the records of the General Indian Court. Created in 1592 and abolished in 1820, the court held wide-ranging jurisdiction over suits involving natives of colonial Mexico. In its two centuries of existence, the largest proportion of cases (administered by the legal aides of the court with the viceroy sitting as judge) heard by the court concerned land.[43] The cases of doña María de Olalla Castro (widow of don Gervacio Díaz, former governor of San Juan) and doña María de Villegas (widow of don Lucas de Santiago y Rojas, former governor of Santiago) are examples of the many land disputes heard by the court. The details of the cases highlight the ample familiarity of natives with the Spanish legal system and their use of the courts available to them to further their personal and communal interests. Interestingly, the few cacicas found in the late colonial records of the General Indian Court were widows. Doña María de Olalla and doña María de Villegas were widows who were now going to exercise their rulership over their meager cacicazgos on their own, renting their lands or collecting terrazgo from tributary natives. Though Spanish authorities recognized the status and ownership of lands of native noblewomen, it was typically male caciques who represented the joint concerns of dynastic rulership before Spanish authorities.[44] As widows with cacicazgos, cacicas stepped into the role of their deceased cacique husbands to maintain an economic system that supported indigenous leadership and, as evidenced in the colonial legal record, did so with savvy.

INDIGENOUS RULE

If we return to the 1785 case against Antonio Adrean y Salas for having stabbed the cacica doña Marcela Antonia de Reyna, further examination helps us to also understand the nature of indigenous self rule in Mexico City and the role of cacicas in said rule. In this case, rather than rely first on a Spanish official from the Catholic Church or a local ronda for assistance in addressing her domestic problems, doña Mónica (the victimized wife) and her neighbors depended on the structures of local indigenous leadership. Doña Marcela, the cacica of the barrio, was the indigenous leader who natives turned to that violent evening to settle the domestic dispute—it was she who was formally notified and whose presence was requested. While aware of the events transpiring the evening of March 20, 1785, don Antonio, a cacique and the cacica's husband, as well as don José de Arias, a cacique y principal, did not meddle in the leadership affairs of the cacica. Rather, the male caciques depended on doña Marcela to resolve grievances within her charge. Similarly, don Leonardo, the cacique and choirmaster, also became "aware of what happened because several persons informed me of the occurrence" and did not interfere.[45] Yet all three of these male caciques readily fulfilled their roles in domestic disputes as official witnesses in a formal legal investigation. Their behavior and participation in the written legal drama delineates the separate but complementary leadership roles of caciques and cacicas that governed native communities in late-colonial Mexico City.

Underscoring familiarity with Spanish legal procedure, doña Loreto and don José were not approached until it was necessary to act within the Spanish arena in order to punish Adrean and secure medical treatment for the cacica's wounds.[46] The result of don José's denunciation was that Spanish officials would now intervene and document a domestic matter involving native leaders from one of the city's parcialidades. As caciques, both doña Marcela's husband and don José would also make certain that the investigation into Adrean's criminal behavior was appropriately carried out. By their authority, caciques notified and encouraged community members to testify, albeit on behalf of the cacica and her daughter.

The specifics of the case against Adrean further detail the late-colonial customary practices of natives seeking solutions through indigenous avenues and leadership.[47] Bourbon authorities were increasingly at odds with the structure and functions of native systems of authority but, as had been common practice in Spanish America in the sixteenth and seventeenth centuries, were willing to allow them to exist and perform as they had for generations. The involvement of doña Mónica's family members in mediating her domestic troubles was intertwined with involvement from local indigenous leaders. Though doña Marcela was the mother of the abused wife she went to aid, her actions were nonetheless reflective of the authority and roles played by male and female caciques. Moreover, when Pedro Leonardo, the apprentice, escaped the home of the quarreling couple to seek help from the cacica, he did so in an apparently typical manner. That is, rather than seeking out the help from a nearby cacique, he directly sought the cacica. Doña Marcela, as witnesses corroborated, arrived as expected and invested in the authority to bring peace to the situation.

As the literature on indigenous leaders in colonial Mexico already makes clear, the cacicas of eighteenth-century Mexico City did not hold political office. Spanish law dictated that women, even indigenous noblewomen, could not be elected to political office. They could not serve as elected caciques on native cabildos or become gobernadoras of either San Juan Tenochtitlan or Santiago Tlatelolco. Like their male counterparts, however, cacicas in sixteenth- and seventeenth-century Mexico City oversaw cacicazgo lands, managed their private properties, held sway over community matters, and were directly involved in the individual affairs of natives.[48] By the eighteenth century their status as local leaders remained, despite the general loss of wealth. In her barrio of Santa Ana, the cacica doña Marcela commanded authority and respect in the domestic and communal realms. She managed her community by becoming directly involved in the interpersonal and family relations of the residents of her barrio. She was also an elderly figure and wielded the political charge of a member of an established lineage of caciques. As such, her authority was part and parcel of the control male and female native rulers had over the governance of their own communities in the viceregal capital. So the case against Adrean is exceptional in that the evening's events did not end with an unwritten customary admonishment by the cacica. Instead, that Spanish text, not intended to highlight the authority of female caciques, evidences the status, roles, and deference paid to cacicas by natives in their communities.

WOMEN AND GENDER

The gender of cacicas was not a factor in their ability to function as local leaders. Challenges to their authority in late-colonial Mexico City were not specifically pegged on their condition as women. Rather, they were challenged through physical violence and legal maneuverings based in Spanish law. Yet, in Mexico City, though cacicas maintained an elevated social status vis-à-vis the members of their communities, they did not wield the high levels of political power that some cacicas in the Andean world practiced well into the late colonial era (see chapter 8). Where cacicas did exercise authority—in familial relations and the Spanish courtroom—deference to the cacicas in these situations was not challenged on the basis of their gender. Perhaps, as David T. Garrett, Kimberly Gauderman, and Chad Black have argued for colonial South America, when it comes to the analysis of native women's activities and gender relations, a "refinement" of patriarchal models of indigenous politics may be necessary.[49] Despite Bourbon regulations seeking to stifle the abilities of women to maneuver their own lives without intervention from their parents, especially their fathers, cacicas in late-colonial Mexico City wielded authority in their native barrios and engaged in a variety of activities without their gender used overtly as a political strategy to curb their communal activities.

CONCLUSION

Natives who resided in late-colonial Mexico City routinely received aid, mediation, and leadership from their communities' male and female caciques. When complaints were taken before Spanish authorities, we find that native men and women did so according to distinct practices that both recognized the machinery of Spanish domination and supported their own systems of indigenous rule. City caciques were still connecting with indigenous practices, specifically the continuation of indigenous self-rule in settling disputes at the community and family levels. What also comes through in the details of late-colonial documentation is a distinctive custom and desire to prevent certain cases from going outside the barrio and before Spanish officials. That a significant number of male and female caciques from various barrios of the parcialidad of Santiago Tlaltelolco became immediately aware of the domestic dispute between doña Mónica and Adrean and the grave injury sustained by doña Marcela as a result of her mediation, speaks to a well-established and maintained apparatus of communication and dispute resolution among the indigenous leadership of Mexico City. This practice seems key in explaining the disproportionate presence of "indios," "caciques," and "cacicas" from parcialidades in the late-colonial Spanish record. Many domestic disputes were resolved at the local level, by local indigenous leaders, particularly cacicas, actively proscribing the necessity to take up matters with Spanish officials but resulting in little written evidence of barrio-level indigenous dispute-resolution practices in the late colonial era.

The details of the case against Adrean also suggest that late-colonial urban natives, and especially urban native women, relied first and more often on family, community, and local cacicas to resolve domestic situations before turning to additional aid from male caciques and Spanish officials. Cacicas, though excluded from Spanish-styled systems of authority within native barrios, retained much local authority nonetheless, and it was a direct and grave challenge to this authority that led to the creation of the case against Adrean. Since doña Marcela was critically wounded in her actions to help stop the violence inflicted on a member of her community, this case, in which multiple caciques and cacicas appear prominently, was recorded in Spanish tribunal records. For Adrean, his drunkenness and physical abuse of his wife usually found him reprimanded by the local cacica. Stabbing his cacica mother-in-law however was an *excess* that found him tortured and ultimately imprisoned, via the Spanish legal system, thanks to the actions and leadership of the indigenous lineage he threatened many times to end.[50]

In all, late-colonial litigation records reveal much more than previously known about the cacicas of late-colonial Mexico City. In 1992, James Lockhart argued that by the late colonial era the term "cacique" referred to any "prominent, propertied person of an officeholding family" and that cacicas, unable to hold political office because of their gender, were simply the women—wives, daughters, and mothers—of such officeholding men.[51] In essence, Lockhart argued that the title of "cacica" was more an indication of familial association with male caciques than of real authority; the title functioning as a mere honorific, such as "doña." Research on Mexico City corroborates this pattern in general but not in the details. The status, actions, communal authority, and legal shrewdness of cacicas were an important factor in the ability of native leaders to carve out and maintain their own spaces of autonomy within the heart of Spanish colonial rule. Cacicas managed and defended cacicazgo lands. In the process, they supported the continuation of an indigenous land-holding system that, in turn, also sustained the honor and status of the cacical class. They further defended that personal and family honor in court when it was challenged by violence against the bodies of their female relatives and community members. They also exercised authority at the community level, complementing the Spanish-recognized political power wielded by male caciques. They served their communities as leaders invested with the authority to mitigate and resolve domestic problems at the local level. Through their activities, these women became active agents in the continuation of indigenous self-rule. Thus together male and female indigenous leaders governed over the native barrios of the city.

More research dedicated to unraveling the historical roles of native women and colonial cacicas might add to the patterns of rule by male and female caciques discussed here. Research by Ronald Spores, Robert Haskett, John Chance, Kevin Terraciano, and Lisa Sousa, among others, has informed our understanding of the economic, familial, and political roles played by cacicas in central and southern Mexico.[52] Research on cacica nuns by Asunción

Lavrin and Mónica Díaz and on native women in *cofradías* (lay religious organizations) by Jonathan Truitt and Edward Osowski has further uncovered the rich history of native women and their engagement with the colonial Church, an important Spanish institution.[53] Continued research on gender relations and the social, political, and economic functions of cacicas in their communities, especially urban ones, can yet uncover more about the complex history of cacicas in colonial Latin America.

NOTES

I am grateful for the insightful comments from the anonymous reviewers who read earlier versions of this chapter. Of course, all mistakes are mine. This chapter is part of a larger book project tentatively titled, *Indigenous Mexico City, 1700–1825*.

Note on translation and spelling: All translations, and any errors in translation, from Spanish and Nahuatl to English are mine. For the sake of consistency and readability, I have also modernized the spelling of names and places throughout the chapter.

1. For a detailed study of the development of Spanish and native rule in Mexico City, see William F. Connell, *After Moctezuma: Indigenous Politics and Self-Government in Mexico City, 1524–1730* (Norman: University of Oklahoma Press, 2011). For detailed discussions and examinations of law and legal culture in Spanish America, see Brian Owensby, *Empire of Law and Indian Justice in Colonial Mexico* (Stanford: Stanford University Press, 2008); Yanna Yannakakis, *The Art of Being In-Between: Native Intermediaries, Indian Identity, and Local Rule in Colonial Oaxaca* (Durham, NC: Duke University Press, 2008); and Bianca Premo, *The Enlightenment on Trial: Ordinary Litigants and Colonialism in the Spanish Empire* (New York: Oxford University Press, 2017). For early modern Spain and the broader Iberian world, see Tomas Duve and Heikki Pihlajamäki, eds., *New Horizons in Spanish Colonial Law: Contributions to Transnational Early Modern Legal History* (Frankfurt: Max Planck Institute for European Legal History, 2015); Tamar Herzog, *Frontiers of Possession: Spain and Portugal in Europe and the Americas* (Cambridge, MA: Harvard University Press, 2015); and Tamar Herzog, *A Short History of European Law: The Last Two and a Half Millennia* (Cambridge, MA: Harvard University Press, 2018).

2. See also chap. 2 in this volume, by Bradley Benton.

3. Robert C. Schwaller, *Géneros de Gente in Early Colonial Mexico: Defining Racial Difference* (Norman: University of Oklahoma Press, 2016).

4. Tatiana Seijas, *Asian Slaves in Colonial Mexico: From Chinos to Indians* (New York: Cambridge University Press, 2014).

5. For examinations and visual depictions of the city's layout and development, from the sixteenth to nineteenth centuries, see Andrés Lira González, *Comunidades indígenas frente a la ciudad de México: Tenochtitlan y Tlatelolco, sus pueblos y barrios, 1812–1919* (Mexico City: El Colegio de Mexico, 1983); and Barbara E. Mundy, *The Death of Aztec Tenochtitlan, the Life of Mexico City* (Austin: University of Texas Press, 2015).

6. For example, see Connell, *After Moctezuma*.

7. Connell, *After Moctezuma*, chap. 5.

8. For an examination of the eighteenth-century increase in criminal prosecutions, the expansion of rondas and other enforcement mechanisms, and statistics on the rates of crime in eighteenth-century Mexico City, see Gabriel Haslip-Viera, *Crime and Punishment in Late Colonial Mexico City, 1692–1810* (Albuquerque: University of New Mexico Press, 1999); and William B. Taylor's classic study, *Drinking, Homicide, and Rebellion in Colonial Mexican Villages* (Stanford: Stanford University Press, 1979).

9. Haslip-Viera, *Crime and Punishment*, chap. 3.

10. Quoted in Haslip-Viera, *Crime and Punishment*, 52. Carlos Francisco de Croix, Marqués de Croix, was viceroy of New Spain from 1766 to 1771. The resultant rise in the criminalization of vagrancy, gambling, and drinking by indigenous and casta in the city led to an increase in criminal cases heard in the city's criminal courts, including the eighteenth-century tribunal of the *acordada*, a tribunal with unrestricted and sweeping jurisdiction over crime in colonial Mexico. For an examination of the acordada tribunal, see Colin M. MacLachlan, *Criminal Justice in Eighteenth-Century Mexico: A Study of the Tribunal of the Acordada* (Berkeley: University of California Press, 1974). For natives and eighteenth-century criminal litigation, see Taylor, *Drinking, Homicide, and Rebellion*.

11. The eighteenth-century reorganization of parish districts in Mexico City (and elsewhere in Spanish America) removed the requirement for indigenous to receive Catholic sacraments (e.g., baptism and marriage) in parishes specifically designated as *doctrinas* (Indian parishes). As of 1772, natives who resided in the city, both *naturales* (born in the city) and *extravagantes* (immigrants to the city), would now lawfully continue a practice that by the late seventeenth century had become commonplace; that is, to receive sacraments at the parishes most geographically proximate to their barrios. For more on this secularization, see the meticulous study by Juan Javier Pescador of the *padrones* (censuses) of the Santa Catarina parish in Mexico City, *De bautizados a fieles difuntos: Familia y mentalidades en una parroquia urbana, Santa Catarina de México, 1568–1820* (Mexico City: Colegio de México, Centro de Estudios Demográficos y de Desarrollo Urbano, 1992). See also Matthew D. O'Hara, *A Flock Divided: Race, Religion, and Politics in Mexico, 1749–1857* (Durham, NC: Duke University Press, 2010), especially chaps. 2 and 3. For more on Bourbon Reforms and the Church in colonial Mexico, see D. A. Brading, *Church and State in Bourbon Mexico: The Diocese of Michoacán 1749–1810* (New York: Cambridge University Press, 1994).

12. Archivo General de la Nación, Mexico City (hereafter cited as AGN), Tribunal Superior de Justicia del Distrito Federal (hereafter cited as TSJDF) 35, expediente 16, fols. 1–8v.

13. Declaración de doña Marcela Antonia de Reyna, india cacique, AGN TSJDF 35, expediente 16, fol. 3v.

14. Declaración de María de la O, india tributaria, AGN TSJDF 35, expediente 16, fol. 6v.

15. Declaración de doña Marcela Antonia de Reyna, india cacique, AGN TSJDF 35, expediente 16, fols. 3r–4r.

16. Declaración de don Antonio Farelos, cirujano, AGN TSJDF 35, expediente 16, fols. 4r–4v.

17. For marriage, adultery, and domestic violence, see Teresa Lozano Armendares, *No codiciarás la mujer ajena: El adulterio en las comunidades domésticas novohispanas, ciudad de México, siglo XVIII* (Mexico City: Universidad Nacional Autónoma de México, 2005); and Victor M. Uribe-Uran, *Fatal Love: Spousal Killers, Law, and Punishment in the Late Colonial Spanish Atlantic* (Stanford: Stanford University Press, 2016). For ethnohistorical studies that include examinations of adultery and domestic violence, see Kevin Terraciano, "Crime and Culture in Colonial Mexico: The Case of the Mixtec Murder Note," *Ethnohistory* 45, no. 4 (Fall 1998); and Lisa Sousa, *The Woman Who Turned into a Jaguar and Other Narratives of Native Women in Archives of Colonial Mexico* (Stanford: Stanford University Press, 2017).

18. To the point about witnesses whose testimony was based on public knowledge of the details of physical abuse shared with neighbors by victimized wives, see Kimberly Gauderman, "The Authority of Gender: Marital Discord and Social Order in Colonial Quito," in *New World Orders: Violence, Sanction, and Authority in the Colonial Americas*, ed. John Smolenski and Thomas J. Humphrey (Philadelphia: University of Pennsylvania Press, 2005). In her assessment and comparison of marital disputes adjudicated by ecclesiastical and criminal courts, she finds that women were more often successful in compelling criminal authorities to intervene in their marriages (by arresting and jailing their violent husbands, for example) especially in cases where women had publicized their maltreatment.

19. One might think that doña Marcela acted as she did only because she was doña Mónica's mother. For archival examples in which cacicas played prominent roles in resolving domestic problems, see Ana Herrera, india principal, contra José María Perez [her husband] y Pascuala María Herrera [her daughter] in 1821, AGN Criminal 529, expediente 9, fols. 375–82v; Inés Fernandez, india casique, contra don Francisco Peredo, *clerigo* (clergy) in 1806, AGN Criminal 641, expediente 29, fols. 372–76r; and María Rafaela Escobar, india principal, contra Thomasa Mora [her daughter] in 1792, AGN TSJDF 35, expediente 42, fols. 1–6r.

20. Declaración de María de la O, india tributaria, AGN TSJDF 35, expediente 16, fols. 6r–6v.

21. Declaración de Balthasar de los Reyes Navarro, mestizo, AGN TSJDF 35, expediente 16, fol. 8r.

22. Declaración de don Leonardo de San Pedro, cacique, AGN TSJDF 35, expediente 16, fols. 5v-6r.

23. According to her study on prostitution in colonial Mexico, "candle" could be a euphemism for the penis, though in this case witnesses describe the cavito as just a candle stub. See Nicole von Germeten, *Profit and Passion: Transactional Sex in Colonial Mexico* (Oakland: University of California Press, 2018).

24. Declaración de María de la O, AGN TSJDF 35, expediente 16, fol. 6r.

25. Declaración de Salvador Domingo de Rojas (viejesito), castizo, AGN TSJDF 35, expediente 16, fol. 7v.

26. Chad Thomas Black, *The Limits of Gender Domination: Women, the Law, and Political Crisis in Quito, 1765–1830* (Albuquerque: University of New Mexico Press, 2011), 246.

27. See Uribe-Uran, *Fatal Love*; and Kimberly Gauderman, "The Authority of Gender."

28. For more on masculinity and the socially prescribed economic obligations of men to the marital household, see Sonya Lipsett-Rivera, *The Origins of Macho: Men and Masculinity in Colonial Mexico* (Albuquerque: University of New Mexico Press, 2019), chap. 4. For marriage, adultery, and economic obligations, see Margarita R. Ochoa, "Illicit Relations in a Multiethnic City: Emotions, Fidelity, and Economic Obligations in Colonial Mexico," in *Courtship, Marriage and Marriage Breakdown: Approaches from the History of Emotion*, ed. Katie Barclay, Jeffrey Meek, and Andrea Thomson (New York: Routledge, 2019).

29. Some important works on the household for colonial Mexico City include Pilar Gonzalbo Aizpuru, *Familia y orden colonial* (Mexico City: El Colegio de México, Centro de Estudios Históricos, 1998); Rosalva Loreto López, ed., *Casas, viviendas y hogares en la historia de México* (Mexico City: Centro de Estudios Históricos, El Colegio de México, 2001); and Silvia Marina Arrom, *The Women of Mexico City: 1790–1857* (Stanford: Stanford University Press, 1989). For more on the households of tribute-paying natives in colonial Mexico City, see Susan Kellogg, *Law and the Transformation of Aztec Culture, 1500–1700* (Norman: University of Oklahoma Press, 1995), 110–11.

30. For definitions and discussion of the legal reasons for and uses of depósitos (or *casas de depósito* [houses of depósito]) and *recogimientos* (jails or houses of seclusion for women), see Josefina Muriel, *Los recogimientos de mujeres: respuesta a una problemática social novohispana* (Mexico City: Universidad Nacional Autónoma de México, 1974), 146–47; Arrom, *Women of Mexico City*, 47, 212–17; Asunción Lavrin, "Sexuality in Colonial Mexico: A Church Dilemma," in *Sexuality & Marriage in Colonial Latin America*, ed. Asunción Lavrin (Lincoln: University of Nebraska Press, 1989), 64; and Lee M. Penyak, "Safe Harbors and Compulsory Custody: Casas de Depósito in Mexico, 1750–1865," *Hispanic American Historical Review* 79, no. 1 (February 1999).

31. For more on social and legal conventions of status, honor, and reputation in colonial Latin America, see Lyman L. Johnson and Sonya Lipsett-Rivera, eds., *The Faces of Honor: Sex, Shame, and Violence in Colonial Latin America* (Albuquerque: University of New Mexico Press, 1998).

32. See introduction to this volume for a lengthier discussion of the trajectory of cacicazgos in colonial Mexico. See also Robert Haskett, *Indigenous Rulers: An Ethnohistory of Town Government in Colonial Cuernavaca* (Albuquerque: University of New Mexico Press, 1991); and John K. Chance, "The Caciques of Tecali: Class and Ethnic Identity in Late Colonial Mexico," *Hispanic American Historical Review* 76, no. 3 (August 1996).

33. Connell, *After Moctezuma*, 153. See also the occupations listed in the 1800 tributary census for San Juan Tenochtitlan as examined in Luis Fernando Granados, "Cosmopolitan Indians and Mesoamerican Barrios in Bourbon Mexico City: Tribute, Community, Family, and Work in 1800" (PhD diss., Georgetown University, 2008). I am currently examining the 1790 tributary census for Santiago Tlatelolco, and, in a preliminary assessment, the occupations of *albañil* (stonemason) and *hilandero* (spinner) are prominent across the district.

34. See Sonya Lipsett-Rivera, "A Slap in the Face of Honor: Social Transgression and Women in Late-Colonial Mexico," in *Faces of Honor: Sex, Shame, and Violence in Colonial Latin America*, ed. Lyman L. Johnson and Sonya Lipsett-Rivera (Albuquerque: University of New Mexico Press, 1998), 154.

35. AGN Criminal 641, expediente 29, fols. 372–76r.

36. AGN TSJDF 35, expediente 42, fols. 1–6r.

37. AGN Criminal 529, expediente 9, fols. 375–82v.

38. AGN Criminal 529, expediente 9, fol. 379v.

39. Connell, *After Moctezuma*, chap. 5.

40. AGN TSJDF 49, expediente 18, fols. 1–46v.

41. For more on Spanish law and custom on partible inheritance and dowries, see Arrom, *Women of Mexico City*, chap. 2; and Asunción Lavrin and Edith Couturier, "Dowries and Wills: A View of Women's Socioeconomic Role in Colonial Guadalajara and Puebla, 1640–1790," *Hispanic American Historical Review* 59, no. 2 (May 1979).

42. AGN Tierras 427, expediente 3, fols. 1–16v.

43. The second largest case load the General Indian Court dealt with consisted of legal complaints by natives against Spanish officials, including priests. See Woodrow Borah, *Justice by Insurance: The General Indian Court of Colonial Mexico and the Legal Aides of the Half-Real* (Berkeley: University of California Press, 1983), chap. 5.

44. For a discussion of *conjunta persona* (joint person), the preference of Spanish authorities to deal with male caciques, and the prominence of cacica widows in the legal record because they were exercising their dynastic rulership on their own, see Kevin Terraciano, *The Mixtecs of Colonial Oaxaca: Ñudzahui History, Sixteenth through Eighteenth Centuries* (Stanford: Stanford University Press, 2001), 179–90.

45. Declaración de don Leonardo de San Pedro, cacique, AGN TSJDF 35, expediente 16, fol. 5v.

46. Though Spanish authorities recognized the status of female caciques, male caciques like don José played a more visible role in legal proceedings within the male-dominated Spanish legal system when the criminal issue involved members of their communities and required the intervention of Spanish authorities. See Kevin Terraciano, *Mixtecs of Colonial Oaxaca*, 180–81.

47. For example see, don Joseph Francisco, cacique principal de San Juan, contra Pedro de Guadalupe, Indio, por tierras in 1725, AGN Tierras 440, expediente 6, fols. 1–6v.

48. For a detailed discussion of the important activities of caciques and cacicas, from the sixteenth through the end of the seventeenth centuries, in Mexico City, see Kellogg, *Law and Aztec Culture*.

49. David Garrett, "'In Spite of Her Sex': The Cacica and the Politics of the Pueblo in Late Colonial Cusco," *The Americas* 64, no. 4 (April 2008), 550. See also Kimberly Gauderman's discussion of the history of the patriarchal model in *Women's Lives in Colonial Quito: Gender, Law, and Economy in Spanish America* (Austin: University of Texas Press, 2003); and Black, *Limits of Gender Domination*.

50. In her testimony, doña Mónica described how Adrean regularly threatened her with his desire "to make carnage of her and her entire [cacical] lineage." Declaración de doña Mónica García, india cacique, AGN TSJDF 35, expediente 16, fol. 5r.

51. James Lockhart, *The Nahuas after the Conquest: A Social and Cultural History of the Indians of Central Mexico, Sixteenth Through Eighteenth Centuries* (Stanford: Stanford University Press, 1992), 133.

52. Ronald Spores, *The Mixtec Kings and their People* (Norman: University of Oklahoma Press, 1967); Ronald Spores, "Mixteca *Cacicas*: Status, Wealth, and the Political Accommodation of Native Elite Women in Early Colonial Oaxaca," in *Indian Women of Early Mexico*, ed. Susan Schroeder, Stephanie Wood, and Robert Haskett (Norman: University of Oklahoma Press, 1997); Robert Haskett, "Activist or Adulteress? The Life and Struggle of Doña Josefa María of Tepoztlan," in *Indian Women of Early Mexico*, ed. Susan Schroeder, Stephanie Wood, and Robert Haskett (Norman: University of Oklahoma Press, 1997); Terraciano, *Mixtecs of Colonial Oaxaca*; and Sousa, *Woman*.

53. For cacica nuns, see Asunción Lavrin, *Brides of Christ: Conventual Life in Colonial Mexico* (Stanford University Press, 2008); and Mónica Díaz, *Indigenous Writings from the Convent: Negotiating Ethnic Autonomy in Colonial Mexico* (Tucson: University of Arizona Press, 2010). For work on native women, cofradías, and the Church, see Jonathan Truitt, *Sustaining the Divine in Mexico Tenochtitlan: Nahuas and Catholicism, 1523–1700* (Norman: University of Oklahoma Press, 2018); and Edward W. Osowski, *Indigenous Miracles: Nahua Authority in Colonial Mexico* (Tucson: University of Arizona Press, 2010).

CHAPTER 4

Sinking Fortunes

TWO FEMALE CACIQUES AND AN *EX-GOBERNADORA* IN THE KINGDOM OF GUATEMALA, 1700–1821

Catherine Komisaruk

The colonial jurisdiction called the Kingdom (*Reino*) of Guatemala encompassed the territory that now constitutes Central America as well as the Mexican state of Chiapas. The region was home to numerous native cultures and polities. In the northwestern reaches of the kingdom, in what is now Chiapas and the Republic of Guatemala, most native societies fell into the ethnolinguistic category that scholars today call Maya. To the east and south—what is now El Salvador, Honduras, Nicaragua, and Costa Rica—cultures varied more widely in ethnolinguistic origins.

The vast majority of ethnohistorical studies of Central America and Chiapas have focused on Maya groups.[1] Analysis of gender and women's lives in the late nineteenth and twentieth centuries is particularly developed in the work of David Carey on the Cakchiquel Maya (of central Guatemala). Additional gendered analyses of the time period have focused on K'iche' Maya (in what is now western Guatemala), Kekchí Maya (northern Guatemala), and Mam Maya (western and northwestern Guatemala) communities.[2] For the colonial period, various works give attention to both women and native people—again, mainly Maya groups.[3]

However, the subject of native women with elite status or political power has been studied mainly for the pre-Hispanic period. Based on visual images portrayed in precontact Maya art as well as hieroglyphic texts, scholars have demonstrated various roles played by noblewomen.[4] These roles were often embedded in marriage. For example, male rulers of major Maya centers sometimes sent elite women from their cities to become wives for noblemen in lesser centers, with the goal of cementing political or economic alliances between communities. Some scholars have viewed such marriages in terms of exploitation of the women.[5] Other work, though, describes these women as "protagonists" who sometimes came to occupy high offices at the sites where they were married—even "offices and positions . . . more important than those of the local men."[6] Although political rule was normally reserved for men, scholars generally agree that women served on occasion as rulers at several Classic Period sites.[7] Not all of these women were outsiders sent as wives; some, for example, had inherited the right to rule from their fathers.[8]

For the colonial period, there is relatively less written on native women with elite status or formalized political power.[9] Alvis Dunn has described native women's recognized leadership in *cofradías* (Catholic lay organizations) in the late colonial era. Works by Severo Martínez Peláez and Kevin Gosner have examined collective riots and uprisings in which native women assumed a sort of de facto political power.[10] A few scholars have identified evidence of noblewomen in the early colonial period; and for the late sixteenth and seventeenth centuries, Robert M. Hill has documented inheritance and marriage patterns in an aristocratic Cakchiquel Maya family.[11] Tadashi Obara-Saeki and Juan Pedro Viqueira Alban mention colonial-era cacicas as a group, in a discussion of native mothers who would perpetuate hereditary cacique populations.[12]

Yet occasional records in Guatemala's colonial archives identify specific native women as "cacique" or "gobernadora" (female governor), and reveal aspects of their lives beyond reproductive roles as mothers of caciques. This chapter draws on the handful of these records that I have located, all from the eighteenth and early nineteenth centuries, from areas now in Guatemala and El Salvador. The records capture moments in the lives of three different women: doña Micaela de Miranda, identified as an *india cacique* (female Indian cacique) in the pueblo of Tecapa (today called Alegría), in what is now the department of Usulután in El Salvador; María Josefa Tzoch, also identified as an "india cacique" in the pueblo of Totonicapán, in the western highlands of Guatemala; and María de Jesús Chiquival, "ex-gobernadora" of the pueblo of Jocotenango, just outside the Guatemalan capital city.[13] (See map 2.) The significance of these women's titles of nobility and political office is not self-evident, for the scholarship addressing native aristocracy and government in the Kingdom of Guatemala has been focused, explicitly or implicitly, on male caciques and officeholders.[14]

What did it mean to be a female cacique or a native ex-gobernadora in the later colonial era? Why were these identities significant—enough so that people made note of them in public written records? This chapter addresses these questions by situating three women from the Guatemalan records in a gendered analysis of native elites' privileges and power.

It is generally agreed that indigenous communities' economic and political roles waned across the colonial period. Not only native commoners but also—especially—caciques and indigenous government officers faced diminishing and often precarious circumstances.[15] Scholars have demonstrated numerous ways in which male native elites in Spanish America advocated for the interests of their communities as well as for their individual interests.[16] As seen in various chapters in this book, elite native women also acted to protect their privileges. Indigenous women strategically deployed colonial legal institutions as well as native social hierarchies to advance their positions. However, as this chapter demonstrates, the colonial laws that underwrote cacique identity and privileges were gendered. An examination of both code law and case law shows a gendered pattern in the long decline of caciques' status. In the Kingdom of Guatemala, the privileges and power of elite native women were more limited, and were eroded faster, than those of elite native men.

This gender difference did not evidently arise through any conscious program of the colonial administration. Rather, it seems to have resulted intrinsically from the gendered structures of native governance under colonial rule and from the long-term social changes that diminished the power of the native nobilities. These social changes carried more force than did any particular Spanish administrative policy, as indigenous populations plummeted and surviving native communities fell increasingly under Hispanic influence. In a process that scholars have called "macehualization," indigenous nobilities were gradually subsumed in the larger category of *principales*.[17] Principales were native political elites whose status and power derived primarily from service in civil and religious offices; they were not necessarily hereditary nobles. In some cases, *macehuales* (native commoners) assumed *cabildo* (Spanish-styled city council) and religious posts simply because their communities did not have enough caciques to serve as officers. Epidemics and high death rates played a role, as did attrition by *mestizaje* (ethnic mixing). With macehualization, formalized service in native cabildos and the church became the primary avenues to elite status and economic privileges. This change had gendered implications: whereas native nobilities had included women since pre-Hispanic times, native officeholders under Spanish rule were exclusively male. Thus women's membership in the native elite was occluded, submerged under broad social transformations.

DOÑA MICAELA DE MIRANDA: HEREDITARY CACIQUE

The case of doña Micaela de Miranda, from the Pipil town of Tecapa (in what is now the department of Usulután, El Salvador), comes to light because she petitioned the *audiencia* (high court) in 1724.[18] (The Pipil are not a Maya group. Their Uto-Aztecan language, called Pipil or Nahuat, survives today in parts of western El Salvador.) It is possible that Miranda traveled to the capital city of Santiago de Guatemala and went to the audiencia's offices there personally. By today's roads, the journey one way is about 230 miles (370 kilometers) and would take about eighty hours to walk, not including rest stops.[19] Perhaps her petition was written closer to her home and sent by mail.[20] In standard form, the petition gives neither the date nor location where it was penned.

Miranda was asking to be recognized as an "india cacique," free of obligations to pay tributes or to perform *tequío* and *servicio personal* (both were forms of tributary labor). The audiencia granted her request. The *fiscal* (audiencia's attorney) noted that Miranda had provided written evidence demonstrating that she was a descendant of caciques who had enjoyed exemption from tribute. In writing his opinion, the fiscal quoted a law promulgated in 1572 and published again in 1680 in the *Recopilación de Leyes de Indias*.[21] The law specified that a cacique's eldest child (or eldest son) would be exempt from tribute requirements and obligatory labor but younger offspring or other descendants would not be exempt. Hence the audiencia ruled that Miranda's eldest child (or eldest son) would receive the privilege of exemption but younger offspring and other descendants would not.[22]

Miranda's case illustrates several points. At a most basic level, it shows that even in the eighteenth century, certain privileges for caciques continued to be observed within the colonial system in the Kingdom of Guatemala. This was despite the decline in the status and privileges of caciques starting early in the colonial period. In addition, the Miranda case confirms that cacique status and privileges were hereditary and could be inherited matrilineally at least some of the time among the Pipil. In contrast, most scholarship on Maya societies seems implicitly to assume that cacique status was inherited through the male line, though at least one study—on Chiapas—finds that status succession was patrilineal in some communities and matrilineal in others.[23] Miranda's petition demonstrates that even as late as the eighteenth century, women could be recognized by the Hispanic state as hereditary caciques and could pass the privileges to their offspring. Her case also highlights the point that native women could be subject to tribute and obligatory labor. Though legislation at various moments in the colonial period aimed to protect women from these requirements, in practice the demands tended to recur.[24] Doña Micaela Miranda sought relief by petitioning the audiencia.

The very fact that she petitioned is a key point. Although the record reveals little further information about Miranda herself, it shows that she used the colonial legal system to advocate for her individual interests as a cacique. She may also have been thinking of the interests of her descendants. Evidently she had been denied those privileges or not recognized as a cacique locally. This was not a completely uncommon scenario for male caciques either, as evidenced by cases in the judicial archives brought by men petitioning for recognition of their status as caciques.[25] There is nothing in the record to indicate that anyone helped Miranda bring her request other than the attorney who penned her petition; she seems to have acted independently. She may have hired the attorney, or she may have relied on the colonial procurator for the poor. (The record doesn't give his name, nor does it indicate whether she used an interpreter. It closes simply with the words *No sé firmar* [I do not know to sign]—the standard signature line for illiterate petitioners. The penmanship and wording, though, convey the attorney's elite Spanish background.) Notably, Miranda had possession of the *escrito*— the paper documenting her noble descent—and she presented it with her case. We don't know who wrote the escrito, or when. But Miranda herself knew its significance.

There is some haziness about gender in both the legal code and Miranda's case. The 1572 law specifies that the tribute exemption applies to caciques and their *hijos mayores*—which can mean either "eldest sons" or "eldest children." The judges' decision in the Miranda case used the same terminology, mentioning her "hijo mayor"—either eldest son or eldest child. No child is named in the record, thin as it is on details about Miranda's life. The rhetoric of the audiencia's decision is brief and closely focused on the law of 1572. It gives the impression that the judges probably did not know whether Miranda had children, much less the gender of her eldest. However, it appears that daughters—eldest if not also younger daughters—were also recognized as caciques: the colonial state declared doña Micaela Miranda herself to be a cacique, exempt from tribute requirements, based on the fact that her ancestors were caciques. Interestingly, her petition and the audiencia's ruling use the word "cacique," not "cacica," in effect interpreting "cacique" as gender-neutral. The code laws used "cacique" as well, without specifying whether the term was meant to include women as well as men.[26] The crown may have left gender unspecified purposefully to allow local norms and local administrators to decide. This sort of flexibility was typical in Spanish governance. Laws issued at the imperial or viceregal level tended to be general guidelines, open to interpretation and the addition of more specific rules provincially and locally.[27] Regardless of the original intent of the edict, in the audiencia's interpretation doña Micaela Miranda was legally a cacique.

Neither the codified law nor the record of Miranda's case clarifies whether both parents had to be caciques in order for their child to be recognized as a cacique. Scholarship on Chiapas has indicated that the offspring of cacique mothers and Spanish or mestizo fathers were typically considered as caciques and hence would have been exempt from tribute.[28] Beginning in the sixteenth century, code law insisted that the children of indigenous mothers and Black fathers (enslaved or free) should be subject to tributes, though the implication here is about macehual mothers, not caciques.[29] Certainly in many such instances, the children were raised outside the mother's native community or they left as youths or adults, and hence could not be made to pay tribute. The same was often true of children of unions between macehuales and Spaniards or *mestizos* (persons of mixed native and European decent). The *Recopilación de Leyes* says nothing about these unions and nothing about whether the children should be subject to tribute.

But what about the children of a marriage between a macehual and a cacique? These children would likely be raised within the native community and as adults would be living in the orbit of tribute demands. Would they be exempt from tribute? This question lies at the center of the case of María Josefa Tzoch of Totonicapán, below.

MARÍA JOSEFA TZOCH: A LEGAL END TO MATRILINEAL CACIQUE DESCENT

María Josefa Tzoch's story comes to light because of a disputed betrothal.[30] Tzoch was the daughter of a cacique in the K'iche' pueblo of Totonicapán, in what is now the northwestern highlands of Guatemala. (The record never mentions her mother.) In 1803 Tzoch and her boyfriend, a macehual, made plans to get married.[31] Soon afterwards, the parish priest of Totonicapán wrote to the province's *alcalde mayor* (chief colonial magistrate) to say that the caciques had jailed one of their own. The prisoner was the cacique Nicolás Tzoch, the father of María Josefa. He was incarcerated, the priest's letter said, because his daughter was engaged to marry a macehual.

The record gives no explanation as to why the caciques objected to the planned intercaste marriage. Perhaps they feared diminished tributes if the couple's children claimed exemption as caciques. (In contrast, if a macehual married a macehual, their offspring would be tributaries.) Or perhaps the match defied *costumbre* (native understandings and cultural practices) surrounding nuptial arrangements. Scholars have described the importance of matchmaking in colonial-era Cakchiquel culture as well as K'iche' and Mam communities in more recent times.[32] As we will see, María Josefa Tzoch and her intended groom were already ensconced in a sexual relationship. We might imagine that their engagement was based on love or lust rather than on the culturally appropriate matchmaking ritual.

The alcalde mayor, a man called don Prudencio Cózar, had long experience in government in the region.[33] He wrote back to the parish priest telling him to suspend the marriage proceedings. Cózar's letter reveals that the couple had been "living wrongly"—that is, in an illicit liaison. It is not clear how Cózar knew this; the priest's letter to him didn't mention it. Perhaps the priest had delivered the letter himself to Cózar and spoken directly with him. In any case, Cózar's reply instructed the priest to put the intended bride in *depósito*. Depósito was placement in a secluded and neutral location, typically the home of a respected elder woman in the community. Often a depósito was meant to protect a girl or woman from coercion in expressing her will to marry. In María Josefa Tzoch's case, the aim seems to have been to remove her from the illicit sexual involvement.[34] Tzoch's premarital affair suggests that courtship in Totonicapán may have been similar to the scenario in the largely Hispanized colonial capital city. High rates of premarital and extramarital sex have been demonstrated for all Hispanized social classes in Santiago in the eighteenth century.[35] Concubinage and extramarital relationships appeared among natives from nearby communities as well.[36]

Having replied to the parish priest, the alcalde mayor, don Prudencio Cózar, then wrote to the kingdom's captain general (who also served as president of the audiencia). His letter indicates that the discord over María Josefa Tzoch's plan to marry a commoner was hardly unusual. "At every turn,"

Cózar wrote, "disputes come up about marriages of *indios caciques* [Indian caciques] with macehuales." He seemed puzzled about the rationale for the disputes. "I know many who are in mixed [cacique-macehual] marriages, but the [Indian] Governor and *Principales de Caciques* have consented to several of these marriages," he noted. (More in the next section about his wording, "principales de caciques.") Yet in other cases, he continued, the caciques "tenaciously oppose, and they pursue and punish, as happened now with Nicolás Tzoch." Cózar acknowledged that a cacique marriage to a macehual could cost the cacique bloodline its loss of privileges. But he argued that this should not completely prohibit such marriages, especially "in the circumstances of the present case and others like it"—presumably referring to the premarital sexual relationship.[37] He asked the audiencia to make a decision not only for the case of the Tzoch marriage but also for future instances that would surely arise.

The audiencia and the *real junta superior* ("royal superior council," a separate council of the captain general) passed the case back and forth and then sat on it for twenty-two months without reaching a decision.[38] Finally, a new interim fiscal in the audiencia offered a clear opinion, and the judges accepted it. The fiscal noted that natives of either sex, like other vassals of the king, were free to marry whomever they wanted, regardless of the *calidad* (ethnicity or rank) of the partner, provided they were of age or had consent from their parents or guardians. However, the fiscal argued, if a female cacique married a macehual man, there should be no privileges or exemptions for their children. On the other hand, if a male cacique married a macehual woman, their eldest child and the firstborn children in subsequent generations should enjoy hereditary privileges. The reasoning, the fiscal explained, was that "the family's calidad is derived from the father and not from the mother." Thus cacique status was to be inherited through the paternal line, not the maternal line.

The judgement was formally decreed in the Tzoch case in November 1805, more than two years after the parish priest of Totonicapán first alerted the alcalde mayor about the jailing of Nicolás Tzoch. It is not known what happened to Tzoch's cacique daughter María Josefa or her macehual lover. If they did finally get married, the audiencia's ruling—at least in theory—denied their children the privileges of cacique status. It also denied those privileges to any children they had together even if they didn't get married, and it denied the privileges to any children María Josefa may have had in a union with anyone else who wasn't a cacique. While the decision in the

Tzoch case recognized female hereditary noblewomen, it limited their privileges in ways that did not limit the privileges of native noblemen. The audiencia had legally ended women's ability to pass their cacique status to their descendants, even while it upheld that ability for men.

Though I have not found evidence as to whether the ruling was enforced, it had a potentially dramatic impact if it was followed across the kingdom, or even in just some of the provinces. It would have significantly reduced the numbers of people eligible for the status and privileges of nobility, in effect constricting the perpetuation of cacique bloodlines. As don Prudencio Cózar's letter indicates, it was not uncommon for caciques to be married to macehuales. Cózar did not explicitly specify whether these marriages often united cacique women with macehual men or whether it was mainly cacique men marrying macehual women. Yet he seemed to find nothing unusual in the betrothal of the cacique María Josefa Tzoch to a macehual. Presumably there were other couples like them.

In 1805 when the interim fiscal wrote his opinion, neither he nor the audiencia's *oidores* (judges) could have foreseen the political changes that would culminate in independence in 1821. From their perspective, their ruling—and its gradual diminishment of hereditary native nobility and privileges—could have continued indefinitely. It wasn't that the colonial administration contemplated eliminating native governance. On the contrary, the Spanish Empire needed indigenous governments to administer native affairs and to help maintain the order that underwrote the entire system of Spanish rule. But native officers could be selected through "election" (the Spaniards' term) by the principales within their communities. The *república de indios* (republic of Indians), after all a Spanish construction, could function without a hereditary native nobility. This point is illustrated in the following case of doña María de Jesús Chiquival.

DOÑA MARÍA DE JESÚS CHIQUIVAL: "EX-GOBERNADORA"

In the known written records, doña María de Jesús Chiquival was never identified as a cacique or hereditary noble. Rather, she was called doña and labeled as the *ex-gobernadora* (female ex-governor) of Jocotenango, a Cakchiquel pueblo located on the northern edge of the capital city.[39] Her late husband, don Diego Casanga, had served as the native *gobernador* (male governor) of Jocotenango on and off and on again over the second half of the eighteenth century.[40] To be clear: people who held political offices in the kingdom's indigenous governments were men, not women. María de Jesús Chiquival was called "ex-gobernadora" because she had been married to the gobernador, not because she herself had been recognized as a member of the native government. Any recognition she may have had was certainly less than that of a male gobernador.

By the eighteenth century if not sooner, the post of native governor was appointive, not hereditary. Indigenous governors were selected by Spanish administrators—the alcalde mayor or the *corregidor* (Spanish district magistrate).[41] The office commanded more power than any other in native municipal governments, and the men appointed as native governors typically had already served in religious and civil offices in their communities. Scholarship has indicated that in the sixteenth and seventeenth centuries, they were often caciques—that is, members of the nobility.[42]

However, the criteria for appointment of native governors seem to have shifted somewhat over time. Historian Greg Grandin has suggested that in the Habsburg era, "moral rectitude and the ability to ensure that Indians fulfilled their religious obligations were important qualifications"; whereas in the Bourbon era, Spanish administrators chose gobernadores "whom, to put it simply, they felt they could work with." Among other things, this meant that those appointed had to be able to speak Spanish.[43] Of course, given the context of increasing Hispanization across the colonial centuries, by the Bourbon era a larger proportion of native people were able to speak Spanish.

Further, by the eighteenth century, in some communities the classification "cacique" was no longer being used. The process of macehualization had reached the point where the hereditary nobility was completely subsumed in the larger category of "principales." Certainly, wealth as well as birth into elite families often positioned native men for office in civil or religious posts—that is, positioned them as principales. But high birth was not required to be a principal. Though principales ran native governments and controlled much of the wealth of their communities, they were not necessarily hereditary nobles. The boundary between nobility and commoners had been blurred.[44]

We can see that in the context of these changes, Spanish officials maneuvered verbally to keep their terminology current. The records on the disputed betrothal of María Josefa Tzoch (seen above) show that in Totonicapán the term "cacique" was still in use in the early nineteenth century. However, the alcalde mayor referred to "principales de caciques"—a turn of phrase mixing two categories that had probably in fact become indistinguishable. In the capital, the interim fiscal took care in his wording to cover various constructions of social categories. He referred to indigenous people who were "nobles or caciques or descendants of these" and later to "a female descendant of a cacique, or any other noble title." The final ruling issued by the audiencia replicated this flexible classification verbatim.[45]

The shifts in sociopolitical categories had gendered implications. Although women had been entitled to inherit noble status as caciques, they could not serve in political offices or in religious offices (other than in cofradías).[46] The category "principales" therefore did not have a clear entrance open to women. In general, principales were men. Thus as the category of "caciques" was absorbed into that of "principales," the structures in which native women could hold formalized elite status all but disappeared. Marriage to a principal was perhaps the only remaining legal structure through which native women could be recognized as elites.

The record of doña María Josefa Chiquival, in its use of the term "ex-gobernadora," alludes precisely to her marriage to the governor—the most powerful principal in the community. To be sure, Chiquival may have been born into a noble family. High birth could explain her use of the honorific "doña," and it could have positioned her for her marriage to the man who would become (or perhaps already was) the governor. But the records of her life—documents dated in 1805 and 1809—never use the term "cacique," and she hardly seems to have had access to privileges of nobility after her husband's death. If she was of noble birth, it wasn't much recognized by the nineteenth century.

As don Diego Casanga's wife, Chiquival had presumably shared in the material benefits of his office. In Spanish colonial law, wealth gained during a marriage was owned jointly by husband and wife.[47] Chiquival and Casanga shared a house and had a family together. Through his position as governor, Casanga controlled significant community wealth in the forms of obligatory labor and money. The pueblo of Jocotenango, just a short walk from the colonial capital, had for centuries provided workers for the city's myriad needs. People from Jocotenango labored in urban jobs ranging from construction to janitorial service, and from grass cutting to wetnursing.[48] Records from the years of Casanga's governorship show that he played a central role in recruiting his townspeople to fill these jobs. He also collected their required cash tributes, and as governor he had access to the *caja de comunidad* (community coffer). He himself was exempt from tribute levy, and his wife therefore was also exempt. In what seems to have been an unusual scenario, in 1797 the audiencia ruled that Casanga as governor would be paid a salary. The salary would be four reales a day; this was a sizable amount, at the upper end of the wage range for urban men skilled in the building trades.[49] Thus among natives, even those in Jocotenango and other communities near the capital city, Casanga and Chiquival fared exceptionally well in financial terms.

Yet the economic privileges they enjoyed were attached to Casanga's position as gobernador, and these privileges evidently were not extended to his wife after his death. Casanga died at some point between 1797 and 1805. He was succeeded in office by a man named Luis Ylarios, not related (as far as I can tell) to Casanga or Chiquival.[50] By this time, Chiquival was exempt from tribute demands because of her age. But a record from 1805 portrays her in reduced pecuniary circumstances.

In that year she petitioned the audiencia, complaining that the town's *juez preventivo* (a Spanish official charged with local judicial matters)—a man named don Francisco Gomes—had taken possession of a *sitio* (small plot) left to her by her husband. She described improvements that she said her husband had paid for—a wall around the property and a *galera* (a shed or small shelter). She had kept a *milpa* (cornfield) and banana or plantain trees there, she said, but now without the key to the sitio, she had been unable to plant and was forced to buy maize for her family at the year's high market prices. She alleged that the juez preventivo had taken the fruit from the trees for the past two years. She was requesting that he be ordered to return the key to her to restore her access to the sitio.[51]

Like the cacique doña Micaela de Miranda nearly a century earlier, María de Jesús Chiquival was petitioning the colonial state in an effort to retain, or to reestablish, her privileges as a native elite. The attorney who drew up her petition used rhetoric typical of appeals to Spanish juridical beneficence. Two standard elements of such rhetoric were claims about the supplicant's poverty and assertions of his or her merit. Chiquival's petition included both. In the closing lines, she asked the court to view her request "considering my family, poverty, and deplorable circumstances as a woman." Then she alluded to merit, as she noted the "exceptions and privileges of my late husband." The implication was that her husband had merited these privileges, and therefore she also should benefit from them.

A written response to Chiquival's petition came from Francisco Gomes, the Spanish juez preventivo for Jocotenango. Gomes vehemently disputed Chiquival's claims. He portrayed a scenario in which Diego Casanga and

María de Jesús Chiquival had obtained privileges at the expense of the townspeople. The sitio that Chiquival was seeking to recover, Gomes said, was "none other than the interior patio of the *casa de cabildo* [town hall]."[52] This patio—at the center of the community's physical space—would have commanded multivalent cultural significance in both Hispanic and Maya understandings.[53] Gomes contended that Casanga had the shed and wall built and banana trees planted, not at his own expense but rather with labor and monetary contributions that he required from his subjects. Further, Gomes argued, Casanga could not have left the sitio to his wife because it was never his; rather, it belonged to the entire pueblo in common. Gomes did not recognize any right for a governor's widow to enjoy the same access to community resources that her husband had enjoyed.

Nor did the current principales recognize such a right, as demonstrated in further details of Gomes's statement. He described how, shortly after he assumed the office of juez preventivo for the pueblo, "the *Justicias* [native cabildo members] and some principales [who may have been past officers]" had come to him and asked him to cut off Chiquival's access to the sitio because they needed to use it. Gomes summoned Chiquival, but she refused to give him the key, arguing that the sitio had been left to her. Then and there the justicias began to quarrel with her. Words escalated on both sides. The indigenous officers called Chiquival and her late husband thieves for having demanded payments from the townspeople every Sunday without telling the people how the payments were invested.

Gomes's account echoes the impression conveyed in other records of Diego Casanga's governorship. For one thing, records from Casanga's lifetime indicate that he had a hand in brokering credit from Spaniards to cover tribute payments for the townspeople. Casanga and other native officers from Jocotenango sometimes collected tribute payments directly from the Spanish creditors. The townspeople whose tributes were thus advanced would then be obligated to work off the debts.[54] Granted, this was not unique to Casanga's administration; the same thing happened in other native communities as well.[55] Records also show that Casanga wielded significant power in drafting indebted laborers and otherwise forcing debtors to pay off their loans. One townswoman testified in a 1797 deposition that Casanga had seized possession of her house and sold it, as if on her behalf, to repay a debt left by her absentee husband. She alleged that Casanga had then promised to restore the house to her in exchange for money that she earned after the sale of the house. She gave him her wages, she said, but then he reneged, demanding further payment.[56]

From their own perspective, indigenous officeholders faced a herculean task in collecting sufficient tributes to meet Spanish demands. Evidence indicates that Diego Casanga himself, like many native officials, struggled to produce tribute when his townspeople had fled.[57] Principales who failed to deliver required tributes to the Spaniards were subject to punishments as severe as jailing and whipping.

Yet the process of tribute collection helped constitute the distinction between native elites and commoners and therefore formed an important basis of elite status and power.[58] As one historian has noted for the community of Quetzaltenango in northwestern Guatemala, the principales "proved particularly vigilant in collecting the tribute."[59] Their role as administrators in the tribute process benefited them.

None of these roles or benefits passed to Casanga's widow, doña María de Jesús Chiquival. Because "ex-gobernadora" was a not a formalized title, it did not confer any rights. In fact, Chiquival did not even use the title "ex-gobernadora" in her 1805 petition; it appears only in a later, unrelated document that we will see below. Her privileges had existed only by way of her marriage to the governor, and they ended when the marriage ended with his death. In the colonial system of appointed and elected offices in native communities, only men were appointed and elected. Women could benefit from certain privileges as wives of male officers, but as the Chiquival case shows, women could be stripped of these privileges when their husbands died or left office.[60] The privileges attached to appointive and elective native offices were not heritable or transferable. For their part, the cabildo members took no pains to protect a widow whose late husband had, in their view, exploited the townspeople in his position as gobernador.

In the dispute over the sitio, the juez preventivo don Francisco Gomes firmly sided with the native cabildo. Gomes said that he ultimately "had to take the key" from Chiquival—forcibly, one imagines—and give it to the justicias. In his statement he complained that Chiquival had left a mess of the milpa after the last harvest. It took six men to clear and smooth out the ground, he said. He denied the veracity of various of Chiquival's statements. Her family consisted of only three people, he said, who with their work earned more than what it cost to maintain them.[61] He argued that her claims about needing to use the patio of the cabildo to grow maize were also untrue. "Every year she plants adequate crops of maize and squash [ayote]" in the town's field, he said, and no one stopped her or charged her anything for using the land there. It is hard to imagine that don Francisco Gomes would himself have observed so much about Chiquival's family and her crops. He probably got some of his information from the native justicias.

The audiencia's fiscal quickly rejected Chiquival's petition. Her request for the sitio had no grounds, he wrote, because she herself in her petition stated that her husband made the improvements to benefit the pueblo. The plot belonged to the cabildo and the *común del pueblo* (community), the fiscal wrote, and it was the pueblo that paid and did the work of making the improvements. "The Indians themselves say so," the fiscal noted, referring to the justicias.[62] It is clear, though, that the fiscal had written his opinion drawing mainly on the statement of the Spanish juez preventivo don Francisco Gomes. It was Gomes who indicated that that sitio was in the patio of the cabildo, and it was Gomes who reported what the justicias had said. The indigenous officers themselves never testified in the case.

Beneath the ruling lies an important facet of native political life under colonial rule. Native communities were formally represented in their interactions with the Spanish state by collective administrative bodies—that is, native governments or cabildos. Records generated by these bodies, as well as records created by the colonial state, often labeled the native government of a given community as "el común" or even "el pueblo"—for example, "el común de Jocotenango" or "el pueblo de Totonicapán," in both cases meaning the cabildo. The fiscal in the Chiquival case wrote, "the Indians themselves say so," when he really meant the Indian justicias (that is, the cabildo members) say so. All these lexical usages in effect equated the cabildo with the community itself. But the cabildo was not the community. The cabildo was only a few people, and these were not just any townspeople. They were caciques or principales, elite members of the community; the very fact of their officeholding conferred privileged status on them if they had not already had it.

Moreover, cabildo members were exclusively male. Native governments served as a structure in which elite native men collectively adjudicated, advocated, and litigated on behalf of the interests of their collectives—that is, of the cabildos. These interests coincided sometimes, but not always, with the interests of their entire communities. No such structure existed in which native women, elite or not, acted collectively.[63] In the Chiquival case, when the Spanish officers—the juez preventivo and fiscal—sided with the justicias, they were siding with a collective of elite native men. Doña María de Jesús Chiquival, in contrast, had appealed to the court as an individual.

This pattern is replicated broadly throughout the colonial archives of the Kingdom of Guatemala. The vast majority of petitions from native people to the Spanish colonial state were brought by native town governments or by factions within town governments—that is, by collectives of male officers. There are only occasional appeals by individual native men and women. Many if not most of the individual men who petitioned were, like doña Micaela Miranda of Tecapa, seeking recognition as caciques with associated tribute exemptions. My impression is that the cases brought by indigenous women varied more widely in their goals, and further, that native women who appealed to the colonial courts were more often commoners than were the native men who appealed.

CODA: SINKING STATUS

In a coda to the story of doña María de Jesús Chiquival, she surfaces as a witness in a colonial court case from 1809.[64] It is here that she is identified as the "ex-gobernadora de Jocotenango." The label is curious because this particular record is largely unrelated to her social status or her late husband's governorship; it is an investigation into the drowning death of her adult grandson, Antonio Casanga (no "don" in his name). Perhaps Chiquival stated she was the ex-gobernadora to establish her prestige or respectability as a witness, or perhaps she wanted to (re)assert her family's importance in the context of loss. Perhaps her status as ex-gobernadora was simply standard identifying information like calidad and age, and had been omitted from her 1805 petition about the sitio just as calidad and age were normally omitted from complainants' petitions.

Though the events in the 1809 case ended in tragedy, the record paints a colorful picture of the young man's escapades with friends in the hours before his death. The witnesses' testimonies illustrate a remarkable degree of interethnic social mixing in a community where native governance was still operating. The key witness, Manuel Matute, remained in legal custody until the investigation was completed. He identified himself as *mulato* (of mixed African and European or native ancestry), a resident of the capital, married, and a *peón* (day laborer). His age was recorded as "over thirty," though his account portrays him as a young soul. He described how on the morning of the drowning he had met up with Casanga and two other friends in the capital. They were on their way to work, Matute said, but first they had a couple of reales of *agua dulce* (a non-alcoholic beverage). Then they went to an *estanquilla* (liquor concession) run by a woman they knew. Casanga ordered a real of aguardiente and the four men drank it all.

Casanga and Matute left the estanquilla together. Finding they had no more cash, they hatched a plan. They went to the house of Casanga's grandmother, doña María de Jesús Chiquival. Matute went inside and told her that the police had arrested her grandson and if she did not send money, he would be put on the chain gang. Matute suggested a peso or six reales. Chiquival said no. Then Casanga went into the house, crying and asking for money. Chiquival still said no.

Finally, the two men headed out to the fields of Jocotenango, where Casanga had left some tools at his milpa. They stopped at a thatched house next to a *zanja* (either a drainage ditch or irrigation canal). Casanga spoke with a native woman there; Matute testified that he did not know what they said because they spoke "en lengua," that is, in Cakchiquel. In any case, Casanga told Matute to wait for him while he went to his milpa on the other side of the reservoir. Casanga jumped over the zanja, and after a short wait, Matute looked up and saw him in the reservoir, flapping his arms. For a moment Matute thought Casanga was swimming. Then he realized that Casanga was still wearing his clothing and hat. He had fallen in.

After shouting for help from the woman in the thatched house, Matute jumped the zanja himself and started into the reservoir after Casanga. But when he couldn't touch the bottom, he turned back. Once the justicias arrived, Matute asked them to tie a rope around his waist to see if he could save Casanga—he knew how to swim a bit, he said—but the justicias were afraid he too would sink. They finally pulled Casanga out with a ladder. "Although they put him head down and he expelled a lot of water," Matute recounted, "there was no sign of life."[65]

At the end of his deposition, Matute was asked about the influence of alcohol. This was a standard question put to defendants and witnesses in criminal proceedings. Matute confirmed that both he and Casanga had been drunk. The court evidently had little doubt about what had happened. They interviewed only a few other witnesses, including Casanga's grandmother doña María de Jesús Chiquival. The remaining testimonies were brief, and they all coincided with Matute's account. The record ends with his release.

There was nothing unusual, nothing to raise the judges' eyebrows, in the events leading up to the drowning. Colonial officials who took judicial depositions often interrupted with reprimands and further questioning—after all, witnesses were under interrogation—and the notaries often documented these interruptions. But there are no signs in the record that the officers investigating Antonio Casanga's death asked anything beyond the standard template. Scholarship has shown that it was common in the world of Guatemala's capital city for men to stop in taverns before work. It was also normal for young adults to fraternize across ethnic lines.[66] Antonio Casanga was part of this world. In reporting his death, the indigenous governor of Jocotenango identified him as "un hijo de este pueblo" (a son of this pueblo). But Antonio Casanga spent his last hours with Hispanized friends whom he met in the colonial capital.

Though Antonio's grandfather had ruled for years as a powerful native governor, the family's fortunes had sunk significantly. The governor's widow, doña María de Jesús Chiquival, was unable to access the labor and wealth he had controlled. When she testified about the day of the drowning, she told the court that she had refused to give Matute or her grandson money because she had none. She seems to have had no children in political office. Her grandson was working as a day laborer.

CONCLUSION

The history of the Casanga-Chiquival family reflects a number of broader trends, some of which have been recognized by historians. One is the process of "macehualization." As caciques' status and privileges declined, the category of "caciques" was increasingly absorbed into the category of "principales." Principales, in turn, could be drawn from among the macehuales, as macehual men could advance their status through alliances with principales and through service in civil and religious posts. Yet in a second trend, the roles of native elites and native governments within the Hispanic world were diminishing. This trend coincided with increasing cultural Hispanization of native communities and their officers. (Note that all the natives in the 1809 record on Antonio Casanga's drowning were bilingual in Cakchiquel and Spanish.) Thus, paradoxically, even as native governments became more Hispanized, they lost importance in the Hispanic sphere. The role of native elites and states was further diminished after independence with the elimination of the separate república de indios.[67] This reduction of the two colonial-era "republics" into a single polity under Hispanic rule in effect elided native states, foreclosing the privileges that caciques and principales had held in the colonial system.[68]

In addition, as this chapter has illustrated, there were gendered processes that have been less recognized. The cases of the three women highlighted above show how elite native privileges were structured along lines of gender.

The records suggest that colonial legal institutions eroded the privileges of elite native women more quickly, and more completely, than those of elite native men. In the Tzoch case, the audiencia interpreted cacique status and privileges as passing through the paternal line only, thereby dissolving cacique women's ability to pass privileged status to their children and to perpetuate cacique bloodlines.

By the nineteenth century, the category "caciques" had ceased to exist in some pueblos in the Kingdom of Guatemala. Even where caciques still played a role, principales commanded greater power. Unlike the category "caciques," which had included both men and women, principales were men. Native women could potentially gain access to the privileges and wealth of principales only through relationships with male principales, but even then their access was not permanent. As in the experience of doña María de Jesús Chiquival, if a woman's marriage to a principal ended—by death or by separation—her fortunes sank. Presumably the same would have been true for a daughter of a principal: she might enjoy material benefits of his office, but these would end when he died or when she left his home to marry or pursue her own fortune—limited though it would likely be.

NOTES

I am very grateful to Ann Jefferson for photographing archival records for me. I also thank the anonymous reviewer whose comments helped me improve the chapter, and the National Endowment for the Humanities, which supported the writing. Any views, findings, conclusions, or recommendations expressed in this chapter do not necessarily reflect those of the National Endowment for the Humanities.

1. Examples include Robert Wasserstrom, *Class and Society in Central Chiapas* (Berkeley: University of California Press, 1983); Robert M. Carmack, John Early, and Christopher Lutz, eds., *The Historical Demography of Highland Guatemala* (Albany: Institute for Mesoamerican Studies of the State University of New York at Albany, 1982); Severo Martínez Peláez, *Motines de indios: La violencia colonial en Centroamérica y Chiapas* (Guatemala City: F&G Editores, 2011); Robert M. Hill II, *Colonial Cakchiquels: Highland Maya Adaptation to Spanish Rule, 1600–1700* (Fort Worth, TX: Harcourt Brace Jovanovich, 1992); Robert Carmack, *Rebels of Highland Guatemala: The Quiché-Mayas of Momostenango* (Norman: University of Oklahoma Press, 1995); Kevin Gosner, *Soldiers of the Virgin: The Moral Economy of a Colonial Maya Rebellion* (Tucson: University of Arizona Press, 1992); Greg Grandin, *The Blood of Guatemala: A History of Race and Nation* (Durham, NC: Duke University Press, 2000); René Reeves, *Ladinos with Ladinos, Indians with Indians: Land, Labor, and Regional Ethnic Conflict in the Making of Guatemala* (Stanford: Stanford University Press, 2006); W. George Lovell, *Conquest and Survival in Colonial Guatemala:*

A Historical Geography of the Cuchumatán Highlands, 1500–1821, 4th ed. (Montreal: McGill-Queen's University Press, 2015); and Aaron Pollack, *Levantamiento K'iche' en Totonicapán, 1820: Los lugares de las políticas subalternas* (Guatemala City: Avansco, 2008). There is also extensive scholarship on Maya societies in the Yucatan region of Mexico; for example, Nancy M. Farriss, *Maya Society under Colonial Rule: The Collective Enterprise of Survival* (Princeton: Princeton University Press, 1984); Matthew Restall, *The Maya World: Yucatec Culture and Society, 1550–1850* (Stanford: Stanford University Press, 1999); and Mark Christensen, *Nahua and Maya Catholicisms: Texts and Religion in Colonial Central Mexico and Yucatan* (Stanford: Stanford University Press, 2013).

2. Examples of Carey's works include *Engendering Mayan History: Kaqchikel Women as Agents and Conduits of the Past, 1875–1970* (New York: Routledge, 2006); and *I Ask for Justice: Maya Women, Dictators, and Crime in Guatemala 1898–1944* (Austin: University of Texas Press, 2013). On the K'iche', Mam, and Kekchí, see, respectively, Grandin, *Blood of Guatemala*; Reeves, *Ladinos with Ladinos*; and Julie Gibbings, *Our Time Is Now: Race and Modernity in Postcolonial Guatemala* (New York: Cambridge University Press, 2020). Ethnographic studies also can illuminate gender, though we should not assume that modern-day structures are the same as those in the colonial era.

3. For example, William Sherman, *Forced Native Labor in Sixteenth-Century Central America* (Lincoln: University of Nebraska Press, 1979), chap. 14; Carmack, *Rebels of Highland Guatemala* (which considers also the nineteenth and twentieth centuries); Hill, *Colonial Cakchiquels*; Gosner, *Soldiers of the Virgin*; Martha Few, *Women Who Live Evil Lives: Gender, Religion, and the Politics of Power in Colonial Guatemala, 1650–1750* (Austin: University of Texas Press, 2002); Robinson Antonio Herrera, *Natives, Europeans, and Africans in Sixteenth-Century Santiago de Guatemala* (Austin: University of Texas Press, 2003), esp. chap. 9; and Catherine Komisaruk, *Labor and Love in Guatemala: The Eve of Independence* (Stanford: Stanford University Press, 2013), esp. chap. 1. Newson considers gender in her studies of Maya as well as other native cultures in Honduras and Nicaragua; see Linda Newson, *The Cost of Conquest: Indian Decline under Spanish Rule* (Boulder, CO: Westview Press, 1986); and Linda Newson *Indian Survival in Colonial Nicaragua* (Norman: University of Oklahoma Press, 1987).

4. For an excellent overview of the literature on pre-Hispanic Maya women and discussion of their various roles, see Susan Kellogg, *Weaving the Past: A History of Latin America's Indigenous Women from the Prehispanic Period to the Present* (New York: Oxford University Press, 2005), 35–41. A valuable collection of works appears in the 2002 volume edited by Traci Ardren, *Ancient Maya Women* (Walnut Creek, CA: AltaMira Press, 2002); Ardren's introductory chapter, "Women and Gender in the Ancient Maya World," gives an insightful overview of the field.

5. John P. Molloy and William L. Rathje, "Sexploitation among the Late Classic Maya," in *Mesoamerican Archaeology: New Approaches*, ed. Norman Hammond (Austin: University of Texas Press, 1974). They write that the "core" (dominant centers) turned high-status women "into a harem of scarce resources exchangeable for other critical commodities" (435).

6. Joyce Marcus, *Emblem and State in the Classic Maya Lowlands* (Washington DC: Dumbarton Oaks, 1976), 154–79, quotations from 157 and 162.

7. Kellogg, *Weaving the Past*, 36–38; Ardren, "Women and Gender," 1–2.

8. J. Kathryn Josserand, "Women in Classic Maya Hieroglyphic Texts," in *Ancient Maya Women*, ed. Traci Ardren (Walnut Creek, CA: Alta Mira Press, 2002), 147–48.

9. On limits to women's power, see Grandin, *Blood of Guatemala*, 38–39.

10. Alvis E. Dunn, "A Cry at Daybreak: Death, Disease, and Defense of Community in a Highland Ixil-Mayan Village," *Ethnohistory* 42, no. 4 (November 1996); Martínez Peláez, *Motines de indios*, 150–55; and Gosner, *Soldiers of the Virgin*.

11. Sherman, *Forced Native Labor*, 304–5, wrote in general terms of native noblewomen. A few works have identified Nahua and Oaxacan women who traveled to Guatemala as part of the Spanish conquest. Some of these women were noblewomen, and all seemed to gain some privileges or status as a result of their participation in the conquest. See Laura Matthew, *Memories of Conquest: Becoming Mexicano in Colonial Guatemala* (Chapel Hill: University of North Carolina Press, 2012), 215–30; and Herrera, *Natives, Europeans, and Africans*, 136. For Hill's work, see *Colonial Cakchiquels*, 33–38.

12. Tadashi Obara-Saeki and Juan Pedro Viqueira Alban, *El arte de contar tributarios. Provincia de Chiapas, 1560–1821* (Mexico City: El Colegio de México, 2017), 180, 602.

13. The research was based in the Archivo General de Centro América (General Archives of Central America, hereafter cited as AGCA) in Guatemala City, which houses colonial-era records from the Kingdom of Guatemala. The records of doña Micaela de Miranda and María Josefa Tzoch were identified in a search of the AGCA's card catalogue under the heading "Indígenas" and subheading "Caciques." The records of María de Jesús Chiquival surfaced in a random sampling of judicial cases dated between 1770 and 1821, carried out in the course of research for a separate project (Komisaruk, *Labor and Love*).

14. The focus on men—which is not illogical given that governance was exclusively by men—does not detract from this scholarship. Examples include Murdo J. MacLeod, *Spanish Central America: A Socioeconomic History, 1520–1720* (Berkeley: University of California Press, 1973); Robert M. Hill II, *The Pirir Papers and Other Colonial Era Cakchiquel-Maya Testamentos*, Vanderbilt University Publications in Anthropology 37 (Nashville: Vanderbilt University, 1989); Carmack, *Rebels of Highland Guatemala*; Herrera, *Natives, Europeans, and Africans*, chap. 9; Matthew, *Memories of Conquest*.

15. On this decline, see, for example Sherman, *Forced Native Labor*, chap. 13; MacLeod, *Spanish Central America*, 137–38, 141–42, 296, 328; Grandin, *Blood of Guatemala*, 44–45; and Obara-Saeki and Viqueira Alban, *Arte de contar tributarios*, 179.

16. For the Kingdom of Guatemala, see, for example, Christopher H. Lutz and Karen Dakin, eds., *Nuestro pesar, nuestra aflicción: Tunetuliniliz, tucucuca: Memorias en lengua náhuatl enviadas a Felipe II por indígenas del Valle de Guatemala hacia 1572* (Mexico City: Universidad Nacional Autónoma de México and Centro de Investigaciones Regionales de Mesoamérica, 1996); MacLeod, *Spanish Central America*, 222; and Wasserstrom, *Class and Society*, 87, 91, 101.

17. For the term "macehualization" and a description of the process, see Rodolfo Pastor, *Campesinos y reformas: la Mixteca 1700–1856* (Mexico City: El Colegio de México, 1987), 323–28, which is on the Mixtec region (in Oaxaca, Mexico). On Guatemala, see Grandin, *Blood of Guatemala*, 44–45; and Reeves, *Ladinos with Ladinos*, 139–40. On Chiapas, see Obara-Saeki and Viqueira Alban, *Arte de contar*, 179.

18. AGCA Signatura A1, Legajo 1584, Expediente 10,288.

19. Distance and travel time were calculated using Google Maps.

20. On the colonial mail system, see Sylvia Sellers-García, *Distance and Documents at the Spanish Empire's Periphery* (Stanford: Stanford University Press, 2014).

21. The *Recopilación* was a compendium of laws that provided bases for judicial decisions through the end of the colonial period. Judges in colonial Central America, even into the early nineteenth century, also routinely cited the *Siete Partidas*, a thirteenth-century Castilian compendium of laws. Their thinking was clearly shaped by centuries-old legal culture, if not also by their contemporary contexts of imperial administrative policies.

22. AGCA Signatura A1, Legajo 1584, Expediente 10,288. For the 1572 law, see Libro 6, Título 5, Ley 18 in Carlos II, *Recopilación de leyes de los Reinos de las Indias*, 5th ed. (Madrid: Boix, 1841), 242.

23. For example, Farriss, *Maya Society*, 239–40; Hill, *Colonial Cakchiquels*, 40–41; Carmack, *Rebels of Highland Guatemala*, 93. Scholarship has also noted that the Spanish authorities sometimes installed caciques of their own choosing; see MacLeod, *Spanish Central America*, 136–38. The study on Chiapas is Obara-Saeki and Viqueira Alban, *Arte de contar*, 179–80, 243–44.

24. Rafael D. García Pérez, "El regimen tributario en las intendencias novohispanas: La ordenanza para la formación de los autos de visitas, padrones, y matrículas de Revillagigedo II," *Anuario Mexicano de Historia del Derecho*, 11–12 (1999–2000); Obara-Saeki and Viqueira Alban, *Arte de contar*, 187–96. See also Charles Gibson, *The Aztecs under Spanish Rule: A History of the Indians of the Valley of Mexico, 1519–1810* (Stanford: Stanford University Press, 1964), 200; Sherburne F. Cook and Woodrow Borah, *Essays in Population History: Mexico and the Caribbean* (Berkeley: University of California Press, 1971), 1:272–278; Christopher H. Lutz, *Santiago de Guatemala, 1541–1773: City, Caste, and the Colonial Experience* (Norman: University of Oklahoma Press, 1994), 24, 74, 277n97. Examples of continuing demands appear in the padrones, which generally indicate that women were taxed for tribute payments through the 1770s. For an example of a woman being charged for *tequíos* (labor drafts), see AGCA Signatura A1, Legajo 2,770, Expediente 24,079 (year 1803).

25. For example, AGCA Signatura A3, Legajo 249, Expediente 5,032; Signatura A3, Legajo 250, Expediente 5,069; Signatura A1, Legajo 6,082, Expediente 55,024; Legajo 6,119, Expediente 56,884; Signatura A3, Legajo 2,800, Expediente 40,485; Signatura A1, Legajo 1,570, Expediente 10,214, fol. 276; Signatura A1, Legajo 1,573, Expediente 10,217, fol. 61; Signatura A1, Legajo 191, Expediente 3,889; Signatura A3, Legajo 439, Expedientes 8,976 and 8,978; Signatura A3, Legajo 241, Expediente 4,797; and Signatura A3, Legajo 819, Expediente 15,093.

26. The law's wording is: "son exentos de pagar tributos, y acudir á mitas los caciques, y sus hijos mayores: y en cuanto á los demas hijos, y descencientes, . . . no se haga novedad, ni las audiencias dén provisiones de exencion" (caciques and their eldest sons [or children] are exempt from paying tributes and doing draft labor: and as for the other sons [or children], and descendants, . . . there should be no exception, nor should the audiencias grant exemptions). (Libro 6, Título 5, Ley 18, in Carlos II, *Recopilacion*, 242).

27. This flexibility was often made explicit. For example, see Libro 6, Título 5, Ley 7 in Carlos II, *Recopilación*, 240. Originally issued in 1578, this law required native men to pay tribute from age eighteen to fifty but ended with a coda stating this would only apply in provinces that did not already have a requirement for some shorter or longer period of years.

28. Obara-Saeki and Viqueira Alban, *Arte de contar*, 180. This contrasts with Laura Matthew's finding (*Memories of Conquest*, 221, 224) for native Mexican elites who participated in the conquest of Guatemala: offspring of unions between these Mexicans and Spaniards were normally considered Spanish.

29. Libro 6, Título 5, Ley 8 in Carlos II, *Recopilación*, 240.

30. AGCA Signatura A1, Legajo 6,091, Expediente 55,307, fols. 129–37.

31. The macehual intended groom was Ignacio Tipaz. I have omitted his name from the narrative above to limit possible confusion among numerous names.

32. Hill, *Colonial Cakchiquels*, 141–42; Charles Wagley, *The Social and Religious Life of a Guatemalan Village* (Menasha, WI: American Anthropological Association, 1949), 37–39; and Barbara Tedlock, *Time and the Highland Maya*, rev. ed. (Albuquerque: University of New Mexico Press, 1992), 74, 110, 117, 156. The matchmaker is highlighted in the classic colonial-era K'iche' text, the *Popol Vuh*.

33. On Cózar, see Jorge H. González Alzate, "COZAR, Prudencio de," Asociación para el Fomento de los Estudios Históricos en Centroamérica, last modified May 20, 2011, http://www.afehc-historia-centroamericana.org/index_action_fi_aff_id_1262 .html; and Martha Few, *For All of Humanity: Mesoamerican and Colonial Medicine in Enlightenment Guatemala* (Tucson: University of Arizona Press, 2015), 94, 137–43.

34. On depósito, see Patricia Seed, *To Love, Honor, and Obey in Colonial Mexico: Conflicts over Marriage Choice, 1574–1821* (Stanford: Stanford University Press, 1988), 75, 78, 271n14.

35. Lutz, *Santiago de Guatemala*, 171–73, 223–37. The demonstration is based on baptismal records. Out-of-wedlock births ranged between 42 and 49 percent of all births among *gente ordinaria* (a category that included those not identified as Indians or Spaniards) and between 26 and 37 percent of all births among *españoles* (Spaniards).

36. For example, AGCA Signatura A2, Legajo 40, Expediente 830 (Felipa Guerra was in an illicit relationship with Martín Cherec); AGCA Signatura A2, Legajo 187, Expediente 3,771, fol. 28; and AGCA Signatura A1, Legajo 4,400, Expediente 36,146.

37. AGCA Signatura A1, Legajo 6,091, Expediente 55,307, fol. 131v.

38. On the real junta, see Timothy Hawkins, *José Bustamante and Central American Independence: Colonial Administration in an Age of Imperial Crisis* (Tuscaloosa:

University of Alabama Press, 2004), 28. The members of the real junta—at least in 1803–1805 when the Tzoch case was heard—were also members of the audiencia, though not all members of the audiencia sat on the real junta.

39. On the founding and early history of Jocotenango, see Lutz, *Santiago de Guatemala*, 19–21. The pueblo of Jocotenango adjacent to the old capital at Santiago (today's Antigua Guatemala) persists as a separate community. At the new location in the Valle de la Ermita (today's Guatemala City), Jocotenango was subsumed as a neighborhood within the city, in what is now Zona 2.

40. Casanga was in office in 1765; see AGCA Signatura A2, Legajo 40, Expediente 830. In 1768, another man, Juan Poyón, was serving as gobernador; see AGCA Signatura A2, Legajo 150, Expediente 2,812, fol. 3v. By 1797, Casanga was in office again; see AGCA Signatura A1, Legajo 254, Expediente 3,063.

41. Following the usage in the colonial Guatemalan records, I use the terms "Spaniard" and "Spanish" to refer to people born in the Americas of Spanish ancestry, as well as to people born in Spain. The term "Creole" (*criollo*) is not generally used in the eighteenth- or early nineteenth-century records from this region, nor is the term *peninsular*.

42. Reeves, *Ladinos with Ladinos*, 140.

43. Grandin, *Blood of Guatemala*, 44. On appointment of noncaciques as gobernadores in early eighteenth-century Chiapas, see Obara-Saeki and Viqueira Alban, *Arte de contar*, 180–81.

44. Pastor, *Campesinos y reformas*, 323–28; Grandin, *Blood of Guatemala*, 44–45; Reeves, *Ladinos with Ladinos*, 139–40; Obara-Saeki and Viqueira Alban, *Arte de contar*, 179. The terms "principal" and "cacique," which had distinct meanings in the eighteenth century, seem to have overlapped in the sixteenth century; see Sherman, *Forced Native Labor*, 264–65; and Lutz, *Santiago de Guatemala*, 32.

45. The wording is "la India descendiente de Cacique, o cualquiera otro título noble." AGCA Signatura A1, Legajo 6,091, Expediente 55,307, fols. 131v, 132v, 133r, 134r.

46. Native men served in church roles as sacristans' assistants (called *sacristanes*), cantors, and *fiscales* (lay assistants to the priest).

47. Silvia Marina Arrom, *The Women of Mexico City, 1790–1857* (Stanford: Stanford University Press, 1985), 67.

48. Lutz, *Santiago de Guatemala*, 23; AGCA Signatura A3, Legajo 223, Expediente 3,986, fols. 22, 25–28; AGCA Signatura A1, Legajo 154, Expediente 3,063.

49. AGCA Signatura A1, Legajo 2,767, Expediente 24,027. I have not found evidence of salaries paid by the Spanish state to other native officers. On salaries of urban workers, see Komisaruk, *Labor and Love*, 44.

50. AGCA Signatura A3, Legajo 251, Expediente 5,122. See also AGCA Signatura A2.2, Legajo 231, Expediente 4,918, fol. 1r., which includes what appears to be Ylarios's signature and a note penned in the same very practiced hand. The note and signature may have been written by a notary or scribe.

51. AGCA Signatura A1, Legajo 5,908, Expediente 50,354. Chiquival's petition appears on fols. 1r and 1v.

52. AGCA Signatura A1, Legajo 5,908, Expediente 50,354, fol. 1v.

53. For a discussion of the significance of the cabildo's patio and other spaces in a conquest-era Yucatec Maya community, see Matthew Restall, "People of the Patio: Ethnohistorical Evidence of Yucatec Maya Royal Courts," in *Data and Case Studies*, ed. Takeshi Inomata and Stephen D. Houston, vol. 2, *Royal Courts of the Ancient Maya* (Boulder, CO: Westview Press, 2001), especially 338–41.

54. AGCA Signatura A2, Legajo 40, Expediente 830 (deposition of Diego Casanga and Gaspar Sic, and that of Simón García).

55. MacLeod, *Spanish Central America*, 296.

56. AGCA Signatura A1, Legajo 154, Expediente 3,063. This episode is discussed further in Komisaruk, *Labor and Love*, 55–58.

57. Komisaruk, *Labor and Love*, 49.

58. Severo Martínez Peláez, *La patria del criollo: Ensayo de interpretación de la realidad colonial guatemalteca* (Guatemala City: Universidad de San Carlos de Guatemala, 1970), 536–55; Sherman, *Forced Native Labor*, 297; Hill, *Colonial Cakchiquels*, 113; Carmack, *Rebels of Highland Guatemala*, 85; and Grandin, *Blood of Guatemala*, 50.

59. Grandin, *Blood of Guatemala*, 73.

60. On a K'iche' governor's widow in similarly reduced circumstances, see Grandin, *Blood of Guatemala*, 39, 43.

61. The Spanish reads: "ganan mas de lo que comen con su trabajo personal" (AGCA Signatura A1, Legajo 5,908, Expediente 50,354, fol. 2v).

62. The Spanish reads: "Así lo da a conocer el Expediente, y lo dicen los mismos Indios" (AGCA Signatura A1, Legajo 5,908, Expediente 50,354, fol. 3v).

63. Women participated as members of cofradías, which were a formalized collective body. However, while cofradías served ritual and financial roles (notably, lending), they did not have an institutionalized role in the political sphere.

64. AGCA Signatura A2, Legajo 231, Expediente 4,918.

65. Matute's testimony appears in AGCA Signatura A2, Legajo 231, Expediente 4,918, fols. 2r–3v.

66. Komisaruk, *Labor and Love*, 160, 224–27.

67. The term "república de indios" refers to native societies and their polities, which were recognized by the Spanish state as existing separately from the "república de españoles" (Spanish society and state) albeit subordinate to Spanish government rule.

68. Miles Wortman, *Government and Society in Central America, 1680–1840* (New York: Columbia University Press, 1982), 183; Farriss, *Maya Society*, 377–80; David McCreery, "Atanasio Tzul, Lucas Aguilar, and the Indian Kingdom of Totonicapán," in *The Human Tradition in Latin America: The Nineteenth Century*, ed. Judith Ewell and William H. Beezley (Wilmington, DE: Scholarly Resources, 1989); Woodward, "Changes in the Nineteenth-Century Guatemalan State and Its Indian Policies," in *Guatemalan Indians and the State: 1540–1988*, ed. Carol A. Smith (Austin: University of Texas Press, 1994); and Grandin, *Blood of Guatemala*, chap. 6.

PART II

South America

Map 4. South America

CHAPTER 5

"Women were governing before the Spanish entered in this kingdom"

THE INSTITUTIONALIZATION OF THE CACICA FROM THE NORTH COAST OF PERU

Karen B. Graubart

Doña Francisca Canapaynina (or Mesocoñera), a young noblewoman from the town of Nariguala, near Piura, was among the first female candidates to litigate successfully for title to her office as cacica in Peru. In 1610, with the assistance of the procurador general de Indios (procurator general for Indians), Francisco de Montalvo, she brought her case for the *cacicazgo* (office of the cacique, sometimes including its political role, services, and property) of Nariguala to Lima's *real audiencia* (royal high court). Supporting witness testimony revealed that, in a number of communities around Piura as well as Trujillo to its south, women had occasionally held political office dating back to before the Spanish conquest. At the conclusion of the litigation in 1614, the judges of the audiencia reinstated doña Francisca Canapaynina in the cacicazgo of Nariguala over her paternal uncle, who had seized the office at the death of his father and doña Francisca's grandfather, the cacique Diego Mesocoñera, taking advantage of "the tender age of his niece."[1] (See fig. 5.1.) Don Francisco Mesocoñera, the uncle, was required to repay doña Francisca "the salaries and privileges that he had enjoyed during the time he served as cacique." Within a few years she had married, and her new husband used the titles of cacique and governor.[2]

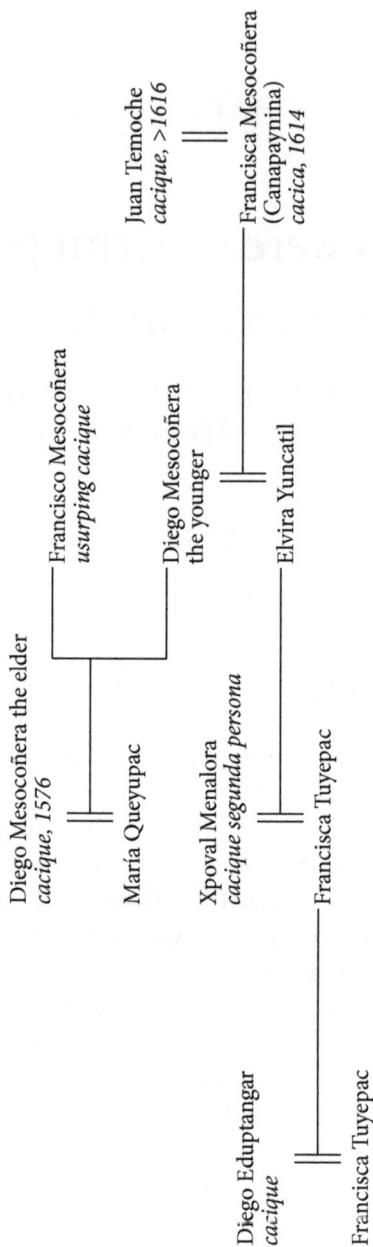

Fig. 5.1. Doña Francisca's genealogy

Doña Francisca was far from alone among northern women holding cacicazgos. Near Guayaquil, doña María Cayche had sued along with her husband for the titles of cacique and cacica of Daule, as the only living legitimate
heirs of their two lineages in 1600.[3] Indeed, doña María had served in the
office since 1595, and her aunt held the cacicazgo of another nearby *ayllu* (local kinship group). And doña Francisca's own lawsuit named a number of
women holding the position near Piura and Trujillo. Her own grandmother,
Francisca Tuyupac, had been refused the office in 1576 after the death of her
father, the sitting cacique Diego Eduptangar, on the grounds that, although
she was his only child, she was a minor. In her place, then-viceroy Francisco
de Toledo appointed a distant relative, Diego Mesocoñera (later known as the
elder). In the document that confirmed Mesocoñera's title, Toledo noted that
the Incas "did not install the eldest children that the dead caciques left but
the [male] child who had the best judgment or other Indians he chose from
among [the cacique's] relatives or those of greatest ability and appropriateness
for the office, without granting them the right of succession."[4] Toledo's analysis placed the north coast in the context of his interpretation of Inca practices, rather than within its own ethnohistory.

Francisca Tuyupac, once she came of age, married the *cacique segunda
persona*, or leader of a secondary or parallel lineage in the town of Catacaos
that had been combined with Nariguala. Their daughter, Elvira Yuncatil,
eventually married the son of the cacique Mesocoñera, known as Diego
Mesocoñera the younger. In this way the younger Mesocoñera's legitimacy
within the community was cemented by joining the two lines.

In contrast, doña Francisca's successful litigation established the precedent
for indigenous women to inherit the office based upon regional pre-Hispanic
uso y costumbre (customary law), in the legal language of the time. At the
death of Diego Mesocoñera the elder in 1610, doña Francisca, the only child of
his late eldest son, was considered a candidate despite being an unmarried
minor. According to testimony, Mesocoñera the elder's second son, Francisco
Mesocoñera, colluded with Spanish officials to obtain legal title to the cacicazgo until doña Francisca and the procurador general filed their papers. They
presented a fixed narrative about pre-Hispanic political customs on the coast
that could displace both the colonial packaging of Inca practice and the ability of Spanish officials to intervene in local affairs.

In that vein, doña Francisca Canapaynina emerges as a legal pioneer, like
the many indigenous men who litigated for their privileges and for the rights
of their communities. These indigenous men have been celebrated in a new

literature that recognizes litigation and petitioning, which inherently required the collaboration of legal experts and networks of knowledgeable
specialists for their success, as intellectual acts.[5] Like them, doña Francisca
collaborated with her Spanish lawyer and the mostly male elders who provided expert testimony for her case. She also drew upon public knowledge
passed between indigenous and Spanish elites about women's roles and
rights. Though she was still legally a child when she litigated to become
cacica, she also functioned as a legal and intellectual linchpin in a transformation that affected subsequent generations.

In late 1612 Francisco de Montalvo presented seven witnesses to testify on
behalf of doña Francisca: four indigenous and three Spanish men who spoke
to the history of chieftainship in the north. Three of the indigenous men were
elders, between fifty and eighty years old. They testified to their knowledge of
practices dating back to the conquest period. The Spanish witnesses were all
vecinos (politically empowered members of the municipality), including the
local *encomendero* (male holder of royal grant of tribute), Capitán Bartolomé
Carreño. All addressed the question of whether "it has been and is the accepted and kept custom in the said *repartimiento* [colonial political unit] of
Nariguala and in all the provinces of the valley since antiquity, before the
Spanish entered in this kingdom, and after, that the *capullanas* [female chiefs]
inherited cacicazgos."[6] Six of the seven witnesses agreed that it was indeed
customary, in the absence of male heirs, that female children would hold and
exercise office (the seventh lacked knowledge), "that the capullanas succeed in
cacicazgos as if they were male and they serve and govern the said cacicazgos."[7]

Each witness named other indigenous women who had held political office within his memory: doña Luisa, capullana cacica of Colán; doña Leonor,
once the capullana and cacica of Menon; doña Latacina, once the cacica segunda persona of Colán; and doña Isabel Socola, who had "received the
salary" as cacica in Socola. The final witness was the encomendero Carreño,
who testified to all of the above and that he had heard "said that in this said
repartimiento of Nariguala women were governing before the Spaniards entered in this kingdom."[8] The encomendero's motivations may have been more
political than historical: he might have had knowledge of favorable marriage
plans for the young woman, had a dislike for the usurping cacique, or been
aware of brewing discontent among the cacique's subjects, which could have
affected his livelihood. In any case, by concurring with their testimony and
establishing a precedent at the conquest, the encomendero contributed to a
reformulation of colonial political policy as well as of preconquest history.

Doña Francisca won her case and became the cacica of Nariguala. Within a few years she had married one don Juan Temoche, who took the titles of cacique and governor and apparently carried out the tasks of the office himself: organizing indigenous labor and otherwise mediating between the community and the colonial authorities. Doña Francisca now used the surname Canapaynina, suggesting that she had adopted Mesocoñera strategically in her suit. Testimony in a subsequent lawsuit indicates that her husband had a strong relationship with Spanish officials including the *corregidor* (royal magistrate), hinting at the reason for the procurador's interest in doña Francisca's succession. If colonial authorities considered that custom allowed indigenous women to hold office, they did not necessarily expect them to exercise its authority and might well see them as the means to their own ends.[9]

Women emerged as successful candidates for cacicazgos due to the convergence of indigenous ethnohistoric narratives, Spanish legal conventions, and the interested use of both by litigating parties. Women had unremarkedly held office within indigenous political units on the north coast before the arrival of Spaniards. With the conquest, the practice continued, if generally without viceregal imprimatur: in addition to the cacicas mentioned in passing in these lawsuits, other women used the title in documents they drew up with notaries. Doña Juana Faringuango, for example, called herself the cacica of Otavalo (Quito) in her will, written in 1560, where she claimed authority over lands and people, though no documentation of her receiving official title exists.[10] Doña Francisca Canapaynina's litigation created a new legal paper trail for female cacicazgo succession, instructing indigenous candidates, as well as Spanish lawyers and viceroys in this narrative. It was likely buoyed by the victories of Spanish women in inheriting *encomienda* (royal grant of indigenous tribute), which served as a template for the demand for female succession in the cacicazgo. In the seventeenth century, the practice proliferated, extending to other regions of Peru that did not have a history of female succession. Cacicas became commonplace because viceregal officials found them an efficient solution to the thorny problem of succession and because indigenous elites found female lineages effective when crafting their own litigation. Female litigants were thus crucial in shifting the succession question away from an argument about continuity in practices towards a way for indigenous elites to claim legitimacy through male and female lines within the new boundaries of colonial institutions.

THE PRECONQUEST ETHNOGRAPHY OF SUCCESSION

Chroniclers described female indigenous leaders in the conquest period.[11] Some, like Oviedo y Valdés, reached for hyperbolic descriptions of Amazons, drawing on the language of marvels associated with the New World.[12] Others—like Sarmiento de Gamboa or the indigenous chronicler Santa Cruz Pachacuti Yamqui—recognized the efforts of Inca women in battle and used the language of political leadership to describe their roles.[13] Those who traveled to the north told more specific kinds of stories. The conquistador Ruiz de Arce stated that when the Spaniards came ashore near Puerto Viejo (modern Ecuador) in 1531 they encountered a woman "who was ruler of this land and everyone obeyed her and regarded her as their ruler."[14] Reginaldo de Lizárraga, a Dominican priest, asserted that the Tallán peoples of the Piura region were solely governed by women, who chose their own husbands and forced discarded spouses to attend their marital rites, sitting alone in the corner while a new husband was feted with drunken revelry. The historian-chronicler Pedro Cieza de León also told colorful stories of female rulers who interacted with Francisco Pizarro and other conquistadors, often challenging their masculinity.[15] Without taking the content of their Amazon fantasies too literally, their recollections of female chiefs line up with repeated indigenous claims in Nariguala that "when the Spaniards entered this kingdom and thereafter capullanas inherited cacicazgos as if they were men, and they serve in them and govern the said cacicazgos."[16]

Chroniclers called the women leaders of the north "capullanas." Pedro Cieza de León argued that Spaniards coined the term from *capuz* (long cloak of Arab origin worn by women in Spain), which indigenous women's dress was said to resemble: "the dress of the women was long and wide like a capuz open on both sides, through which they stick their arms."[17] Historian María Rostworowski suggested it came from a now-lost indigenous language spoken in Catacaos and Piura: *capuc*, referring to female gender (as in *icuchin capuc* or "female child") with the suffixes *-lla* and *-na*, indicating respectively status and gender.[18] If true, this analysis would substantiate the existence of a distinct analytic category for elite women in that language, as there was in Quechua (e.g., *ñusta* for a woman of royal blood, *palla* for a noblewoman, and *coya* for a woman who married a ruler). It also provides a way to think about possible distinctions between coastal and highland practices.

Andean society was composed of various interlocking levels of political and social structure: smaller kin groups, which may have functioned relatively independently at times; larger hierarchical networks created by intermarriages between elites of these communities; and more provincial or "imperial" structures such as those forged by the Chimús on the north coast and the Incas in the central highlands. Environment also mattered. Highland society was characterized by vertical archipelagos, with nesting levels of geographically dispersed ayllus united through shared reciprocal labor relationships.[19] In contrast, lowland coastal deserts (known as *llanos* in the colonial period) were home to more centralized and contiguous units, dependent upon the sea as well as on agricultural land in valleys dependent upon complex shared irrigation practices.[20] Scholarship has also focused on the different economic relationships in the two regions: coastal leaders claimed ownership over all territory, leasing it to their subjects for rent payments in goods, while highland societies appear to have organized landholding and use communally, with transient occupancy. The coast shows evidence of markets and artisanal specialization, while redistributive processes within highland ayllus gave members access to diverse products without dependence on markets.[21] Even after two waves of imperial conquest, coastal political organization remained distinct from that of the highlands—the model best-known by Spanish administrators—and was probably inconsistent across time and space. Under Spanish rule, litigants over cacicazgos learned to claim "traditional" social relations that favored their candidates, utilizing strategies that they knew would be well received by the courts, yielding even more contradictory narratives about these practices.

Succession practices might not have been precisely fixed at all. Ethnohistorical studies of coastal Peru and Ecuador indicate that succession in the immediate preconquest period in these regions was probably "designed for optimal flexibility" in order to prefer more able candidates within the lineage over structural rigor.[22] An office could pass equally through male siblings or through male issue, and the likelihood of regular political challenge was a benefit of the system, ensuring competent heirs. This flexibility also created the possibility of lengthy turmoil and malicious interventions. Cabello Balboa noted in the sixteenth century that, within the memory of his informants, the cacique of Lambayeque had put his own brothers to death in order to eliminate them preemptively as political rivals.[23]

Flexible succession might have been characteristic of central highland communities too, though Inca practice shifted in the late empire. Andean politics was deeply rooted in bloodlines and kinship, and as the Incas began imperial expansion they used polygamous marriage to link themselves to dominated groups, leaving large numbers of potential heirs.[24] The Inca Pachacuti seems to have established the practice of marrying his full sister in order to produce a legitimate—and singular—heir, to avoid the chaos usually unleashed at the Inca's death.[25] The two generations after Pachacuti did marry their sisters to produce successors, although the dying Huayna Capac either changed his mind or was otherwise influenced in his choice of a successor, causing the civil war between two sons that ended with the Spanish conquest. Inca succession was certainly not rigid nor a particularly ancient institution.

Nonetheless, all of those heirs were male. Studies of highland politics have found little evidence of female rulers before the colonial period. On the contrary, they suggest that their well-known parallel inheritance patterns might have made succession *less* likely to go through the female side, preferring nephews over wives and daughters.[26] Even with flexibility among close male relatives, there were institutional preferences. The sixteenth-century chronicler Hernando de Santillán noted that while Andean *kurakas* (ethnic leader, cacique) might have the ability to choose anyone to succeed them, they generally followed fairly strict generational sequences, preferring brothers, then their own sons or nephews.[27] The sole, and somewhat shaky, counterexample is that of Contarguacho, daughter of the kuraka of Huaylas, who married the Inca Huayna Capac to forge a political alliance and was said to be the leader of some eighteen thousand subjects. Contarguacho's status was elevated to señora or ruler in a petition presented, after her death, by her daughter doña Inés Huaylas (Qispi Sisa) to cement her own royal privileges under Spanish control.[28]

If women were not sole rulers in the highlands, they did occupy public and symbolic space. While the Incas calculated descent through the male lineage, elite Inca women were designated with titles, such as ñusta, palla, and coya, that invoked both political roles and membership in royal lineages.[29] Guaman Poma's famous parallel portraits of Incas and coyas, their wives, argue for a female role in politics and religious practice, and after the Spanish conquest, Inca women litigated over control of resources including land and people. Ethnic groups outside the Inca orbit used elite women to forge alliances across the empire, making them crucial political players. Gender parallelism was a complex matter, neither reducible to equality nor simply a symbolic fiction: male rulers were complexly dependent upon female relatives.

Given the realistic limitations of Cuzco's ability to intervene in the affairs of its vast tributary regions, the Incas presumably exercised little direct control over local kurakas. Only occasionally, as when there might be fear of insurrection, did they choose or impose candidates.[30] More likely the Incas exercised some ratification process confirming local decisions and pressured kurakas to cooperate. The office of kuraka also carried the expectation that the holder would provide adequate reciprocal services to the community and could not therefore be purely mechanical: a community could fail to obey an incompetent or bad kuraka.[31]

Pre-Hispanic polities across the Andes displayed diverse mechanisms for succession, though all hinged upon the identification of a limited bloodline from which candidates could be presented. Evidence from the north coast points to a flexible system whereby candidates emerged from among a group of relatives, creating both legitimacy and the possibility of conflict. In none of these cases was there a necessary preference for female rule, but in the absence of strong male candidates or the presence of a superior female one, women could and did hold the office of kuraka or capullana in the north.

THE COLONIAL CACICAZGO

The colonial cacicazgo, a well-documented institution, was also complicated and heterogeneous. Succession played out both in the local political sphere— between members of indigenous polities but with the intervention of Spanish encomenderos, priests, and political officials—as well as through royal courts, where titles were confirmed and issued, creating a paper trail and legal precedent. The colonial cacique, who might have questionable lineage, was a particularly political animal, legitimizing authority by simultaneously meeting the demands of Spanish officials and the cultural expectations of indigenous subjects. Legitimacy depended on actual as well as perceived abilities—in both the indigenous and Spanish political spheres—and was subject to contestation on many fronts.[32]

The Spanish colonial project in the Americas depended heavily upon indigenous self-governance, delegating limited jurisdiction to native rulers. This was in part a mechanism for constraining conquistadors by limiting their jurisdiction over the monarch's new vassals. The crown rewarded conquistadors with encomienda, which provided an income derived from indigenous labor through the intermediation of their caciques, but declined to give them claims over those subjects' lands or legal jurisdiction. Each reorganized indigenous population unit, the repartimiento (so-called because it represented the distribution of indigenous labor), was entitled to its own uso y costumbre, guaranteeing it the right to its own leadership and forms of justice insofar as those did not contravene the laws of the Crown or the

Church.[33] That right included the form of succession in what became known generically as the cacicazgo.

Nonetheless, indigenous polities experienced constant political intervention, often through the demands of encomenderos, priests, merchants, and colonial officials. Their own polities were a source of strain, as encomienda grants fragmented and reconstituted existing populations, grouping them under a *cacique principal* (primary cacique) chosen from what might have been a number of local headmen and establishing from the latter group a cacique segunda persona subservient to the cacique principal. In the late sixteenth century most indigenous polities were physically moved to new sites, called *reducciones* (Spanish-style indigenous towns), where they could be reorganized for religious tutelage and economic efficiency.[34] Reducciones were intended to form *pueblos de indios* (Indian towns) built on a grid with a new political leadership (the *cabildo*, or Spanish-styled city council), which theoretically excluded caciques and was intended as a challenge to cacical power. By the seventeenth century, the cacique's main job was collecting tribute and organizing men to carry out *mita* (forced labor draft). When women held the office of cacica, their husbands were usually given the title of *gobernador* (governor), with the expectation that they carried out these duties.

On the north coast, depopulation made the reconstitution of small communities even more dramatic. Communities quickly adapted to Spanish legal culture, becoming quite successful litigators. Competing claims and conflictive lines of legitimation played out at multiple levels of jurisdiction. For example, two encomiendas were created out of the pre-Hispanic settlement of Callanca: Callanca (with its original cacique, Quico Chumbi) and Reque (headed by his relative Xancol Chumbi, appointed by the encomendero for his service to Spaniards during the conquest). Xancol Chumbi's subjects considered him illegitimate and too aggressive in tribute collection, and they assassinated him. He was succeeded briefly by his brother, then his son, and then someone "elected by the Indians by order of the encomendero," probably to reinstate a sense of legitimacy.[35] In the face of this, colonial legitimacy had to be produced through the creative manipulation of genealogies, physical documents, and the narrative of an historical past.[36]

"USE AND CUSTOM": THE CREATION OF SUCCESSION IN INDIGENOUS COMMUNITIES

Spanish jurists and bureaucrats sought a framework for legitimate succession to apply to all indigenous communities. Viceroys collected information about preconquest social organization in order to clarify and make uniform the "use and custom" of Indian repartimientos, the aspects of local political organization theoretically not imposed, although always overseen, by the Spanish Crown. Viceroy Francisco de Toledo (r. 1569–82), like his predecessors, carried out extensive reviews and established legal formulas and procedures which had effect long after his departure from office. Toledo was concerned with stabilizing a local indigenous elite which would "be the instruments of execution, in the spiritual as well as temporal," that is, providing for religious as well as political leadership.[37] He sought to streamline legitimate indigenous successions that would support these goals as well as end what he considered indigenous litigiousness and conflict.

In 1569, Toledo asked that the administrators of the general census of the indigenous population ascertain who had held the cacicazgo at the time when Spaniards first entered into the land, whether they had legitimate issue still alive, and

> what order they had in the time of the Inca of succession in cacicazgos and *principalazgos* [hereditary elite privileges]; whether the sons succeeded the fathers by way of succession, and which of the sons succeeded, if it was the eldest or the most able or he who was named by the Inca; or if, when the cacique was dead, the Inca himself according to his own will named a successor for such offices who might not be a son or descendant of the dead man, even if he left children.[38]

These instructions reveal that Toledo was aware of the existence of flexible succession, in particular of the possibility of the succession of the "most able," though he clearly favored the patrilineal bloodline. His information-gathering created conflict, as inspectors intervened in contemporary succession contests. In 1571 he clarified his instructions, demanding that inspectors simply write reports regarding the cacique and his children, so that the viceroy himself could choose successors.[39] The redefinition of succession as patrilineal pushed the fact-finding mission aside in the service of political expediency.

Similarly, political questions tended to overrule even notions of bloodline inheritance. In a case regarding succession in Carabuco in 1575, Toledo

ordered that, in accordance with his reading of Inca practice, the most intel-
ligent or able son, or the most sufficient candidate among all his relatives,
was to be chosen by the viceroy (standing in for the Incas), rather than simply
the eldest son of the late cacique. "Sufficiency" was reduced to two characteristics: competence and Christianity, to discourage idolatry among the
caciques.[40] Bloodline succession—the centerpiece of Spanish inheritance
law—had now been shunted aside in favor of the colonial government's drive
to micromanage cacicazgos. Legitimate inheritance was packaged as a rein-
terpretation or reinvigoration of Inca policy, with "most able" reduced to a
candidate's malleability to the aims of the colonial state. This and subsequent
orders established the new boundaries for debate over succession, demanding that bloodline inheritance within cacicazgos be largely respected but
with the right of refusal retained for the Crown and viceroy, based upon
some criterion of aptitude for colonial office. This policy was flexible and
ambiguous, leaving Spanish authorities with the final say, but also creating a
space for interpretations of preconquest history by those who could speak in
the public realm.

WOMEN AND SUCCESSION IN
PERUVIAN ENCOMIENDAS

There was one other key source of influence on colonial succession practices:
Spanish women who successfully sued to inherit encomiendas. In doing so,
they normalized female succession patterns in the Andes and provided an
important example for indigenous women, with whom they intimately
interacted. Colonized social spaces were notably integrated: indigenous
laborers occupied households, enterprises, and urban centers, and rural indigenous towns might be home to Black slaves and Spanish workers as well
as receive regular visits from Spanish administrators, priests, and merchants. But indigenous elites were especially situated in Spanish milieus,
through attendance at *colegios* (educational institutions), participation in the
church, residences in urban neighborhoods, and joint enterprises of all kinds.
Elite indigenous girls might be placed in convents or Spanish households to
learn respectable skills.[41] Moreover, because of their universal characterization
as legal *miserabiles* ("unfortunates," who deserve legal protection), indigenous
litigants received access to free legal representatives, *procuradores de causas*
(assigned legal advocates), who assisted them in their claims. As scholars
have demonstrated, all of these connections were fertile environments for

indigenous men and women to learn the skills of litigation and effective self-fashioning.

Succession practices for encomienda, which were aggressively debated in the middle of the sixteenth century and likely discussed around many dinner tables, would be an obvious source for caciques' own presentation of their rights to succession. The initial encomiendas—there were some five hundred in Peru in the 1540s—were granted almost exclusively to Spanish men, usually soldiers who had fought in the conquest or on the Crown's side in the subsequent civil wars.[42] Within a few decades, the question of their succession was prominent. Attempts to resolve it intersected with attacks on the institution of encomienda across the kingdom and the "perpetuity controversy" in Peru, where encomenderos demanded the right to pass their titles to their descendants in perpetuity as well as to have legal jurisdiction over Andean subjects held in encomienda. A bribery scandal ended that conversation, leaving encomienda succession defined for three lives: a surviving spouse could inherit the title from a deceased encomendero, and then a child could succeed, before the privileges reverted to the Crown.[43] Thus the second generation of encomenderos included the conquistadors' wives, sons, and daughters. A list of the individuals holding encomiendas in 1561 includes not only women but also a great number of men who obtained their title by marrying the widows of encomenderos.[44]

Elite Spanish women, as Helen Nader reminds us, "lived in a dual system, one in which patriarchy coexisted with matriarchy."[45] While many institutions excluded women from public life, they also made it possible for women to manage, buy, sell, and inherit property; exercise guardianship over minor children; and act consequentially in many spheres. Women's dowries and labor were the basis for many households' prosperity, and women retained theoretical ownership of that capital even if their husbands were temporarily empowered to invest it.[46] Elite women became especially significant when familial control over resources was at stake: the stability of the Spanish monarchy, for example, regularly hinged upon the ability of female heirs to take the throne.

The New World encomienda provided a special case of *mayorazgo* (entailed estate inherited by right of blood). While women inherited more or less equally with men within most Spanish law, *feudos* (large entailed properties) were not divisible and their inheritance was restricted to the eldest male issue. But in New World encomiendas, women could succeed their husbands and daughters could inherit from fathers. This special dispensation was made in order to attract more men (and families) as stable settlers, as well as to avoid impoverishing widows.[47] Succession to the daughter was preferred over the widow, but in the absence of heirs, or when children were minors, the Crown preferred to name widows *encomenderas* (female encomienda holders) and encourage them to remarry rapidly.[48]

Spanish women were well-represented as holders of encomiendas in northern Peru, where cacicas also flourished. Of twenty-four encomiendas in Trujillo in 1561, three were directly administered either by a woman or by a couple where the succession went through the wife.[49] By the turn of the seventeenth century the situation was more dramatic, as women made up a growing share of the diminishing population of surviving encomenderos.

Women were not automatically granted the next life of the encomienda: they had to make an application, usually emphasizing the woman's poverty and her late husband's selfless service to the Crown. These provide important testimony of female succession in the north. In 1601, doña Ana de Velasco y Avendaño successfully sued for the encomienda of Jayanca, near Trujillo, when her father, don Miguel de Avendaño, died just a year after being awarded an annual income in remuneration for his military service in Peru and Chile. Doña Ana de Velasco, left "very poor" by her father's death, was granted the encomienda recently left vacant by the death of doña Ysabel Palomino, who had herself inherited it from her late husband don Manuel Criado de Castilla. The provision explicitly gave the right of succession to the eldest legitimate son or daughter of doña Ana (with her husband, Juan de Calderón, who made the application in doña Ana's name).[50]

In many cases, widows (or daughters) acted as a placeholder until an appropriate male could exercise office.[51] Widows found themselves under pressure to remarry quickly, and an encomienda grant was an attractive asset to suitors. But many elite women, particularly in northern Peru, were known for their business acumen and the wielding of power through their encomiendas. Ana Pizarro, Florencia de Mora, and Beatriz de los Ríos all succeeded their husbands and, despite remarriages, notoriously retained active control over their own business interests. Doña Florencia ran an *obraje* (textile enterprise), a cattle ranch, and her own encomienda, all in highland Huamachuco and was known for her charitable works as well as her iron will.[52] In nearby highland Cajamarca, doña Beatriz de Ysásaga and doña Jordana Mexia, widows of two conquistadors, were regularly in the courts in the 1570s, suing each other over the possession of particular indigenous pueblos as part of their own encomiendas.[53] These women joined the ranks of other prominent businesswomen, forming a visible and voluble corps of

Spanish women involved in the social, economic, and political life of the region. But the encomenderas, in particular, modeled successful maneuvering through the courts by women who could articulate their rights to succession based upon both law and personal histories.

By winning their cases, encomenderas normalized female succession both for indigenous candidates and for the Spanish officials who would judge their cases. Northern caciques regularly took female encomenderas to court over financial issues and presumably saw them as models for their own juridical practices and business enterprises. They interacted with them in cities like Trujillo, where both were likely to have had homes. The case of north-highland Cajamarca—which had no known tradition of preconquest cacicas but a number of prominent ones after the arrival of its powerful encomenderas—is especially suggestive of the ways that this legal discourse about female succession traveled between elites.[54]

In the sixteenth century, litigation over cacicazgos was silent on the topic of gender, although women held the office. But in the seventeenth century, in northern Peru, indigenous women (with their lawyers) produced a narrative centering the role of female succession before the conquest. As colonial officials continued to push for predictability and uniformity in indigenous succession, this language became embedded in its formal codification. The model of mayorazgo, the feudal entailment that encomienda approximated in the New World, became the definition of customary inheritance in the indigenous world. For example, the jurist Juan de Solórzano y Pereira, in his 1647 legal compendium, *Política indiana*, corrected Toledo's more narrow formulation by asserting that natives had the right to determine "succession by right of blood in imitation of mayorazgos." That is, the right to administer succession was left in indigenous hands, but the method of determining succession was now to be limited to "succession derived from fathers to sons."[55]

Once "most able" was replaced by the mayorazgo, the problem of female inheritance became prominent. When the bloodline had no males, the possibility of counternarratives (of ability or election, for example) reestablished themselves, creating power vacuums that could be manipulated by local players. In this case, Spanish officials saw female succession as a way to resolve many crises, as it had with encomiendas. Solórzano noted that Viceroy Toledo was unwilling to allow women to exclude any male kin, even of more remote descent. But because of the tendency on the north coast to allow indigenous women, especially when married, to hold office, he argued, "this custom ought to be observed where it is proven and is accompanied by acts that suffice to introduce it, because we do not find a lack of examples of offices, duties and dignities of much greater import in which females succeed although they have mixed jurisdiction; so we see that they are competent to inherit kingdoms, states and lordships, feudos and mayorazgos."[56] In this case, offering daughters as successors, but only in the absence of sons, decreased the likelihood of contested succession and provided the viceroy with a wider range of potential candidates when intervention proved necessary.

CACICAS BEYOND CAPULLANAS

Throughout the seventeenth century many northern Andean women called themselves cacicas, sometimes in order to claim office or benefits, at others simply as a title of respect or an honorific. In 1679, an extremely long and contentious litigation over the cacicazgo of Túcume and Mochumi ended in favor of doña María Josepha Mincha. Three women had vied for this cacicazgo, each asserting their legitimacy in the absence of male heirs. Doña María Josepha eventually won because, as the sister of the late cacique, she demonstrated legitimacy through bloodline and was treated as such. Another claimant, doña Catalina, was dismissed by witnesses because "if she were [the cacica] . . . the Indians of the repartimiento would treat her as their señora and they don't, they view her like any other [plebeian] Indian . . ." Another stated that "he knows her as a woman and an *india* [non-noble Indian woman] like all the rest, that although she knows how to speak Spanish in the end she is an india."[57] Both the local community and the representatives of royal power gestured towards chiefly legitimacy, which increasingly meant noble lineage, no matter the gender of the claimants.

While a woman might inherit the cacicazgo, it was not always clear that she would govern. The office itself was shrinking in the seventeenth century: the task of the cacique was, in the blunt words of one document, "dispatching *mitayos* [mita laborers] . . . and collecting tribute with punctuality" in exchange for "salary and services and care for fields as established by the schedule."[58] The husbands of cacicas often took on these duties, often receiving the title "governor." This expectation was usually clarified in the title, as for the cacicazgo of Huamán in 1673: "Because when succession and the right of cacicazgos are deferred to women who are married, it is convenient that the governance be in the hands of the husbands, if they are competent, because the Indians obey them and respect them as husbands of their cacicas."[59]

But cacicas also proliferated in the central and northern sierra, strongholds of the Incas before the conquest with no heritage of capullanas. Cajamarca in particular had numerous colonial cacicas, who appear with great frequency in the archival record carrying out the duties of their office. These included the two youthful cacicas, doña Feliciana and doña María de Barrionuevo, who jointly won back doña Feliciana's cacicazgo from their uncle after Feliciana attained majority in 1681; doña María de los Reyes, cacica of Guacapongo, who litigated on behalf of the "community of Indians" against an indigenous *alcalde* (an elected leader of a town) for abuses and mistreatment in 1678; and doña Clara Cabuslachos, cacica of the province of Cajamarca, who went to court in 1631 over her land holdings.[60] Doña María Collquisilles, the cacica of Otusco, died in 1636, leaving a vast estate of personal goods, animals, and family lands she described in two wills.[61] Doña María left her estate to three "orphan *mestizos* [persons of mixed indigenous-Spanish descent]" she had raised (sometimes referred to as her children in the documents), as well as to her brother; she made only fleeting mention of her husband in her first will and never identified him as her husband in the second. She appears to have served as the cacica, and documentation throughout largely refers to her by that title. That her use of the office's privileges may have been contested is suggested, however, by her statement that "by provision of the lord viceroys, my parents were granted two mitayos to guard their livestock, and I have been robbed of the said provisions, I order my executors to search for them so that my inheriting children can take advantage of them for the guarding of the livestock of the ranch for which they were assigned."[62] The proliferation of cacicas may have had to do with both Cajamarca's proximity to Trujillo (the latter with a tradition of cacicas) and the powerful and autonomous Spanish encomenderas who held labor grants in both regions.

Elsewhere, women calling themselves cacica also proliferated, though some of these were simply asserting an elite bloodline rather than claiming an office. In 1616 in the central highlands town of Chincha, doña Juana Curilla, "cacica principal of the valley of Chincha," sued the corregidor's lieutenant over some lands that were taken from her, which she claimed to have inherited from her ancestors. The opposing counsel referred to her as "Juana Curilla yndia," rather than cacica and based his defense on witnesses who testified as to how stupid, corrupt, and immoral indigenous people were.[63] No documentation in that file supports her claim to be cacica, which was not relevant to her suit, but the title apparently afforded her some status when battling the bureaucracy.

On the other hand, in highland Jauja in 1629, doña María Llaxachumbi sued for possession of the cacicazgo of her ayllu, which came to her "by direct male line." The lawsuit was filed by her husband, don Diego Clemente Tisi Guaman, who argued that his young wife had been displaced from the cacicazgo founded by her grandfather, don Juan Chivan, because she was young and unmarried at the time of his death. Her own father seemingly did not serve due to an unnamed "incapacity," and an interim cacique was appointed: Vicente, the son of one of don Juan Chivan's daughters. The interim cacique sought to make himself permanent, but once doña María came of age and married, the couple sought physical title, claiming they were already carrying out all aspects of the office. They received it, but the suit lasted twenty years, ending in 1649. The question of gender was never raised in the litigation: the most compelling evidence was likely a tributary census from 1635 that listed don Diego as the cacique and Vicente as an untitled tributary, proving that don Diego and doña María were acting as leaders.[64]

Ysauel Caja y Yapa "cacica" made her will before a Lima notary in 1701. Nothing in her will indicates that the title "cacica" was more than an honorific: she was the daughter of don Francisco Yapa and Catalina Josepha of San Juan de Coyata, neither of whom were titled, and was married to Bartolomé Rosales, a native of Guacho. She made no mention of a cacicazgo within the will, and it is possible that "cacica" (like "palla" or "ñusta" in the previous century) simply became a strong honorific of the period.[65]

These and other cases illustrate the ways in which the title "cacica" came to be used with growing frequency by elite indigenous women over the seventeenth century, departing from its origins in the north and its links to the real exercise of power to have broader and more ambiguous significance. The dilution of the meaning of the term, which accompanied the declining significance of the rural indigenous elite overall, allowed it eventually to become a mere marker of status. Elite men also increasingly used their female ancestors to assert their legitimacy, perhaps drawing upon traditions of parallel descent in highland society, and they also used young elite wives as ways to achieve legitimacy in the merged lineages of the shrinking Andean political world. But the institution of the cacica provided a space for elite women to promote their own interests, within the bounds of colonial society.

CONCLUSION: MAGDALENA MALLAO
AND THE CHILD CACICA

By the middle of the seventeenth century, indigenous women had normalized succession as cacicas. No longer confined to their northern origins, cacicas appeared in a variety of strategic situations, the answer to certain Andean power struggles. In the final case presented here, there was no local tradition of female succession to speak of. This lawsuit moved forward because cacicas had become part of a generalized preconquest past, now integral to colonial customary law. The suit was brought in 1643 before the *real audiencia*, the royal high court, over urban lands in Huánuco, in the central sierra. In it, notions of legitimacy and illegitimacy, tradition and law all intermingle as litigants struggled over power in the guise of resources. Female succession in cacicazgos became not only relevant to a particular woman's ability to claim resources, but part of a larger discourse of indigenous customary law.

The suit began when don Pedro Ayra and his niece doña Francisca Ayra (married at the time to the cacique don Juan Bautista Curicaya) tried to throw Magdalena Mallao, an elderly indigenous woman, out of a house and two pieces of land they owned in the city of León de Huánuco. Mallao had lived in the house and made use of the surrounding farmland for some years prior to the complaint, while the owners were living away from the city. Don Pedro and doña Francisca returned and found themselves unable to remove Mallao from their property. Although they initially stated that Mallao had "invaded" their house, in their interrogatories they clarified that they had indeed, "from the pity they had for the said doña Madalena Mallao, being poor and having no house to live in, consented to her living in a chamber on the lot of land, sowing for her food on a piece of land."[66]

Don Pedro and doña Francisca's ownership of the two lots stemmed from a legal donation made by doña Francisca Ruray after the death of her husband don Francisco Ayra, the cacique of Ychuc. That couple had only one child who survived don Francisco, named Leonor, and she passed away within six months of her father's death. In 1601 doña Francisca Ruray, aging and with no living children of her own, decided to transfer her property to some of her late husband's illegitimate children, of which there were at least five. That donation recognized don Pedro Ayra, the legitimate son of don Francisco's illegitimate son don Andrés, and three other *hijos naturales* (children born to individuals without legal impediment to marry): don Santiago Ayra, don Tomás Ayra, and don Domingo Ayra. Doña Francisca Ayra, the copetitioner with don Pedro, was the legitimate daughter of don Santiago Ayra, granddaughter of the caci-que, and heir to her father's share of the property.

The confusion over the property had to do with the vagaries of law regard-ing children born outside of wedlock. Much of the witness testimony dealt with establishing which of don Francisco's children were "bastards" (born while he was married to another woman) or hijos naturales. The latter could be legally recognized by a parent and inherit part of their estate, but bastards could not: doña Francisca's use of the instrument of donation rather than naming the children in her will likely reflects her concern that, as inheritance, the property transfer would be contested over bastardy and delay execution. The second issue was whether don Francisco and doña Francisca had legally recognized the children as hijos naturales, a requirement for their ability to inherit. Litigation proceeded around the legal niceties of the donation and subsequent wills. In the midst of this wrangling, Magdalena Ayra or Mallao entered, claiming to be yet another of don Francisco's illegitimate children, and demanded to share in the property and live peaceably alongside them.[67]

The question of legitimacy and inheritance had long been on the minds of all the participants. Don Santiago Ayra in his own will of 1606 stated that only he, the eldest of the cacique's illegitimate children, was natural and all the others were bastards.[68] However Magdalena introduced another will during her appeal to the high court. It belonged to doña Leonor Lliuyac Mallo, the daughter of the late cacique don Francisco, who had died in 1586. Doña Leonor in this will called herself cacica principal and named Magda-lena Mallao as her sister. Doña Leonor left a small amount of cash and some sheep to her mother, doña Francisca Ruray, but left the great majority of her estate including the house and lands in question to her sister Magdalena, "because I have raised her since she was small." And she left this parting shot for the other future claimants:

> all the rest of my relatives and bastard brothers have done great inju-ries to my father and to me in taking away many houses and haciendas that were my father's, and the title that my father left me to the caci-cazgo; they have insulted me and their parents without any right whatso-ever ... and thus they do not deserve to inherit my goods for being such bad Christians ... and to the said doña Madalena Mallao ... I leave her the said lot with the consent of my mother and may none of my relatives interfere in this, let her enjoy it freely, and it is my will and may she plead with God for my soul.[69]

Don Pedro and doña Francisca immediately declared the will a fake, and not without reason: doña Leonor was only eight or nine years old when she died and hardly able to construct such a document. And if it was authentic, why did Magdalena Mallao wait so long to produce it? Their witnesses, mainly elderly indigenous men, continued to argue over the marital status of don Francisco and doña Francisca Ruray at the birth of various children, all agreeing that Magdalena's status as bastard entirely disqualified her from inheritance. On the other hand, Magdalena Mallao's witnesses, mostly Spanish women and mestizas, testified that they knew of the existence of the will and that it was valid. Friends and relatives of the late priest whose signature was on the document verified his handwriting and the fact that they had heard him speak of it or even seen it themselves.

In the end, the high court failed to overturn the findings of the lower and awarded possession of the house to Magdalena Mallao. The frankly unbelievable story of a will made by a nine-year-old girl and secreted for forty years triumphed over the machinations of the local indigenous elite. Magdalena Mallao won her house due to her connections to Spanish society rather than by excavating the local ethnography of her community.

Doña Francisca Ayra's support came entirely from local indigenous officials, drawing on the weight of the status of her husband and uncle. On the other hand, Magdalena Mallao had a mestiza daughter with whom she was sharing the disputed house. Her witnesses included a "mestiza dressed like an india," the niece of the Spanish priest who witnessed doña Leonor's will, a master blacksmith, the town councilman, and his sister. Their testimony centered on gossip they heard in Spanish households, which established public knowledge of the will and inheritance. While the legal character of the will of a child (girls under the age of twelve were explicitly prohibited from creating a will)[70] should have been questionable, and its rhetorical style and sudden appearance strongly suggest it was faked, the authorization of a Spanish priest and public discourse in the Spanish community validated it. Leonor's claim to be cacica upon her father's death was never challenged in the trial and only served to underscore the role of the successful narrative in supporting this rather political agenda.

Magdalena Mallao's improbable story illustrates how doña Francisca Canapaynina's cacical claims achieved hegemony and lost specificity in colonial Peru. If the ethnohistory of the north coast's capullanas provides a point of origin for colonial cacicas, their histories became more complicated. Capullanas—elite women who held office in preconquest north coast polities—were transformed into colonial cacicas, whose ability to rule autonomously was curtailed but who could be effective conduits for lineage, salaries, and power, to themselves and the men around them. They fashioned narratives of lineage that borrowed from Spanish women's success with inheriting encomiendas, including the expectation that they would marry men who could carry out the tasks associated with the office. They learned from the litigious environment of the early colony to construct narratives that met the expectations of Spanish authorities but also drew upon highly localized notions of chiefly legitimacy and nobility. They drafted new genealogies, swapped surnames, and sought witnesses among indigenous elders and Spanish citizens who could lend weight to their accounts. Their ability to litigate for titles and resources drew upon interwoven Spanish and indigenous societies and the ways that indigenous customary law was reinvented as an interested refraction of Spanish practices. The victories of colonial cacicas, such as they were, were contingent upon their ability to manage multiple discourses in the legal arena as well as gain the support of their putative subjects.

NOTES

1. Archivo General de la Nación (Lima, Peru), Derecho Indígena (hereafter cited as AGN DI) Cuaderno 627 (1610). This case was first analyzed and excerpts published as María Rostworowski de Diez Canseco, *Curacas y sucesiones: Costa norte* (Lima: Minerva, 1961).

2. Rostworowski, *Curacas y sucesiones*, 225.

3. Archivo General de Indias (Seville, Spain) (hereafter cited as AGI) Quito 26. On the case's ethnographic merits, see Luis Miguel Glave, "Hombres del mar: Caciques de la Costa ecuatoriana en los inicios de la época colonial." *Procesos* 40 (2014).

4. AGN DI 627 (1610), fol. 22.

5. For example: Gabriela Ramos and Yanna Yannakakis, eds., *Indigenous intellectuals: Knowledge, Power, and Colonial Culture in Mexico and the Andes* (Durham, NC: Duke University Press, 2014); and José Carlos de la Puente Luna, *Andean Cosmopolitans: Seeking Justice and Reward at the Spanish Royal Court* (Austin: University of Texas Press, 2018).

6. AGN DI 627 (1610), fol. 37.

7. AGN DI 627 (1610), fols. 57–58.

8. AGN DI 627 (1610), fols. 65v–66.

9. Rostworowski, *Curacas y sucesiones*, 225.

10. Chantal Caillavet, "Como cacica y señora desta tierra mando. Insignias, funciones y poderes de las soberanas del norte andino (siglos XV–XVI)." *Bulletin de l'Institut Français d'Études Andines* 37, no. 1 (October 2008).

11. Caillavet, "Como cacica y señora"; and Karen B. Graubart, "Indecent Living: Indigenous Women and the Politics of Representation in Early Colonial Peru." *Colonial Latin American Review* 9, no. 2 (December 2000).

12. Gonzalo Fernández Oviedo y Valdés, *Corónica de las Yndias y la Conquista del Peru* (Salamanca: Juan de Junta, 1547), 388.

13. Joan de Santa Cruz Pachacuti Salcamaygua, *Relación de las antiguedades deste reyno del Piru: Estudio etnohistórico y lingüístico*, ed. Pierre Duviols and César Itier (Lima: Institut Français d'Etudes Andines y Centro de Estudios Regionales Andinos Bartolomé de las Casas, 1993), 19v; and Roberto Levillier, *Don Francisco de Toledo, Supremo organizador del Perú: Su vida, su obra (1515–1582)* (Madrid: Espasa Calpe, 1955), 73.

14. Juan Ruiz de Arce, "Advertencias de Juan Ruiz de Arce a sus subcesores," in *Tres Testigos de La Conquista Del Perú: Hernando Pizarro, Juan Ruiz de Arce y Diego de Trujillo*, 3rd ed., ed. Conde Miguel Muñoz de San Pedro Canilleros (1543; repr., Madrid: Espasa Calpe, 1964) 81.

15. Reginaldo de Lizárraga, *Descripción del Perú, Tucumán, Río de La Plata y Chile* (Madrid: Historia 16, 1986), chap. 8; and Pedro de Cieza de León, *Crónica del Perú, tercera parte*, ed. Francesca Cantù (Lima: Pontificia Universidad Católica del Perú, Fondo Editorial, 1989), 62–69.

16. AGN DI Cuaderno 627 (1610), fol. 50v.

17. Pedro de Cieza de León, *Crónica del Perú, primera parte*, ed. Franklin Pease G. Y. (1553; repr., Lima: Pontificia Universidad Católica del Perú, Fondo Editorial, 1989), 192.

18. María Rostworowski de Diez Canseco, "La mujer en el Perú prehispánico," *Instituto de Estudios Peruanos Documento de Trabajo 72* (1995), 12.

19. For example, see John V. Murra, *Formaciones económicas y políticas del mundo andino* (Lima: Instituto de Estudios Peruanos, 1975); Franklin Pease G. Y., *Curacas, reciprocidad y riqueza* (Lima: Pontificia Universidad Católica del Perú, Fondo Editorial, 1992); and Karen Spalding, "Kurakas and Commerce: A Chapter in the Evolution of Andean Society," *Hispanic American Historical Review* 53, no. 4 (November 1973).

20. For example, María Rostworowski de Diez Canseco, *Costa peruana prehispánica* (Lima: Instituto de Estudios Peruanos, 1989); Susan E. Ramírez, *The World Upside Down: Cross-Cultural Contact and Conflict in Sixteenth-Century Peru* (Stanford: Stanford University Press, 1998); Patricia Netherly, "Local Level Lords on the North Coast of Perú." (PhD diss., Cornell University, 1977); and Glave, "Hombres Del Mar."

21. See Brooke Larson, Olivia Harris, and Enrique Tandeter, *Ethnicity, Markets, and Migration in the Andes: At the Crossroads of History and Anthropology* (Durham, NC: Duke University Press, 1995); José Carlos de la Puente Luna, "That Which Belongs to All: Khipus, Community, and Indigenous Legal Activism in the Early Colonial Andes," *Americas* 72, no. 1 (January 2015); and Glave, "Hombres Del Mar."

22. Netherly, "Local Level Lords," 202; see also Frank Salomon, *Native Lords of Quito in the Age of the Incas: The Political Economy of North-Andean Chiefdoms* (New York: Cambridge University Press, 1986).

23. Miguel Cabello Balboa, *Miscelánea antártica* (Sevilla: Fundación José Manuel Lara, 2011), 468.

24. Susan E. Ramírez, *To Feed and Be Fed: The Cosmological Bases of Authority and Identity in the Andes* (Stanford: Stanford University Press, 2005); Catherine Julien, *Reading Inca History* (Iowa City: University of Iowa Press, 2000).

25. María Rostworowski de Diez Canseco, "Succession, Coöptation to Kingship, and Royal Incest Among the Inca," *Southwestern Journal of Anthropology* 16, no. 4 (1960); Susan A. Niles, *The Shape of Inca History: Narrative and Archaeology in an Andean Empire* (Iowa City: University of Iowa Press, 1999), 302, 305–6.

26. Salomon, *Native Lords of Quito*, 133. In contrast, see Estela Cristina Salles and Héctor Omar Noejovich, "La herencia femenina andina prehispánica y su transformación en el mundo colonial," *Bulletin de l'Institut Français d'Études Andines* 35, no. 1 (April 2006).

27. Hernando de Santillán, "Relación del orígen, descendencia, política y gobierno de los Incas," in *Crónicas peruanas de interés indígena*, ed. Francisco Esteve Barba, vol. 209 of *Biblioteca de autores españoles* (Madrid: Atlas, 1968), 109.

28. Sara Vicuña Guengerich, "Inca Women Under Spanish Rule: Probanzas and Informaciones of the Colonial Andean Elite," in *Women's Negotiations and Textual Agency in Latin America, 1500–1799*, ed. Mónica Díaz and Rocío Quispe-Agnoli (New York: Routledge, 2017).

29. On Inca women, see Sara Vicuña Guengerich, "Capac Women and the Politics of Marriage in Early Colonial Peru," *Colonial Latin American Review* 24, no. 2 (April 2015). On Andean gender roles more broadly, see Irene Silverblatt, *Moon, Sun, and Witches: Gender Ideologies and Class in Inca and Colonial Peru* (Princeton: Princeton University Press, 1987); and Karen B. Graubart, *With Our Labor and Sweat: Indigenous Women and the Formation of Colonial Society in Peru, 1550–1700* (Stanford: Stanford University Press, 2007).

30. Pease, *Curacas, reciprocidad y riqueza*, 20.

31. Pease, *Curacas, reciprocidad y riqueza*, 21; Spalding, "Kurakas and Commerce," 584–5.

32. See Spalding, "Kurakas and Commerce"; Karen Vieira Powers, "A Battle of Wills: Inventing Chiefly Legitimacy in the Colonial North Andes," in *Dead Giveaways: Indigenous Testaments of Colonial Mesoamerica and the Andes*, ed. Susan Kellogg and Matthew Restall (Salt Lake City: University of Utah Press, 1998); Rafael Varón Gabai, *Curacas y encomenderos: acomodamiento nativo en Huaraz, siglos XVI y XVII* (Lima: P. L. Villanueva, 1980); and Marina Zuloaga, *La conquista negociada: Guarangas, autoridades locales e imperio en Huaylas, Perú (1532–1610)* (Lima: Instituto de Estudios Peruanos-Instituto Francés de Estudios Andinos, 2012).

33. See Karen B. Graubart, "Learning from the Qadi: The Jurisdiction of Local Rule in the Early Colonial Andes," *Hispanic American Historical Review* 95, no. 2 (May 2015).

34. Akira Saitō and Claudia Rosas Lauro, *Reducciones: La concentración forzada de las poblaciones indígenas en el Virreinato del Perú* (Lima: Pontificia Universidad Católica del Perú and National Museum of Ethnology, 2017); Jeremy Ravi Mumford,

Vertical Empire: The General Resettlement of Indians in the Colonial Andes (Durham, NC: Duke University Press, 2012); and María Rostworowski de Diez Canseco, *Señoríos indígenas de Lima y Canta* (Lima: Instituto de Estudios Peruanos, 1978).

35. Rostworowski, *Curacas y sucesiones*, 209. See also Jorge Zevallos Quiñones, *Los cacicazgos de Lambayeque* (Trujillo, Peru: Gráfica Cuatro, 1989), 113–15.

36. On the larger role of genealogy in creating colonial legitimacy, see María Elena Martínez, *Genealogical Fictions: Limpieza de Sangre, Religion, and Gender in Colonial Mexico* (Stanford: Stanford University Press, 2011).

37. Levillier, *Don Francisco de Toledo*, 2:lxxi.

38. Maria Justina Sarabia Viejo, *Francisco de Toledo: Disposiciones gubernativas para el virreinato del Perú* (Sevilla: Escuela de Estudios Hispano-Americanos de Sevilla, 1986), 1:19.

39. Sarabia Viejo, *Francisco de Toledo*, 1:139.

40. Sarabia Viejo, *Francisco de Toledo*, 2:113–4.

41. See Kathryn Burns, *Colonial Habits: Convents and the Spiritual Economy of Cuzco, Peru* (Durham, NC: Duke University Press, 1999); Monique Alaperrin-Bouyer, *La educación de las élites indígenas en el Perú colonial* (Lima: Instituto Francés de Estudios Andinos, 2007), chap. 8.

42. Only one woman was directly granted an encomienda, doña Francisca Pizarro, the illegitimate daughter of the conquistador Francisco Pizarro (who granted her the title in 1540) and Quispe Sisa (Inés Huaylas Yupanqui), the daughter of the Inca Huayna Capac. See María Rostworowski de Diez Canseco, *Doña Francisca Pizarro: Una ilustre mestiza, 1534–1598* (Lima: Instituto de Estudios Peruanos, 1989), 36–37, 69.

43. On the controversy, which also included a bid from Andean kurakas, see Mumford, *Vertical Empire*, chap. 4. The limits on encomienda were originally set out in the New Laws of 1542, which led to a civil war in the Andes and ended with the treatment of Andean encomiendas as privileges that had to be authorized by the Crown.

44. Teodoro Hampe Martínez, "Relación de los encomenderos y repartimientos del Perú en 1561." *Historia y Cultura* 12 (1979).

45. Helen Nader, *Power and Gender in Renaissance Spain: Eight Women of the Mendoza Family: 1450–1650* (Urbana, IL: University of Illinois Press, 2004), 3.

46. Graubart, *With Our Labor*.

47. Juan de Solórzano Pereira, *Política indiana* (Madrid: Diego Díaz de la Carrera, 1648), 2: 246.

48. Ana María Presta, "Portraits of Four Women: Traditional Female Roles and Transgressions in Colonial Elite Families in Charcas, 1550–1600," *Colonial Latin American Review* 9, no. 2 (2000): 251.

49. Hampe Martínez, "Relación de los encomenderos," 101–3.

50. Biblioteca Nacional del Perú (hereafter cited as BNP) B137 (1601).

51. Ana María Presta, "Detrás de la mejor dote, una encomienda: Hijas y viudas de la primera generación de encomenderos en el mercado matrimonial de Charcas, 1534–48," *Revista Andina* 8 (1997): 27–46.

52. Archivo Regional de La Libertad (hereafter cited as ARLL) Protocolos Notariales Mata 25, fols. 71, 187, 229v.

53. ARLL Corregimientos, Causas Ordinarias (hereafter cited as CCO), Legajo 151, Expediente 126; AGN Juicios de Residencia Legajo 2, Cuaderno 5 (1582).

54. On the political machinations of Cajamarca's nobility, see Aude Argouse, "¿Son todos caciques? Curacas, principales, e indios urbanos en Cajamarca (siglo XVII)," *Bulletin de l'Institut Français d'Études Andines* 37, no. 1 (2008): 163–84. For examples, see below.

55. Solórzano y Pereira, *Política Indiana*, 1:408–9.

56. Solórzano y Pereira, *Política Indiana*, 1:410.

57. BNP B1486 (1679), fol. 50. It is fascinating that Doña Catalina, although an "india like all the rest," knew how to write and sign her own name, unusual for indigenous women.

58. BNP B1087 (1629), fols. 2, 6. On the changing duties, see Spalding, "Kurakas and Commerce"; Ramírez, *World Upside Down*.

59. ARLL CCO Legajo 202, Expediente 1,407 (1673).

60. BNP B1385 (1681); Archivo Documental de Cajamarca Corregimientos Causas Criminales (hereafter cited as ADC CCO) Legajo 2 (1678); ADC CCO (1631).

61. ADC CCO Legajo 25 (1636).

62. ADC CCO Legajo 25 (1636), fol. 2v. This may reflect a reduction in or contest over privileges associated with the office; see Graubart, "Learning from the Qadi."

63. BNP B1051 (1616).

64. BNP B1087 (1689).

65. "Testamento de Ysauel Caja y Yapa cacica," Archivo Arzobispal de Lima, Testamentos 134:9 (1701).

66. AGN DI Legajo 103 (1639), fol. 47.

67. Throughout the litigation Magdalena Mallao referred to herself as Magdalena Ayra, although no other participants did: as with doña Francisca above this might have been a strategic claim. She also cast aspersions on don Pedro's claims by calling him "don Pedro Guaclla, a.k.a. Ayra" and the "so-called cacique of Singa." AGN DI Cuaderno 101 (1643), fols. 40, 29.

68. AGN DI Cuaderno 101 (1643), fol. 18.

69. AGN DI Cuaderno 101 (1643), fol. 33.

70. Robert I. Burns, ed., *Las Siete Partidas*, trans. Samuel Parsons Scott (University of Pennsylvania Press, 2000), 522.

CHAPTER 6

Public Voice and Political Authority

NATIVE FEMALE LEADERSHIP IN THE
SIXTEENTH-CENTURY NORTHERN ANDES

Chantal Caillavet

As a point of entry into native female authority in the northern Andes
before the Spanish irruption, I use the theoretical and methodological insights contained in the convergent works of two historians as a
means of understanding the gendered changes generated by colonization.
These authors underline the *silences* that so encapsulate the female experience in western history and find their exact counterpart in colonial societies
in the New World.

It is certainly an ambitious goal to retrieve female testimonies from written sources in the context of a society in which women themselves did not directly produce archival material. A pioneering study by Michelle Perrot argues
that the sources traditionally used to write history are the work of men, who
project onto women certain repetitive images which often slide into clichés.
She encourages us to establish a closer understanding of the real, recover
women's voices, and move away from traditional male discourse.[1] This approach is especially stimulating for the northern Andes, where indigenous
societies did not have written records and our only available sources were
written by the Spanish colonizers.

It is more specifically the nexus between public power and the female
sphere which requires exploration, according to Mary Beard.[2] This is where
the fundamental male-female differentiation is located. Political power resides

in the voice of authority, which proves to be a masculine reserve. And, in consequence, female silence is held to be self-evident. Beard cites an ancient expression in Homer's *Odyssey*: when the youthful Telemachus imposes silence on his mother (and for good measure affirms his male status) by arguing that "speech will be the business of men, all men, and of me, most of all; for mine is the power in this household."[3] The western world has inherited so many mental and political categories from classical antiquity that Beard invites us to analyze the strength and enduring nature of their projection. I think we can apply this dichotomy in Spanish America, as a key cultural import from Europe. I believe this analytical framework can be valuable in directing us towards a definition of female power in other cultures. How can we establish a link between public voice and political power in the pre-Hispanic north Ecuadorian Andes? How was authority exercised and distributed between female and male ethnic leaders both before and after the installation of Spanish rule?

SOURCES AND METHODOLOGY

The climatic conditions of the northern Andes—and, specifically, their high rate of precipitation—have not allowed for the survival of pre-Hispanic remains of a similar quality to those located in drier parts of the Andes. Among the archaeological remains of men and women, the tombs of the Lady of Cao Viejo, also known as the "priestess of Chornancap," help us to define the spaces of power occupied by women.[4]

Among the surviving pottery of Ecuador are statuettes of women with high-prestige decoration (e.g., body painting, jewelry, and clothing) and vessels for coca consumption comparable to that of their male counterparts and which distinguish them from nonelite women. These have been found on both the Pacific coast and in high-altitude areas near the present-day border between Ecuador and Colombia. (See map 3.)

But it is above all close attention to written sources, in accordance with Perrot's reflections, which will allow us to retrieve the testimonies of colonial women and bring them out from the shadows of their habitual silence. Narratives of the Spanish conquest and early colonization all belonged to an epic literary genre monopolized by men—soldiers, priests, and high-ranking officials—who produced chronicles, *probanzas de méritos* (merit inquests), and *relaciones* (accounts), in which they only rarely cited female protagonists. When referenced, women were, according to these accounts, inevitably subject to men or played only minor roles in historical events. Yet, abundant administrative and judicial archival sources recorded the voices of colonial women.

At first glance, administrative records may not appear promising given their formulaic structures. Such formats provided little room for self-expression or revealing digressions. Yet, numerous notarial acts testify to the ways that the native elite entered the colonial system through marriage contracts, testaments and inventories of goods, and judicial litigation that were as much female as masculine in character. It is within this body of documentation that we can find details of women's lives.

Testaments have long been viewed as an invaluable source in European history: they are sufficiently abundant for us to be able to build up fairly complete series, while they supply detailed information about an individual's place in society.[5] For southern Europe in particular (and specifically the official model that predominated in Spanish colonial society), they explicitly regulate funerals in a Christian context and manage the transmission of material goods as well as the avenues to power and its prerogatives. As a documentary corpus, testaments allow us to establish a solid body of information on the testators and their place in society through standardized features in notarial acts. But it is precisely when testators diverged from habitual practices that we can "read between the lines." A silence or absence may be as significant as a specific indication, whether profuse or laconic: all mistakes, omissions, or departures from the norm are markers in such crucial areas as identity, self-designation, kinship ties, the right to possession or usufruct of an inheritance, authority over others, the place occupied or claimed in society as well as the underlying explanation, which may be implicit, for the choice of legatees. William Phillips's "Testaments in the Spanish World in the Early Modern Period" has proved a valuable synthesis on the study of testaments as a source of social history in the Hispanic sphere in the sixteenth century and helps us to interpret the nature of practices in the recently colonized American territories.[6]

Extensive use of this exceptionally informative source (grouping together both testaments and posthumous inventories) has likewise informed a number of studies of colonial Spanish American society. In particular—to draw closer to the heart of this article—it has highlighted the ways in which the native population sought recourse through an alien legal framework.[7] Some historians have analyzed the authority of ethnic leaders as revealed by their testaments.[8] Others have focused on a narrower corpus allowing for the parallel study of the wills of men and women in order to clarify gender differences.[9] Here I will follow a similar approach, selecting testaments of ethnic leaders from the northern Andes, half of them female and half of them male, as well as leadership couples, in the rare cases where the sources have allowed me to do so. The work in this chapter is based on a body of fourteen texts, in which the testators were indigenous leaders in an area spanning from the present-day Colombian border (in the north) to the central Andean region of Ecuador farther south. They feature individuals from five ethnic groups (Pasto, Otavalo, Panzaleo, and Latacunga, alongside a member of the Inca elite of Quito). They were dictated between 1560 and 1606, just a few decades after the foundation of the city of Quito (December 1533). These testaments thus cover a crucial period for analyzing the early stages of colonization.[10]

A one-to-one comparison of testaments permits identification of the respective traits of female and male power, teasing out singular features in the female exercise of authority, which could not otherwise be fully achieved through a uniquely female series of texts. The testators of the combined testaments include four couples. The side-by-side examination of their wills adds an extra dimension. It provides information on their relationship in the light of pre-Hispanic or colonial traditions, and clarifies the intergender power relations operating in each period. These parallel texts clarify each other. This methodology helps us to shed light on the female voice in gender terms.[11]

The narrative of one of the earliest Spanish observers offers a striking male interpretation of indigenous female power and demonstrates how European male discourse produced coded images of women. In 1531, the chronicler Diego de Trujillo was part of a small group of conquerors led by Francisco Pizarro, who advanced along the Ecuadorian coast towards Cajamarca. Trujillo blithely described a "lady" who headed an indigenous community in the Manabí region as a "rich widow."[12] We should add that under Spanish law and custom, women were generally subordinate to their fathers and, after marriage, to their husbands. As widows, however, women had less familial restrictions, though, if a widowed woman did not have the economic means by which to support herself, she was forced to depend on the economic support of her family and remain under its authority. In contrast, a widow from a wealthy family retrieved the management of the dowry that her father had transferred to her husband at marriage at the time of her husband's death. It is uniquely in these circumstances that a woman holds a legal status according her both autonomy and power. And this is what colors the perception of a Spanish chronicler about a woman who, with no male counterpart, wields authority over an ethnic group. We should not therefore believe the image conveyed by this comment about a high-ranking woman who is wrongly believed to have inherited this power from her deceased husband, in the manner of a queen regent in Europe. A male Spaniard of this period does not have the conceptual framework that allows him to envisage a female ethnic leader, apparently independent of any known past or present male authority. Yet this is precisely the case of this female ruler on the Pacific coast.[13]

IN SEARCH OF THE PUBLIC VOICE

Notarial acts, in the presence of a figure who assures its legality, reproduce the public voice of an individual before witnesses. When a testament is created, it is dictated and the oral discourse is registered, sometimes following translation from a vernacular language. The voices of all seven male and seven female leaders can be heard in the body of texts I have compiled. We shall explore the expression and content of their voices. Although the traditional Catholic objective is to look after one's soul through a testament, it is clear that both male and female ethnic leaders from the earliest colonial period structure this legal document towards a different goal. Indeed, they seek to transmit their entire authority through inheritance to one or more heirs chosen for that purpose, transferring their power to others and making associated bequests of symbolic objects, labor, property, goods, lands, and other natural resources. For ethnic leaders, it is imperative to adapt the form of dealing with death imposed by the colonizers to their own advantage. Only in that way can ethnic leaders maintain their place in their local hierarchies, thereby connecting the living and the dead and perpetuating dynastic links. Through adaptation of testaments, they also assure that continuity is recorded by the Andean collective mind, as Susan Ramírez stresses. The Andean conception of community was, ideally, "an authority and his kin who participated in the cult of their ancestors in order to preserve their world."[14]

Let us identify the different formulas that ethnic leaders used to express their authority. We should not be misled by the formal expressions inherent in any testament: by its very nature, it records the exercise of individual authority to dispose freely of goods and rights. Consequently, all testators—male and female, rich and poor, and irrespective of their social status—announce *quiero y es mi voluntad* (I desire and it is my will), *mando* (I order), and/or *quiero que se cumpla porque así es mi voluntad* (I desire that it be fulfilled because it is my will). But the documents that concern us here transmit the imperative character of their discourse through details that justify the possession of political authority and the voice that reflects it. In 1560, doña Juana Faringuango affirms her own public voice of authority by saying *que sirva como lo digo yo* (he is to work as I myself say), referring to the work of a servant whom she has willed to her granddaughter. Both males and females present themselves as ethnic leaders.[15] The 1580 testament of doña Francisca Sina Sigchí even makes a bold claim rarely encountered in notarial records. In the absence of a better legal recourse, she dictates a testament, which is not a response to the urgency of her imminent death (as she makes clear in the text). Instead, it is an inventory of her rights as ruler, with its associated goods and prerogatives, which she feels obliged to defend against incessant usurpations by her cacique husband. It is an act of vindication, and all the witnesses she chooses are Spaniards because it is henceforth colonial law that is the guarantor of the new order. Doña Francisca's intentions are clear in this act, which is a public proclamation of her authority as a ruler, using language that is altogether exceptional for archival documentation. She declares that she is "not ill and suffers from no pains" and that she wants to make a "statement" (*exclamación*) "so that [her] heirs and successors are protected and have their rights respected."[16] Thus, she seeks to protect her own lineage vis-à-vis that of her husband.

These male and female leaders designate themselves using the equivalent and symmetrical Spanish terms of *señor/señora* (supreme lord/lady), cacique/cacica (lord/lady), *principal/principala* (secondary lord/lady). Similarly, I have demonstrated that the Otavalo ethnic group uses the title *ango* (title of political authority) indiscriminately for both male and female leaders.[17] Testaments are drawn up in the first person, and males and females introduced themselves by specifying their links to the most prestigious lines. That is, the relationships that defined their places in the hierarchy of power, both at that time and for eternity, as they will maintain their position as *mallquis* (dead ancestors). In 1560, doña Juana Faringuango identifies herself as "señora, cacica, and *mother* of don Alonso Otavalango, señor of this land." In 1569, the cacique don Hernando Pillas Ynla referred to himself as "*brother* of don Luis Ango, my cacique and principal governor."[18]

The authority of a leader is described in the same terms for both sexes with regard to their power over others. In their testaments, these men and women made bequests to their servants (variously referred to as *criados, servicios,* and *yanaconas*) and native subjects. These terms referred to the different modes of domination from which the leaders benefited and which underwrote their political power. That domination may have been rights over persons and their labor, personal in nature, through their obligation to work the land, or over members of a subjugated ethnic group. The ethnic group perceived their lords, men or women, as such authority.[19] In effect, doña Juana Faringuango uses the alien form of the colonial testament to settle "an Indian matter" between representatives of the indigenous elite in power. She was clearly not demanding the application of Spanish law but the protection of the preeminent ethnic leader against a likely future interference by other leaders against her heir. Her only witnesses are the two principal leaders of the ethnic group.[20] A female leader's authority within the ethnic group is recognized by both her subjects and peers.

Doña Francisca Sina Sigchí was a particularly active and independent cacica. As corroborated by the testament of her husband (who was the principal cacique), she exercised her role as an authority figure by settling conflicts among her native subjects. After a group had fled from the lands to which she had assigned them, she went after them and persuaded them to return. This gives us an example of a defining characteristic of cacical power: "I declare that I acquired the Angaraes Indians, promising them lands and dwellings for their sustenance and I brought them from Cotocolla and they fled from me. I went in person to Hambato to get them and brought them from Hambato and imposed my will on them and thus I gave them lands of mine in the orchards of Mulinbilí."[21]

Male and female caciques also expressed their authority through their diplomatic role in relations and negotiations among the ethnic leaders of other groups and the Spaniards. The symbolic objects that are associated with this role (e.g., vessels always given in pairs for libations between leaders and politico-religious rituals) are owned by both men and women and bequeathed as symbols of power to those who inherit their position. For example, doña Catalina Faringo Ango belonged to the female lineage of the principal leader Otavalango Ango. She passed down vessels that played an essential role in interethnic diplomatic rituals in the Cuzco tradition: "I bequeath to my son another pair of silver *mates* [bowls] and also a pair of silver *aquillas* [goblets], I bequeath them to my said son because they are from his mother."[22] This full-scale involvement of female leaders in diplomacy and the handling of conflicts is confirmed by a detail in the chronicler Cieza de León's account of the civil wars in the Quito and Otavalo regions. In 1546 in Otavalo, doña Juana Faringuango warned the viceroy Blasco Núñez of the presence in

Quito of the rebel Gonzalo Pizarro and his faction.[23] This major ethnic leader likely sided against the rebel faction in order to break free of the domination of her *encomendero* (male holder of a royal grant of indigenous tribute), Pedro de Puelles, Gonzalo Pizarro's second-in-command. Thus, she demonstrates a power to intervene politically at a high level. This is corroborated by the fact that in her testament she does not refer to a husband, not even to the father of her son, the paramount lord. In this autobiographical text she clearly showed her authority as an independent woman.

Male and female leaders possessed and transmitted valuables that were symbols of power in equivalent ways. Particular items of clothing of exquisite quality and body decoration (for example, *collarejos de chaquira de la tierra* [necklaces]) were passed on to the next person to hold the title regardless of gender, and their symbolic role and content has been the subject of a number of studies.[24] It is noteworthy that objects with a religious dimension, such as "mirrors of the Indians," probably used in divinatory practices, and drums for ritual celebrations, were owned by both male and female leaders. This suggests that a shamanic role was one of the attributes of the ethnic leader, irrespective of their gender.[25]

It would appear, then, that male and female ethnic leaders affirmed their public voice and exercised an authority acknowledged by both their peers and subjects, both in the same way and with the same perceived importance. Nevertheless, a closer analysis of the bequeathed attributes of power shows that there was sexual differentiation in some areas. Only male ethnic leaders bequeathed spears, launchers, and trumpets, that is, warrior paraphernalia.[26] On the other hand, female cacicas in the northern Andes bequeathed specific types of shells and precious stones associated with fertility. Doña Juana Faringuango bequeathed an item of exceptional value in Andean culture: a large shell plated in gold. (See fig. 6.1.) Semantically, this object belongs to the same field as "the wealth of women [and] female fertility."[27] Doña Juana also bequeathed a necklace of unidentified 'green beads', using the expression *una chaquera de berde*. They may have been emeralds or other green gemstones that were highly prized among indigenous cultures, whose symbolism has only been partly deciphered.[28] By fusing marine shells with gold, thereby endowing a raw material of little intrinsic value with sacred meaning, the fashioned gold objects become symbols of authority and prestige that accompany male and female ethnic leaders in their burials.[29]

Fertility proves to have been the domain of female leaders, while warfare was that of male leaders. As ethnic authorities, both male and female leaders

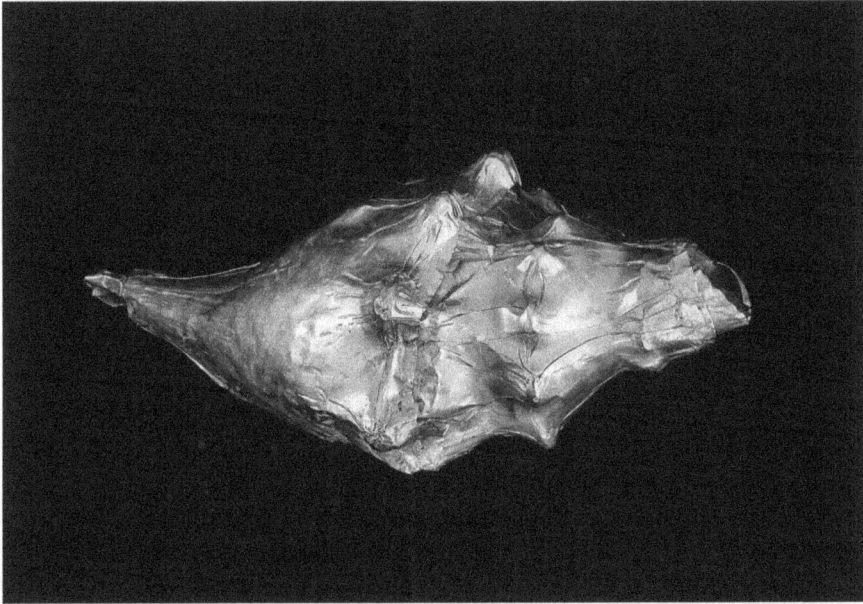

Fig. 6.1. A marine shell covered in gold from the Cauca Valley (Colombia), measuring 5.8 by 11.8 in. (14.8 by 30 cm). (Banco de la República, Colección del Museo del Oro, Pieza 003316. Bogotá, Colombia. Photo by Rudolf Schrimpff.)

controlled these fields essential for the survival of a group. The leaders were responsible for the appropriate rituals, while the balance between the sexes permitted the reproduction of the cosmic order. This gendered division was active at ideological and practical levels in the organization of kinship ties: male ethnic leaders were polygamous but female leaders counterbalanced male power through their control of matrimonial alliances. In the following discussion I argue that male ethnic leaders reached their position of authority via a necessary dependence on the female branch of the lineage.

The polygamy of ethnic leaders of the northern Andes has been carefully analyzed for the "Incaized" valley of Chillos, a prosperous enclave close to Quito that provided the ethnic lord with great wealth as the beneficiary of the artisanal and agricultural work of a large household. The same picture emerges for ethnic groups that were never, or only briefly, under Inca control, which leads me to view it as a pre-Inca native tradition.[30]

The testaments of the Otavalo ethnic group refer to family units in Spanish terms, classifying children as "natural, legitimate, and bastards." However, this placed children in categories outside the pattern of native marriage alliances: a cacique, a principal wife, and secondary wives. Only the children of Christian marriages were considered legitimate. Other children, born previously by the same wife or other women, were "natural," while the children of secondary wives born after the Christian marriage were "bastards." Colonial law deprived illegitimate children of their right of succession to the title of cacique. But in texts that referred to precontact practices, it is clear that it was not necessarily the son who was designated to succeed his father—it could be a "nephew" or a "brother."[31] In fact, polygamy seems to have been based on the personal prestige acquired by having an abundant household workforce together with the material prosperity that it helped to generate. But no evidence suggests that political authority was dependent on it.

Matrimonial alliances and family dynamics are problematic to interpret given that native kinship terms have been erroneously transformed into nonequivalent categories in Spanish. Nevertheless, for all the pitfalls, it is evident that the feminine branch played an important role in the mechanisms of succession. Hence, female leaders could, in their testaments, unambiguously favor a female of their lineage, that is, a son's daughter. Thus, doña Francisca Sina Sigchí appears to have "selected" the daughter of her son Tito Hacho, from among her five sons and eight daughters, for the position of ethnic leader of her Angaraes natives, although we do not know her selection criteria (Tito Hacho was in fact the only one of her sons to be favored through inheritance).[32] She designated the future cacica as *nieta* (grandaughter) or *hija* (daughter). It is a similar story with doña Juana Faringuango, who only leaves a bequest to one woman, namely the "daughter of the son" who succeeds to the position of cacique. This female descendant inherits a high-ranked servant who appears to have been a kind of steward.[33] Another illustrative case is that of the Pasto cacica, doña Catalina Tuza, a widow and without issue, who named a cacique who was the husband of her niece as successor.[34]

Male ethnic leaders apparently respected this type of transmission of indigenous political authority. In Panzaleo, don Diego Collín named two *sobrinos* (nephews) who would inherit positions of cacique, and he specified that one of them was his niece's son.[35]

In the two cases cited, where female heirs were named, descent by the same female lineage was indicated by the use of the same indigenous anthroponym (which was often associated with the same baptismal name). Thus, the granddaughter who would become cacica of the Angaraes had exactly the same name as her grandmother: doña Francisca Sina Sigchí. Similarly, doña Juana Faringuango favored her granddaughter, doña Ana Faringuango. [36] The cacicas of Otavalo demonstrated a similar pattern, complicated by the imposition of the Spanish custom of rulership passing from father to son only. The previously mentioned cacica doña Juana Faringuango shared the pre-Hispanic patronym, Faringuango, with doña Catalina Paringuango, a daughter of the supreme leader Otavalango. The latter shared a Christian name and pre-Hispanic anthroponym with the wife of his son.

This son of doña Catalina Paringuango was the "grandson" of the cacique Otavalango (according to the western kinship system), but the young cacique seems to have been excluded from the succession because, according to Spanish law, rulership did not transfer through daughters. But from 1563, at the age of 14, don Alonso Anrrafernango Puento Maldonado contested the appointment of a son of Otavalango and, on behalf of his mother, doña Catalina Paringuango, claimed the position of paramount leader, which he said was his by virtue of being the son of Otavalango's daughter. It was only towards the end of his life that don Alonso achieved his ambition to become "cacique and governor of the Otavalo *repartimiento* [indigenous labor draft]."[37]

Does this suggest a possible model of matrilineal filiation, which is well documented in neighboring pre-Hispanic Colombian territory? Under the system of avunculism, in which the nephew succeeds his maternal uncle, this nephew was the son of the oldest sister of the cacique, and in turn he transmitted the position to a nephew, son of the oldest of his sisters.[38] In the case of Otavalango's succession, the sons who succeed him consecutively, following Spanish law, were the sons of a cacica of Axangue, from the Pillaxos ethnic group living in hot lands. However, it is possible that their mother came from a less prestigious lineage than Otavalango's own daughter who would pass on the cacicazgo (office of the cacique, including sometimes its political role, services, and property) to her son, a position that, as we saw, don Alonso Anrrafernango Puento Maldonado himself claimed in accordance with indigenous tradition.[39]

Although we have few well-documented examples of transmission of pre-Hispanic political power, we can draw on numerous lawsuits preserved in the archives relating to the succession to cacicazgos, which drag on from one generation to another throughout the colonial period. From the sixteenth century onwards, we encounter men drawing on Spanish law to usurp power against the claims of the women insisting on the legitimacy of the female lines according to traditional norms.[40]

In the northern Andes, male power was reached through female lines, which played a decisive genealogical role in succession. Male principal leaders obtained their position through either their mother or their paternal aunt, which could point to a female route to power through the alternating succession of women belonging to maternal but also paternal lines. This led to rivalries between the female lines, whose deep-rooted character, which sprung from the intrinsic nature of pre-Hispanic political dynamics, was reflected in subsequent colonial litigation. It is in this context that we can appreciate why the cacica doña Francisca Sina Sigchí left bequests to two of the natural and bastard sons of her husband (apparently, he had nine). She designated them as *entenados* (step-sons). No doubt the mothers of these two boys were women belonging to doña Francisca's lineage or classified symbolically as such.[41]

Other scenarios of succession, poorly understood by the Spaniards, appear to reflect the situational kinship that Ramírez suggests, taking account of similar processes in Africa: to inherit a position is also to inherit its accompanying kinship status. Thus, a "nephew" may occupy a higher place hierarchically than an older relative once he himself has become an "uncle."[42] We have seen an example of this in the Pasto cacica doña Catalina Tuza, who bequeathed her position of cacique to the husband of her *sobrina* (niece), but repeatedly referred to him as her *suegro* (father-in-law).[43]

Symbolic kinship terms were tied to hierarchical relations following proximity to the person holding authority, with the Inca at the head of this pyramid. The only legitimate sons were those that the lord had with his sister, in a system of maximum endogamy where the relationship between spouses represented the closest one possible. A documented example of this is the couple formed by siblings doña Francisca Sina Sigchí and don Sancho Hato (that is, *hermano / a carnal de padre y madre* [sibling / of the carnal relationship of father and mother]), a union that had been celebrated according to Inca usage.[44] Similarly, the case of doña Juana Faringuango, Otavalango's mother, obeys a comparable logic because the Spanish term that she employed in her testament, linking her heir to the lord as his filial protégé, is manifestly translated from Quechua. This important cacica employs an originally Quechua expression *huaccha*, which refers to the Andean notion of an orphan who is poor by virtue of being deprived of family support and solidarity and, consequently, needs protection from the lord. Directly translating this Quechua term into Spanish, she designates her "son" (probably grandson) as *pobre y servicio* (poor and in service) of the current supreme ethnic leader, don Luis Ango, Otavalango's son and successor, and hence insists on his allegiance to him. And she asks this lord to ensure that this descendant, whom she favors, will not be defrauded by other caciques.[45]

These links between male and female lords, firmly based on their power as rulers, conveys a picture of balanced and interlinked gender relations, both in the exercise of their authority and in the transmission of their titles. Susan Kellogg coined the expression "parallel and equivalent" in reference to male and female Mexica ethnic leaders. Here, I would concur with Karen Powers's nuance for the northern Andes, characterizing their power as "parallel and complementary."[46]

COLONIZATION AND THE EROSION OF FEMALE POLITICAL POWER

If we compare the features defined here as characteristic of female political authority with the evolution that can be observed in later documentation, we can see the logical ways in which Spanish culture took root. Colonization opened a divide between male and female leaders on the sole basis of gender. Even the most powerful women were subject to men. Doña Catalina Tuza accepted this innovation by recognizing that, according to Spanish law, the male is the heir to effective and symbolic power.[47]

Testaments are especially revealing about the fields of Christianization (and the framework they provided for managing the hereafter) and Westernization (through bequests that provide information about material culture). This type of historical source contains indicators that signpost the divergences by gender in the adoption, whether accepted or imposed, of the rules of colonial life. Henceforth women, irrespective of their social position, were obliged to define themselves in relation to the other gender, as wives or widows, as though they were lifelong minors. Similarly, they had to accept their loss of legal independence.[48] One observation—elicited from the presence of couples in the selected documentation—raises a highly significant point: while in 1560 none of the leading male or female lords (whether testators or witnesses) possessed the foreign skill of writing, over the course of the following years nascent literacy (promoted through schools for the native elite) was exclusively reserved for males.[49] No cacica knew how to sign their testaments, while male caciques learned to do so by 1580. Female leaders had to "entreat" a man to do it on their behalf.[50] Women were therefore excluded from the vital new instrument of self-affirmation. Oral communication became merely a secondary and partial means to express authority, which was henceforth displaced by writing—an exclusively male terrain among both the Spanish colonial and native elites.

Colonization likewise displaced the symbolic charge of the objects that functioned as emblems of authority. The Spanish *vara de alcalde* (staff of office) was only attributed to a man, reinforcing a leading male cacique's power.[51] On the other hand, the indigenous jewelry transmitted by male and female ethnic leaders to their successors of either sex was stripped of its significance. The testaments show that female ethnic leaders now bequeathed them only to their female descendants, and so they acquired the status of valuable, but humdrum, women's jewelry. They became part of the goods specifically reserved for women in the domestic sphere, such as hand looms, jars to make chicha, and grinding stones.[52]

In elite colonial society, cacicas (like wealthy Spanish women) were legally subject to their spouses. Western norms of sexual behavior and gender relations were likewise imposed.[53] Some rare documentation provides clues as to sexuality and the manifestation of Old World patriarchy in native society. In 1577, for example, an indigenous man recorded before a notary that he forgave his wife and the cacique who were guilty of adultery. The document referred to an earlier notarial document that the wife did not seem to have followed. Consequently, the new act, which included clauses in the *perdón* (pardon), required that the wife did not travel without her husband's explicit permission.[54]

The portrait of a cacica of Otavalo "of ill repute" emerges through several contemporary testimonies. This cacica doña Ana Ango Quilago, high-status daughter of the cacique of Saranze, don García Anrrango ("no hera yndia que servía a nadie por ser hija de cacique" [she was a native women who served no one because she was the daughter of the cacique]), who was then in Quito, sought to escape from the hold of the powerful encomendero of Otavalo and return home to Otavalo. The witnesses follow the dominant discourse of the encomendero and hence the description of her as *destrayda e desasogada* (uncontrolled and free), a woman of reprehensible sexuality.[55] Among the accusations made by the Spaniards (the encomendero and witnesses on his behalf), the indigenous husband, and an important native cacica were that doña Ana was living as a concubine. But if her father, the cacique, defends her denouncing the ill treatment to which she was subjected by her husband's parents, the voice of this woman has come down to us as a woman who took the initiative of rebelling and then fleeing with her husband.[56] Both Spanish and indigenous witnesses recorded insults to male honor, for which women held prime responsibility. And it was a cacique who had drawn defamatory graffiti, using charcoal on the white wall of the chapel in Otavalo, denouncing the cuckolding of the husband.[57] Public notoriety was an aggravating factor in the offense committed, which explains, as Natalie Zemon Davis reminds us, why the murder of an adulterous wife by a husband was considered "excusable homicide" in the courts of law and public opinion.[58]

Restrictions on the freedom of movement of the wife appear to be the highest priority for a deceived husband. Can we detect, through this aspiration, any behavioral traits of the female indigenous elite? While acknowledging that we lack documentary sources on pre-Hispanic patterns of sexuality and its place in gender relations, it is striking that doña Francisca Sina Sigchi's action against her husband's abuse of power demonstrates that she has taken the initiative to track down her fugitive subjects and therefore enjoys freedom of movement without any interference from her husband.[59]

Freedom of movement, decision making, and assertion of the right to give orders were inseparable from the exercise of authority. In this respect, it is possible that female independence was uniquely a cacical privilege and that the lot of nonelite women was far less favorable, involving submission to native men. Furthermore, the litigation cited above underlines the intent of female leaders to continue exercising their role and traditional power in parallel to male political power. This demonstrates the strength and durability of female lines that at least survived as the ideal model of family organization in the face of the imposition of a kinship system that dispossessed them of their share of power and "silenced" them.

Can we also hypothesize a concomitant displacement of the authority of these female lines into the religious domain of Christian practice? In their testaments, both male and female ethnic leaders adopted colonial norms in equal measure: they made legacies to the church, ordered numerous masses, and founded capellanías (perpetual loans to a chapel), which reinforced the power of their male descendants.[60] Nevertheless, an analysis of an oft-overlooked source, the archives of native cofradías (confraternities, Catholic lay organizations) demonstrates a significantly higher proportion of female participation in confraternity activities in data from the early seventeenth century. For example, the proportion of female penitents exceeds that of

males in each of the *ayllus* (local kinship groups) of the exclusively indigenous confraternity of San Juan in Otavalo. In all, 165 females participated as
opposed to 118 men (58 percent of total membership). However, this balance
does not appear to match the breakdown of membership by sex in confraternities in Spain, which were dominated by male members.[61] Moreover, many
historical references suggest that some native women held a preeminent role
(perhaps as colonial cacicas) by virtue of their positions as *fundadoras*
(founders) who directed worship in the confraternity, kept in their homes
the saints' statues, clothes, ornaments, and banners used for the processions.
This illustrious title could be inherited by a son (*fundador*) or by a daughter
(fundadora), within a completely indigenous sphere of religious organization.
This appears to draw on the idea of the "founding ancestor" (male or female)—a
fundamental concept that linked a population to a territory sacralized by a
pre-Hispanic ancestor and his or her burial place.[62]

Should we see in these features a testimony to the importance of the female role in directing the sacred sphere? Spiritual leadership was a role that
cacicas had previously shared on an equal footing with male leaders, but did
they manage to preserve it under Spanish domination? Or does this evidence
indicate instead that female leaders made up for their loss of political power
by participating in the control—not least economic—of the confraternities,
a colonial system open to native women? It is important to note that the confraternities owned abundant lands and herds of animals, which made them
important centers of economic activity.

CONCLUSIONS

In this chapter, I examine a corpus of documents featuring the same number
of testaments drawn up by male and female leaders and then contrast this
documentation with complementary sources, such as litigation. This comparative approach provides insights into the gender dimension of indigenous
power in the northern Andes. It also provides us with access to the female
voice, which is so often silenced in early Spanish accounts not to mention the
broader historical narrative.

Gender roles can be seen as "equal and complementary," in so far as leaders, both women and men, counted on exactly the same authority, a representative role and acquiescence from their subjects. Their public voice was
recognized, and they held the same attributes of power. Only two areas of
power were gender specific: women leaders controlled fertility in its symbolic

and ritual aspects, while men were responsible for waging of war. This complementarity was also seen in their equivalent roles in patterns of succession: male polygamy conferred prestige and economic power on the lords, while the female role in the choice of female and male successors came from the involvement of female lines in providing the lords with several spouses. In this way, female lines shared control of the offspring and played an active role in dynastic strategies.

In contrast to the dominant European narrative of the contact period, a sharply different picture emerges of colonial intervention radically transforming the respective roles of female and male indigenous leaders over the early decades of colonial rule. The complete submission of women to men, occasionally mitigated by astute strategies, involved their exclusion from political power over succession and was manifested in the redistribution and reclassification of their former symbolic attributes of power. Even their freedom of movement was reinterpreted as reprehensible, licentious behavior in the colonial mindset.

Female ethnic leaders were excluded from the new colonial rituals of power, which reflected the transition from the authority of the publicly spoken word to that of the written record. Women's active participation in Catholic confraternities may have been an adaptive strategy to retain control of the religious sphere even while their public authority was otherwise being expunged.

NOTES

1. Michelle Perrot, *Les femmes ou les silences de l'Histoire* (Paris: Flammarion, 1998); Michelle Perrot, "Faire l'histoire des femmes: bilan d'une expérience" in *Masculin—Féminin: questions pour les sciences de l'homme*, ed. Jacqueline Laufer, Catherine Marry, and Margarat Maruani (Paris: Presses Universitaires de France, 2001), 229–44; and Michelle Perrot, "L'histoire ouverte," *Critique* 843–44, no. 8 (2017).

2. Mary Beard, "The Public Voice of Women," in *Women and Power: A Manifesto* (New York: Liveright, 2017).

3. Beard, "Public Voice of Women."

4. Santiago Uceda Castillo, curator, "Le Pérou avant les Incas" (exhibition, Musée du quai Branly-Jacques Chirac, Paris, 2017–18).

5. Martin de la Soudière, "Les testaments et actes de dernière volonté à la fin du Moyen Âge," *Ethnologie Française* 5 (1975); Philippe Ariès, *L'homme devant la mort* (Paris: Seuil, 1977); Bartolomé Bennassar, "Los inventarios post-mortem y la historia de las mentalidades," in *La documentación notarial y la historia*, ed. Antonio Eiras Roel (Santiago: University of Santiago de Compostela, 1984); Agustín Rubio Semper, "Piedad, honras fúnebres y legados piadosos en Aragón (Calatayud) en la Baja Edad

Media," in *Muerte, religiosidad y cutura popular: siglos XIII–XVIII*, ed. Eliseo Serrano Martín (Zaragoza: Instituto Fernando El Católico, 1994); and Carlos M. N. Eire, *From Madrid to Purgatory: The Art and Craft of Dying in Sixteenth-Century Spain* (Cambridge: Cambridge University Press, 1995).

6. William D. Phillips Jr, "Testaments in the Spanish World in the Early Modern Period," in *Historia del derecho privado*, ed. M. J. Peláez (Barcelona: Promociones Publicaciones Universitarias, 1989).

7. Sarah L. Cline, *Colonial Culhuacan, 1580–1600: A Social History of an Aztec Town* (Albuquerque: University of New Mexico Press, 1986); Frank Salomon, "Indian Women of Early Colonial Quito as Seen through Their Testaments," *Americas* 44, no. 3 (1988); Matthew Restall, *Life and Death in a Maya Community: The Ixil Testaments of the 1760s* (Lancaster: Labyrinthos, 1995); Nadine Béligand, "De la forme au contenu. Propriété et parenté indiennes à travers les testaments nahua de la vallée de Toluca à l'époque coloniale," in *Des Indes Occidentales à l'Amérique Latine. A Jean-Pierre Berthe*, ed. Alain Musset and Thomas Calvo (Paris: ENS/Fontenay-Saint Cloud, 1997); Stephanie Wood, "Matters of Life and Death: Nahuatl Testaments of Rural Women, 1589–1801," in *Indian Women of Early Mexico*, ed. Susan Schroeder, Stephanie Wood, and Robert Haskett (Norman: University of Oklahoma Press, 1997); Susan Kellogg and Matthew Restall, eds., *Dead Giveaways: Indigenous Testaments in Colonial Spanish America* (Salt Lake City: University of Utah, 1998); and Mark Christensen and Jonathan Truitt, eds., *Native Wills from the Colonial Americas* (Salt Lake City: University of Utah Press, 2015).

8. María Rostworowski de Díez Canseco, *Curacas y sucesiones. Costa norte* (Lima: Minerva, 1961); María Rostworowski de Díez Canseco, *Etnia y sociedad: Costa peruana prehispánica* (Lima: Instituto de Estudios Peruanos, 1977); Udo Oberem "Don Sancho Hacho, ein 'cacique mayor' des 16 Jahrhunderts," *Jahrbuch für Geschichte von Staat, Wirtschaft und Gesellschaft Lateinamerikas* 4, no. 1 (1967); Ronald Spores, "Mixteca *Cacicas*: Status, Wealth, and the Political Accommodation of native Elite Women in Early Colonial Oaxaca," in *Indian Women of Early Mexico*, ed. Susan Schroeder, Stephanie Wood, and Robert Haskett (Norman: University of Oklahoma Press, 1997); Chantal Caillavet, "Ethnohistoire équatorienne: un testament indien inédit du XVIè siècle," *Caravelle* 41 (1983); Susan E. Ramírez, "Rich Man, Poor Man, Beggar Man, or Chief: Material Wealth as a Basis of Power in Sixteenth-Century Peru," in Kellogg and Restall, *Dead Giveaways*.

9. Chantal Caillavet, "Caciques de Otavalo en el siglo XVI: Don Alonso Maldonado y su esposa," *Miscelánea Antropológica* 2 (1982); Susan Kellogg, "From Parallel and Equivalent to Separate but Unequal: Tenochca Mexica Women, 1500–1700," in *Indian Women of Early Mexico*, eds. Susan Schroeder, Stephanie Wood, and Robert Haskett (Norman: University of Oklahoma Press, 1997); and Susan Kellogg, "Indigenous Testaments of Early-Colonial Mexico City: Testifying to Gender Differences," in Kellogg and Restall, *Dead Giveaways*.

10. Chantal Caillavet, "Masculin-Féminin: les modalités du pouvoir politique des seigneurs et souveraines ethniques (Andes, XV–XVIe siècle)" in *Les autorités indigènes entre deux mondes*, ed. Bernard Lavallé (Paris: Sorbonne Nouvelle, 2004).

11. For a full list of this documentation, see Caillavet, "Masculin-Féminin," 87–89.

12. "Pasó adelante a un pueblo en la mesma provincia de Puerto Viejo que era señora de él una viuda rica" (he passed on to a town in the same province of Puerto Viejo, which was ruled by a wealthy widow), in Diego de Trujillo, *Una relación inédita de la conquista: la crónica de Diego de Trujillo*, ed. Raúl Porras Barrenechea (Lima: Universidad Nacional Mayor de San Marcos, 1970), 45.

13. For other examples, see Rostworowski, *Curacas y sucesiones*, and Caillavet, "Masculin-Féminin."

14. Susan Ramírez, *To Feed and Be Fed: The Cosmological Bases of Authority and Identity in the Andes* (Stanford: Stanford University Press: 2005), 224–25.

15. Saying *como tal señora* (as a lady) and *como tal señor* (as a lord). See the testament of doña Juana Faringuango, 1560, in Chantal Caillavet, "'Como caçica y señora desta tierra mando . . .'. Insignias, funciones y poderes de las soberanas del norte andino (siglos XV–XVI)," *Bulletin de l'Institut Français d'Etudes Andines* 37, no. 1 (2008): 59; Udo Oberem, "Testamentos de Doña Francisca Sina Sigchi y de Don Sancho Hacho de Velasco," *Boletín del Archivo Nacional de Historia* 16 (1966), 1580 and 1587, respectively; and the testament of Don Diego Collín, 1598, in Caillavet, "Ethnohistoire équatorienne," 5–23. The testaments of Doña Sina Sigchí and her husband are from the private archives of the historian Carlos Manuel Larrea, which he donated to the collection of the national Ecuadorian Archives, the Archivo Nacional de Historia in Quito (hereafter cited as ANH/Q) and published in their *Boletín* the same year (1966). I was unable to locate these valuable documents in the ANH/Q, and have therefore followed Larrea's transcriptions.

16. Oberem, "Testamentos de Doña Francisca," 13.

17. Caillavet, "Masculin-Féminin," 47.

18. Emphasis added. Caillavet, "Como caçica," 79. Archivo del Instituto Otavaleño de Antropología, Otavalo. 1a Notaría, Paquete especial, Varios Años, Caja 1b, Document 2, and also ANH/Q, Tierras 13, Document 1689, vol. 3, 18, fol. 18v.

19. John V. Murra, "Nueva información sobre las poblaciones yana" in *Formaciones económicas y políticas del mundo andino* (Lima: Instituto de Estudios Peruanos, 1975), 225–41; María Rostworowski de Díez Canseco, "La estratificación social y el Hatun Curaca en el mundo andino," *Histórica* 1, no. 2 (1977); Frank Salomon, *Native Lords of Quito in the Age of the Incas* (New York: Cambridge University Press, 1986); Susan E. Ramírez, "The 'Dueño de Indios': Thoughts on the Consequences of the Shifting Bases of Power of the 'Curaca de los Viejos Antiguos' under the Spanish in Sixteenth-Century Peru," *Hispanic American Historical Review* 67, no. 4 (November 1987); Ramírez, "Rich Man, Poor Man"; Ramírez, *To Feed*; and Juan Villamarín, "Chiefdoms: The Prevalence and Persistence of 'señoríos naturales,' 1400 to European Conquest," in *The Cambridge History of the Native Peoples of the Americas*, vol. 3, ed. Frank Salomon and Stuart Schwartz (Cambridge: Cambridge University Press, 1999).

20. Caillavet, "Como caçica," 19.

21. Oberem, "Testamentos de Doña Francisca," 14, 18.

22. Caillavet, "Ethnohistoire équatorienne"; and Caillavet, "Caciques de Otavalo," 49, fol. 69r, 54, n12.

23. Pedro de Cieza de León, *Las guerras civiles del Perú*, vol. 2 of *Obras completas*, ed. Carmelo Sáenz de Santa María (Madrid: Consejo Superior de Investigaciones Científicas/Instituto Gonzalo Fernández de Oviedo, 1984–1985), 495.

24. To cite only those concerning the northern Andes, Salomon, *Native Lords*; Caillavet, "Caciques de Otavalo"; Caillavet, "Ethnohistoire équatorienne"; Caillavet, "Como caçica"; and Warwick Bray, "Emblems of Power in the Chiefdoms of the New World," in *Circa 1492: Art in the Age of Exploration*, ed. J. A. Levenson (Washington: National Gallery of Art, 1991).

25. Frank Salomon, "Shamanism and politics in late-colonial Ecuador," *American Ethnologist* 10, no. 3 (1983); Ramírez, *To Feed*, 135–37; and Caillavet, "Como caçica," 68–69, n24–n25 for the archaeological references to these objects. In our corpus, two cacicas bequeath "mirrors" to their heirs: doña Juana Faringuango of the Otavalo ethnic group in 1560 (Caillavet, "Como caçica," 80) and doña Luisa Tota (Otavalo) in 1596 (Cristóbal Landázuri, *Los curacazgos pastos prehispánicos: agricultura y comercio, siglo XVI* [Quito: Instituto Otavaleño de Antropología/Banco Central del Ecuador, 1995], 189). The caciques of Panzaleo and Otavalo each bequeath two ceremonial drums, and the Pasto cacica bequeaths one that seems to be covered in "jewels" and other precious adornments: "un tambor de madera con todas alhajas" (a wooden drum with all the jewels), don Diego Collín in Caillavet, "Ethnohistoire équatorienne," 19; don Alonso Maldonado in Caillavet, "Caciques de Otavalo," 48; and doña Catalina Tuza in Landázuri, *Curacazgos pastos prehispánicos*, 214.

26. Don Hernando Pilas Ynla in ANH/Q, Tierras 13, Document 1689, vol. 3, 18, fol. 16v: *lanzas de la tierra* (regional-style spears). Don Diego Collín (1598) in Caillavet, "Ethnohistoire équatorienne," 16: "tengo 2 chambachuques como es costumbre tener los caciques señores" (I have 2 spears as is customary for the supreme caciques to have), and "estólicas con sus varas" (spearthrower with its spears). Don Alonso Maldonado in Caillavet, "Caciques de Otavalo," 48: "trompetas viejas" (old trumpets).

27. Thanks to archaeological evidence we can identify this as *Lobatus gigas* (formerly known as *Strombus gigas*) a marine shell; it appears as a specifically female item in southern Colombia where it is associated with the burials of women and newborn babies. In present-day ethnic groups in Colombia, women wear this shell and the necklaces from which beads are taken. For a more detailed analysis, see Caillavet, "Como caçica," 65–77. On the archaeology of the Cauca valley and ethnographic references on the Kogi groups of the Sierra de Santa Marta and on the Uwas of the Amazonian region, see Marianne Cardale de Schrimpff, Leonor Herrera, Carlos Armando Rodríguez, and Yolanda Jaramillo, "Rito y Ceremonia en Malagana (Corregimiento de El Bolo, Palmira, Valle del Cauca)," *Boletín de Arqueología* 14, no. 3 (September 1999): 52.

28. As well as emeralds, greenstones such as jade, green obsidian, and *lidita* (radiolarite) have also been found in archaeological contexts, the latter being associated with female statuettes in burials. See Cardale et al., "Rito y Ceremonia," 48–52, for the Cauca valley.

29. Bray, "Emblems of Power," 535–37.

30. Salomon, *Native Lords*, 129–31. The Spanish *visitador* (inspector) of the Quixo ethnic group in the Amazonian foothills refers to the ethnic leaders' polygamy using a catching metaphor: "duermen entre ellas como gallos entre gallinas" (they slept among women like roosters among hens). Udo Oberem, "Diego de Ortegóns Beischreibung der 'Gobernación de los Quijos, Zumaco y la Canela.' Ein Ethnographischer Bericht aus dem Jahre 1577," *Zeitschrift für Ethnologie* 83 (1958): 236.

31. Salomon, *Native Lords*, 133–34. Rostworowski, "La estratificación social," 262–65.

32. Oberem, "Testamentos de Doña Francisca," 14.

33. "Mando para la hija [sic] Diego Anrrango doña Ana Farenguango un yndio mi servicio llamado Rodrigo Faremba que sirba y mire" (I bequeath to the daughter of [sic] Diego Anrrango, doña Ana Farenguango, my Indian servant called Rodrigo Faremba so that he serves her and checks for her) in Caillavet, "Como caçica," 79.

34. "Mando a doña Esperanza mi sobrina mujer de don Pedro Cellín una tierra ... declaro y mando por sucesor mío a don Pedro Cellín porque no tengo otro heredero legitimo para poder gobernar a los yndios mando que sea mi principal y gobernador de estos cuarenta y cuatro indios tributarios" (I bequeath to doña Esperanza, my niece and wife of don Pedro Cellín, a piece of land ... I declare and command don Pedro Cellín as my successor because I have no other legitimate heir with the power to govern the Yndios. I command him to be my principal and governor of these forty-four tributary Indians), in Cristóbal Landázuri, *Curacazgos pastos prehispánicos*, 213–14.

35. "Don Miguel Saltacasic Zumba mi sobrino hijo de doña Ysabel Casachiní mi sobrina, conforme al horden natural de esta tierra" (Don Miguel Saltacasic Zumba my nephew, son of doña Ysabel Casachiní my niece, in accordance with the natural law of this country), in Caillavet, "Ethnohistoire équatorienne," 21.

36. The Spaniards transcribed the same aboriginal phoneme by "p" and "f" indiscriminately.

37. Caillavet, "Caciques de Otavalo," 39.

38. Tomás López Medel, "Tratado de los tres elementos," *Cespedesia* 43–44, no. 9 (1982); and Juan Villamarín, "Kinship and Inheritance among the Sabana de Bogota Chibcha at the time of Spanish Conquest," *Ethnology* 14, no. 2 (1975): 177.

39. See Chantal Caillavet, "Ethnohistoire des communautés indiennes d'Otavalo, Andes de l'Equateur" (PhD diss., University of Bordeaux III, 2009), 630–631 for a testimony of 1578: "Otavalo Ango cacique principal deste repartimiento tuvo por su hijo legitimo en su ley y porque a la sazon no se casaban al dicho don Diego Chalam Puento en la cacica de Asangui" (Otavalo Ango, supreme leader of this ethnic group, had don Diego Chalam Puento as his legitimate son by the cacica of Asangui; this was according to his own law because they were not married at that time).

40. See, for example, a series of court documents from 1540 to 1780 about the right to a cacicazgo in Calpi (Riobamba) where the female branches are represented. These documents are transcribed in "Cacicazgos de los indios Llangarimas," *Boletín del Archivo Nacional de Historia* 10, no. 16 (1966). See also Karen Vieira Powers, "A Battle of Wills: Inventing Chiefly Legitimacy in the Colonial North Andes," in Kellogg and Restall, *Dead Giveaways*.

41. Oberem, "Testamentos de Doña Francisca," 14.

42. Susan E. Ramírez, "Historia y memoria: la construcción de las tradiciones dinásticas andinas," *Revista de Indias* 66, no. 236 (2006): 37, 52–54.

43. Zuidema established this point in his analysis of the complex system of Inca kinship, which was adopted in the northern Andes to a greater or lesser extent according to the degree of Incaization. R. Tom Zuidema, *La civilisation Inca au Cuzco* (Paris: Presses Universitaires de France, 1986); and Landázuri, *Curacazgos pastos prehispánicos*, 213–14.

44. Salomon, *Native Lords*. Zuidema, *Civilization Inca au Cuzco*, 46. "Me casó el Inga por sus leyes" (the Inca decreed my marriage in accordance with his laws), in Oberem, "Testamentos de Doña Francisca," 13, 17.

45. Karen Spalding has analyzed the meaning of this term in "Social Climbers: Changing Patterns of Mobility Among the Indians of Colonial Peru," *Hispanic American Historical Review* 50 (1970): 654. On this point, Zuidema specifies that the original Quechua term *huaccha concha* means "poor nephew" or "orphan nephew" and refers to children that the Inca has procreated by non-Inca women; they likewise hold a place as secondary children, younger sons, and in Spanish terminology they are designated sobrinos. The title pobre y servicio demonstrates kinship ties with the lord, holding the status of "son of a younger brother." Zuidema observes that these secondary children are classified as "sons of a sister," a designation ascribed to the female lines from which they come, and that therefore indicates matrilineal status. Zuidema, *Civilisation Inca au Cuzco*, 36–38, 46–47; Caillavet, "Como caçica," 80; Archivo General de Indias, Seville (hereafter cited as AGI/S), Quito 172, fols. 6r–6v: "Expediente del protector de Indios a Juan de Luján por azotar a un cacique de Tumbaco," in his testament of 1649, the cacique don Francisco Cachoango designated his sons by the terms hijo or sobrino according to the place they occupy in the hierarchy of siblings.

46. Kellogg, "From Parallel and Equivalent"; and Karen Vieira Powers, *Women in the Crucible of Conquest: The Gendered Genesis of Spanish American Society, 1500–1600* (Albuquerque: University of New Mexico Press, 2005), 15–16, 41.

47. Doña Catalina Tuza said, "vayan heredando el dicho patronazgo [de su capilla] excediendo siempre por linea recta el varon a la mujer aunque sea menor de edad" (go on inheriting the patronage [of her chapel] always along the straight line from the man to the woman, even if he is a minor), in Landázuri, *Curacazgos pastos prehispánicos*, 212.

48. The sister of the ethnic lord Otavalango married the son of the Inca Atahualpa. She makes her testament in 1596 and presents herself as "yo doña Beatriz Ango biuda muger que fui de don Francisco Atagualpa" (I, doña Beatriz Ango, widow of Francisco Atagualpa), in ANH/Q, 1a Notaría, vol. 3, fol. 383r. The cacica of Otavalo, who died in 1606 before her husband, declared: "vieren como yo doña Lucía Coxilaguango mujer ligitima de Don Alonso Maldonado gobernador de este repartimiento de Otavalo" (see how I, doña Lucía Coxilaguango, legitimate wife of Don Alonso Maldonado, governor of the Indians of Otavalo), in Caillavet, "Caciques de Otavalo," 51.

49. Powers, *Women in the Crucible*, 44.

50. Testament of doña Juana Faringuango in Caillavet, "Como caçica," 80. Doña Catalina Tuza (1606): "y porque no sé firmar rogué al padre Fray Juan Nuñez . . . que fuese testigo y firmase por mi" (and because I do not know how to sign, I begged fray Juan Nuñez . . . to witness and sign for me), in Landázuri, *Curacazgos pastos prehispánicos*, 215. Doña Lucía Coxilaguango (1606): "por no saber escrevir rogué a Lazaro de la Torre testador que firme por mi" (for, not knowing how to write, I begged Lazaro de la Torre, witness, to sign for me), in Caillavet, "Caciques de Otavalo," 53.

51. Frank Salomon, "Don Pedro de Zámbiza, un varáyuj del siglo XVI," *Cuadernos de historia y arqueología* 42 (1975).

52. In 1611, doña Ana Farinquilunguango bequeathed "un par de topo de plata a mi nuera Beatriz . . . las dos botijas grandes para hazer chicha . . . y telares de los naturales . . . Para mi hermana Juana Cuxilaguango una piedra de moler" (a pair of silver clasps to my daughter-in-law Beatriz . . . and the two big pots to make chicha . . . and the looms of the Indians . . . For my sister Juana Cuxilaguango a grinding stone), in ANH/Q Indígenas, Caja 41, Documento 6, vol. 3/5 (1724), fol. 9v. Bequest of doña Lucía Coxilaguango (1606) of jewelry to her three daughters: "una sarta de chaquira de plata . . . Otra sarta de chaquira de plata mezclada con corales de azul . . . Otra chaquira mezclada de blanco y azul" (a string of silver beads . . . another string of silver beads mixed with blue coral . . . another string of mixed white and blue beads), in Caillavet, "Caciques de Otavalo," 51.

53. Powers, *Women in the Crucible*, 39, 67.

54. "Yo Rodrigo Darcos escribano de Su Magestad doy fe a los señores que la presente vieren como en sierto perdón que ante mi otorgó Francisco Moenango a Juana su mujer e don Diego Guambo de sierto adulterio que avian cometido fue condicion que la dicha Juana no saliese a parte nynguna *sin licencia de su marido* y debaxo esto hizo el dicho perdon" (I Rodrigo Darcos notary of His Majesty declare that the pardon that Francisco Moenango accorded to Juana his wife and don Diego Guambo of the adultery that they had committed was on condition that the said Juana did not go anywhere *without her husband's permission,* and this was a condition of the said pardon; emphasis added), in AGI/S Escribanía de Cámara 922a, 3a Pieza, fol. 124v. This procedure recalls the "letters of pardon" in sixteenth-century France, magisterially studied by Natalie Zemon Davis, that illuminate everyday life and criminal activity, and are of especial interest here in referring to conjugal violence perpetrated by men on women. Natalie Zemon Davis, *Fiction in the Archives: Pardon Tales and their Tellers in Sixteenth-Century France* (Cambridge: Polity Press, 1987), especially chap 3: "Bloodshed and the Woman's Voice."

55. Witnesses described how she, "andaba destrayda e desasogada . . . se avía hechado con un cacique de Guaycan llamado Don Pedro . . . y había tenido cuenta con un español llamado Baltasar Rodríguez" (was uncontrolled and free . . . she slept with a cacique of Guaycan called Don Pedro . . . and she had an affair with a Spaniard called Baltasar Rodríguez), in AGI/S Escribanía de Cámara 922A 3a Pieza, fols. 889r, 179v–180r, 877v.

56. Miguel de Cantos, the corregidor of Otavalo, recalled: "un día pasando este testigo por la puerta del dicho capitán Rodrigo de Salazar salio tras del la dicha doña

Ana mujer del dicho Machín y lo alcanço en la plaza de San Francisco y le dixo a este testigo llorando que le faboreciese a ella y a su marido para bolverse a su tierra porque el dicho su encomendero los tenía sercados en su casa e servicio" (once this witness was walking by the gate of the said Captain Rodrigo de Salazar when the said doña Ana, wife of the said Machín, came out and caught up with him in San Francisco Square, and crying she implored this witness to help her and her husband return to their lands because the said encomendero was keeping them locked up inside his house and at his service), in AGI/S Escribanía de Cámara 922A 3a Pieza, fols. 862v, 870v, 882r, 260r–v, 264r.

57. The graffiti read that "la dicha doña Ana vivía desonestamente e por tal era avida y tenida en tanta manera que en las paredes de una ermita que está en Otavalo . . . estava escrito con carbón 'Machín cornudo' y que procurando de saver quien lo avía escripto ansi me dixo avello escripto don Agustín yndio cantor el caci-que" (the said doña Ana was living in dishonor, and such was her reputation that "Machín cuckold" was written in coal on the walls of a hermitage in Otavalo, and when I tried to ascertain who had written it, don Agustín, the cacique and singer in church, told me that he had done so), in AGI/S, Escribanía de Cámara 922a, 3a Pieza, fols. 867v, 179v. "Andaba destrayda e desasogada" (she was uncontrolled and free) is the kind of language that would refer to an escaped mare.

58. Davis, *Fiction in the Archives*, 95.

59. Oberem, "Testamentos de Doña Francisca," 14, contains the testimony (cited above) describing how she tracked down her indigenous subjects in Ambato.

60. In 1596, doña Beatriz Ango asks to be buried in Franciscan robes, names her grandson patron of her chapel, orders masses, and gives lands to the church; ANH/Q, 1a Notaría, vol. 3 (1593–97), fols. 383–84r. In 1606, doña Catalina Tuza be-queaths numerous goods to her chapel and its confraternity and orders many masses for the salvation of her soul, which are dedicated to various saints (of both sexes) and archangels; Landázuri, *Curacazgos pastos prehispánicos*, 211–14.

61. Caillavet, "Ethnohistoire des communautés," 415–17.

62. Caillavet, "Ethnohistoire des communautés," 409–20.

CHAPTER 7

Cacicas, Land, and Litigation in Seventeenth-Century Chincha, Peru

Liliana Pérez Miguel and Renzo Honores

From the first decades of the post-conquest era, litigation was a common facet in Spanish American courts. The use of rooms of justice as a space for resolving disputes was a feature that both Spaniards and natives shared.[1] Notions of Castilian law were appropriated by indigenous subjects as early as the mid-sixteenth century. In the historiography of native actors in the Spanish legal world, caciques who bring litigation have been studied whereas their female counterparts have received less attention, at least for the Andean region.[2] Native female litigants were visible users of colonial courtrooms. They demanded the protection and recognition of their personal and patrimonial rights, employing a variety of legal strategies that were the result of indigenous participation in the legal arena since the sixteenth century.[3] In 1577, for example, a native commoner, Inés Tocto, filed a suit to recover her salt pans and a plot of land in Cuzco.[4] Like her, cacicas, such as the ones examined in this collection and in this chapter, turned to the courts to defend their assets and receive recognition of their noble status. By maneuvering within the legal system, invoking doctrinal principles and developing legal narratives, they became central agents in the making of the colonial juridical orders.[5]

This chapter examines the judicial cases of two cacicas, doña Juana Curilla and doña Magdalena Chimaca, from the valley of Chincha, south of Lima. (See map 7.1.) Both women litigated before the *Real Audiencia* (royal high court) of Lima between 1616 and 1620, a time of gradual maturity of colonial law.[6] Their cases are not about succession to a *cacicazgo* (office of the cacique, including sometimes its political role, services, and property) but about how two women identified as cacicas used the judicial machinery to defend their land rights, dowries, and social reputation. The valley of Chincha, located in the region of Ica (in the Peruvian central coast), was home to an important principality in pre-Columbian Peru. Its political relevance was such that it named a portion of Tahuantinsuyu: Chinchaysuyu.[7] From 1592 to 1593, Chincha had been the setting of the process of *composición de tierras*, a governmental confirmation or legalization of land titles through the payment of a sum of money. This process marked a turning point in land dispossession of indigenous peoples.[8] In the following years, indigenous lords argued that these lands were part of their communities, family, or personal patrimony, and they did not hesitate in using all strategies at their disposal to recover or keep them. The cases of doña Juana Curilla and doña Magdalena Chimaca exemplify the participation of indigenous women in these legal battles and the complexity and fluidity of their legal experiences in Spanish courts.

Doña Juana Curilla, the "principal cacica of the valley of Chincha," together with doña Juana Canchulla, her niece, sued Gaspar de Oya Osores, a lieutenant of the *corregidor* (Spanish magistrate) in Chincha, for the return of forty *fanegadas* of land.[9] The women claimed to be the legitimate owners and possessors of the lands in question, whereas Oya, they argued, was a usurper. In the case of doña Magdalena Chimaca, a cacica married to Bernabé de Morales, a Spaniard, she demanded the nullity of a land sale, arguing that her lands had been "irregularly" transferred to don Rodrigo de Guzmán y Ayala, another Spaniard. While her marriage to Morales is an example of the close relationships between cacique families and Spaniards in the early seventeenth century, the cacica's case was also about spousal violence and abuse of power. Doña Magdalena not only accused her husband of having unlawfully sold her lands but also of domestic violence and intimidation.

It is important to note that neither doña Juana Curilla nor doña Magdalena Chimaca were actual rulers. Yet their titles of cacicas, understood as principal or lordly women, were strategically deployed within legal channels, affording these cacicas countless interactions with Spanish officers and legal facilitators. This chapter argues that cacicas who brought litigation, though not always successful, were important agents in the making of the colonial legal system, a role that has been mainly emphasized for their male counterparts.[10] In similar fashion to caciques, doña Juana and doña Magdalena

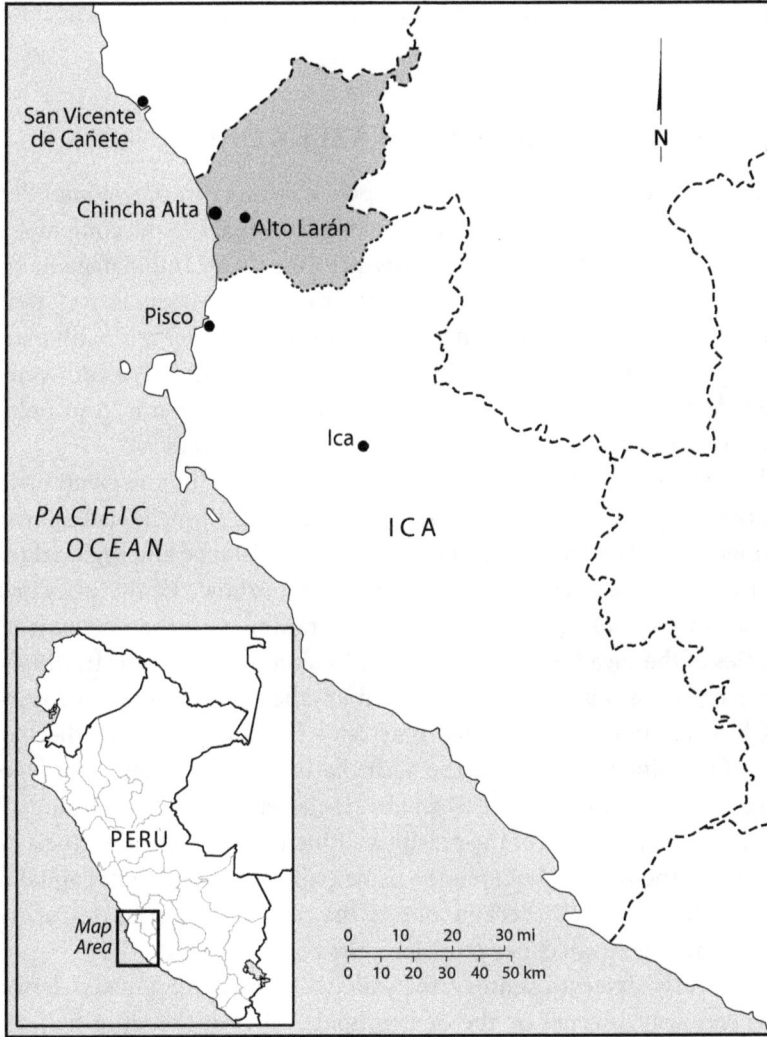

Map 5. Ica Region

went to the forums—in Chincha and Lima—and recruited a series of witnesses who supported their testimony, narrated stories, and produced a repertory of the legal past. These litigants *rethought* and re-created the Castilian and pre-Hispanic legal institutions via their pleas and allegations, in which they introduced their own experiences, notions of justice, and pre-Columbian narratives.[11] Overall, the cases of doña Juana and doña Magdalena not only shed light on the position of cacicas in colonial Andean society, but also offer information on their "social dramas."[12]

THE SCENARIO: THE VALLEY OF CHINCHA

Chincha was an important valley and political entity in precolonial Peru.[13] The small, fertile valley is located in the northern part of the contemporary region of Ica and its homonymous province. The Chico and Matagente rivers irrigate the valley. Chroniclers such as Pedro Cieza de León, in 1553, praised the valley's fertility, describing it as "one of the greatest in Peru" with marvelous irrigation channels and high quality fruits.[14] Several sixteenth-century testimonies also pointed out the valley's cultural, economic, and political importance during the Inca Empire and early colonial era.[15]

The principality of Chincha was thus also a powerful one given its location, diversity of natural resources, and population. Chincha had an important merchant class who were in charge of long-distance and regional trade, serving as central agents in the economic importance of the principality. They acquired *mullu* (Spondylus shell) by trading with the northern communities of the Inca Empire. Likewise, they obtained copper by trading with southern groups. Fishermen constituted another relevant group of workers for Chincha, and their presence illustrates the importance of the Pacific Ocean for Chinchano society. The Chincha Islands with their rich deposits of *guano* (bird droppings used as fertilizer) also enriched the economy of the lordship.[16] The main seat of the pre-Inca Chinchanos was the Centinela complex. When the Incas conquered the principality, they settled its capital near this complex.[17] Chincha became one of the central territories of Cuzqueño lords during the Inca's expansion along the Peruvian coast.

In the early sixteenth century, the valley was densely populated; however, it was seriously affected by the demographic crisis of the latter half of the century.[18] Smallpox destroyed the valley's populace at the end of the sixteenth century, and the number of male tributaries substantially declined. The population of Chincha was entrusted in *encomienda* (royal grant of tribute) to king Charles V, in 1538. However, during the civil wars of 1544–48, the valley and its tributaries were administered by the Pizarros, the leading clan of Spanish conquerors in Peru.[19] After their management, the encomienda returned to the hands of the king. In 1542, the Dominicans settled in the area, building a convent under the direction of Friar Domingo de Santo Tomás.[20] The good relations between the archbishop of Lima, Jerónimo de Loaysa, and the governor of the territory, Vaca de Castro, were central. The order was influential in the elaboration and circulation of critical ideas about the conquest and the negative effects of the Spanish exploitation (especially by the *encomenderos* [male encomienda holders]). Dominican activities in the valley were of such significance that when the town of Chincha was officially christened, its name honored the order: Santo Domingo de Chincha (or Chincha Alta).

In the 1550s, Viceroy Andrés Hurtado de Mendoza, second marquis of Cañete (r. 1556–60) ordered an inspection to scrutinize the geography and society of the valley. Cristóbal de Castro, a Dominican friar, and Diego de Ortega Morejón, the corregidor, wrote a detailed report, which was the first on Chincha under Spanish rule.[21] As part of an ongoing but slow-moving Spanish campaign to learn the customary laws in the Andes, the report included specific information on the pre-Columbian tributary system, cultural customs, history, and the laws of the natives of Chincha.[22] In that report, Castro and Ortega Morejón also indicated that the rulers of Chincha were conquered by the Incas in the time of Tupa Inca Yupanqui (r. 1470s–90s).[23] However, the first great paramount leader before the Incas was the lord Guavia Rucana.[24] Castro and Ortega Morejón also mentioned how the political system of the Chinchas changed with the Incas, who appointed their own local authorities and ordered new tributary obligations. In that document, the authors provided information about male caciques only.[25]

Land was an important resource in colonial society. During the time of García Hurtado de Mendoza, the fourth marquis of Cañete (r. 1590–96), the viceroy ordered the composición de tierras. Composición was a fiscal measure oriented to enrich the royal treasury.[26] The process generated enormous indigenous opposition, and in the seventeenth century, several caciques went to the Audiencia of Lima to legally demand new land inspections as well as the annulment of the legal titles awarded during the land campaign. As mentioned earlier, legal challenges to the land campaign were not only carried out by male leaders. Doña Juana Curilla's legal case is an example of female challenges to the composición process. In the midst of territorial dispossession, litigation over land turned into an important legal arena in the seventeenth century.

CACICAS AND INDIGENOUS WOMEN'S RIGHTS IN A COLONIAL CONTEXT

Although the institution of indigenous lordship was pre-Columbian, it had a special relevance in the colonial period. As Raúl Adanaqué points out, caciques played a leading role in the development of the viceregal economy and society, by constituting the bridge between the indigenous population and the Spaniards. In addition, caciques were key actors in the recruitment of indigenous laborers for farming, mining, and public works. These colonial indigenous leaders were not strictly male, as cacicas also exerted power and authority in Andean society. These cacicas, however, did not constitute a matriarchal government. Rather, colonial indigenous lordships were patriarchal and hereditary by definition. Nevertheless, cacicas could inherit the lordship in absence of male candidates.[27] Karen Graubart's research indicates that although women had rights to linear succession according to Castilian law, men were usually preferred. Yet political succession could be flexible. In some cases, the brothers of caciques were preferred over the next generation of the deceased indigenous lord's children and nephews.[28]

Lordships were not always considered patrimonial rights, as opposed to landed property. While in theory Castilian law recognized the patrimonial rights of females, they were under the legal tutelage of a male guardian. Nonetheless, in the midst of the complex dynamics between law and reality, women were visible legal agents and employed Spanish juridical channels to their own benefit. For example, Castilian law required that during marriage a woman's patrimony be administered by her husband and that he be given "full capacity" for legal acts. However, the property belonged exclusively to the woman and her assets could not be transferred without her legal consent.[29] Castilian civil law regulations were codified in the medieval Siete Partidas (1256–65) and the early modern Leyes de Toro (1505). Civil law regulated the individual within its juridical space whereas canon law, another important legal space, regulated marriage and canonical divorce.

Litigation by both men and women depended on the participation of legal facilitators. In the early modern period, the system of legal representation was dual and *abogados* (advocates) and *procuradores de causa* (solicitors) participated in the representation of litigants in trial. While advocates provided the legal arguments in a judicial dispute, procuradores (solicitors) were the procedural experts of the case. Given the "minority" of female litigants, these experts assumed their representation and legal counseling.[30] Indigenous litigants (both male and female) were considered under the Roman legal status of *miserabiles* ("unfortunates": those deserving of royal legal protection).[31] This meant that they required, due to their legal minority, the presence of officers for litigation activities. Because of their legal status of miserabiles, their cases were considered *casos de corte* (protected legal category allowing petitioners to have their case bypass lower courts and be heard by an audiencia) and would be judged by the audiencia, the high court of justice, in the first instance.[32] Lower courts were the scenarios for the collecting of oral and documentary (or notarial) evidence. As the two legal cases that are the focus of this chapter came from the region of Chincha, they were initiated and judged in the Audiencia of Lima. However, witness testimonies and the collection of oral and documentary proofs occurred in the valley of Chincha. Once all evidence was compiled, the litigants sent out a dossier to Lima as a formal and sealed document. In Lima, the testimonies were attached to the general proceedings.

Since the times of viceroy Francisco de Toledo (r. 1569–81), a system of public representation was created to monitor and provide legal counseling to indigenous litigants. Two agents, one a *protector general de naturales* (main advocate for indigenous legal cases in the audiencia and chief advisor of the viceroy in indigenous matters) and the other a *procurador general de naturales* (main solicitor of the audiencia for natives' lawsuits) represented indigenous litigants before the audiencia and the seats of *corregimientos* (high courts). The system was not uniform. In Lima, the protector was usually a distinguished member of the legal profession, and the procuradores were facilitators commissioned for the post. Protectores developed legal arguments based on a series of legal sources, and procuradores crafted the procedural strategy for each legal case. In 1610, for example, two *capullanas* (female chiefs) argued that according to their own customary practices women could serve as legitimate rulers.[33] The reasoning was based on the invocation of customary law, and in this sense the litigants enjoyed a legal space in which they could provide their own versions of justice and law from time immemorial.

The ideas and principles of law were re-created in the courts by litigants through their own cases. Despite the role of facilitators, litigants expressed their own voice. The legal arguments in colonial courts were created from several legal sources in a pluralistic mode of forensic discourse. The key importance of colonial documents is that they represent the positions of litigants—in moments of inequality or even outright injustice—allowing us to appreciate their voice and activities. They were cocreators of their social lives and legal definitions of justice. The Spanish legal system, characterized by the use of pluralistic legal ideas, permitted the presence of indigenous narratives and legal defenses.

THE CASE OF DOÑA JUANA CURILLA: LAND
USURPATION, COMPOSICIONES, AND WITNESSES

On March 25, 1616, doña Juana Curilla, cacica of Chincha, and her niece, doña Juana Canchulla, sued Gaspar de Oya Osores in the Audiencia of Lima. The defendant, the lieutenant corregidor of Chincha, was accused of encroaching upon forty fanegadas of land that belonged to doña Juana and her niece.[34] The petition was signed by Leandro de Larrínaga Salazar, the protector general de naturales and presented by Pedro de Valencia Bohórquez the procurador general de naturales in the audiencia. Larrínaga was a prominent jurist of the city, a professor at the University of San Marcos, and the head of an influential family of Limeño lawyers.[35] In the suit, Larrínaga also asked that the case be classified as a caso de corte because the litigants were indios and requested that all evidence be collected locally in the corregimiento of Chincha.[36] His adherence to the *real provisión* (royal decree) mandating the caso de corte classification was an initial victory for the claimants because it meant a legal case would be opened, legal inquiries would take place in the valley, and an implicit recognition of a certain level of truthfulness to the cacica's petition.[37]

The second stage was the process of collecting testimonies, especially the oral versions provided by witnesses. Oral depositions played a central role in civil and canon litigation since these testimonies were privileged legal proofs in both jurisdictions.[38] In theory, notarial and written documents enjoyed higher credibility over oral declarations. However, at the discretion of the judges, more value could be given to oral testimonies. Using both written and oral testimonies, doña Juana Curilla's trial turned into a battle of witnesses and their credibility.

Doña Juana Curilla selected her witnesses. The *alcalde* of the Santa Hermandad (a kind of rural police officer) conducted the declaration of testimonies and appointed the *lengua* (translator).[39] In colonial times, lenguas were key legal agents due to their proximity to litigants, and they disseminated legal ideas. Their role was not of a simple interpreter in a courtroom, but they were central legal agents for indigenous litigants.[40] Meanwhile, in Lima, Valencia Bohórquez, the procurador, had prepared a questionnaire containing nine items. Doña Juana Curilla's witnesses included members of the local elite as well as commoners. Some of them were senior residents, whose narrations constituted privileged instruments in the trial since the matter concerned crucial past events. Their words served as a reconstruction of deeds and facts that supported the plaintiffs' viewpoint.

Witnesses narrated the history of the valley and the role and rights of doña Juana Curilla and doña Juana Canchulla. Doña Juana's position in the community was that of a cacica and a member of a local landholding dynasty. The witnesses recalled the history of the valley through the mid-sixteenth century and identified don Francisco Napan Lucana as the founding figure of Chincha, grandfather of doña Juana Curilla, and great-grandfather of doña Juana Canchulla. After his death, the witnesses claimed, the lands passed to his heirs, doña Juana Curilla and don Tomás Quipo, her brother. When the process of composiciones took place, they added, Lázaro Pérez de Idiáquez, an official in charge, reconfigured the land property in the valley of Chincha.[41]

In the trial, doña Juana Curilla was obligated to present two different groups of witnesses in two rounds. The declarations of the first group, made up of six witnesses, started on August 27, 1616. The first witness was the sixty-nine-year-old don Pedro Hatunca, the past governor of the valley. He said that he had known doña Juana Curilla since her birth. He also indicated that he knew Gaspar Oya de Osores for at least twelve years. Don Pedro testified that the lands in dispute belonged to doña Juana Curilla's ancestors, who "had cultivated wheat, corn, and beans for more than thirty years" on the lands. According to him, these actions illustrated the "long possession" of the family and its full patrimonial rights over the lands.

Possession was a crucial concept in civil law and a common argument in seventeenth-century Peruvian courts. Don Pedro Hatunca also mentioned that Lázaro Pérez de Idiaquez had seized the lands, which were later occupied by Gaspar de Oya Osores.[42] Hatunca's version was corroborated by a second witness, a different elder, who said that don Francisco Napan Lucana, "grandfather of doña Juana Curilla and great-grandfather of doña Juana Canchulla, had possessed the lands as his own, for a long time, and enjoyed and cultivated them because he had inherited them from his parents."[43] This witness indicated that he knew this because he had heard it from other elders in the community and that this fact was known by all the inhabitants in the area.

Doña Juana Curilla also presented elder female witnesses: Ana Alto, Isabel Ochama, and María Omoto.[44] All were in their seventies and born in the valley. They confirmed the version of the long possession of the land by don Francisco and his heirs, the practice of agriculture, and the rights of doña Juana. Their testimonies were coherent and supported doña Juana's primary argument. They also provided information on the kinship between doñas Juana Curilla and Juana Canchulla. The latter seems to have been the daughter of Tomás Quipo; thus the niece of doña Juana. The main strategy of doña Juana was to prove with her witnesses that the lands in the valley had been possessed by members of her lineage for a long time and that they were wrongfully seized in the composiciones and later unlawfully occupied by Oya Osores.

The second group of deponents, whose testimonies were rendered in October, comprised six other witnesses. Interestingly, a significant part of this case was a battle over testimonies and their impartiality. In all of these procedural activities, doña Juana Curilla and her niece participated actively by selecting witnesses and attending the judicial acts. The cacica was especially engaged with the case in the audiencia and in local justice.

While the legal actions of doña Juana Curilla started on March 20, 1616 and were undertaken in the form of evidence in August of that same year, the response of Oya Osores was late. He started his actions in September with Joan Lorenzo de Cela as his procurador. A prominent facilitator in the Audiencia of Lima, he—along with the licentiate Duarte, Oya Osores's lawyer—observed the proceedings of the opposite side. Duarte argued that all the witnesses, even the scribes, were clients of Juana Curilla—whom they referred to as an "india" rather than as "cacica"—and her family and therefore, should be declared null and without judicial relevance.

The main claim by both men was that the deponents were clients of doña Juana Curilla, and were also her drinking buddies. Duarte added, "it is not even necessary to give credit to all the *probanza* [evidence] made by the opposite side because the witnesses of it are drunken facile Indians brought up by the aforementioned [Juana] and her parents [and], as many of them declared, induced and taught by the opposite party and of their ayllos [sic]."[45] The lieutenant Gaspar de Oya Osores denied the accusations against him, arguing that the forty fanegadas were sold in accordance to Castilian law. Oya Osores claimed that he had bought them from a Captain named Juan de Barrios.

The accusation of immoderate drinking was common in colonial times, and it was used as an example of the excesses and inferiority of the indigenous population. Thus, colonial authorities or chroniclers, among others, referred to the "continuous drunkenness of the Indians," which was responsible for such evils as weakness or rebellion.[46] But this argument was also used to discredit the legal testimonies. Also, in the procedural theory of the seventeenth century, litigants had the right to question the reliability of testimonies. *Tachas* (the disqualification of a witness) was a common strategy in colonial litigation. Hevia Bolaños, the seventeenth-century author, argued that it was a prerogative of the litigants.[47] In addition, the legal proceedings became tournaments of procedural aspects. Procuradores, who were the masters of litigation, were the main agents in the detection of procedural irregularities.

Due to the accusations about the reliability of the witnesses and diligence of the notary and interpreter, doña Juana Curilla decided to present a new inquest (*probanza*). The deposition of the witnesses began on February 1, 1617. Her primary objective through the questionnaire was to demonstrate that the witnesses, interpreter, and notary were unbiased and they were neither her clients nor her relatives. Doña Juana also emphasized that the witnesses were "good Indians and good Christians who speak truth and are not drunks or servants."[48] The second group of witnesses of doña Juana Curilla emphasized their neutrality and interest in the truth. They said that none were clients of the claimant, and they were only interested in declaring the facts. Juan de Alonso, the lengua, participated as translator and interpreter in this stage of the trial.

On the other hand, Oya Osores presented a different narrative that challenged the testimony of doña Juana. He argued that the lands were allotted during the time of the composición. During this land campaign, lands considered to be vacant were, essentially, given away.[49] To determine if a piece of land was vacant, authorities needed to carry out an inquiry that included the testimonies of several witnesses. In that sense, the legal arguments of Gaspar de Oya Osores were based on the procedural and formalistic technicalities. He said that the process of composición transferred the land and whoever was the recipient of the land could sell it to any available buyer. This was the factual circumstance that allowed him the rights to the disputed lands. Another important element of his defense was that he had only bought twenty-one fanegadas—not forty—and he denied the versions of doña Juana and Canchulla. In short, the lands he bought were legally acquired. These legal and formalistic aspects marked the system of land property in colonial Peru. Nonetheless, the dispossessed litigants went to the audiencia and the viceroy to request the return of their precious resource.[50]

Gaspar de Oya Osores also offered a probanza in which his witnesses repeated his version of the facts. Francisco de Córdoba declared that all of Curilla's witnesses were her clients and servants of her family and their *ayllus* (local kinship groups).[51] Another witness added that several of doña Juana's deponents "simply declared what she wanted."[52] The outcome of this case was somewhat predictable. Oya Osores was a lieutenant, a high official in the city. He purchased the lands legally because the very process of composición determined the legality of the acts. It was precisely the Real Audiencia de Lima that pronounced a sentence in August of 1617 recognizing Oya de Osores as the legitimate owner of the lands.

In colonial times, Spanish courts did not indicate the foundations of their legal reasoning. A sentence was seen as warranty of a correct procedure, inversely to the current view. In this case, it seems that the court recognized Oya de Osores's evidence and arguments regarding the legality of the composición and the free transference of lands. It is important to mention that the audiencia expressed its rules in laconic mandates, rather than in a series of legal arguments, as it happens in current litigation. So, in the first episode of this procedure, the gradual dispossession of indigenous lands in the central valley was justified in a context of depopulation. In 1618, Gaspar de Oya Osores, who had continued as an officer in Chincha, was part of a *juicio de residencia* (administrative review after a bureaucrat's term in office) in the town. At that time, he was accused of not being severe enough with certain regulations. Yet, in most of the charges of that trial he was declared innocent.[53]

Doña Juana Curilla lost her case as did many other natives affected by the composiciones in the valley of Chincha. Neither her title of cacica and the narrative of her aristocratic lineage, the role of founding figures in her family, nor her political influence in the Chincha valley were enough to tip the balance in her favor. Yet her case serves to illustrate the different ways in which litigants sought to use and influence the law. In seeking justice, she still contributed to the making of the colonial juridical process. Just as her male counterparts, she participated actively in all the stages of the procedure, interacted with facilitators, provided narratives, and also journeyed from Chincha to Lima at various times. The several towns around the city of Lima became corridors for litigious natives interested in obtaining justice, and even if they did not always obtain it, they were a force that worked underneath the visible colonial powers.

DOÑA MAGDALENA CHIMACA: DOWRY, RURAL PATRIMONY, AND DOMESTIC VIOLENCE

The legal case of the cacica doña Magdalena Chimaca illustrates the invocation of civil laws to defend female patrimonial rights and the sanctioning of domestic violence in colonial times. Like doña Juana Curilla and doña Juana Canchulla, doña Magdalena demanded the restitution of her lands from a reputed usurper. These rural dominions, however, were part of her dowry. Doña

Magdalena was part of a cadre of wealthy natives in seventeenth-century Peru; a woman from a family of caciques in the valley of Chincha.

She married a destitute Spaniard named Bernabé Morales. According to witnesses, Morales was a penniless individual with a very meager patrimony at the time of the wedding. Upon his marriage to this affluent woman, he received a fabulous dowry of about 12,000 pesos, which included, among other properties, jewelry, land, and slaves. During the marriage, Morales acquired a negative reputation as a gambler and negligent administrator of his estate; accusations that would be especially emphasized by doña Magdalena's legal defense and witnesses. According to doña Magdalena, her husband forced her to sell a rural piece of property, the size of four fanegadas, in the valley of Larán (referred to in the document as *el pago de Larán*). She sold to a man named Rodrigo de Guzmán for the "low" price of 7,700 pesos. The cacica claimed that she never agreed to this transaction. Rather, she had been forced to sell her lands under the violent pressure of her husband, who on several occasions had beaten her, "with much slapping and kicking and by dragging her by the hair, swearing that he would kill her," if she did not concede.[54] Thus, "pressed against all her will and forced with the just fear of death," she granted the sales letter, not without requesting the approval of the viceroy Luis de Velasco (r. 1596–1604) or the audiencia.[55] This sale was the main reason for the dispute, yet the lawsuit gives us rich information on the gender and racial relationships in colonial Chincha.

Morales enjoyed the prestige, wealth, and reputation of his wife and her family. He became an important, albeit controversial, local character. But why did doña Magdalena marry Bernabé Morales despite his supposed poverty? Chimaca's case reminds us of what Steve Stern called the "tragedy of success," whereby powerful or fortunate individuals engaged in relationships with the Hispanic world only to buttress colonial domination.[56] While no further references are given about Chimaca's motivations to marry Morales, the text of the case suggests that this was a marriage of convenience.

In 1619, Gonzalo Ortiz de Mena, procurador general de naturales, submitted doña Magdalena's legal proceedings. As in doña Juana Curilla's case, the protector general requested that the case should be considered as a caso de corte.[57] The general plea demanded the annulment of Bernabé Morales's sale because it had violated numerous rules of Castilian civil law. The lands were part of doña Magdalena's dowry, her consent was unlawfully forced, and the property belonged exclusively to her patrimony as part of her dowry.[58] The use of violence generated sanctions in civil and canon law. In civil law, coercion was seen as an example of an infraction against free will. In canon law, the use of violence was a factor to demand a canonical divorce by mistreatment. Violence also affected free will in canon law.[59] The suit was addressed to don Rodrigo de Guzman, the buyer, and Diego de Guzmán, his son. The case also provides numerous details of doña Magdalena's patrimony, the testimonies of witnesses, and her role as a litigator.

During the proceedings, doña Magdalena narrated the circumstances that explained the fraudulent and compulsory sale of her estate. She calculated that the pago de Larán was worth at least 20,000 pesos, yet it had been sold for a third of its value. She tried to void the transaction several times. However, because her husband was in jail, charged for not paying his rural workers' wages, she could not overturn the sale.[60] In the absence of her husband, the current viceroy, Luis de Velasco, would have to have authorized the sale. However, whether he approved the sale or not, the transfer of the property was carried out after 1612.[61]

By the time doña Magdalena sued Rodrigo de Guzman, she must have been familiar with the network of protectores, abogados, and procuradores de naturales as well as with the genre of memoriales. A "memorial" was an exposition of facts and legal problems through forensic language, demanding the intervention of an authority.[62] This type of legal literature was popular in the legal culture of Lima in the early seventeenth century. Some memoriales were printed and used in legal cases pending in the audiencia. In the 1619 claim, her advocate was the native protector general, don Leandro de Larrínaga Salazar, who had been the lawyer for other cacicas, such as Doña Juana Curilla above. He was accomplished with this sort of litigation.

As in doña Juana Curilla's trial, doña Magdalena collected her evidence in the valley of Chincha. The valley became the epicenter of her legal activities to carry out the probanza. Doña Magdalena presented six witnesses to demonstrate her own version of the events. In her reconstruction of how things happened, she emphasized how she inherited the fanegadas of pago de Larán from her father, don Jerónimo Guayla, in 1599. She also highlighted that Bernabé Morales was a "poor man" with no patrimony who took advantage of their marriage. Antonio de Torres y Mendoza, the lieutenant corregidor, declared in favor of doña Magdalena, saying she was a wealthy and prominent figure in the area emphasizing her possession of jewelry and Black slaves.[63] In contrast, he added that Morales was a "penniless man" whose only patrimony was the shirt he wore at his wedding. Bernabé Morales was also characterized as a compulsive gambler with a long history of debts, who had been merely interested in Magdalena's patrimony. His marriage was a "convenient" economic strategy.

Doña Magdalena's lands were fertile and highly productive. Moreover, in a probanza of July 27, 1619, witnesses testified that the lands were so fruitful due to a permanent source of water. The sale of pago de Larán financially affected the couple because they lost an important source of income. Rather than her condition as cacica, the witnesses focused on Morales's economic exploitation of doña Magdalena, their unequal status, and the conjugal violence. They asserted how Morales mistreated and physically punished doña Magdalena. Her witnesses not only offered details about the land and the property rights of doña Magdalena but also narrated episodes of domestic violence. Augustin Quispe, choirmaster of the local church of Santo Domingo, for instance, declared that during his classes he had heard doña Magdalena's screams in the town of Santo Domingo de Chincha. When he went to her home once, he saw doña Magdalena terribly beaten and crying. This situation happened time and time again, he added.[64]

According to doña Magdalena herself, she suffered the fate of African slaves due to her long sufferings.[65] Other testimonies referred to the "weakness" of women. Indianness was also linked with pusillanimity. These stereotypes were especially exacerbated when referring to native women.[66] Gaspar Guerra, *ladino* (fluent in Spanish), and a principal of the ayllu Aya stated that doña Magdalena was unable to resist the pressure exerted on her by her husband due to her condition as a woman.[67] The assumption of the subordinate status and diminished capacity of women had a long history in sixteenth-century Castile. Writers, theologians, and jurists penned on the physical and mental feminine weaknesses.[68] Some of these authors judged women as "frivolous" and as "liars." A priest named Rodrigo Acuña y Silva, for example, was a prolific author of misogynist literature rooted in medieval Castile.[69] These ideas, and the status of the Amerindians as legal minors, turned native women into permanent inferiors in the eyes of the law. However, these arguments could and were challenged in court. In Castilian civil law—influenced by Roman legal tradition—the doctrine of *imbecellitas seu fragilitas sexus* (the naïve and fragile sex) was invoked to restrict juridical capacity of females to sign contracts and conduct business.[70] Likewise, in criminal law, judges were to impose lighter penalties on women. Doña Magdalena and her professional facilitators argued during several stages of the trial how Bernabé Morales had abused her good faith, acted irresponsibly, and taken advantage of her feminine condition. The imbecellitas sexus doctrine was used to protect and reassert doña Magdalena's rights.

The testimony about the abuse suffered by Magdalena was typical of lawsuits intended to obtain both divorce and marriage annulments. It contains several of the ingredients that other authors, such as Bernard Lavallé, describe as common to these processes, such as *sevicia* (excessively cruel or violent treatment beyond that allowed by law). As Lavallé points out, these testimonies must be handled with great caution and criticism, since they were used to obtain a favorable result in the courts. In this case, the nullification of a land sale.[71] In addition, these testimonies were often influenced by the protector general himself. Gonzalo Ortiz de Mena, doña Magdalena's protector, likely advised his clients on the type of data to include and highlight, based on his previous experiences of success or failure in these types of lawsuits. However, it would be misleading to limit these statements to a mere judicial strategy and forget the personal and credible dimensions of doña Magdalena's experiences. Historical sources reveal the physical abuses that many of doña Magdalena's contemporaries suffered in seventeenth-century colonial Lima.[72]

The sale of pago de Larán was the result of endless incidents of coercion. Don Pedro Atunca, cacique, maintained that doña Magdalena, panicked by the violent environment in which she lived, was forced to sell her lands. Magdalena responded that the transfer should have had the participation of the corregidor of Chincha. At the end, doña Magdalena Chimaca's judicial strategy was successful: the audiencia ruled in her favor. The Audiencia of Lima ordered the sale null and void and declared that pago de Larán should be returned to her by employing the *retitutio in integrum* (restitution to original condition) doctrine, a legal principle in favor of indigenous litigants. Doña Magdalena should also receive the revenues that pago de Larán had produced during the period in which this property was in Guzmán's hands.

The result of this trial must be seen as an example of the intersections of gender, race, and status as much as the strength and tenacity of doña Magdalena in recovering her possessions and obtaining justice. She was so engaged in this trial that she went to Lima at least twice, including when she was seriously ill. Some 1681 testimonies from outside the proceedings shed light on other aspects of her life. For instance, we learn about her piety and devotion to Isabel Flores de Oliva (the future Santa Rosa de Lima), which was recorded by the Dominican chronicler and writer, friar Juan de Meléndez. Friar Meléndez narrates doña Magdalena's miraculous healing through relics left by Santa Rosa de Lima. In this story, Meléndez extolled the piety of doña Magdalena and detailed her quick recovery to health.[73]

We can speculate that in Lima, doña Magdalena consulted with her protector and the network of legal specialists for native legal matters. She could have also exposed her case to the *oidores* (high court judges), the viceroy, and other indigenous litigants. Although we have no records that she undertook those activities, we know that other litigants did.[74] In Lima, doña Magdalena could have observed the prolific circulation of printed allegations. Litigants paid for the printing of their legal defenses, which were used to put pressure on the oidores. Doña Magdalena could have been familiarized with this production and circulation of legal ideas. Likewise, given the centrality of Lima, doña Magdalena could have met notable jurists and procuradores, whose offices were in and outside the audiencia building. The audiencia was one block away from the Convent of Santo Domingo, which doña Magdalena visited frequently. In addition, doña Magdalena likely met other indigenous litigants, including caciques and nobles, who provided her valuable information for the defense of her rights. In sum, all these circumstances could have enriched her legal knowledge and strengthened her search for justice.

FINAL REFLECTIONS

The cases of doña Juana Curilla and doña Magdalena Chimaca allow us to sketch two portraits that illustrate how indigenous women who used the title of cacica connected it with their land dispossession and defense of their integrity and honor. Their determination was an example of legal appropriation and development of beliefs about their own rights. Their privileged position, as local nobility, allowed them to access these judicial circuits and the personnel devoted to indigenous litigation in the Limeño forum. Common native women also made use of the legal channels, but they had less visibility than their noble counterparts. Nonetheless, the social and legal status of these aristocrats did not assure their legal victory. Doña Juana Curilla's case shows the limits of female indigenous litigation. What's more, these judicial cases also show the adversities and tribulations meted out to women and natives in a colonial society.

Despite real obstacles, like illness or alleged poverty, they started legal actions, chose witnesses, and supplied factual and legal information for the court's investigation. Rather than being passive actors in the corridors of justice, doña

Juana Curilla and doña Magdalena were active parties in the legal process and construction of their own identities. Their experiences allow us to observe the complexity and fluidity of the legal experiences of native women in colonial times. What's more, their cases open a door to understanding how colonial law was also made from below and by indigenous women despite social constraints and regulations.[75]

NOTES

1. On Spanish legal culture in the early modern period, see Betahny Aram's article "From the Courts to the Court: History, Literature, and Litigation in the Spanish Atlantic World," *Colonial Latin American Review* 21, no. 3 (December 2012). Her work illustrates the legal horizon of the period and the massive use of courts. For the prolific use of tribunals in mid-sixteenth-century New Spain by native people, see the classic work of Woodrow Borah, *Justice by Insurance: The General Indian Court of Colonial Mexico and the Legal Aides of the Half Real* (Berkeley: University of California Press, 1983).

2. For some studies on cacicas (and litigators) of the Andean central and northern coast from the late fifteenth through the seventeenth century, see Chantal Caillavet, "'Como caçica y señora desta tierra mando . . .'. Insignias, funciones y poderes de las soberanas del norte andino (siglos XV–XVI)," *Bulletin de l'Institut français d'études andines* 37, no. 1 (October 2008). See also María Rostworowski de Diez Canseco, "Los curacas costeños," *Historia* 23, no. 2 (1999): 292–96; María Rostworowski de Diez Canseco, *Recursos naturales renovables y pesca, siglos XVI y XVII: Curacas y sucesiones, costa norte* (Lima: Instituto de Estudios Peruanos, 2005), 217–25; and Karen Graubart, *With Our Labor and Sweat: Indigenous Women and the Formation of Colonial Society in Peru 1550–1700* (Stanford: Stanford University Press, 2007), 158–85.

3. While Karen Graubart (chap. 5) suggests that these women also made use of a model of legal maneuvering established by Spanish *encomenderas* (female holders of royal grants of tribute), who tended to be the widows of the first conquistadors, we argue that indigenous legal knowledge was decisive in their disputes. For an alternative analysis on encomenderas in the Andes and their employment of the legal circuits, see the forthcoming book by Liliana Pérez Miguel, *Mujeres ricas y libres: Mujer y poder: Inés Muñoz y las encomenderas en el Perú (s. XVI)* (Sevilla: Centro Superior de Investigaciones Científicas, Universidad de Sevilla y Diputacion de Sevilla, 2020).

4. Her case was about thirty salt pans and a half *topo* (measure that is equivalent to 1.5 Spanish leagues [4.5 miles or 7.2 kilometers]) of land. A detailed discussion on this case and a transcription of the document is in Jorge A. Guevara Gil, *Propiedad agraria y Derecho colonial: los documentos de la hacienda Santotis, Cuzco (1543–1822)* (Lima: Pontificia Universidad Católica del Perú, Fondo Editorial, 1993), 216–33, 411–47.

5. Juridical orders here contain a plurality of legal systems. In colonial times, several ingredients from diverse sources composed the law. For a discussion on the

plural nature of Spanish American colonial law, see Susan Kellogg, *Law and the Transformation of Aztec Culture, 1500–1700* (Norman: University of Oklahoma Press, 1995), 85–120; and Brian Owensby, *Empire of Law and Indian Justice in Colonial Mexico* (Stanford: Stanford University Press, 2008), 211–49.

6. The judicial proceedings are held at the Biblioteca Nacional del Perú: doña Juana Curilla's case is B-1051, 1616 (or 2000001472) and doña Magdalena Chimaca's trial is B-1488, 1605 (or 2000001901).

7. "Tahuantinsuyu" is a Quechua word that refers to the four parts into which the Inca Empire was divided: Antinsuyo, Contisuyo, Collasuyo, and Chinchaysuyo. Tahuantinsuyu is another name for the Inca Empire. For more, see Noble David Cook, *La catástrofe demográfica andina: Perú 1520–1620* (Lima: Fondo Editorial, Pontificia Universidad Católica del Perú, 2010), 216.

8. Luis Miguel Glave, "Propiedad de la tierra, agricultura y comercio, 1570–1700: El gran despojo," in *Compendio de historia económica del Perú*, vol. 2, ed. Carlos Contreras (Lima: Instituto de Estudios Peruanos, Banco Centra del Reserva del Perú, 2009).

9. A fanegada was an area measurement of 1.25–1.75 ac (0.5–0.7 ha).

10. For caciques and litigation in sixteenth-century colonial Peru, see José Carlos de la Puente Luna, *Los curacas hechiceros de Jauja: Batallas mágicas y legales en el Perú colonial* (Lima: Fondo Editorial de la Pontificia Universidad Católica del Perú, 2007), 133–62; and José Carlos de la Puente Luna, *Andean Cosmopolitans: Seeking Justice and Reward at the Spanish Royal Court* (Austin: University of Texas Press, 2018).

11. After the sixteenth century, caciques used the Castilian concept of natural lord. This notion recognized the inherent rights to be a legitimate lord (or lady) relating with the premises of natural law, one of the important sources of the legal system; see Robert S. Chamberlain, "The Concept of the *Señor Natural* as Revealed by Castilian Law and Administrative Documents," *Hispanic American Historical Review* 19, no. 2 (May 1939); Jan Schröder, "Legal Scholarship: The Theory of Sources and Methods of Law," in *The Oxford Handbook of European Legal History*, ed. Heikki Pihlajamäki, Markus D. Dubber, and Mark Godfrey (Oxford: Oxford University Press, 2018), 552–553. Caciques and indigenous subjects collected oral testimonies and elaborated sophisticaded *probanzas de méritos* (proofs of merit) to demonstrate their rights, in Sara Vicuña Guengerich, "Inca Women Under Spanish Rule: *Probanzas* and *Informaciones* of the Colonial Andean Elite," in *Women's Negotiations and Textual Agency in Latin America, 1500–1799*, ed. Mónica Díaz and Rocío Quispe-Agnoli (New York: Routledge, 2017); and Jorge A. Guevara Gil, *Diversidad y complejidad legal: Aproximaciones a la Antropología e Historia del Derecho* (Lima: Pontificia Universidad Católica del Perú, Fondo Editorial, 2019), 313–15. Licentiate Polo Ondegardo depicted with surprise how indigenous litigants had become skillful users of the Castilian law in Cuzco; Polo Ondegardo, "Informe del licenciado Polo Ondegardo al licenciado Briviesca de Muñatones sobre la perpetuidad de las encomiendas en el Perú," in *Pensamiento colonial crítico: Textos y actos de Polo Ondegardo*, ed. Gonzalo Lamana Ferrario (Lima: Instituto Francés de Estudios Andinos, Centro Bartolomé de Las Casas, 2002), 144. In the seventeenth century,

indigenous *cabildos* (municipal administration) of colonial Peru, invoked Castilian law in its judicial decisions and also introduced their own definitions of customary law; see Karen Graubart, "Containing Law within the Walls: The Protection of Customary Law in Santiago del Cercado, Peru," in *Protection and Empire: A Global History*, ed. Lauren Benton, Adam Culow, and Bain Attwood (Cambridge: Cambridge University Press, 2017); and José Carlos de la Puente Luna and Renzo Honores, "Guardianes de la real justicia: Alcaldes de indios, costumbre y justicia local en Huarochirí colonial," *Histórica* 40, no. 2 (December 2016). In all these processes, caciques transformed and adapted the Castilian law for local needs.

12. On legal cases as "social dramas" and examples of personal experiences of social change, see Susan Kellogg, *Law and the Transformation of Aztec Culture*, 37–82.

13. Juan Carlos Crespo, "La relación de Chincha (1558)," *Historia y Cultura* 8 (1974); Julian Idilio Santillána, "La Centinela: Un asentamiento Inka-Chincha. Rasgos arquitectónicos estatales y locales," *Arqueología y Sociedad* 10 (1984); and Teodoro Hampe Martínez, "Notas sobre la encomienda real de Chincha en el siglo XVI (Administración y tributos)," *Revista de Historia de América* 100 (July–December 1985).

14. "Y es cosa hermosa de ver sus arboledas, y acequias y quantas fructas ay por todo él," in Pedro de Cieza de León, *Crónica del Perú: Primera parte*, ed. Franklin Pease G. Y. (Lima: Pontificia Universidad Católica del Perú, Fondo Editorial, 1984), 220. Cieza also indicated the cultural and religious importance of Chincha in pre-Columbian times.

15. Juan Carlos Crespo, "Chincha y el mundo andino en la relación de 1558," *Histórica* 2, no. 2 (December 1978).

16. Marco Curatola, "Guano: Una hipótesis sobre el origen de la riqueza del señorío de Chincha," in *Arqueología, antropología e historia en los Andes: Homenaje a María Rostworowski*, ed. Rafel Varón Gabai and Javier Flores Espinoza (Lima: Instituto de Estudios Peruanos and Banco Central de Reserva del Perú, 1997), 230, 234–36, argues that the wealth of the lordship of Chincha was the result of these large deposits of nitrates, especially on the Chincha Islands.

17. Santillána, "Centinela," 17–18.

18. Noble David Cook, "Population Data for Indian Peru: Sixteenth and Seventeenth Centuries," *Hispanic American Historical Review* 62, no. 1 (February 1982); Cook, *Catástrofe demográfica andina*, 217.

19. The encomienda of the Chincha Valley was granted by the governor, Francisco Pizarro, to his brother Hernando in merit for his service in the conquest of the Peruvian territory. However, shortly after receiving this encomienda, Hernando was forced to renounce it, since it was requested by the king as head of the province. Rafael Varón Gabai, *La ilusión del poder: Apogeo y decadencia de los Pizarro en la conquista del Perú* (Lima: Instituto de Estudios Peruanos, Instituto Francés de Estudios Andinos, 1997), 318–20.

20. O. P. Isacio Pérez Fernández, *Bartolomé de Las Casas en el Perú: El espíritu lascasiano de la primera evangelización del imperio incaico (1531–1573)* (Cusco: Centro de Estudios Rurales Andinos Bartolomé de Las Casas, 1986), 102.

21. The report was concluded in Santo Domingo de Chincha on February 22, 1558.

22. At that time, others created similar legal reports in other areas. For example, the royal inspector, Damián de la Bandera, wrote in 1557 about the native society of Huamanga (in south-central Peru), their tributary system, pre-Columbian laws, and their land tenure characteristics; "Relación general de la disposición y calidad de la provincial de Guamanga, llamada San Joan de la Frontera, y de la vivienda y costumbres de los naturales de ella, año de 1557," in *Relaciones geográficas de Indias: Perú*, ed. Marcos Jimenez de la Espada (Madrid: Biblioteca de Autores Españoles 1965).

23. "Vino por estos llanos un ynga llamado Capa Yupangue que fue el primer ynga que oyeron decir el q(ua)1 vino con gran cantidad de jente" (an Inca called Capa Yupangue came through these plains, which was the first Inca they heard who came with a great amount of people), in Crespo, "Relación de Chincha," 93. Capa Yupangue was Topa Inca Yupanqui who ruled after the death of his father, Pachacutec. Topa Inca Yupanqui conquered vast dominions and expanded Tahuantinsuyu.

24. In the words of Castro and Ortega Morejón, "Conviene a todos los curacas antiguos destos valles en que antes que fuesen sujetos a los Yngas governava y era señor de este valle de Chincha Guavia Rucana cuya casa el día de (h)oy [in 1558] está en pie" (before the Incas subjected all the ancient curacas from these valleys, the governor and lord of the valley of Chincha was Guavia Rucana, whose house is still standing today [in 1558].), in Crespo, "Relación de Chincha," 93.

25. Crespo, "Relación de Chincha," 93. Women were mentioned as part of families, labor, and tribute; see Crespo, "Relación de Chincha," 97, 99. In spite of the omission of females from the records of the ruling families, we still consider their authority associated with the indigenous rulership (cacicazgo) since pre-Columbian times and more concretely since the dominion of the area by the Incas. See Karen B. Graubart, *With Our Labor*, and Raúl Adanaqué, *Poder y riqueza: caciques y principales (siglos XVI–XVIII)* (Lima: Editorial Quellca, 2014).

26. Guevara, *Propiedad agraria*, 174–81.

27. Adanaqué, *Poder y riqueza*, 13.

28. Graubart, *With Our Labor*, 166.

29. Eugene H. Korth and Della M. Flusche, "Dowry and Inheritance in Colonial Spanish America: Peninsular Law and Chilean Practice," *Americas* 43, no. 4 (April 1987); M. C. Mirow, *Latin American Law: A History of Private Law and Institutions in Spanish America* (Austin: University of Texas Press, 2004), 56.

30. Per Siete Partidas, females were under the legal guardianship of their fathers, male relatives or husbands; Mirow, *Latin American Law*, 56. In the field of contract law, females were under specific requirements and restrictions to transfer their assets, establish contracts, and draw up legal agreements. In colonial Andes, Roman law rules like Ley de Justiniano and Senado Consulto Veleyano were used in contracts in which females were involved, see Guevara, *Propiedad agraria*, table 16, items 11 and 12. Historiography, however, argues that women exerted legal autonomy despite these rules; see Asunción Lavrin and Edith Couturier, "Dowries and Wills: A View of Women's Socioeconomic Role in Colonial Guadalajara and Puebla, 1640–1790," *Hispanic American*

Historical Review 59, no. 2 (May 1979); Ana María Presta, "Doña Isabel Sisa: A Sixteenth-Century Indian Woman Resisting Gender Inequalities," in *The Human Tradition in Colonial Latin America*, ed. Kenneth J. Andrien (Wilmington, DE: Scholarly Resources, 2002); and Kimberly Gauderman, *Women's Lives in Colonial Quito: Gender, Law, and Economy in Spanish America* (Austin: University of Texas Press, 2003), 30–47.

31. Borah, *Justice by Insurance*, 13, 83; Woodrow Borah, "El status jurídico de los indios en la Nueva España," *América Indígena* 45, no. 2 (April–June 1985); Caroline Cunill, "El indio miserable: Nacimiento de la teoría legal en la América colonial del siglo XVI," *Cuadernos Intercambio* 8, no. 9 (2011).

32. Alonso de Villadiego Vascuñana y Montoy, *Instrucción política y práctica judicial: conforme al estilo de los consejos, audiencias y tribunales de corte y otros ordinarios del reino* (Madrid: Oficina de Antonio Morin, 1766), 25–27.

33. AGN-DI Legajo 31, Cuaderno 627 (1610), fols. 1r–2v, Lima, September 7, 1610, see Rostworowski, *Curacas y sucesiones*; Graubart, "Containing Law"; Graubart, *With Our Labor*; Gaubart, this volume, chap. 5; and Kellogg, *Law and the Transformation of Aztec Culture*, 13–21. Customary law was an important source of law in seventeenth century. Due to the fact that it was an open territory for legal definitions, indigenous leaders and litigants provided narratives to indicate what was their customary legal order.

34. BNP, B1051 (1616), fols. 1r–1v, Lima, March 18, 1616.

35. Guillermo Lohmann Villena, *Los regidores perpetuos del cabildo de Lima (1535–1821): Crónica y estudio de un grupo de gestión* (Seville: Excma. Diputación Provincial de Sevilla, 1983), 2:162–63. The lineages of lawyers were common in the colonial era. Other prominent lineage of men of law was the family Diez de San Miguel of Huamanga, with an active participation of its members in the forums of Lima and Huamanga.

36. BNP, B1051 (1616), fol. 1v.

37. Real provisión was a crucial legal instrument. This document had the seal of the king, a symbol of royal authority, and had the signature of all members of the audiencia.

38. R. C. van Caenegem, "History of European Civil Procedure," in *Civil Procedure: International Encyclopedia of Comparative Law*, ed. Mauro Capelletti (New York: Oceana Publications, 1973); Yanna Yannakakis, *The Art of Being In-between: Native Intermediaries, Indian Identity, and Local Rule in Colonial Oaxaca* (Durham, NC: Duke University Press, 2008); and Yanna Yannakakis, "Hablar para distintos públicos: testigos zapotecos y resistencia a la reforma parroquial en Oaxaca en el siglo XVIII," *Historia Mexicana* 55, no. 3 (January–March 2006).

39. The Santa Hermandad was a patrol or policing force in the rural areas surrounding the town. There are currently no studies for Peru on this important group.

40. On their important roles in the colonial courts of New Spain and Peru, see the studies of José Carlos de la Puente Luna, "The Many Tongues of the King: Indigenous Language Interpreters and the Making of the Spanish Empire," *Colonial Latin American Review* 23, no. 2 (2014); Caroline Cunill, "Un mosaico de lenguas: Los intérpretes de la Audiencia de México en el siglo XVI," *Historia Mexicana* 68, no. 1 (2018); and Luis Miguel Glave, "*Simiachi*: El traductor o lengua en el distrito

de la Audiencia de Lima," in *Las lenguas indígenas en los tribunales de América Latina: Intérpretes, mediación y justicia (siglos XVI-XX)*, ed. Caroline Cunill and Luis Miguel Glave Testino (Bogotá: Instituto Colombiano de Antropología e Historia, 2019).

41. "Ydiaques repartio dichas tierras a los naturales deste pueblo de Santo Domingo de Chincha y preguntado por qué dixo que por poder que para ello le avian ymbiado de Lima" (Ydiaques distributed these lands to the natives of the town of Santo Domingo de Chincha and when asked why stated that he was given this power and sent from Lima), in BNP, B1051 (1616), fol. 36v.

42. BNP, B1051 (1616), fol. 30 r.

43. BNP, B1051 (1616), fol. 50 r.

44. Alto was recorded as being born in the valley of Chincha, Ochama from the town of Santo Domingo de Chincha of the *ayllu* (local kinship group) Chicon, and María Omoto from the town of Santo Domingo de Chincha, of the ayllu Lurin.

45. BNP, B1051 (1616), fol. 53r.

46. Rebecca Earle, "Algunos pensamientos sobre 'El indio borracho' en el imaginario criollo," trans. Iván Martínez Jimenez, *Columbia: Red Revista de Estudios Sociales* 29 (2008): 22.

47. Juan de Hevia Bolaños, *Curia Philipica* (1797; repr., Madrid: Lex Nova. S. A., 1989), 1:93–94. Procuradores objected to the witnesses of another party in a process called *prueba de tacha* (test and disqualification of witnesses), which could be done after the publication of the testimonies. The first edition of Hevia's *Curia Philipica* was in 1603.

48. "Buenos indios i buenos cristianos i que tratan verdad i no son borrachos ni criados," in BNP, B1051 (1616), fol. 57r. Some of the indigenous witnesses presented by doña Juana were don Pedro Hatunca, Çiprian Quispe, Ana Alto, Isabel de Ochama, Alonso Choclla, Juan Ruraico, María Omoto, Martin Pachaico, Juan Jaico, Diego Quipai, Martin Guailas, and Luis Quispi.

49. *Tierras vacas* was a legal term that meant the absence of a recognizable owner or possessor of these lands. In the mid-sixteenth century, the allotment of lands, which were considered vacas, stirred up the litigation by caciques before the Audiencia of Lima. On early sixteenth century land tenure, see Robert G. Keith, *Conquest and Agrarian Change: The Emergence of the Hacienda System on the Peruvian Coast*, Harvard Historical Studies 93 (Cambridge, MA: Harvard University Press, 1976); Luis Miguel Glave and María Isabel Remy, *Estructura agraria y vida rural en una región andina: Ollantaytambo entre los siglos XVI y XIX* (Cusco: Centro de Estudios Rurales Andinos, Bartolomé de Las Casas, 1983); Susan E. Ramírez, *Provincial Patriarchs: Land Tenure and the Economics of Power in Colonial Peru* (Albuquerque: University of New Mexico Press, 1986); and Guevara, *Propiedad agraria*.

50. Colonial caciques went to Lima to litigate and observe the state of their trials and businesses. This phenomenon caused the criticism of Spanish jurists. One example of the caciques' legal activities is don Cristóbal Choquecasa in the early seventeenth century; see José Carlos de la Puente Luna, "Choquecasa va a la Audiencia: Cronistas, litigantes y el debate sobre la autoría del Manuscrito Quechua de Huarochirí," *Histórica* 39, no. 1 (July 2015).

51. BNP, B1051 (1616), fols. 101v–102v.

52. "Tiene por cossa cierta declararian a la medida del deseo de la dicha doña Juana," in BNP, B1951 (1616), fols. 57r, 109r.

53. BNP, B893 (1618).

54. "Doña Magdalena Chimaca, Cacica Principal del Valle de Chincha, mujer legítima de Bernabé de Morales, español, contra don Rodrigo de Guzmán y Ayala sobre unas tierras"; "con muchos bofetones y coces y arrastrándola por los cabellos y jurando que la había de matar," in BNP, B1488 (1605), fol. 4r [2000001901].

55. "Apremiada contra toda su voluntad y forzada con el justo temor de la muerte," BNP, B1488 (1605), fol. 4v.

56. For an indispensable reading of the natives' challenges in the colonial period, see Steve Stern, *Peru's Indian Peoples and the Challenge of Spanish Conquest: Huamanga to 1640*, 2nd ed. (Madison: University of Wisconsin Press, 1993), 158–83. Stern, *Peru's Indian Peoples*, 114–37, also explores the significant role of Spanish justice in the indigenous colonial experience in Huamanga.

57. BNP, B1488 (1605), fols. 10v, 11r.

58. BNP, B1488 (1605), fol. 11v.

59. Patricia Seed, *To Love, Honor, and Obey in Colonial Mexico: Conflicts over Marriage Choice, 1574–1821* (Stanford: Stanford University Press, 1988), 32–30.

60. Prison sentences for debts were common in colonial Peruvian justice. In 1580, Antonio de Porras, a Spaniard who lived in Ollantaytambo, was accused of not honoring his obligations with his workers. Afterwards, he proved his innocence and left the jail; see Glave and Remy, *Estructura agraria*, 134.

61. If Viceroy Velasco gave the fiat, the sale should have occurred between 1599 (when Chimaca received the lands from her father) and 1604 (the end of Velasco's tenure). In the years of tension for the pago de Larán between doña Magdalena and Bernabé (around 1612 and 1619), the viceroys were marquis of Montesclaros (r. 1607–15) or the Prince of Esquilache (r. 1615–21). Montesclaros had a reputation of being a "pro-Indian" viceroy. In 1617, doña Magdalena was in Lima.

62. This was a legal practice associated with *arbitrismo* (political and legal literature in search of specific royal policies). In seventeenth century, an *arbitrista* was an author who addressed memoriales to the royal authorities (the king, viceroy, and Council of the Indies) narrating precise problems and proposing urgent solutions. They sought their intervention for the enactment of specific legislation. The structure of arbitrista genre was reutilized in printed allegations that circulated in rooms of justice as well as religious sermons in preaching, see Carlos Gálvez Peña, "'El mejor arbitrio, el sermón': Discurso religioso y representación política en el Perú del siglo XVII," *Anuario de Estudios Americanos* 71, no. 1 (January–June 2014). For a discussion of arbitrismo and its relevance in seventeenth-century Peru, see Fred Bronner, "Peruvian Arbitristas under Viceroy Chinchón, 1629–1639," *Scripta Hierosolymitana* 26 (1974).

63. Antonio de Torres y Mendoza conducted research in 1618, a juicio de residencia. "Juicio de residencia tomado por el factor Antonio de Torres a don Francisco de Xeria," in BNP, B893, fol. 618 [2000001322]:

64. In his testimony: "algunas veces estando él dando lecciones de canto a los dichos muchachos oía que Magdalena daba gritos y al ir a casa a ver lo que pasaba la veía maltratada y llena de golpes" (sometimes, when he was giving singing lessons to the boys, he heard Magdalena screaming and when he went to the home to see what had happened, he saw her mistreated and full of bruises), in BNP, B1488.

65. This was a constant trope in the cases of domestic abuse; see Bernard Lavallé, "Divorcio y nulidad de matrimonio en Lima (1650–1700): la desavenencia conyugal como indicador social," *Revista Andina* 4, no. 2 (December 1986): 442.

66. Alonso de la Peña Montenegro, a prominent theologian in the seventeenth century, argued that "no hay mujer española tan pusilánime como el indio más atrevido" (there is no Spanish woman as fainthearted as the most daring Indian), in *Itinerario para Parochos de Indios: En que se tratan las materias más particulares, tocantes a ellos para su buena administración* (Antwerp: Casa de Juan Bautista Verdussen, mercader de libros, 1726), 162.

67. BNP, B1488 (1605).

68. María José Collantes de Terán de la Hera, "La mujer en el proceso inquisitorial: Hechicería, bigamia y solicitación," *Anuario de Historia del Derecho Español* 77 (2017): 56–57.

69. In the words of Rodrigo Acuña y Silva: "Las mujeres son versátiles, dolosas, falaces, mentirosas, frívolas y corruptibles, además de propensas a la acusación y proclives al odio y la ira" (women are versatile, malicious, fallacious liars, frivolous and corruptible, as well as prone to accusation, hatred, and anger), in Collantes, "La mujer," 58. Rodrigo Acuña y Silva's, *Tractatus de Confessaris Solicitantibus* (Valladolid: Juan de Rueda, 1620) represented the mysoginistic view of the theological thought in seventeenth-century Castile (see Collantes, "La mujer," 56–59).

70. Enrique Gacto Fernández, "Imbecellitas Sexus," *Cuadernos de Historia del Derecho* 20 (2013).

71. Lavallé, "Divorcio y nulidad."

72. For a discussion of colonial domestic violence, see Victor M. Uribe-Uran, *Fatal Love: Spousal Killers, Law, and Punishment in the Late Colonial Spanish Atlantic* (Stanford: Stanford University Press, 2015).

73. Juan de Meléndez, *Tesoros verdaderos de las Yndias en la historia de la gran provincia de San Juan Bautista del Perú de el Orden de Predicadores* (Rome: Imprenta de Nicolás Angel Tinassio, 1681), 2:440, indicated that "una india noble de Chincha, descendiente de sus reyes llamada Magdalena Chimaco llegó a estar impedida de dolores de cuerpo gastó mucha hacienda sin reparo en médicos y medicinas" (a noble Indian woman from Chincha and a descendant of local royalty, Magdalena Chimaco was impeded by body aches. She spent much on doctors and medicines without success). However, because she could not recover her health, she went to Lima. In the capital, the stories of the miraculous power of Santa Rosa were popular. Doña Magdalena used relics associated with the saint (a palm leaf and a piece of her veil and robe) by putting them on her chest and "pidiendo con mucha confianza salud a la Virgen Rosa" (asking the virgin Rosa for health with much confidence), she recovered the next day. Afterwards, she decided to visit Rosa's tomb to express her

gratitude. Finally, doña Magdalena "se volvió a los valles de Chincha sin mal nin-guno dentro de pocos días" (within a few days, she returned to the valley of Chincha without any ailment) (Meléndez, *Tesoros verdaderos*, 2:440). Isabel Flores de Oliva died in Lima in August 1617, and Magdalena must have been in Lima between late August and September of that year.

74. La Puente Luna, "That Which Belongs."

75. Cornelia Hughes Dayton, *Women before the Bar: Gender, Law & Society in Connecticut, 1639–1789* (Chapel Hill: The University of North Carolina Press, 1995); Bianca Premo, "On Currents and Comparisons: Gender and the Atlantic 'Turn' in Spanish America," *History Compass* 8, no. 3 (March 2010); Yanna Yannakakis, "Indigenous People and Legal Culture in Spanish America," *History Compass* 11, no. 11 (November 2013); and Thomas Duve, "Indigenous Rights in Latin America," in *The Oxford Handbook of Legal History*, ed. Markus D. Dubber and Christopher Tomlins (Oxford: Oxford University Press, 2018).

CHAPTER 8

A Royalist Cacica

DOÑA TERESA CHOQUEHUANCA AND
THE POSTREBELLION NATIVES OF THE
PERUVIAN HIGHLANDS

Sara Vicuña Guengerich

A t nearly 13,000 feet (4,000 meters) above sea level, on a grassy plain with rounded hills forming undulations on the west lies the province of Azángaro. In the vicinity of the majestic Lake Titicaca, Azángaro was the home of doña Teresa Choquehuanca, the daughter of the powerful *kuraka* (ethnic leader, cacique), don Diego Choquehuanca.[1] The Choquehuancas could trace their genealogy to before the Spanish conquest as descendants of Aymara lords and Inca emperors.[2] In the community of Azángaro Anansaya, they claimed to have ruled since the times of the Incas, and by the eighteenth century, they became the most powerful cacical family of the region.[3] Born in the mid-1740s, doña Teresa became a *cacica y gobernadora* (a female indigenous leader with the role of mustering tribute and native labor) in the aftermath of the Tupac Amaru Rebellion (1780–82) due to her loyalty to the Spanish Crown and her native noble blood.

Perhaps the rich documentation about this woman has been largely overlooked because the native nobility who remained loyal to the Crown during the era's indigenous uprisings gained a traitorous stigma or because she was considered as merely an interim cacica ruling in the absence of a male heir. As a member of this royalist collectivity and a woman, doña Teresa's case has been doubly silenced from the historical record. An examination of the available documentation on doña Teresa, however, allows us to examine the trajectory of her political conduct in relation to the Spanish Crown and to her community. As it did other caciques from this late colonial period and region, the Spanish system expected her to oversee the distribution of communal resources and the collection of tribute and *mita* (forced labor draft) at the mines while also allowing her private gain. When she did so by re-creating the power and influence of her male predecessors—through land expropriation from her rural dependents, entrepreneurial self-gain activities, and personal political alliances—she was ultimately challenged with vicious gendered protests from her defiant native subordinates. Her responses to these challenges exemplify how cacicas attempted to battle a series of cultural forces and broader economic trends to maintain their authority at a time of a general weakening of this institution.

In past decades, a series of studies have provided evidence of late-colonial female rulership for which archival materials are significant, albeit fragmentary. David Garrett's study of hereditary cacicas in the bishopric of Cuzco brings to light numerous examples of cacicas who ruled in their own name as well as through their husbands or proxies. He asserts that cacicas served a dual purpose: as heiresses they reproduced intergenerational hierarchies and as wives they allowed cacical authority to move between different noble patrilines, thus addressing competition among indigenous noblemen for *cacicazgos* (office of the cacique, including sometimes its political role, services, and property).[4] Yet he also encourages us to further explore the realm of the economic, familial, and personal authority of these cacicas to understand how they played a role within Andean indigenous politics. The extant documentation about doña Teresa's ancestors and their cacicazgo, business records within the main regions of the Titicaca basin, accession to cacica, *probanzas de méritos* (merit inquests), and legal battles, as well as the testaments of her relatives in relation to her, yield a narrative where she emerges as a purposeful historical subject.[5] She was wealthy, took the royalists' side in indigenous-Spanish conflicts, and in contrast to most cacicas discussed in this volume, actually served as a gobernadora. The position that she claimed within the colonial system in an era of political and economic adversity made her a rich target for opposition. The conflicts surrounding her authority illustrate the relationship cacicas had with *principales* ("hereditary nobles," who sometimes exercised political influence) as well as with commoners, suggesting the different expectations indigenous people had for a female ruler and illuminating how Andean gendered conceptions could be used against her.

THE CHOQUEHUANCA FAMILY'S NETWORK

The historiography on the Choquehuanca lineage has emphasized the importance of its male members in a long list of legendary caciques since the time of the conquest.[6] The women are less known, but no less important. In the five generations prior to doña Teresa's birth, the Choquehuancas' wealth tactics had centered on the control of communities through a series of strategic marriages. These included hypergamous alliances between Aymara lords and Inca women, crossed alliances between distinct cacical lineages around the Titicaca basin, endogamic alliances within the local communities of Azángaro Anansaya and Urinsaya, and interethnic alliances with descendants of Spanish settlers or *criollos* (American-born Spaniards).[7] These unions expanded their pasturelands for this region's abundant stock of herds, enabling their appropriation of native labor and tribute.[8] They also contributed to shaping the identity of native elites in the way they positioned themselves among one another. (See fig. 8.1.)

Doña Teresa's parents, don Diego Choquehuanca and doña Melchora Bejar y Vega, were an example of a mixed criollo-Aymara-Inca marriage. Doña Melchora's family was engaged in pastoral and mining ventures in the region. They had allegedly ruled the town of Putina prior to the 1720s, and the eighteenth-century limestone church standing there was built with their donations.[9] Don Diego was not only a member of an affluent native family, but he had also been educated in the school of caciques of San Borja, perhaps along with the future rebel Tupac Amaru II.[10] In sum, the eighteenth-century Choquehuancas, unlike many native nobles, even those of Cuzco, had the solvency and the cultural capital to be recognized as provincial elites by Spaniards. Moreover, they considered themselves an amalgamation of the Inca, Aymara, and Spanish higher strata.

Growing up, doña Teresa and her six siblings lived in a two-story house with eleven rooms, two patios, and two kitchens—a residence only comparable to that of a Spanish official. Each child—Roque, Blas, José, Gregorio, Dionisia, María, and Teresa—had a room of their own, furnished with desks, chairs, beds and lavish linens, and trunks for their Andean and European clothing. They probably ate together in the dining room, which had benches and a sizable table, and as they gathered with their parents or other important community members in the main lounge, the children may have sat on the wooden floors covered by imported rugs, gazing at the walls covered by nearly twenty paintings of former ancestors, the Virgin Mary, and Jesus. The

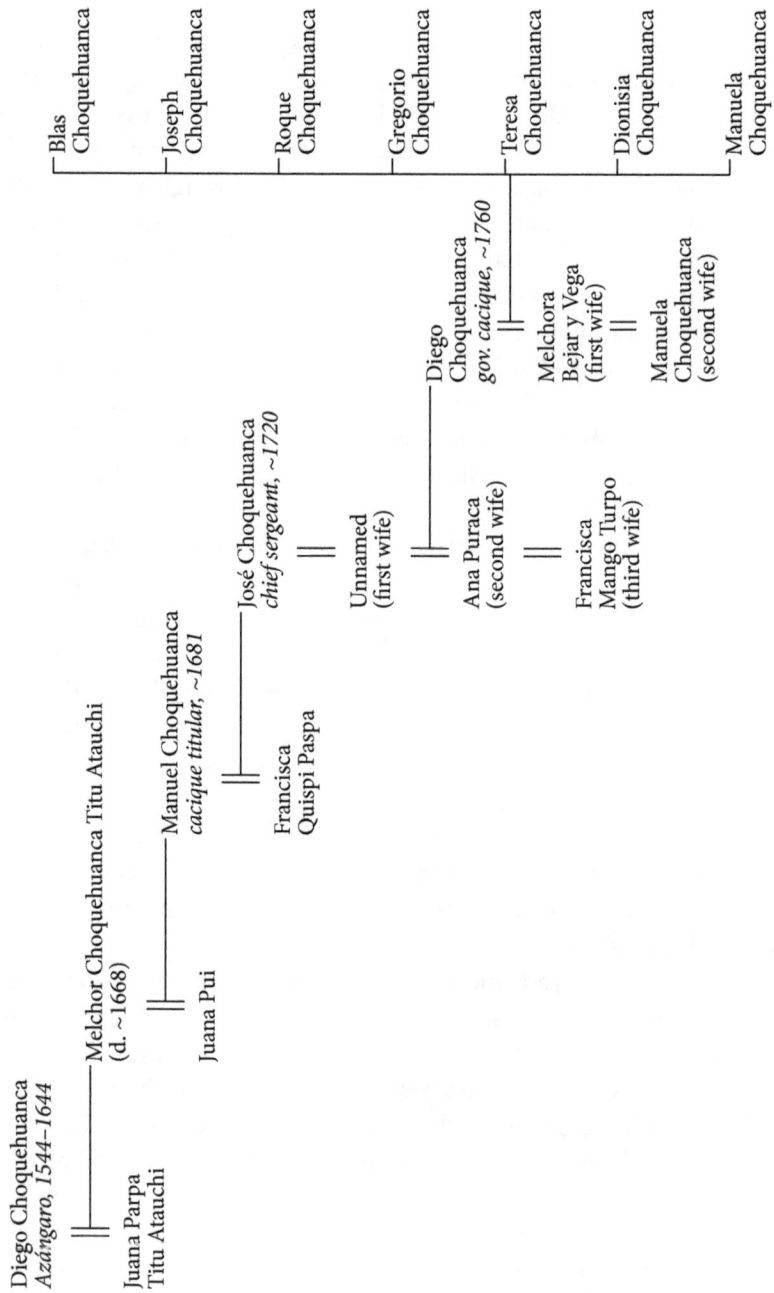

Fig. 8.1. Choquehuanca genealogy

Diego Choquehuanca
Azángaro, 1544–1644

Juana Parpa
Titu Atauchi

Melchor Choquehuanca Titu Atauchi
(d. ~1668)

Juana Pui

Manuel Choquehuanca
cacique titular, ~1681

Francisca
Quispi Paspa

José Choquehuanca
chief sergeant, ~1720

Unnamed
(first wife)

Ana Puraca
(second wife)

Francisca
Mango Turpo
(third wife)

Diego
Choquehuanca
gov. cacique, ~1760

Melchora
Bejar y Vega
(first wife)

Manuela
Choquehuanca
(second wife)

Blas
Choquehuanca

Joseph
Choquehuanca

Roque
Choquehuanca

Gregorio
Choquehuanca

Teresa
Choquehuanca

Dionisia
Choquehuanca

Manuela
Choquehuanca

statues of saints distributed around the house reminded the children of the Christian doctrine they learned on Sundays at the town church.[11]

Doña Teresa's family also possessed several estates, worth 14,000 pesos, and more than 14,000 camelids. With such a long line of noble and affluent ancestors, doña Teresa and her siblings were likely expected to attain similar standings in colonial society, and they did. They were all more than just lettered natives. Blas and José attained the title of *justicias mayores* (native deputies), and both were also substitute kurakas with military ranks. Gregorio and Dionisia entered the religious life. Dionisia became a white-veil nun at the Santa Catalina convent in Arequipa, and Gregorio came to be the benefice of the Metropolitan Cathedral in La Plata.[12] While Roque, María, and doña Teresa sought marriage alliances with Spanish criollos, doña Teresa also became a successful businesswoman, *segunda persona* (secondary leader to primary kuraka) of the cacicazgo while her father was still alive, and subsequently confirmed as cacica y gobernadora.[13] Since the formal or official authority of any cacique in the public space mattered only to Spaniards, some of doña Teresa's personal characteristics, as well as her relationships with the principales and commoners of an *ayllu* (local kinship group), help us to explore how cacicas might have been chosen to rule and what their powers and limitations were within indigenous politics in this region.

DOÑA TERESA'S PERSONAL TRAJECTORY

As a young adult, doña Teresa became the owner of an *obraje* (textile enterprise).[14] A determined woman, she likely learned the business trade from her ancestors—during the seventeenth century, the abundant camelid and sheep fiber of Azángaro was processed in obrajes that employed hundreds of natives through which they paid a third of their tribute allowances. Considering that to complete a *pieza de ropa* (item of clothing) demanded the labor of at least six people[15] and scarcity of native labor was a problem for highland elites, doña Teresa likely needed to secure a constant labor supply.[16] She did so by marrying another prominent landholder with access to workers, the Biscayan don Domingo de Irastorza.

Upon their marriage, she brought 3,000 pesos in dowry, which would add to the "abundant wealth" he possessed.[17] Doña Teresa and don Domingo carried out their business ventures together for a few years. On her initiative, they expanded the amount of livestock and textile production, and they also distributed an assortment of *efectos de Castilla* (goods produced in Spain) along the Collao region, which included the provinces of Lampa, Azángaro, Puno, and Chucuito, with the help of middlemen.[18] As the practice of the *reparto de comercio* system (forced distribution of European wares to natives) had been legalized between 1751 and 1756, it is arguable that doña Teresa and her husband cooperated with the *corregidor* (royal magistrate) of Azángaro, Fernando Inclán y Valdéz, distributing high-priced goods to the native population.[19] The couple continued their partnership until 1761, when don Domingo died. Upon his death, doña Teresa compelled her husband's heirs to return the value of her dowry to her estate lest his private estate be forfeited.[20] Apparently, she continued her ventures as a widow, with the help of agents, as evidenced by a 1762 suit in which she was accused by commoner natives of taking lands from three ayllus.

The complainants asserted that doña Teresa had built three large rooms, probably to expand her obraje, on the very spot where one of the expelled community peasants stood, and she had done it "at the cost of the Indians, without paying them anything."[21] Doña Teresa justified her actions by arguing that these had been the Choquehuancas' lands since the late sixteenth century but they had only recently started to exploit them. Her father backed up her claims and justified this economic maneuver, for which he was also accused for abuses.

That same year, the indigenous inhabitants of Muñani complained that don Diego Choquehuanca was evading royal tribute by keeping a number of natives from entering into the tribute list, so that he could collect their levies for his personal account. He was also charged with making twelve-year-old boys pay 2 pesos of tribute every six months when, as minors, they were legally exempt from tribute obligations, and declaring *yanaconas* (paid personal dependents without kinship ties to the community) to be *originarios* (indigenous persons with claims and obligations within communities of origin) so that they too would pay a tribute of 3 pesos every six months.[22] As Nils Jacobsen points out, these legal battles among native communities, their caciques, and corregidores were not only symptomatic of the cycle of rebellions that would ensue in the following decades but also the legacy of colonialism that polarized society into antagonistic groups, which eventually affected the implementation of economic policies and the effectiveness of labor recruitment, taxation, and other native resources.[23] As the case of the Choquehuancas exemplifies, these antagonisms first pitted native commoners against nobles and later loyalists against insurgents.

The claim that don Diego patronized the lesser community's native officers, for instance, occupies center-stage in the official complaints. The ayllu leaders accused don Diego of jailing the former *alcalde de naturales* (an elected indigenous leader of a town), ripping out his hair and confiscating part of his livestock under the pretext of a shortfall in tribute.[24] Yet, in the midst of these ethnic conflicts, the colonial Spanish courts were an arena for testing the powers of native litigants. The Choquehuancas proved to be more powerful than their adversaries as not only were all these accusations dismissed by the *audiencia* (royal high court) of Charcas, now with jurisdiction of the Titicaca basin, but in November of that year the court confirmed don Diego Choquehuanca's rights to the Muñani lands. The formal procedure of taking possession was carried out in 1765.[25] This official confirmation only reaffirmed the feeling of superiority of the Choquehuancas over the rest of the natives, driving a wedge deeper between the two.

Of the forty-six caciques appearing in the 1754 tribute list for the province, none came close to the wealth and power of this cacical family.[26] Moreover, by the early 1770s Azángaro was in its prime. On his journey through this region, the Spanish geographer Cosme Bueno asserted that "this province was extremely abundant in livestock, which constitutes the principal base for its commerce, as well as camelid and sheep fibers, tallow and hogs."[27] By this time, the Choquehuancas' network had covered the main regions of the transit corridor along the shores of Lake Titicaca with eleven estates in the Azángaro province itself. (See map 6.) The great road that connected Lima with the crucial mining center of Potosí extended to the western border of the province of Azángaro for 12 to 19 miles (20 to 30 kilometers). Another road that fed into the major transverse road at Lampa connected the altiplano with Arequipa and its coastal valleys.[28] The strategic location of Azángaro had been perfect for doña Teresa's commercial activities. She had accumulated significant wealth in gold and silver coins and other items to the point that her own father had borrowed money from her at various times.[29] Like doña Teresa, other native entrepreneurs also benefited from these roads until the late 1770s, but in the following two decades, the fiscal aspects of the Bourbon Reforms exacerbated the disruptions of trade systems in the southern Andes.[30]

By 1778, trade had fallen under the control of royal authorities, and Charles III issued a royal ordinance allowing direct exchanges between four ports in the west coast of South America. The opening of commerce between Buenos Aires and Upper Peru would create widespread competition of internal and global markets. Overproduction of Andean textiles, for example, now faced unprecedented competition from European textiles. Furthermore, the years

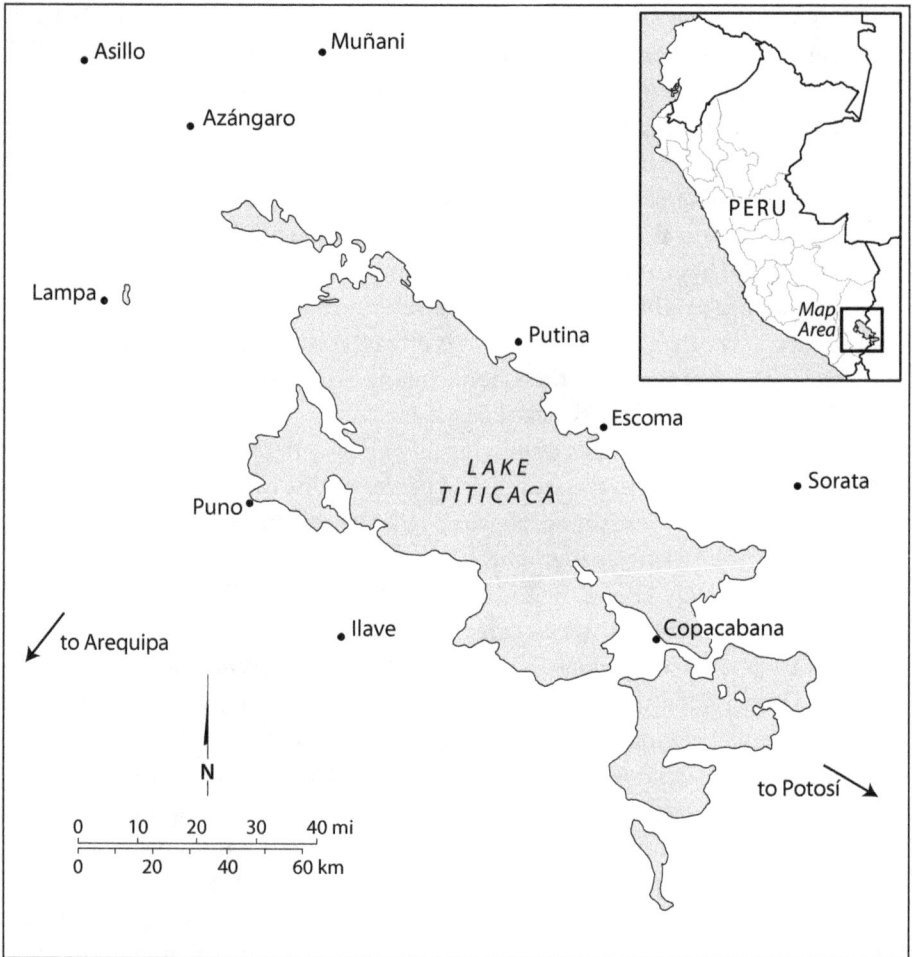

Map 6. Major Towns of the Titicaca Basin

1778 and 1779 brought extreme cold weather to the highland regions, damaging crops and making travel more difficult.[31] The Choquehuancas—as well as other cacique businessmen, such as José Gabriel Condorcanqui, a muleteer in this region—experienced this crisis, but reacted differently. In addition to an economic decline, the tense and fragile alliances among natives, clear from decades prior, resulted in the complex cycle of social movements in which doña Teresa and other native noblewomen took part.

THE CHOQUEHUANCAS AND THE
TUPAC AMARU REBELLION

By 1780 the kuraka of Tungasuca, José Gabriel Condorcanqui, rebelled against the Spanish Crown under the moniker Tupac Amaru II. Recognized by many as the rightful heir of the last Inca ruler but most of all carrying out revenge against the natives' oppressors, he managed to rally thousands of combatants united against the economic burdens imposed by the Bourbon Reforms. Seeking to enlist the support of powerful kurakas, Amaru wrote letters to don Diego Choquehuanca, explaining his efforts. Not only did don Diego oppose the movement, but he immediately denounced the rebel to the nearby corregidores.[32] He also mobilized his sons, don Joseph and don Gregorio, to shore up their defenses and disseminated the rebel's plans, which he had obtained from a reliable source.[33]

The Choquehuancas, like several other noble natives, remained intentionally loyal to the Bourbon Crown. They were loyal to both the monarchy and the idea of nobility that they had so strategically forged throughout the colonial period. When Amaru proclaimed he would extirpate all corregidores and mitas with the true king's authority, adding that he was "the last descendant of the last king of Peru,"[34] he was fighting against all that the economically successful cacique families of the region held dear. Amaru's message thus resonated primarily with some members of the Andean nobility and made a huge impact among the commoners.

Some of these nobles, many of them unsuccessful kuraka aspirants, supported the insurgent movement. For instance, Pedro Vilcapaza, a *ladino* (fluent in Spanish) from Muñani whose ancestors had been long-term rivals of the Choquehuancas, became a major rebel figure in the area north and west of Titicaca.[35] The commoner natives of the Titicaca basin also championed the movement. In addition, Tupac Catari (formerly Julián Apaza) led another massive uprising in other regions of Upper Peru, which paralleled, joined, and contravened the Tupac Amaru rebellion.[36] Amaru's army had recruited people from several surrounding towns including Chucuito, Lampa, Puno, Carabaya, and Azángaro. Those who did not join the uprising fled to Arequipa.

In the meantime, some of the royalists had captured Amaru's nephew, Simon Noguera, and executed him in public. Enraged by the death of Noguera and thinking he had been killed by Choquehuanca's forces, Amaru assaulted the cacique's family and their numerous estates with fury.[37] A description of his entrance into Azángaro describes how "Tupac Amaru ransacked the houses of don Diego and don Joseph Choquehuanca leaving not a single stake standing in the wall, and he executed the same thing in other villages spreading horror and fright and taking the lives of the corregidores and chapetones."[38] Azángaro soon became the rebels' headquarters as it provided them with much needed funds from properties seized at obrajes and livestock estates. During the raids, thousands of heads of livestock that belonged to the Choquehuancas were stolen by rebels and local commoners as the whole family fled in different directions.

The description of these attacks and the events that happened afterwards are vividly narrated in doña Teresa's letters to officials at the Audiencia de la Plata and retold in her 1794 probanzas de méritos that reached the Spanish king. These sources can be read against the numerous documents related to the rebellion. In both instances, doña Teresa describes how she and her family witnessed the destruction of all their possessions and were forced to separate and flee Azángaro. Don Diego managed to march down to Arequipa, where most of the corregidores took refuge, aided by his two sons, Joseph and Gregorio, who were actively fighting against Amaru's forces in the Titicaca region. As doña Teresa, her daughter, her sister María, her brother Blas, and other relatives were fleeing to Sorata, doña María drowned in the Escoma River.[39]

Sorata, capital of the province of Larecaja (see map 6), became the refuge of the royalists, including the native elites. Doña Teresa's party managed to arrive and remained safe briefly until the insurgents laid siege to the city. Pedro Vilcapaza oversaw the siege, with thousands of rebels surrounding the town. The royalists of Sorata confronted the mutineers with their own ammunition, and Blas died while fighting. A testimony of this siege states that "bullets were flying everywhere, killing all kinds of people from all ages, daily."[40] Other Choquehuanca relatives were captured and hanged. Moreover, in the following weeks, the population ran low on food. Hunger must have been unbearable, as doña Teresa claims, "We went to the extremes of eating wild animals."[41] In fact, desperate refugees, said friar José Eustaquio Caravedo, "ate the meats of mules, dogs, cats, mice and other filthy animals."[42]

Once Sorata was defeated, declared another witness, Andrés (Mendiguri) Tupac Amaru, the rebel's cousin, and Gregoria Apaza, Tupac Catari's sister, entered the town riding horses, dressed elegantly as Incas. They fashioned a tribunal in the main plaza condemning many to die and confiscating their wealth. The only ones who were able to save their lives were the women who resigned themselves to be stripped of their *mantillas* and *faldellines* (lace veils and fancy dresses) and wear instead the rags of the commoner natives.[43] Doña Teresa confirms this in her depositions saying that she, along with other women and children, were left almost naked.

Most of the seized items were sent to Amaru's headquarters in Azángaro. Some goods, however, remained in the hands of Gregoria Apaza, who, in the words of historian María Eugenia del Valle, "was passionate about the possibility of becoming rich, not only to be well-dressed, meet all her needs and have a Spanish servant, Josefa Anaya, but most of all to feel like a great lady, the *talla* who gives away presents, grants petitions, lends money and distributes her resources when everyone else is hungry."[44]

Gregoria's actions serve to exemplify how some natives took advantage of the situation to become leaders and to personify the characteristics they wanted to see in one. Del Valle also adds that in Sorata, it was the natives who treated Gregoria like a cacica and a gobernadora, sitting her in a chair like a queen and referring to her as *señora y madre* (lady and mother).[45] Something similar happened to Micaela Bastidas, Tupac Amaru's wife, whom the natives called *Mamanchic* (mother) and duly obeyed, respected, and even feared for the enormous zeal with which she pursued the rebellion.[46]

In comparison to these women, doña Teresa was repudiated, seen "as the daughter of a traitor cacique" by most of the insurgents.[47] She fled Sorata several times, only to be repeatedly captured by the rebels. She remained captive there for two months until she managed to escape by foot from Ilabaya to the town of Copacabana, in present-day Bolivia. She claimed to have walked 16 leagues (ca. 55 miles [88 kilometers]) alone with "indescribable efforts."[48] Her depiction of the sufferings she endured is characteristic of the major narratives evoking the misery of the royalist soldiers in Sorata, La Paz, and Cuzco as they trekked through the mountains dressed mostly in rags and constantly vulnerable to rebel hit-and-run attacks. Teresa's goal of reaching Copacabana, a well-known sanctuary, plays a symbolic role in her narrative. The Sanctuary of Our Lady of Copacabana was the bastion of the native nobility's Christendom, a point of contention in the midst of this rebellion.[49] At a time when everyone questioned one another's Christianity, her arrival to this holy place, at least in her narrative, foretells the victory of the Christian royalist faction. Amaru's forces could not reach her there. Yet her brothers, fighting along with a royalist commander, came to her rescue.

By 1782, Amaru had been captured and killed and his rebellion defeated, but the insurgent movement would continue. By this time doña Teresa was returned to Azángaro, to find a devastated local livestock economy. During the years of the Great Rebellion, soldiers and peasants raided animals from abandoned or unprotected estates to enrich themselves. In the words of the parish priest of Juliaca, a few miles from Azángaro: "The estates of the churches, convents, monasteries, and private persons are seen today in the utmost decadence; many years will still pass by to rebuild them. Many houses in the towns and other places are burned, through actions of both Indian rebels and Spanish troops, who destroyed the towns. In some places, one is caused to cry upon seeing their ruins."[50]

The Choquehuancas were perhaps the ones who lost the most. By 1783, don Diego and his son Joseph began expropriating thousands of heads of livestock from several indigenous communities, which they claimed had been stolen from their estates during the rebellion.[51] These actions were opposed by both the corregidor, don Lorenzo Zata y Zubiria, and his agent, don Mariano Correa, who allegedly had their own economic interests competing against the Choquehuancas. One of doña Teresa's letters to the Audiencia de Charcas denounced the excesses of these men and their native allies and included the testimonies of other natives that claimed that the corregidor and his agent were forcing abusive repartos de comercio upon them.[52] Evidently, the commercial relationship of the Choquehuancas with the corregidores deteriorated at this time.

In the aftermath of the Tupac Amaru rebellion, the Spanish Royal Council was apprehensive about the native elite and would not consider requests from natives claiming descent from the Incas. A 1782 administrative order even reached the Peruvian viceroyalty audiencias prohibiting the *oidores* (high court judges) of Lima and Buenos Aires from admitting any new proofs of nobility and confiscating the *Royal Commentaries of the Incas* written by the Inca Garcilaso.[53] Nonetheless, records of Inca and non-Inca women petitioning for cacicazgos, and obtaining them, steadily emerge from the archive after 1784.[54] It should not be surprising, then, that the daughter of a long-time loyal cacique would also request a reward, as she was aware of her rights and obligations, the Spanish gendered discourses of that era, and the legal system, as well as had the ability to initiate litigation.

In her 1793 inquest, Teresa petitioned the confirmation of her titles as the cacica y gobernadora of Azángaro Anansaya because she had been the acting cacica and serving with a "manly spirit" since 1787 while her father was still alive.[55] Many things had happened by then, which she mentions in this document. Her father, the elder kuraka, received the title of gobernador. She had been married again, this time to the sergeant don Nicolás de la Cámara, an obscure creole. Her brother don Joseph was declared a knight of the order of Santiago and named "faithful and distinguished cacique"[56] before he died in 1787 leaving her a small inheritance, some debts, and the responsibilities of helping her aging and ill father with the cacicazgo.[57] Her noble counterparts from Azángaro Urinsaya, the royalist Mango Turpos, had recently been granted cacicazgos elsewhere.[58] Thus, doña Teresa's request had a precedent. It also suggests her sense of governance that, albeit justified by the colonial system, allowed for women rulers within pueblo politics.

In 1792, the newly appointed *intendente* (a Bourbon-era official) of Puno, the marquis of Casa Hermosa, had installed doña Teresa as interim cacica upon the death of her father. He described her installation: "Taking doña Teresa Choquehuanca by the hand, I gave her real, factual and corporeal possession of this office, and sitting her in the *duo* [ceremonial chair], she received this appointment without contradiction so that no one deprives her of it without a hearing . . . and all the Indians embraced her and proclaimed her as their legitimate [cacica], displaying their satisfaction and contentment."[59] Among those present at doña Teresa's installation were also the bishop's deputy, the alcaldes de naturales, and some prominent members from the Calsina and the Vilcapaza clans, the Choquehuanca's long-time adversaries.

From the Spanish officials' vantage point, doña Teresa had been identified as a descendant of a noble native line, already experienced serving as segunda persona to her father and someone who had amassed past economic successes. The alleged native reactions to her installation suggest a recognition of her backing by the colonial state, but as Sinclair Thomson reminds us, for Andean natives, the negotiation of a cacique involved a set of traditionally defined expectations for conduct, which was in effect until the late colonial era. Some of those expectations were economic and had a dual role. On one hand, caciques engaged actively in colonial commerce and sometimes accumulated substantial private fortunes. On the other, in exchange for their privileged access to community lands and labor, traditional norms of economic reciprocity obliged the caciques to show their generosity with their subordinates.[60] Doña Teresa's administration of the cacicazgo fulfilled one of those economic roles but not the other. When she began in this office, she requested royal permission to rent the lands of Caravilque to tenants outside the community. While she seems to have done this to alleviate the higher taxes of that decade in comparison to the decline in number of tributary originarios, she also accumulated the rental profits for her own gain.[61]

The response from the Azángaro natives to this and other economic ma-
neuvers was immediate. In 1793, the natives of Checayani denounced doña
Teresa to the marquis of Casa Hermosa. Their main complaint was that she
treated them like "slaves," saying they were yanaconas of her "hacienda"
when they considered that estate their "ayllu."[62] She did not reply to the complaint for several months. Rather, she and de la Cámara continued working
on her proof of merits to obtain the confirmation to this cacicazgo. Her 1794
probanza, a summary of doña Teresa's full dossier of 1793, is a rhetorical piece
that centers on her loyalty, Christianity, and rank. It also reflects the Spanish
gender discourses of the era (e.g., "a pious woman infused by God with a virile spirit, who fought against the enemies of the king").[63] While likely written
by Nicolás de la Cámara himself, the document is devoted entirely to doña
Teresa's experiences in the Tupac Amaru rebellion. It was endorsed by the
marquis of Casa Hermosa, who in turn sent it to viceroy Juan José Vertiz.
Both officials highlight doña Teresa's courage during this upheaval and state
that, as an interim cacica, doña Teresa "fulfills these obligations with virile
spirit, collecting the tributes and delivering them herself, like her father did
when he was an active cacique propietario."[64] Casa Hermosa and viceroy Vertiz endorsed doña Teresa and her husband to receive a royal reward, alleging
that her father and brothers died without enjoying theirs.[65]

By 1796, doña Teresa was in her fifties and a widow again. Her wealth had
increased following her father's death in 1792, and she and her daughter,
doña María del Carmen Mendoza, were the *apoderadas* (legal agents) of all
the papers accumulated by the Choquehuancas and deeds to many of their
properties.[66] In addition, she had been confirmed as cacica gobernadora by
the superior government, but not without the opposition of the natives. The
indigenous of Checayani, for instance, persisted in their accusations, this
time demanding that she present the deeds to the property and yanaconas
she claimed. Otherwise, they requested to be free from tribute obligations.[67]
Reading the complaints of the natives against the demands of the new tribute collection, however, provides a contextualized vision of doña Teresa's position in her term as cacica gobernadora. The politics of the marquis of Casa
Hermosa were focused on the restructuring of tribute. He organized tributary *revisitas* (reinspections to revise the findings of earlier inspections) to
increase the number of tributaries, legalized land titles, and reduced tax eva-
sion, for which he also gained several enemies, accusing him of the misap-
propriation of funds.[68] As a cacica in this period, doña Teresa was immersed
in the reformist program of late-colonial fiscal pressures. Her appointment

had also meant a contract with colonial officials, and she was conscious of her position in this system.

She had been in the midst of long-standing ethnic conflicts for most of her adult life, but she had seen time and time again how royal mandates had worked in her family's favor. This time, however, she would face a new set of challenges. By 1797, she found out that several of her native subordinates had sent out four different complaints about her performance as cacica to the marquis of Casa Hermosa. The charges against her provide an interesting window into pueblo politics in a moment of general protests against tribute payment. They also illustrate the relationship cacicas had with principales as well as commoner natives as they suggest what indigenous communities expected from a noble female ruler.

While the natives' main allegation was the excessive tribute that doña Teresa collected, their gender expectations of their cacica occupy a significant portion of their complaints. The principales, for example, accused doña Teresa of wanting to take revenge against them because she was "propelled by her hatred toward us."[69] After all, some of them, like Vilcapaza and Calsina, were related to those who actively participated in the Tupac Amaru rebellion. For these men, doña Teresa's government was unconventional for various reasons. For one, instead of engaging in court litigation on their behalf, they claimed she was unable or unwilling to instruct them in their own legal procedures against the "enemies that usurped our lands."[70] In addition, unlike traditional Andean kurakas who would collect tribute themselves, they claimed, she usually sent her proxies (*mandones* [cacique's employees], *hilacatas* [low-rank native authorities], or *domésticos* [domestic servants]), whom they contended, "do not follow our traditional ancient customs."[71] Here, they were probably referring to the ritual drinking caciques provided to the natives of their ayllus, conveying power and responsibility—because it was through drinking that caciques gained respect.[72] Under her rule, the principales claimed, the commoners had lost respect for their superiors.[73] In sum, doña Teresa failed the principales' expectations to behave as a male leader.

The commoner natives, on the other hand, had a different set of gender expectations from their cacica. While they denounced how doña Teresa continued selling them high-priced items through her proxies, most of their complaints made reference to doña Teresa's lack of a maternal character.[74] The accusations are rife with phrases such as "we live like abandoned orphans," "she does not protect us," "she is indifferent to us" (*nos trata con desamor*), and "she does not promote harmony among us."[75] This is the case, they argued, because "she does not live among us, rather she only comes to get the tribute or sends her mandones to get it."[76] For the commoners, then, it seems to have been more important that doña Teresa would exercise this office like a symbolic "mother" caring for her children, but she did not. In other words, she was neither sufficiently masculine to the principales nor feminine enough to the commoner natives to be an adequate cacica.

The whole set of allegations were ultimately shaped by an attorney that incorporated additional gender discourses that were used against her. References to doña Teresa as "fickle," "stubborn," and "incompetent" were tied directly to her gender. Other attacks referred to her age, claiming that "she gets tired easily," "she sleeps until midday," and is "constantly sick, every day with something new," things, they claimed, a young kuraka would not do.[77] In addition, the document includes some of the alleged abuses of the commoners protesting that doña Teresa "wanted to be treated like a queen," being carried in her duo by at least twenty-five natives who were forced to do so "if they wanted to avoid her wrath."[78]

The general native discontent with this cacica soon became bullying. Assertions such as "we don't want to honor this woman named Teresa using the title of cacica," or "every time she comes around, we insult her in unison, laughing and making fun of her," are part of the commoners' testimonies.[79] Their main goal, as they said, was that doña Teresa "voluntarily step down from this office and the true deserving heir to the cacicazgo be installed."[80] This alleged heir was none other than Manuel Choquehuanca, doña Teresa's nephew (Blas's son), who had been too young to assume the cacicazgo when don Diego died but who nonetheless did not appear in don Diego's testament as his successor.

Doña Teresa's case exemplifies the struggles that other cacicas may have experienced in late-colonial Peru because of their gender, social rank, and the positions they claimed within this system. The Spanish put great emphasis on social status, even within native society as in the case of doña Teresa. It is clear that by emphasizing and encouraging subtle distinctions between different subject groups, Spanish authorities would prevent a unified rebellion against their rule. Doña Teresa, and others like her, were acceptable rulers for the Spaniards because of their loyalty, rank, and "virile" traits. The Spanish learned that many Andean women could be as fierce and aggressive as the insurgent women had proven on and off the battlefields during the Tupac Amaru rebellion, but loyalty to the Crown was a must for this office, in this era. For the natives, however, cacicas still had to find a political balance. As nobles, they had to honor internal indigenous hierarchies and traditional customs. As women, they had to extend their protective power and maternal qualities for the well-being of the commoners.

Both expectations, however, failed to recognize that cacicas were also political beings—more so if they were educated, wealthy, and shrewd, like doña Teresa. She understood the demands and advantages of her position, and she had her own agenda. In a similar fashion to other local kurakas, doña Teresa profited from the trade between Arequipa and Azángaro during her term. Nonetheless, when the tributary numbers fell in 1797, she also requested a *rebaja* (tribute reduction) from the colonial government.[81] In some instances, as doña Teresa declared, she had to cover part of the *tasa* (tribute rate) of her own pocket, something that an impoverished kuraka would not have been able to do. Thus, when she faced the natives' complaints, she became enraged. In her response to these accusations, doña Teresa reminded her subordinates that she was their "legitimate cacica y gobernadora" and labeled these accusations as "inflammatory libels" written by "ill-persuaded Indians against my honor and reputation, so that I may be removed from the cacicazgo."[82] Speaking directly to the marquis of Casa Hermosa, she argued that all these accusations first needed to be legally proved before she would even consider stepping down from this *ministerio* (office), because the natives, she added, "still owe me their delayed tributes."[83]

The native commoners could not present additional documents against their cacica. Nonetheless, they resorted to presenting copies of the previous complaints on her performance. The cacica noted that the latter had no legal value yet had "all the intention to slander her," and she additionally questioned that they could have written it. Rather, she blamed "external forces" for ultimately persuading them to have such a low perception of her.[84] She accused these "forces"—undoubtedly the principales, aided by don Miguel de Urbiola, the deputy mayor and enemy of Casa Hermosa—of plotting against her.[85] Labeling these accusations as "a new rebellion" guided by the "seditious spirit" of the principales and other renegades she was also capitalizing on Spanish fears of social unrest.

Doña Teresa reminded the Spanish officials of the loyalty of her family and of her "blind adherence to and love for the sovereign king," for which she had been rewarded with this cacicazgo.[86] She also stated that her own father had trusted her as the executor of all his properties and possessions and that she had conducted herself according to the recently established *intendencia* (territorial subdivision in the viceroyalty) government rules. Apparently, her nephew, don Manuel Choquehuanca, had already started his political career by now.

A noncompliant member of the Choquehuanca family, don Manuel was likely aware of the Crown's resolution to pacify all indigenous after the Great Rebellion through the temporary abolition of tribute.[87] He began agitating among the natives, encouraging them to pay only half of the required tribute as a strategy to seize the cacicazgo from doña Teresa.[88]

Collecting the native tribute in such conditions was arguably the toughest part of being a cacique, let alone a cacica. Many times, as doña Teresa repeats in her defense, she had to request credit advances when she could not cover the deficit of unpaid tribute with her own money. Producing this testimony must have been a frustrating and stressful task for her amid the attacks and defenses. "To calm my nerves" (*por consultar mi sosiego*), as she stated at one point, doña Teresa decided to step down as cacica y gobernadora and requested the authorities to name her nephew "or anybody else whom your highness may want" as tribute collector.[89] From that moment forward, don Manuel would be the second-in-command in the cacicazgo, but she would remain the cacica propietaria, which indicated that her title was recognized by the superior courts and not just by the natives.

With this clever move, although she later acknowledged was done "in a moment of wrath," doña Teresa rectified this situation in her favor.[90] She would retire to her estate in Muñani, as she herself requested, and don Manuel would have to deal with the *rezagos* (belated tribute payments) that the hilacatas still owed, which amounted to more than 300 pesos.[91] He would also have to persuade Spanish officials to adopt the economic policy of tribute reduction. Don Manuel would ostensibly renounce the cacicazgo in 1799, only to seek reinstatement in 1808.[92] By 1805, doña Teresa was dead and the debates and struggles about the legitimacy of indigenous nobles, role and succession of kurakas, continuation of mita, and weight of taxes on indigenous people invigorated the independence movements of the following years.

CONCLUSION

By empowering local kurakas and their families to rule over commoners since the time of the conquest, Spanish colonial policies contributed to the rise of cacicas, such as doña Teresa Choquehuanca, in late-colonial Andean society. As previous scholarship on cacicazgos has demonstrated, cacicas served a dual purpose: as heiresses, they reproduced intergenerational hierarchies, and as wives, they addressed competition among native noblemen for cacical authority.[93] The well-documented life of doña Teresa helps us expand our

understanding of this dual function and explore cacicas as purposeful historical subjects, that is, as individuals able to contest an oppressive system or claim
a position within it.[94]

Doña Teresa's ascension to cacica gobernadora in the aftermath of the Tupac Amaru rebellion was the result of her long-established reputation as a
member of a royalist noble family, businesswoman who collaborated with
Bourbon economic reforms, and former interim cacica trained in this office by her own father. Yet her appointment was also cause for contention
among the Azángaro natives who resented royalist natives and rejected
their clientelism. The use of Andean gender conceptions against doña Teresa exemplify the tensions of different cultural forces in an era of political
and economic adversity. Doña Teresa's politics and her gender complicated
her specific situation and the history of the cacicazgo in this region. Yet, in a
period of general weakening of this institution, her case exemplifies the ability of noble cacicas to influence colonial governance. Royalist cacicas, more
than traitors, are historical subjects, not simply objects acted upon by men
(native and nonnative), colonial power structures or community traditions
and practices.

NOTES

1. I am grateful to the John Carter Brown Library, which supported writing for
this chapter and other ongoing projects through a National Endowment for the Humanities fellowship. I am also indebted to David Garrett, who graciously shared initial
references to several documents about doña Teresa Choquehuanca with me, as well as
to my generous colleagues Liliana Pérez-Miguel, Marcos Alarcón, and Kathryn Santner, who helped me locate additional sources for the Choquehuanca family in Perú.
Alcira Dueñas, my colleagues in the Women Faculty Writing Program at Texas Tech
University, and the anonymous reviewers of this collection read earlier versions of this
chapter and made useful suggestions. Nonetheless, all interpretations, are my own
responsibility.

2. In Andean ethnography and ethnohistory, the Aymara people were organized within regional kingdoms or ethnic federations that came under Inca rule by
the early fifteenth century. In the Tawantinsuyu realm controlled by the Inca, the
region known as Qollasuyu, which covers the area to the north and northeast of
the Lake Titicaca, is recognized as Aymara territory. For a comprehensive study of the
complex civilizations around Lake Titicaca see Charles Stanish's *Ancient Titicaca: The
Evolution of Complex Society in Southern Peru and Northern Bolivia* (Berkeley: University of California Press, 2003).

3. Anansaya and Urinsaya (also spelled Hanansaya and Hurinsaya) were dual
units of sociopolitical organization in the Andes, often translated as upper and

lower moieties respectively. In Azángaro, the Choquehuancas had ruled the Anansaya moiety while the Mango Turpos were rulers of Urinsaya.

4. David Garrett, "In Spite of Her Sex: The Cacica and the Politics of the Pueblo in Late Colonial Cusco," *Americas* 64, no. 4 (April 2008): 551.

5. Inspired by scholarship on other subordinate and silenced historical subjects (i.e., Afro-Latin Americans and Blacks in the Age of Revolutions), I engage with Michel-Rolph Trouillot's definition of a purposeful historical subject as someone able to articulate an interior self, be that to contest an oppressive system or claim a position within it. See especially chap. 7 in Michel-Rolph Trouillot, *Silencing the Past: Power and the Production of History* (Boston: Beacon Press, 1995).

6. Numerous scholars have explored the real or fabricated genealogical claims of the Choquehuancas to Alonso Tito Atauchi, son of Huascar Inca, who allegedly obtained royal recognition from Charles V in 1544 and 1549. See, for example, Francisco Mostajo, "Los Chuquihuancas hasta la época de Tupac Amaru," *Revista de la Universidad de Arequipa* 25 no. 38 (1953); Fortunato Turpo, *El templo de oro y los Choquehuanca* (Azángaro, Perú: Bicentenario de la Independencia, 1945); Leonardo Altuve, *Choquehuanca y su arenga a Bolívar* (Buenos Aires: Planeta, 1991); Augusto Ramos Zambrano, "Los Choquehuanca de Azángaro en el proceso de la Independencia nacional," in *Pueblos, provincias y regiones en la historia del Perú*, ed. Jessica Bendezú and Margarita Salazar (Lima: Academia Nacional de la Historia, 2006); Augusto Ramos Zambrano, *J. D. Choquehuanca: El cantor de Bolívar. Los caciques Chukiwanka y sus testamentos* (Lima, A. F. A. Editores, 2012); and Nuria Sala i Vila, "Indígena y abogado: el caso de J. D. Choquehuanca de Azángaro," *Histórica* 42, no. 2 (2018).

7. Ariel Morrone's work, "Mujeres cacicales en el tablero colonial. Familia, parentesco y poder étnico en el lago Titicaca (1580–1750)," *Andes Antropología e Historia* 1, no. 29 (2018), traces the place of cacical women from the Titicaca basin within marriage, *mestizaje* (the blending or mixing of cultures and people), inheritance, succession, and access to land from a sociopolitical perspective. The reconstructed genealogy of the Choquehuanca fit Morrone's marriage strategy models in each generation.

8. The strategies of monopoly, clientelism, and land appropriation through marriage alliances are suggested in Azángaro in Nils Jacobsen's *Mirages of Transition: The Peruvian Altiplano, 1780–1930* (Berkeley: University of California Press, 1993). Nuria Sala i Vila's unpublished essay "Reciprocidad, riqueza y prestigio político en un curacazgo entre Colonia y República" also addresses the strategies of wealth accumulation of the Choquehuanca caciques (personal communication). The networks of cacical families and provincial nobilities in the Titicaca basin have been thoroughly studied in David Garrett's *Shadows of Empire: The Indian Nobility of Cusco, 1750–1824* (New York: Cambridge University Press, 2005).

9. Altuve, *Choquehuanca y su arenga*, 52.

10. Alcira Dueñas, *Indians and Mestizos in the "Lettered City": Reshaping Justice, Social Hierarchy and Political Culture in Colonial Peru* (Boulder: University of Colorado Press, 2011), 15.

11. Don Diego's 1792 testament lists these and numerous other items. See the entire transcription in Ramos Zambrano, *J. D. Choquehuanca*. Summaries of the possessions of Diego Choquehuanca are also mentioned in Altuve, *Choquehuanca y su arenga*, 31; and Garrett, *Shadows of Empire*, 131.

12. The transcribed testament of don Diego provides useful information about his listed children as well as of one don Antonio Choquehuanca, his son, who died in 1764 or shortly thereafter. The testaments of don Joseph and don Gregorio provide rich information about themselves and some interesting details about doña Teresa and doña María. I chose to use these names for the latter, rather than María Teresa and María Manuela, as cited in some sources, to avoid confusion. Less information is provided about don Roque. Thanks to Kathryn Santner's research, which she graciously shared with me, we know that doña Dionisia had a significant dowry and an indigenous servant girl named Polonia, who may have been her slave within the convent. In 1750 there were fifty-seven nuns of the black veil, eighteen of the white veil, and fifty-one *donadas* (religious servants). They were attended by two hundred servants. Only affluent women could aspire to become a nun in this convent.

13. For Guaman Poma, the segundas personas were caciques in charge of one thousand tributaries. See Magdalena Chocano, "Contrastes y paralelismos provinciales: La autoridad indígena entre Lucanas y Conchuco," *Élites indígenas en los Andes. Nobles, caciques y cabildantes bajo el yugo colonial*, ed. David Cahill and Blanca Tovías (Quito: Abya Yala, 2003), 111.

14. Several large obrajes in Azángaro were owned by caciques, wealthy mestizos, Spanish creoles, and even religious communities. See Jacobsen, *Mirages of Transition*, 35.

15. Jacobsen, *Mirages of Transition*, 35–39. For the example of the Chucuito obrajes, see Bianca Premo, "From the Pockets of Women: The Gendering of the Mita, Migration and Tribute in Colonial Chucuito, Peru," *Americas* 57, no. 1 (July 2000).

16. Jacobsen, *Mirages of Transition*, 21–27, 37, 101, 134, 287, 331, refers to several epidemics from the sixteenth through the eighteenth centuries in the Peruvian altiplano, which caused frequent labor shortages for mita, obraje, and *jornalero* (day laborer) workers.

17. Ramos Zambrano, *J. D. Choquehuanca*, 191.

18. Archivo Regional del Cuzco, Peru (hereafter cited as ARC) Cabildo, Legajo 33 (1769).

19. The cacica of Asillo, a nearby town, filed a petition opposing the reparto that Inclán y Valdez carried out with the help of some caciques. See Jacobsen, *Mirages of Transition*, 94.

20. Garrett, *Shadows of Empire*, 140. ARC-Cabildo, Legajo 33 (1769).

21. Quoted in Jacobsen, *Mirages of Transition*, 84. The ayllus implicated were those of Ñequeñeque, Picotani, and Chuquini. See Jacobsen, *Mirages of Transition*, 370n23.

22. Jacobsen, *Mirages of Transition*, 85, 91.

23. Jacobsen, *Mirages of Transition*, 4, 129.

24. Jacobsen, *Mirages of Transition*, 158; Garrett, *Shadows of Empire*, 157.

25. Jacobsen, *Mirages of Transition*, 84.

26. Jacobsen, *Mirages of Transition*, 83.

27. Cosme Bueno, *Geografía del Perú virreinal (siglo XVIII)*, ed. Daniel Varcárcel (Lima: Instituto de Historia de la Universidad de San Marcos, 1951), 115.

28. Jacobsen, *Mirages of Transition*, 38, 249.

29. Ramos Zambrano, *J. D. Choquehuanca*, 191.

30. The prolific research about the impact and the effectiveness of the Bourbon Reforms has been assessed by Allan Kuethe and Kenneth Andrien in *The Spanish Atlantic World in the Eighteenth Century: War and the Bourbon Reforms, 1713–1796* (Cambridge, UK: Cambridge University Press, 2014). See also the introduction and chap. 3, from Margarita R. Ochoa, in this collection for a discussion of the Bourbon Reforms.

31. Charles Walker, *The Tupac Amaru Rebellion* (Cambridge, MA: Harvard University Press, 2014), 19.

32. Walker, *Tupac Amaru Rebellion*, 96. The letters by Tupac Amaru and Diego Choquehuanca are transcribed in Ward Stavig and Ella Schmidt, *The Tupac Amaru and Catarista Rebellions: An Anthology of Sources* (Indianapolis: Hackett, 2008).

33. The Spanish colonel Pedro de la Ballina communicated Tupac Amaru's plan to don Diego. He had learned about these plans while he was captured in Tungasuca by the insurgents. He managed to escape, pretending to be doña Teresa's husband, and convinced Tupac Amaru's men he would persuade his "father-in-law" to join the rebellion (Ramos Zambrano, *J. D. Choquehuanca*, 22). This episode of the Tupac Amaru rebellion has created significant confusion about La Ballina's identity and his relationship with the Choquehuancas.

34. Walker, *Tupac Amaru Rebellion*, 145.

35. The Vilcapazas had been unsuccessfully competing for the cacicazgo of Azángaro Ananasaya since the 1670s. See Mostajo, "Los Chuquihuancas," 412–13. The Great Rebellion was an ideal time to confront the Choquehuancas and stand out as leaders. See Walker, *Tupac Amaru Rebellion*, 186.

36. Charles Walker, *Smoldering Ashes: Cuzco and the Creation of Republican Peru, 1780–1840* (Durham, NC: Duke University Press, 1999), 33.

37. Walker, *Tupac Amaru Rebellion*, 96.

38. Jan Szeminzki, *La Utopía tupamarista*, 2nd ed. (Lima: Pontificia Universidad Católica del Peru, 1993), 156. *Chapetones* referred to Spanish people in general.

39. Biblioteca Nacional del Peru (hereafter cited as BNP), C4652, MS 78.

40. María Eugenia del Valle, *Historia de la rebelión de Tupac Catari, 1781–1782*, 3rd ed. (La Paz: Biblioteca del Bicentenario de Bolivia, 2017), 150.

41. Archivo General de Simancas (hereafter cited as AGS), Legajo 6810, 28, Nicolás de la Cámara, Honores (1794–95), fol. 3v.

42. Walker, *Tupac Amaru Rebellion*, 200.

43. Del Valle, *Historia de la rebelión*, 178.

44. Del Valle, *Historia de la rebelión*, 206. *Talla* (also spelled *Ttalla*) is the Aymara word for noblewomen. Ludovico Bertonio translates it as a "mujer del señor principal del pueblo y sus parientas cercanas. Mujer respetable" (woman of the

primary lord of the town and his close female relatives. A respectable woman.). See his *Vocabulario de la Lengua Aymara* (1612; repr., La Paz: CERES, 1984), 53.

45. Del Valle, *Historia de la rebelión*, 207.

46. Leon Campbell, "Women and the Great Rebellion in Peru, 1780–1783," *Americas* 42, no. 2 (October 1985): 170; Sara Guardia, *Mujeres Peruanas. El otro lado de la historia* (Lima: Minerva, 2002), 120.

47. AGS, Legajo, 6810, 28, fols.4r–5v.

48. AGS, Legajo, 6810, 28, fol. 4r.

49. Copacabana had been a pre-Columbian native shrine, and in the colonial period some members of the native elite linked it to their own lineages. For an account of the conversion of some Inca natives there, see Verónica Salles-Reese, *From Viracocha to the Virgin of Copacabana* (Austin: University of Texas Press, 2010). Also, during the Tupac Amaru rebellion, the profound Christianity of Micaela Bastidas and Tupac Amaru played a key role in the fate of this movement. These native leaders refused to silence priests within the areas they controlled who preached against the insurrection.

50. Jacobsen, *Mirages of Transition*, 47.

51. Archivo y Biblioteca Nacional de Bolivia (hereafter cited as ABNB), Ec 1789, 43.

52. ABNB, Rück 86.

53. José Torre Revello, *El libro, la imprenta y el periodismo* (Mexico City: Universidad Nacional Autónoma de México, 1940), 189–90.

54. See the cases of Rita Tamboguacso, María Ramos Tito Atauchi, and Martina Chiguantupa, cited by Garrett, "In Spite," 555. Other cases are Juana Yupanqui, Archivo Regional La Libertad, Peru (hereafter cited as ARLL), Corregimiento, Causas ordinarias, Expediente 2,148, Legajo 236; Juana Capistrana, ARLL, Real Hacienda, Tributos, Expediente 585, Legajo 145 (1786); Manuela Pomacallao, BNP, C2006 (1792); and Bartola Palma, BNP, D338 (1819), among others.

55. AGS, Legajo, 6,810, 28, fol. 2r.

56. Archivo Histórico Nacional, Spain (hereafter cited as AHN), OM-Expedientillos, N.9395.

57. "Testamento de Jose Chukiwanka Vejar" in Ramos Zambrano, *J. D. Choquehuanca*, 199–206.

58. Garrett, *Shadows of Empire*, 220; ARC, Causas Civiles, Legajo 61 (1792).

59. Archivo Histórico de Límites, Lima (hereafter cited as AHL), Legajo 459, PRA, 291. The ceremonial chair had belonged to her father, as attested by don Gregorio in his testament. He states that doña Teresa took the mule and this chair "por su gusto" from their father's possessions when he died. See Ramos Zambrano, *J. D. Choquehuanca*, 221.

60. Sinclair Thomson, *We Alone Will Rule: Native Andean Politics in the Age of Insurgency* (Madison: University of Wisconsin Press, 2002), 42.

61. AHL, Puno, Real Hacienda, Expediente 89 (1797). Rentals were customary in the eighteenth century and were initiated at times of financial need in the community. The accumulated profits, nonetheless, could go directly to the hands of the caciques. For an account of the declining numbers of originarios to *forasteros* (natives

and their descendants who left their home ayllus and were integrated into indigenous society through a variety of relationships with established communities), see Jacobsen, *Mirages of Transition*, 130; and Ann W. Wightman, *Indigenous Migration and Social Change. The Forasteros of Cuzco, 1570–1720* (Durham, NC: Duke University Press, 1990).

62. AHL, Legajo 459, PRA, 291.

63. AGS, Legajo 6,810, 28, fols. 1r–16v.

64. AGS, Legajo 6,810, 28, fols. 1r–16v. The term *cacique propietario* (proprietary cacique) meant that the he or she had been ratified in this office by the superior government. See Scarlett O'Phelan, *Kurakas sin sucesiones, Del cacique al alcalde de indios, Perú y Bolivia, 1750–1835* (Cuzco: Centro Bartolomé de las Casas, 1997), 20.

65. De la Cámara requested to be a royal accountant in a nearby *caja* (royal till). AGS, Legajo 6,810, 28, fols. 3r–16r.

66. See "Testamento del canónigo Gregorio Choquehuanca" in Ramos Zambrano, *J. D. Choquehuanca*, 214–25.

67. AHL, Legajo 461, PRA, 343.

68. See Serena Fernández Alonso, "Un noble canario en el gobierno local indiano: El Marqués de Casa Hermosa en la Intendencia de Puno," in *Coloquio de Historia Canario-Americana* 9 (Las Palmas, Spain: Cabildo Insular de Gran Canaria, 1990); and Alfredo Moreno-Cebrian, "El Marqués de Casa Hermosa, corregidor de Huaylas," *Anuario de Estudios Atlánticos* 24 (1978).

69. AHL, Legajo 461, PRA, 343.

70. AHL, Legajo 461, PRA, 343.

71. AHL, Legajo 461, PRA, 343.

72. Micaela Bastidas, for example, had gained the respect of the native combatants by various actions, including providing them with coca and brandy. See Campbell, "Women," 173; and Jane Mangan, *Trading Roles: Gender, Ethnicity, and the Urban Economy in Colonial Potosí* (Durham, NC: Duke University Press, 2005), 82–83.

73. AHL, Legajo 461, PRA, 343.

74. Although by this time the reparto had decreased across the colonies, it continued in Azángaro until the end of the colonial era. See Jacobsen, *Mirages of Transition*, 97.

75. AHL, Legajo 461, PRA, 343.

76. AHL, Legajo 461, PRA, 343.

77. AHL, Legajo 461, PRA, 343.

78. AHL, Legajo 461, PRA, 343.

79. AHL, Legajo 461, PRA, 343.

80. AHL, Legajo 461, PRA, 343.

81. Jacobsen, *Mirages of Transition*, 98.

82. AHL, Legajo 461, PRA, 343.

83. AHL, Legajo 461, PRA, 343.

84. AHL, Legajo 461, PRA, 343.

85. Her brother, don Gregorio, also accused Urbiola of deposing his sister as cacica on his testament, in Ramos Zambrano, *J. D. Choquehuanca*, 221. See also

Nuria Sala i Vila, *Y se armó el tole tole. Tributo indígena y movimientos sociales en el virreinato del Perú, 1790–1814* (Arequipa: Instituto de Estudios Regionales José María Arguedas, 1996), 127.

86. AHL, Legajo 461, PRA, 343.

87. References to the character of don Manuel are provided in don Gregorio's testament in Ramos Zambrano, *J. D. Choquehuanca*, 214–25). For more on the temporal abolition of tribute, see Christine Hünefeldt, *Lucha por la tierra, y protesta indígena. Las comunidades indígenas del Peru entre colonia y república, 1800–1830* (Bonn: Bonner Amerikanische Studien, 1982), 1663–67.

88. Sala i Vila, *Y se armó*, 407.

89. AHL, Legajo 461, PRA, 343.

90. AHL, Legajo 461, PRA, 343.

91. AHL, Legajo 461, PRA, 343.

92. Garrett, *Shadows of Empire*, 246n51.

93. Garrett, "In Spite," 551.

94. Trouillot, *Silencing the Past*, chap. 7.

CHAPTER 9

Peacemaker Cacicas in the Río de la Plata Southern Frontier

Florencia Roulet

T he impetus of Spanish conquest and colonization in the Río de la Plata region slowed down at the end of the sixteenth century following the founding of several cities, in particular Buenos Aires, Santa Fe, Córdoba, San Luis de la Punta, and Mendoza. Two centuries later, Spanish territorial expansion did not surpass the line of forts and guards erected some tens of miles to the south of those urban centers. Most natives of the *pampas* (South American plains)—nonsedentary hunters, fishers, and gatherers—could not be subjected to the controlling power of colonial society, and their territories remained outside Spanish control. The colonial space at the southern end of the Americas was thus shaped by a fundamental dichotomy. On one side, the territory was organized around settlements scattered as microscopic spots along huge distances and connected by insecure trails. Most of the Spanish and *mestizo* (person of mixed descent) population lived in or around these urban environments, where were concentrated the economic, defensive, and sociable activities of Spanish society. On the other side was what the Spanish referred to as *tierra adentro* (inlands), the endless grasslands belonging to independent indigenous nations. Over time, a frontier emerged between these two zones, a dividing line, which would serve as both a theater of war and a meeting place. (See map 7.) It is here, along the margins of Spanish rule, that this chapter examines the agency of native women who belonged to indigenous nations identified as *indios bárbaros* (savages) in Spanish bureaucratic language.[1]

The ethnographic information about natives living in the pampas and Patagonian regions is scarce in early chronicles of conquest and slaving expeditions.[2] While those inhabiting the vicinity of Buenos Aires were initially known as Querandíes and the tall natives of the South Atlantic coastal line were labeled Patagones, the designations Pampa—for indigenous nations living in the plains south of the colonial cities of Buenos Aires, Santa Fe, and Córdoba—and Serranos—for those living on the mountain ranges of Tandilia and Ventania, in the south of the actual Buenos Aires province, as well as for some Andean groups migrating to the plains—prevailed in the seventeenth century. By that time, the regular presence of *indios de Chile* (Chilean Indians), sometimes called Aucas, was also recorded east of the Andes, where they traded their textiles for horses and wild cattle captured by local Pampas. In the eighteenth century, several new ethnic identities emerged in the region—the Tehuelchús, south of the Colorado River; the Ranquelches in the dry central pampa; the Pehuenches on the eastern slopes of the Andes; and the Huilliches or southern people, south of the Río Negro—through varied processes of ethnogenesis[3] that implied migrations and intermarriages as well as political and military alliances that led to phenomena of ethnic reconfigurations, strongly influenced by each group's policies vis-à-vis the colonial power. In that century, Jesuit missionaries were the first to produce some detailed descriptions of native nations, but their presence in indigenous territories south of Buenos Aires was short-lived (1740–52).[4] However, administrative records were produced in the wake of ongoing tensions between Spanish and natives in the outskirts of the Spanish periphery.[5]

The case of Río de la Plata allows us to explore the important roles played by some native women in negotiating peace treaties between warring Spanish and native parties in a context of intermittent war that lasted from 1740 to 1790. Their efforts resulted in formal agreements and allowed indigenous men and women to trade their furs, feathers, woolen blankets, ponchos, leather reins, and lassos in the frontier forts and cities, for the "vices" of the colonial economy: alcohol, tobacco, sugar, and yerba mate. While most indigenous women are either omitted from the record or identified simply as *chinas*—a term synonymous with native women in the Río de la Plata region[6]—female peacemakers were identified as cacicas by Spanish officials.[7] This colonial category allowed them to distinguish from among the *chusma* (captured human war booty) those women deemed strategically important in peace negotiations due to their close kinship ties with powerful caciques.[8] In times of peace, we also find some cacicas among commercial parties and in the company of caciques in their official visits to colonial centers. Of all cacicas in the late-colonial southern frontier, only a handful bear an imposed Spanish name and sometimes a surname indicating their filiation.

These women who acted in preliminary peace talks, however, either representing their male relatives or as mediators to win their favor, showcase an unexpected female prominence in diplomatic negotiations and a type of political power that emerged in the context of interethnic relationships born from the colonial encounter.[9]

THE RÍO DE LA PLATA SOUTHERN FRONTIER: A STAGE OF WAR, DIPLOMACY, AND TRADE

After the foundation of the southernmost colonial settlements in the late sixteenth century, Spanish colonizers made brief and violent raids into native territories in search of three resources essential to their predatory cattle economy: wild cows, native captives, and salt. While groups of vaqueros hunted cows for their hides, expeditions referred to by a variety of terms, including *batidas, corredurías,* and *campeadas,* raked the countryside to capture entire indigenous groups and force them to work for *encomenderos* (holders of a royal grants of indigenous tribute) in the cities.[10] At the same time, *malocas* (slaving raids) assaulted indigenous settlements, killing men and capturing women and children. In the eighteenth century, Jesuit missionaries would also enter the wilderness of the pampas to "reduce" souls.[11] But, the vast plains favored native flight and condemned Spanish colonists to a chronic scarcity of indigenous labor. For more than a century, the natives of the pampas had suffered these aggressions powerlessly. The combined effects of the wars of conquest, epidemics, labor exploitation, and forceful relocations decimated the indigenous population. Yet the new animal species introduced by Europeans led to deep changes in the material life of native societies and allowed for a demographic recovery that was noticeable by the mid-eighteenth century. After adopting the horse as a means of transportation, weapon of war, and favorite foodstuff, they increased their mobility, military efficacy, and autonomy. Influenced by natives of the Chilean Araucanía who crossed the Andes, the indigenous of the pampas also embraced Araucanian warfare technology developed during the Wars of Arauco (1536–1660): leather armor and long spears with iron points. They also gradually adopted their language, Mapudungun, as a lingua franca for intercultural communication. Around 1700, pampas natives were reacting to Spanish raids by killing cow hunters and travelers. And, in 1740, after Spaniards slaughtered two indigenous tribes and captured hundreds of women and children, more than a thousand warriors from diverse nations united to attack the rural population near Buenos Aires. This native assault was the first act of war since the time of Spanish conquest. It resulted in one hundred dead and an almost equal number of captives. Paradoxically, this act of war became the necessary preamble to peace talks on conditions of relative parity. Now Spaniards as well as natives had dead to mourn and captives under their power. Violence had given way to negotiation.[12]

In 1741, in tacit acknowledgment of indigenous political autonomy, the governor of Buenos Aires sent an expedition to request "peace and good correspondence with the said Indians."[13] The following year, the Jesuits sent a captive woman to negotiate with Cangapol, also known as cacique Bravo, the top indigenous leader of the natives from the mountains south of Buenos Aires. The woman was Bravo's sister, captured some years before in a maloca and incorporated into the first Jesuit mission founded in the region. According to Pierre François-Xavier de Charlevoix, a Jesuit chronicler, Bravo's sister was a determined woman who promised to convince her brother to send deputies to negotiate a solid and lasting peace with the Spanish governor, as it indeed happened some months later via a formal treaty.[14]

This anonymous woman is the first to appear in the colonial papers from Río de la Plata with a leading role in the negotiation of a peace treaty. In his chronicle, Charlevoix does not call her cacica, but he does grant her the merit of engaging her brother in a peace deal and convincing him to allow two more Jesuit missions to be built in his territory. Through the actions of Bravo's sister we see the emergence of the cacica figure. Those women belonged to egalitarian societies where caciques had only limited power: deciding the movements of the group, defining—through a collective decision-making process—the parameters of political and military alliances or the involvement in war actions, and leading the war parties. Identified as cacicas by Spaniards due to their condition as daughters, sisters, or wives of recognized native leaders, these women had the privilege and the capacity to influence the decisions of caciques, bending them often towards peace.[15]

The colonial record, written overwhelmingly by Spanish and creole men who assumed and justified the double supremacy of colonizers over natives and of men over women, overlooks indigenous agency, especially that of native women. The diplomatic action of cacicas who emerge from the record thus stands out even more when we consider that this was a political realm that Spaniards kept aside for only men. Cacicas in the southern Río de la Plata frontiers assumed peacemaking functions analogous to those of Comanche women in the Texas borderlands during the same time period.[16] In both cases, these women owed their broker positions not only to their kinship ties with powerful caciques but also to their status as former captives or hostages, an experience that often acquainted them with the Spanish language and allowed some of them to develop personal contacts among Spanish officials. Their performance in diplomatic dealings is a clear hint of female agency in power relations and, as Juliana Barr points out, of "the predominance of native codes of peace and war" in interethnic relations.[17] The prevalence of native ways of dealing with otherness is apparent in frontier situations where European powers could not readily impose their political hegemony and different cultures had to "search for accommodation."[18] In the Río de la Plata southern frontier, following a diplomatic tradition originated in the Chilean frontier, *parlamentos* (treaty negotiations) became a hybrid and transcultural institution, resulting from a cultural compromise. While these cacicas may appear to have been the political pawns of the natives who sent them, it was ultimately up to these women to negotiate with colonists according to their own criteria. "In a sense, Spaniards fell into the trap of indigenous ways of negotiation because, being unable to impose themselves by force, they had no choice but to accept, under the terms of parlamento, this type of ritual gathering that the Mapuche had practiced long before their arrival."[19]

Most cacicas appear so fleetingly in our sources that we only get a glimpse of their actions.[20] Yet a few of them would reinforce their influence as mediators between cultures. This chapter intends to retrieve the scattered traces of these women: the Pampa María Francisca from the Buenos Aires frontier and the Pehuenches Ignacia Guentenao and María Josefa Roco from the Mendoza frontier.[21] I will sketch their biographies and restore, whenever possible, their gestures and words, estimating the relevance of their political functions in the eyes of their own communities. Although fragmentary and incomplete, the portraits presented in this chapter allow us to realize the respectability and influence achieved by peacemaker cacicas among their peoples.

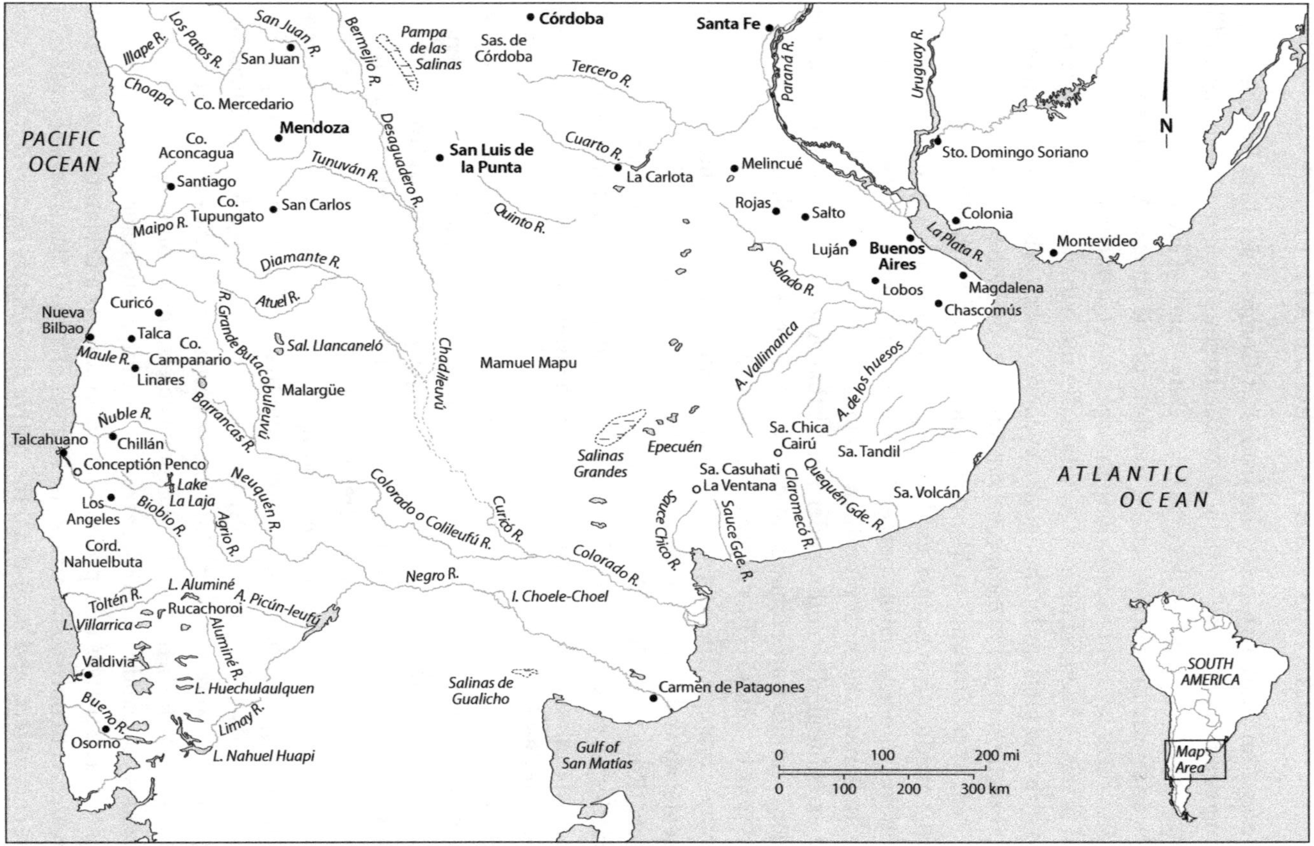

Map 7. Colonial Río de la Plata and Chile Southern Frontier

MAKING WAR TO NEGOTIATE PEACE

At dawn on March 13, 1780, the troops of Commander José Francisco de Amigorena assailed the settlement of the famous cacique Guentenao in El Campanario, some 390 miles (628 kilometers) south of Mendoza. Many caciques and warriors were absent at the time of the attack. After the fighting ended, there lay 106 dead. Among the dead was Guentenao himself, "the eldest of this Pehuenche nation." Additionally, more than one hundred women and girls and boys under the age of eleven were taken prisoners. And, though a few men managed to escape, others "chose to die rather than surrender."[22]

Soon after returning to Mendoza, and inspired by the Chilean model of treaty-making, Amigorena used his captured human booty to lure the Pehuenches into negotiating peace. A native woman was to bring a message to Ancán Amún, the most prominent cacique, informing him of the success of the expedition. The commander hoped that Ancán Amún would "ask for peace" and offer an exchange of captives to recover the Pehuenche families in Spanish hands.[23] Two captive cacicas would play a crucial role in Amigorena's strategy. The first was Ignacia Guentenao, the daughter of the late Guentenao and wife of his successor, the cacique Roco. The other was María Josefa, Roco's daughter. Amigorena, aware of the value of women in these societies, expressed in the "bride's price" that grooms had to pay to their brides' families, believed that the Pehuenche would do everything to recover their families.[24]

On the eastern end of the frontier line, on the night of August 27 of the same year, a group of natives assaulted the district of Luján, in the Buenos Aires countryside. They killed about fifty people and took captives of both sexes. Three days later, a "Christian" man—as Spaniards and creoles are often referred to on the record—freed by the natives arrived in Luján with a message from the caciques. According to the *cristiano*, the natives were "ready to negotiate peace on the condition that the Indians who were prisoners in the city [of Buenos Aires] were freed, in exchange for the Christian captives they were taking."[25] But viceroy Vértiz ignored the caciques' request. He instead banished several indigenous chiefs, imprisoned by treachery the previous year, and ordered the arrest of all indigenous traders arriving at the frontier. The natives interpreted those decisions as a declaration of war and threatened to once again attack the district of Luján. There were several violent encounters, and each time, the native messengers declared that "if the Christian[s] do not give them peace and send them the Indian women and men who are in Buenos Aires to exchange them for the [other] many Christians they have there, there would be constant warfare everywhere to take revenge."[26]

In Buenos Aires as well as in Mendoza, natives and Spaniards resorted to the same logic to force negotiations between themselves. First, they intimidated the enemy through sudden assaults, killing as many men as they could and taking captives as a valuable human booty so as to later discuss the conditions of peace from a strong position. Natives, though, were at a disadvantage. A Spanish raid on a *toldería* (indigenous settlement) usually resulted in the capture of the wives, daughters, and sisters of the caciques while native assaults tended to spare the cities where the families of the most prominent colonizers lived. Natives attacked the scattered rural Spanish settlements and abducted poor peasants who had no economic means or political contacts to lobby for the release of their beloved ones. The vocabulary used to qualify those acts of war—and, as a result, the representation of violence—also changes depending on which side of the border it originated. The terms "expedition," "punitive campaign," and others were used when Christians were the aggressors. In turn, "hostility," "insult," "invasion," "assault," and—from the nineteenth century onward—*malón* when the protagonists were natives.[27]

In the spiral of violence fueled by men in the southern frontier, the cacicas would be the sowers of peace. In February 1781, Lorenzo Calfilqui, the principal cacique of the Auca (Pampa natives from the mountains south of Buenos Aires) resumed his peace proposals sending a Spanish captive, Pedro Zamora, with two indigenous women tasked with claiming two of Calfilqui's abducted female relatives. Our sources do not state who those women ambassadors were, nor the kind of kinship relationship the prisoners had with Calfilqui. Later documents, however, suggest that one of the emissaries was Calfilqui's wife. We cannot help but notice that, while Calfilqui was asking for the release of those women, his own brother, the cacique Cayupilqui, had been held prisoner in Buenos Aires for more than a year. When making demands for the return of his imprisoned relatives, Calfilqui did not privilege men.

This second diplomatic opening was more successful because the circumstances had changed. Several events were going on around that time. For one, the Túpac Amaru rebellion (1780–81) was upsetting the viceroyalty of Peru, while in Río de la Plata there were rumors of mobilization of thousands of native warriors in the Gran Chaco region and from Chile to the pampas. In addition, Viceroy Vértiz was worried by the news of a British expedition to assault Montevideo.[28] Derogating from his previous practice to deny a peace agreement with the frontier natives, Vértiz sent an expedition to the mountains, led by pilot Pablo Zizur, with instructions to take "several Indian men and women to hand them over to the cacique Lorenzo [Calfilqui], conduct preliminary peace agreements with him and his allies, and inspect the territory."[29] Once in the toldería, Zizur noted the presence of "the cacica" beside Calfilqui, but he did not provide a name.[30] After listening to his brother Cayupilqui—who had been released to travel with Zizur—and the detailed description of his sufferings in prison, Calfilqui declined to travel to Buenos Aires. Since Calfilqui's presence in the Spanish city was the main condition for a treaty, the peace agreement was postponed.[31] In 1784, Calfilqui's wife would be sent to Buenos Aires again, with another woman and Christian captive to negotiate peace following a Spanish expedition that assaulted native settlements, killing natives and taking women and children captive. In the records of this event she was named María Francisca.[32]

MARÍA FRANCISCA, CALFILQUI'S SPOKESPERSON

The cacica's Christian name suggests that before assuming the role of Calfilqui's emissary she had had some contact with Spaniards. Yet she was not fluent in Spanish for we know that another native woman who traveled with her was the only one described as having been "quite proficient in the Spanish language."[33] It is likely that María Francisca had been previously captured in an assault on her camp or treacherously imprisoned while trading in the frontier. In either case, she would have been confined to the Casa de Recogidas, known as La Residencia, a detention center for women of loose morals (e.g., prostitutes and young women reluctant to marry or living in concubinage), noncompliant spouses, and female indigenous captives with their children.[34] Her affiliation as well as her past, however, are a mere conjecture. Was she Calfilqui's only wife? It is most unlikely. Such an influential chief, who "governs them all" and whom the others "ask advice before taking any determination," solemnized his political alliances through marital exchanges that linked him with other lineages.[35] Yet Zizur only mentions one cacica and adds that Calfilqui had no children.[36] María Francisca might have been one of the two women accompanying Pedro Zamora in 1781 because, when Pablo Zizur reached the first tolderías a few months later, he was told that Calfilqui was making preparations to attack the frontier because of "the delay of [his] wife and the other individuals that he had sent with her."[37] Here, it is worth noting the different insights of the cacica's role. The Spaniards seem to have perceived Zamora, the male captive, as Calfilqui's ambassador and the two women only as witnesses of the proposed exchange of captives. The natives, in turn, considered Calfilqui's wife as his spokesperson. This misinterpretation reminds us of Richard White's notion of "creative misunderstandings" and James Lockhart's concept of "double mistaken identity," according to which "each side of the cultural exchange presumes that a given form or concept is functioning in the way familiar within its own tradition and is unaware of or unimpressed by the other side's interpretation."[38] While it seemed natural for native societies structured by kinship relations to trust a woman with a delicate political function, Spaniards conceived power as exclusively masculine and often failed to acknowledge the intermediary role bestowed on these women. In fact, María Francisca was her husband's ambassador, while the captive Pedro Zamora was just sent to be redeemed in exchange for the female relatives the cacique was claiming.[39]

In 1784, when María Francisca arrived to the frontier with another china fluent in Spanish along with the captive Bernardo López, the new viceroy, marqués de Loreto, received them reluctantly. Only a few months before, while natives were insistently demanding peace, a coordinated general expedition had assaulted their settlements from the frontiers of Buenos Aires, Córdoba, and Mendoza, killing hundreds of them and capturing their families.[40] Loreto was thus suspicious that their mission was a scheme to neglect the patrolling of the frontier and causing the natives to attack in retaliation. He did not even believe María Francisca was Calfilqui's wife, let alone his spokesperson.[41] Yet Calfilqui himself had sent María Francisca in his place as he was wary of the Spaniards. He could not forget that in 1779, still in times of peace, Viceroy Vértiz had arrested several caciques—Catumillac, Linco Pagni, Valerio, and Calfilqui's own brother, Cayupilqui—who had gone to Buenos Aires to trade. Vértiz had put some of them in jail and exiled others to Montevideo and to the Malvinas Islands. Wary of Spanish promises, Calfilqui would refuse for years to travel to Buenos Aires.

In 1784, María Francisca and her female companion returned to native territory with a treaty proposal from the viceroy, who demanded the caciques' presence to reach a formal agreement. Two months later, both women traveled again to Buenos Aires with three native men sent on behalf of the caciques, while Calfilqui chose to stay with his warriors in their territory. María Francisca explained that the chiefs "were frightened to come because they thought they would be harmed by the Christians and . . . they wanted to see how things worked with those second emissaries." The commander of the frontier himself admitted that "they had some grounded reasons to be afraid of coming because I have heard that on our side they have sometimes been betrayed in their good faith."[42] Lorenzo did not, however, blatantly refuse to go to the capital but asked for some guaranties: he would travel only if Christians sent hostages to his settlement, including "a high-ranking military person" (i.e., a sergeant).[43] As his demand was not fulfilled, he prudently refrained from visiting the capital. Calfilqui's fear of Spanish betrayal explains sending his wife as an ambassador. But there is a second reason, one that the viceroy may not have understood. As Juliana Barr notices in the Texan frontier, in native gender diplomacy that associated men with war and women with peace, "relations with women opened up the potential of expressing peace rather than hostility, and alliance rather than enmity."[44] Likewise, in the pampas, the mere presence of a cacica as emissary was in itself a sign of peaceful intentions, despite Spanish misunderstandings of indigenous gendered diplomatic practices.[45] While war and hunting parties were entirely composed of men, indigenous commercial and diplomatic missions always included women.

In January 1785, confirming Calfilqui's suspicions, a Spanish expedition assaulted the indigenous settlements in Sierra de la Ventana but was defeated by natives. Despite this unjustified aggression, the caciques immediately renewed their call for peace. Over time, war gradually gave way to peaceful interactions. In the following years the annual expeditions to extract salt in native territory resumed, and some partial peace agreements were negotiated with several caciques on those occasions. Indigenous messengers traveled to the capital without being pestered; the chiefs asked for presents from the viceroy and obtained them. In exchange, they promised to prevent attacks from enemy native nations and help Spanish troops who crossed their territories. They even requested credentials or passports allowing them to trade in every frontier of the viceroyalty. Viceroy Loreto could ascertain that the natives were visiting the city in huge parties to trade and that their demonstrations left no doubt about their peaceful intentions.[46]

During one of these expeditions to Salinas Grandes, in May 1790, the Spanish commander Juan Antonio Hernández managed to overcome Calfilqui's long-standing reluctance to sign a formal peace treaty. The cacique accepted to enter the Spanish camp, along with another dozen allied chiefs, after Hernández agreed to send his own son among the natives as a hostage during the peace talks. Three months later, with the guarantee of a Spanish party of soldiers retained in his settlement, Lorenzo Calfilqui finally traveled to Buenos Aires to sign a complementary treaty with the viceroy. No document mentions whether María Francisca formed a part of his entourage. We only have the description of Juan Antonio Hernández, who boasted of having negotiated a successful peace treaty with "the great cacique Calfilqui, powerful enemy and the owner of the broadest fields that we know in these regions." Finally meeting him personally in Salinas had been no small achievement. After all, Lorenzo had been "the terror, the dismay and the most cruel plague for us Christians," noted for "the huge number of his followers and for his distinguished courage and audacity." Hernández describes how the population of Buenos Aires celebrated Calfilqui's entry in the capital with a great quantity of people following him in the streets up to the viceroy's residence.[47]

The following year, María Francisca traveled at least twice to Buenos Aires. In March, joining perhaps a trade party, she was urgently called by the new viceroy, Nicolás de Arredondo, when she was on her way back to the mountains. She was asked to return to the capital "to talk with Madame, the vicereine, and to give news of the said cacique [Lorenzo]." At last, not only was María Francisca acknowledged as a valid partner in political talks, but the viceroy himself thought it appropriate to include his own wife in the conversation, a totally exceptional event. Native ways of negotiation were influencing colonial gender politics.

In August, sent by Calfilqui, María Francisca crossed the frontier to meet the viceroy after "news had arrived [in native lands] that preparations were made in Buenos Aires to assault them."[48] Once assured that the rumors were fake, she went back to her lands to apprise her husband. In perpetual movement between indigenous and Spanish territories, she may have been one of the seven chinas of his retinue the following year, when he returned to the capital.[49] We will not know for sure as the frontier documentation does not mention her any more. Though we lose traces of her, we retain that her diplomatic skills made possible peace negotiations that survived Calfilqui's death in 1796 and lasted until 1820.

IGNACIA GUENTENAO, AMIGORENA'S EMISSARY

In 1780 in Mendoza, at the western end of the Río de la Plata frontier, commander José Francisco de Amigorena bragged about his accomplishments in the expedition to El Campanario. He had allegedly captured a "granddaughter of the cacique Guentenau, recognized among them as cacica, even if single, for there was no man in their nation who could buy her for 100 wages, the value attributed to her according to their rituals."[50] Let's consider the rich information provided by this testimony. Amigorena tells us that, despite being single, a woman could be considered as cacica by her own people on the basis of the prestige of her lineage. His early understanding of female rank in Pehuenche society suggests that, on one side, most women gained access to this position only when married to an indigenous leader and, on the other, that there were exceptions to this rule when the political influence associated to a woman's family translated into a high bride's price. This price made them an impossible match for any man but a wealthy cacique. He was, however, wrong in identifying this particular captive as Guentenao's granddaughter. Among the many prisoners he carried to Mendoza, he had taken Guentenao's daughter, whom he soon called Ignacia. This woman was married to Roco, Guentenao's successor. Amigorena had accommodated her and her four children, a boy and three girls, in his private house.[51] He had also captured another of Roco's wives, doña Agustina; his sister doña María with her two sons; and his beloved daughter, María Josefa—probably the young single woman he initially took for Guentenao's granddaughter. Officers in Mendoza knew that "her father loves her in a singular way and distinguishes her among all the others."[52]

In the months that followed the expedition, María Josefa Roco would be carefully retained as a hostage, while Ignacia would be used as a messenger, carrying Amigorena's peace proposals to her husband and her three brothers—Piempán, Longopán, and Antipán—"who were the remaining chiefs of her nation." Ignacia had a double legitimacy as a mediator with the Spaniards. She was first recognized as Roco's wife, then as Guentenao's daughter, which incidentally meant that she could have a direct influence on her brothers. Acting as a go-between, she had promised several times that she would ask "the friendship, confederation, and alliance of all those from her nation" and assured that, in the event of a peace agreement, they would be ready "to subject themselves in Mendoza's frontier, wherever [Amigorena] chose to assign them."[53] Leaving behind her three daughters as hostages, Ignacia and her son left Mendoza in November. A month later she was back with her brothers, but her husband pretended to be sick and unable to travel. On December 14, 1780, the Pehuenches "doña Ignacia Guentenao as well as doña María Yanqueípi, along with her brothers, Piampán and Llongopán; her brother-in-law, Antipán; and Peñalef" appeared before the members of the Cabildo, offering "a safe peace with this city."[54] With the absence of Roco, the agreements were considered preliminary. After the peace talks, Ignacia, María and their relatives were sent to native territory to bring back Roco and the rest of his men in order to conclude the treaty, while "the principal cacica, doña María Josefa and all the others who had been and still are in this city" were retained as "prisoners or hostages."[55] People in Mendoza knew that "the main objective of these infidels [was] to recover the captive doña María Josefa" and hoped that Roco would finally come, as he did.[56] On April 7, 1781, he appeared with his subordinate, Machiyaso, before the cabildo. Both agreed to settle with their families next to the frontier and contribute to its defense against Pampas, Ranquelches, and Huilliches in exchange for the return of their families and the promise that they could barter salt, ponchos, and other goods in Mendoza.[57] This treaty is the birth record of the group of "frontier Pehuenches" that would last a quarter of a century and the first of a long series of agreements to foster both a military alliance and trade with all the Pehuenche groups living on the eastern slopes of the Andes.[58]

In May of that year, Roco and his brothers-in-law—probably with Ignacia and her son, who are not mentioned as hostages any longer—had settled on the frontier near the fort of San Carlos but did not get their families back. The cabildo would only restore the captives in September, retaining as hostages "the people of most character and esteem among them," most notably María Josefa, Agustina (Roco's wife), and María (Roco's sister), as well as many other women and children.[59] Some months later, Roco suddenly broke camp and escaped to El Campanario. Soon after, fearing retaliation, the cacique sent Ignacia back to Mendoza, asking Amigorena to "forgive him for having run away from the frontier" and "accept him back under any of his conditions."[60] Like Calfilqui, Roco preferred to be represented by his wife when the situation was uncertain. He hoped that Amigorena would see Ignacia, who had lived in his house and knew how to talk to him, as a symbol of peace. Indeed, after listening to her, Amigorena forgave Roco and authorized him to remain in El Campanario.

One may wonder if Ignacia was acting in these circumstances as a mere puppet in the hands of men who manipulated her. Yet I doubt this was the case. Of course, she was not a free woman negotiating with Mendoza's commander on an equal footing. While she was left in an extremely vulnerable position due to her father's death and the slaughter of her relatives in the settlement as well as her abduction and the captivity of her three daughters retained as hostages, Amigorena's narrative suggests that she was acting on her own initiative. Amigorena's initial aim was just to use the human booty he captured in El Campanario to redeem Christian captives in native hands. But Ignacia

suggested a different deal. Knowing that the Pehuenches had no Christian captives to offer in exchange for the prisoners retained in Mendoza, she made a
lucid evaluation of her people's situation. They had been struck by the Spanish
campaign but already weakened by successive epidemics and years of conflict
with the Pampas, Ranquelches, and Huilliches. Thus, she fostered the option of
a Pehuenche settlement in the frontier. She was aware that "today these Pehuenches are few and afraid that the Guilliches will kill them."[61] The vicinity of
the Pehuenches to the Spaniards would constitute a defense and refuge in case
of an attack by their native enemies and would bring closer a market interested
in their products. Sent by Amigorena, Ignacia promoted the creation of a Pehuenche enclave in Mendoza's frontier to her brothers and husband, persuaded
that this was the best means to enhance her people's interests. When Roco finally abandoned the frontier, her brothers remained there and led, one after
the other, the group of frontier Pehuenches until 1787, when the last of them—
Antipán—fled from a devastating smallpox epidemic to join Roco.

Ignacia's diplomatic activities were not confined to Mendoza. Doña Ignacia is found in Chile with her husband, visiting the highest political authority and then traveling to Mendoza to trade and give news to Amigorena.[62] In
the winter of 1787, while the camp of Ancán Amún, the principal cacique,
was being attacked by his Huilliche enemies, one of his brothers traveled to
Mendoza with Ignacia Guentenao to ask their Spanish allies for two hundred armed soldiers to aid in their defense.[63] Ignacia's familiar presence
would have made it easier to introduce the cacique's brother and recall to the
people of Mendoza the promise of military assistance inserted in the treaties. Even if much smaller than requested, the military help was finally delivered. Learning about it, the caciques dispatched the young Jacinto, the son of
Ignacia and Roco, to manifest their delight.[64]

We find Ignacia Guentenao one last time in the fort of San Carlos the following year. She was sent by her husband to inform on the location of the
Pehuenche settlements. After that, she is not mentioned again in our sources.
In 1793, Roco's two sons traveled to the frontier and the following year one of
them, described as the "little captain Paynechiñé," arrived as his messenger.[65]
One decade later, after the deaths of his father and uncles, the "little captain"
would lead one of the Pehuenche tribes. It is uncertain whether Paynechiñé
and Jacinto, Ignacia's son, were the same person. The fragmentary nature of
the sources makes it difficult to know the extent to which Ignacia's offspring
retained a leading role in the Pehuenche political system after her death.

MARÍA JOSEFA ROCO: FROM HOSTAGE
TO AMBASSADOR

Held as a hostage in 1781, when she had already spent almost two years in captivity, María Josefa disappears from the written record for many years. We do not know when she was returned to her father, when she got married, or if she had any children. Fifteen years after the first treaty, while the Pehuenches of Malargüe were in war with their southern relatives from Balbarco, "two cacicas, who were Roco's daughters, and a *chinillo* ["little *chino*," or "little boy"]," visited Amigorena to ask him for confirmation of rumors that the Spaniards were making military preparations to either join forces with enemy natives or attack them. As "there was no Indian man ready to go to Mendoza to find out the truth" about those rumors, the two cacicas traveled to Mendoza to talk to Amigorena. Although their names were not registered in the records, one of them may have been María Josefa. This report informs us that, in times when Pehuenche men were afraid of approaching the city, native women felt safe, "with the confidence of having spent seven years in [Amigorena's] house as hostages, and they now leave undeceived by those news."[66] Once again, women were sent as emissaries when men feared Spanish aggression. Not only did they embody a pacific attitude but their personal ties to Spanish officials were used to sound out the other's intentions. What can also be underscored from this passage is the many years the women spent as hostages in Amigorena's house—which likely made them fluent in Spanish—and the fact that they are called cacicas for being Roco's daughters. The latter would not be the case for the male children of caciques. Males did not automatically inherit their father's rank. They were first chinillos, then *mocetones* (lads). Once they became adults they were promoted to *capitanejos* (captains), and they would only be recognized as caciques after having exerted commanding functions. While the son of a cacique aspiring to chiefdom had to prove through a long cursus honorum that he possessed all the qualities of leadership—courage, generosity, eloquence, and wisdom— women derived their respected position of cacica from kinship relations.

Some years later, we find María Josefa Roco involved in an important peace talk, organized in Mendoza's frontier by commander Amigorena in 1799, to reconcile the Pehuenches with their long-lasting enemies, the Ranquelches. At this meeting, Antepán, Roco's brother, was informed that one of his wives was sick, and he returned to his camp sending as his deputy his son

Caripan and María Josefa.[67] In the minutes of the encounter, María Josefa is the only woman mentioned among the caciques as acting "by herself and in the name of her father, cacique Roco."[68] This would be the last diplomatic act of José Francisco de Amigorena, who would pass away some weeks later. With Amigorena's death, followed soon after by those of Roco (1801); his brother-in-law Antepán (1802); and his brother, the other Antepán (1803), the first cycle of the Spanish-Pehuenche alliance was closed and a new generation of younger caciques would emerge. As former captives, Paynechiñé, Caripan, and María Josefa had been exposed to the ways of the Christians. They knew the symbolic and material advantages of an alliance, which made them feel stronger in front of their many native enemies, but were also aware that they would pay the highest human and material costs of the war against the enemies of the crown.[69]

Paynechiñé would succeed his uncle Antepán as the head of his toldería. Soon after, his sister María Josefa, who was already a widow, traveled to Buenos Aires as his ambassador to meet the viceroy.[70] This happened in 1804, when José de Cerro y Zamudio, a Chilean traveler who intended to open a new road connecting Buenos Aires to Chile through indigenous territory, arrived to his location and promised that if the Pehuenches escorted him to the capital they would be able to sell "their ponchos, woolen [blankets], and other products."[71] Motivated by these potential advantages, Paynechiñé and Pichicolemilla, the principal caciques, named Caripan and María Josefa their ambassadors. They would accompany Cerro y Zamudio with two other Pehuenches: María del Carmen—María Josefa's niece—and the cacique Juan Neculante.

Before leaving, María Josefa asked Cerro y Zamudio that a report concerning "her nobility and the merits she had contracted serving His Majesty" be made for the viceroy and other officials in Buenos Aires. In this text, she included her memory of "the time of the uprising of these frontiers by the infidel nations." Pressured by the natives, the people of Mendoza decided "that the said doña María Josefa should go to native territory to reduce the principal leaders of the Pehuenche nation, and in fact she brought them to this city to treat the peace, that lasts until today."[72] We know that the cacica was particularly retained in Mendoza as a captive in 1780 and later as a hostage, while Ignacia negotiated with Roco and her brothers. Was María Josefa attributing to herself the diplomatic skills of her father's wife? Was she referring instead to her diplomatic approach to Amigorena in 1796, when Pehuenches were torn by an internal war? Were her words misunderstood? In any case, we are dealing with a "captive discourse," one that is translated from Mapudungun to Spanish, with the potential of diluting the native voice as it was transformed into European writing, with the imposition of western logic to the indigenous statement.[73] That is, we are not hearing María Josefa's voice, but Cerro y Zamudio's distorted rendition of it. Yet we can still read how the cacica invoked the nobility of her origins and the merits of her peacemaker functions while providing a version of the history of interethnic relations that is radically different from that suggested by Spanish sources. According to her, the Pehuenche chiefs had agreed to make peace with Mendoza not as losers but from a position of leverage "while Spaniards were cornered by the rigor of the said Indians." This might have been the consecrated discourse inside the Pehuenche community, one that preserved their reputation as fearsome warriors. Lastly, the Chilean traveler makes note of "the veneration and respect that the cacica [María Josefa] enjoys in all the land." Commander Teles Meneses validated María Josefa's assertions, adding that "she not only belonged to the most distinguished lineage of Pehuenche Indians from the frontier" but she was "the widow of one of the most renowned caciques." She had been the means through which a lasting peace "persists without alteration until now due to the love and respect that all other Indians feel for her."[74]

Endowed with this formal recognition of her leadership, María Josefa arrived in Buenos Aires not as an indistinguishable china or as any other cacica but as a respected ambassador who was received by the consulate, cabildo, and viceroy. Once back in Pehuenche territory, a large parlamento was held on the shores of the Diamante River during which the natives ceded a portion of their lands for the erection of a new fort, San Rafael, that would constitute Mendoza's new frontier. María Josefa is mentioned in two articles of the treaty, and we know that she intervened in the discussions to stress, against the reluctant opinion of many fellow countrymen, that she supported the erection of a hamlet and a church next to the new fort, in the spot called Agua Caliente, arguing that the king "offered it to her for her happiness."[75]

After the parliament, a meeting among Pehuenches was held in order to persuade those who were still reticent of the advantages of a new deal with the Spaniards from Mendoza. Two caciques—Carilef, the chief of the frontier Pehuenches, and Caripan, who was ambassador to the viceroy—took the floor before María Josefa. In his speech, Carilef referred to her as "a noble cacica," who was "worthy of all honor and praise" for having been the first to permit baptism, "opening the doors of happiness" for the whole community.

When it was her turn to speak, María Josefa recalled her visit with the viceroy, when she also met the vicereine and her children. Allegedly, María Josefa judged the Spanish proposals as genuine due to the kindness of this family.[76] After all, she had seen the viceroy acting as a husband and a father, by which she meant including his wife and children in the diplomatic talks and distributing presents and good advice to the native ambassadors. With the authority derived from her lineage and her function as observer and participant, she attested to the sincerity of Christian intentions.

María Josefa Roco, the former captive and hostage, orphan, and childless widow (thus freed from the family ties that kept her in the Pehuenche world), had become a mediator between cultures. The following year, in 1806, she inaugurated, together with her niece María del Carmen, "the new Indian *reducción* [in the Río de la Plata southern frontier: a forced permanent resettlement of previously wandering indigenous groups]" next to the fort of San Rafael. By that time, María del Carmen was willing to marry a Christian soldier. Though an unusual marital option for a native woman from prestigious origins, her choice was probably motivated by her intended conversion to Catholicism.[77] We find María Josefa mentioned for the last time during the turbulent years of the wars for independence, when Spanish soldiers securing the San Rafael fort were taken to San Carlos and rumors spread among natives that they were going to be killed. María Josefa and the caciques asked for mercy for "their brothers and countrymen, for they were [also] born in the Indies." They implored the soldiers to return to the fort to fulfill their protective function as provided for in the 1805 treaty: if Pehuenches had then given up some lands—they recalled—it was "for their inhabitants to work to subsist and . . . for a village for their fellow countrymen who decided to convert to Christianity." Once the message was delivered, while the caciques returned to their lands, María Josefa "stayed [in San Carlos] waiting for an answer to carry the good news to her countrymen."[78] With one foot on either side of the frontier, the Pehuenche María Josefa spoke for her people and expected to be the channel through which the words of Spanish men would flow. She was first valued as the most cherished daughter of an eminent chief, then as the widow of "one of the most renowned caciques," and finally as Paynechiñé's sister. With age and a long experience of Spanish-native relations, María Josefa's prestige depended no longer on her male relatives but rather on her own diplomatic skills and her experience as mediator with a voice to be heard.

CONCLUSIONS

The three cacicas—María Francisca, Ignacia, and María Josefa—illustrate the political prominence of indigenous women in the late-eighteenth-century southern Río de la Plata frontier. Subjected to the physical violence of captivity and held as prisoners and hostages, they took advantage of their difficult experiences to create social links and become familiar with Spanish culture. Their intimate knowledge of the two worlds and the social weight attributed to their kinship ties with the prominent caciques transformed them into key players in treaty-making. Their trajectories were not necessarily exceptional, as many other cacicas accomplished similar roles but left fewer traces in the archives.

These women acted in contexts of tension where men had good reasons to fear prison, deportation, and death had they appeared before Spanish officials. Giving cacicas the role of emissaries, indigenous leaders delivered a double message to their counterparts. On the one hand, they were sending their most beloved wives and daughters as ambassadors, hoping that their female condition would protect those women from imprisonment or exile. On the other hand, cacicas were indicating through symbolic language that the presence of women was a visible indicator of the peaceful intentions of the men who sent them. Even in those instances when diplomatic negotiations were not entrusted to female go-betweens, women had been present in the preliminary discussions, ceremonies that formally accepted treaty conditions, ritual demonstrations, and celebrations that followed the ratification of a peace treaty. Native commercial and diplomatic parties arriving to colonial centers included in all cases chinas, who regularly traveled long distances to make business or negotiate agreements. While not always visible to Spaniards, everywhere in the southern Río de la Plata frontier, indigenous women were intimately involved in interethnic relations. As Juliana Barr suggests, women acting "as mediators of peace did not simply signal cross-cultural rapport, but rather the predominance of native codes of peace and war."[79] According to those codes, while war was men's privileged sphere of action, women expressed peaceful intentions. The cacicas opened up negotiations, carried preliminary peace proposals between parties, and acted as social agents endowed with personal initiative—Ignacia suggested that her people could settle next to the frontier; María Josefa requested a reducción in her lands for those Pehuenches who accepted baptism. Conciliatory and pragmatic, inspired by their will to ensure their peoples' survival, they accomplished broker functions that turned them into agents of change not only among their countrymen but also in interactions with colonial power. Even the viceroys, adapting to native codes contrary to their perception of politics as an exclusively masculine realm, ended up asking their wives to be present in their encounters with the cacicas.

The political roles cacicas fulfilled bear witness to the value that was placed upon them in their societies. However, no cacica exerted government functions. While they wielded a strong influence on their male relatives in political matters, they did not decide on war and peace, political alliances, seasonal displacements of tolderías, or commercial initiatives. Their power was limited to representation and persuasion. Kinship and dialogue were their weapons; peace was their horizon. A dignified peace, one that would make possible, after years of cruel wars, the cessation of hostilities, reunification of families, prosperity of trade, acquisition of prestigious goods through presence in colonial centers, and Spanish military aid in their conflicts with other natives. This was a peace agreed upon through treaties that recognized native peoples of the Río de la Plata frontier as sovereign indigenous nations.

NOTES

1. *Indios bárbaros* referred to "Indians independent of Spanish rule." The gloss in this chapter follows David Weber's choice to translate *bárbaros* as "savages," even if the words are not exactly synonymous; *Bárbaros: Spaniards and Their Savages in the Age of Enlightenment* (New Haven: Yale University Press, 2005). See also Juliana Barr, *Peace Came in the Form of a Woman: Indians and Spaniards in the Texas Borderlands* (Chapel Hill: University of North Carolina Press, 2007), 10. I use the term "native" to avoid discussing here the complex issue of ethnic identities. For a broader discussion of indigenous identities, see Lidia Nacuzzi, *Identidades impuestas: Tehuelches, aucas y pampas en el norte de la Patagonia* (Buenos Aires: Sociedad Argentina de Antropología, 1998); and Florencia Roulet, *Huincas en tierra de indios: Mediaciones e identidades en los relatos de viajeros tardocoloniales* (Buenos Aires: Eudeba, 2016).

2. See Juan Francisco Maura, *Carta de Luis Ramírez a su padre desde el Brasil (1528): orígenes de lo 'real maravilloso' en el Cono Sur* (Valencia: Lemir, 2007), https://parnaseo.uv.es/Lemir/Textos/Ramirez.pdf; Álvar Núñez Cabeza de Vaca, *Relación de los naufragios y comentarios* (Madrid: Librería General de Victoriano Suárez, 1906), vol. 1, http://www.cervantesvirtual.com/descargaPdf/relacion-de-los-naufragios-y-comentarios-de-alvar-nunez-cabeza de-vaca-tomo-1-788658/; Ulrich Schmidl, *Viaje al Río de la Plata, 1534–1554* (1567; repr., Buenos Aires: Cabaut y Cía., 1903]); Juan de Garay, "Repartimiento de los indios de esta ciudad [de Buenos Aires] hecho por

el general Juan de Garay, año de 1582," in *Colección de obras y documentos relativos a la historia antigua y moderna de las provincias del Río de la Plata*, ed. Pedro de Angelis (Buenos Aires: Plus Ultra, 1969); Silvia Tieffemberg, *Argentina: Historia del descubrimiento y conquista del Río de la Plata de Ruy Díaz de Guzmán* (Buenos Aires: editorial de la Facultad de Filosofía y Letras, 2012), http://publicaciones.filo.uba.ar/sites/publicaciones.filo.uba.ar/files/Argentina. Historia del Descubrimiento y Conquista del Río de la Plata de Ruy Díaz de Guzmán_interactivo.pdf; Martín del Barco Centenera, "La Argentina o Conquista del Río de la Plata," in *Colección de obras y documentos relativos a la historia antigua y moderna de las provincias del Río de la Plata*, ed. Pedro de Angelis (Buenos Aires: Plus Ultra, 1969).

3. For a discussion of the concept of ethnogenesis and its history, see Guillaume Boccara, "Colonización, resistencia y etnogénesis en las fronteras americanas," in *Colonización, resistencia y mestizaje en las Américas, siglos XVI–XX*, ed. Guillaume Boccara (Quito: ediciones Abya-Yala, 2002).

4. See, for instance, José Cardiel, "Diario del viaje y misión al Río del Sauce por fines de marzo de 1748," in *Publicaciones del Instituto de Investigaciones Geográficas de la Facultad de Filosofía y Letras*, serie A (Buenos Aires: Instituto de Geografía, 1930); François-Xavier de Charlevoix, *Histoire du Paraguay* (Paris: Chez Didot, Giffart et Nyon, 1757); Thomas Falkner, *A Description of Patagonia and the Adjoining Parts of South America* (1777; repr., Chicago: Armann & Armann, 1935), http://www.rockvillepress.com/TIERRA/TEXTS/FALKNER.HTM#Intro1; Tomás Falkner, "Derrotero desde la ciudad de Buenos Aires hasta la de los Césares, que por otro nombre llaman la 'Ciudad encantada,'" in *Colección de obras y documentos relativos a la historia antigua y moderna de las provincias del Río de la Plata*, ed. Pedro de Angelis (1760; repr., Buenos Aires: Plus Ultra, 1969); María Laura Salinas and Julio Folkenand, *Cartas Anuas de la Provincia Jesuítica del Paraguay: 1714–1720, 1720–1730, 1730–1735, 1735–1743, 1750–1756, 1756–1762* (Asunción: Centro de Estudios Antropológicos de la Universidad Católica, 2016); Joseph Sánchez Labrador, *Los Indios Pampas, Puelches, Patagones* (Buenos Aires: Viau y Zona, 1936).

5. This chapter is based heavily on unpublished administrative sources, such as diaries of military campaigns into indigenous territories, reports of frontier officers noting the entry and exit of indigenous parties, declarations of captives escaped from natives and of natives captured by Spaniards, proceedings of local cabildos, correspondence between governors and the Spanish Crown, memories of viceroys, minutes of parlamentos (diplomatic encounters between natives and Spaniards), and peace treaties.

6. Whereas in the Río de la Plata region "china" meant only native woman, in the colonial Andes the same term referred specifically to native female servants.

7. There is no feminine form in Mapudungun (the language of the Mapuche) for the neutral word *lonko* (lit., "head," "hair"), designating the leader. A feminine form could be *domo lonko* (woman leader), but there is no evidence that this expression was used before Spanish arrival. From personal communication with Gertrudis Payás.

8. *Chusma* was a term used by the Spanish in this frontier region to refer to the human booty of interethnic warfare, made up of noncombatant people captured

during the military campaigns; from Real Academia Española, *Diccionario de la Lengua Española*, 23rd ed. (Madrid: Real Academia Española, 2014), https://dle.rae.es/chusma.

9. Florencia Roulet, "Embajadoras y hechiceras indígenas: El poder de las mujeres en la frontera sur," *Todo es Historia* 489 (April 2008).

10. An encomienda was a grant of Indian labor and tribute to a Spaniard. See James Lockhart, *The Nahuas after the Conquest: A Social and Cultural History of the Indians of Central Mexico, Sixteenth Through Eighteenth Centuries* (Stanford: Stanford University Press, 1992), 4–5.

11. The main proclaimed goal of Spanish conquest of the Americas was to "reduce" heathens to Christianity and political life through evangelization in permanent settlements called *reducciones*. In eastern and southern South America, this project entailed a "drastic scheme of forcing a complete social transformation, from shifting horticultural and/or hunter-gatherer ways of life to a would-be utopian village theocracy under the rule of [priests]," in Juan Carlos Garavaglia, "The Crisis and Transformations of Invaded Societies: The La Plata Basin (1535–1650)," in *The Cambridge History of the Native Peoples of the Americas*, ed. Frank Salomon and Stuart B. Schwartz (Cambridge: Cambridge University Press, 1999), vol. 3, part 2:17–18.

12. Florencia Roulet, "Violencia indígena en el Río de la Plata durante el período colonial temprano: un intento de explicación," *Nuevo Mundo, Mundos Nuevos* (2018), https://doi.org/10.4000/nuevomundo.72018.

13. Letter from Miguel de Salcedo, governor, to the king. Buenos Aires, November 11, 1741, Archivo General de Indias (hereafter cited as AGI) Buenos Aires, 302.

14. Pierre François-Xavier de Charlevoix, *Histoire du Paraguay* (Paris: Dessaint & Saillant, 1756), vol. 6, chap. 21:161; Abelardo Levaggi, *Paz en la frontera: Historia de las relaciones diplomáticas con las comunidades indígenas en la Argentina (siglos XVI–XIX)* (Buenos Aires: Universidad del Museo Social Argentino, 2000), 105–8.

15. For a discussion on the nature and limits of women's power in indigenous societies of the Río de la Plata southern frontier, see Roulet, "Embajadoras y hechiceras indígenas."

16. Barr, *Peace Came*.

17. Barr, *Peace Came*, 2.

18. Richard White, *The Middle Ground: Indians, Empires, and Republics in the Great Lakes Region, 1650–1815* (New York: Cambridge University Press, 1991), ix.

19. José Manuel Zavala, *Les Indiens Mapuche du Chili: Dynamiques interethniques et stratégies de résistance, XVIIIe siècle* (Paris: L'Harmattan, 2000), 128.

20. I mention many of them in Florencia Roulet, "Mujeres, rehenes y secretarios: Mediadores indígenas en la frontera sur del Río de la Plata durante el período hispánico," *Colonial Latin American Review* 18, no. 3 (December 2009); and Roulet, "Embajadoras y hechiceras indígenas."

21. By the end of the eighteenth century, in the Buenos Aires frontier, the ethnonym "Pampa" referred to natives inhabiting the plains and sierras south of the city, some of them formerly called Aucas, from mixed ethnic origin. They spoke Mapudungun and based their economy on pastoral activities and trade. The Pehuenches

(meaning "people from the *pehuén*" or *Araucaria araucana,* an evergreen coniferous tree with edible seeds found in the Andean forests of Southern Chile and Argentina) were indigenous from the Cordillera. Many of them, pushed by Spanish pressure on their lands, had migrated east of the Andes in the second half of the century and then to the north, near the vicinity of Mendoza's frontier. They were also shepherds and traders and spoke Mapudungun, and their women were reputedly excellent weavers.

22. José Francisco de Amigorena, "Diario de la expedición que de orden del Exmo. Señor virrey acabo de hacer contra los indios bárbaros peguenches," in *Colección de Obras y Documentos Relativos a la Historia del Río de la Plata,* ed. Pedro de Angelis (1780; repr., Buenos Aires: Plus Ultra, 1969), 4:210, 212, 213.

23. Letter from José Francisco de Amigorena to the viceroy Juan José de Vértiz, Mendoza, July 23, 1780, Archivo Histórico de Mendoza (hereafter cited as AHM), Carpeta 55, Documento 4.

24. Among the indigenous of the Pampas and southern Andes, marriages were celebrated in two ways: one, with the consent of the bride and her parents, only after the groom had "paid" a price in kind (e.g., horses, textiles, spurs, reins, and other valuable goods in a nonmonetary economy) to her family; or, two, through abduction, typically without the woman's consent and without having paid her family. The abduction method of marriage was a strategy deployed mostly with captives taken from enemy groups.

25. "Estaban resueltos à admitir la paz con la condición de que pusiesen en libertad los indios presos que se hallan en la ciudad [de Buenos Aires], en canje de los cautivos cristianos que llevaban" (declaration of the captive Fermín Restoy in Luján, August 31, 1790, Archivo General de la Nación (hereafter AGN), Sala 9, 1-6-2). On the context of those events, see Eduardo Crivelli Montero, "Malones, ¿saqueo o estrategia? El objetivo de las invasiones de 1780 y 1783 a la frontera de Buenos Aires," *Todo es Historia* 283 (1994).

26. "Si el cristiano no le da la paz y le envían las indias e indios que están en Buenos Aires para canjearlos por los muchos cristianos que tienen allá, habrá guerra continua por todas partes a fin de vengarse" (declaration of Alcaluan, Indian, in Chascomús, December 1, 1780, AGN Sala 9, 1-4-3).

27. Derived from the verb *malocan* (to fight, to make war), the word *malón* referred to a native attack on an enemy toldería or on a colonial settlement, capturing cattle, women, and children.

28. Juan José de Vértiz, "Memorias," *Revista del Archivo General de Buenos Aires* 3 (1871): 421–22.

29. "Varios indios e indias para entregar al cacique Lorenzo, tratar con éste y sus aliados las paces e inspeccionar la campaña," in Pablo Zizur, "Diario que yo don Pablo Zizur Primer Piloto de la Real Armada boi á hacer desde la ciudad de Buenos Aires hasta los establecimientos nuestros en la Costa Patagonica; por comisión del Excelentísimo Señor Virrey; a fin de conducir varios indios y indias para entregar al cacique Lorenzo, tratar con éste y sus aliados las pases, y inspeccionar la campaña," *Revista del Archivo General de la Nación,* 3, no. 3 (1973): 67.

30. Zizur, "Diario," 75–76.

31. Zizur, "Diario," 102.

32. Letter from Francisco Balcarce to the viceroy, marqués de Loreto, Luján, June 17, 1784, AGN Sala 9, 1-6-2.

33. "Una china muy ladina [que] se ha criado en estos partidos," in letter from Francisco Balcarce to Viceroy Loreto. Luján, June 17, 1784, AGN Sala 9, 1-6-2.

34. See Natalia Salerno, "Cautivas indígenas. Abusos, violencia y malos tratos en el Buenos Aires colonial," in *Devastación: Violencia civilizada contra los indios de las llanuras del Plata y Sur de Chile (siglos XVI a XIX)*, comp., Sebastián Alioto, Juan F. Jiménez, and Daniel Villar (Buenos Aires, Prohistoria: 2018).

35. "Que gobierna a todos . . . van a tomar parecer para cualquiera determinación," in declaration of Pedro Zamora. Buenos Aires, February 22, 1781, AGN Sala 9, 1-7-4.

36. Zizur, "Diario," 82.

37. "En virtud de la demora que se experimentaba en la venida de Buenos Aires de la mujer del cacique Lorenzo y demás individuos que había mandado con ella," in Zizur, "Diario," 79–80.

38. White, *Middle Ground*, x; James Lockhart, "Double Mistaken Identity: Some Nahua Concepts in Postconquest Guise," in *Of Things of the Indies: Essays Old and New in Early Latin American History* (Stanford: Stanford University Press, 1999), 99.

39. Pedro Zamora declared that he had volunteered to go to Buenos Aires "to bring the Indians peace and two chinas retained in the Residencia, in exchange for his, his wife and his daughter's freedom" (se brindó él prometiendo el llevárselas [las Paces], y dos Chinas que hay en la Residencia, por cuya entrega le darían libertad a él y a su mujer, y a su hija), in declaration of captive Pedro Zamora. Buenos Aires, February 22, 1781, AGN Sala 9, 1-7-4.

40. Kristine L. Jones estimates native peoples of the Southern Cone as "numbering at least between 100,000 to 300,000 individuals" by 1880 (including Chile's native population, much higher than the Pampa and Patagonia population), but she stresses that "until a systematic demographic study is conducted any population estimate of these people prior to their military conquest can only be a rough estimate—most likely an underestimate," in "Warfare, Reorganization, and Readaptation at the Margins of Spanish Rule: The Southern Margin (1573–1882)," in *The Cambridge History of the Native Peoples of the Americas*, ed. Richard E. W. Adams and Murdo J. MacLeod (Cambridge: Cambridge University Press, 1999), 2:138–39. These native peoples were "conquered" only after the military campaigns that took place from 1878 to 1884 in Argentina (1882–84 in Chile).

41. In a letter to Francisco Balcarce, Loreto expressed his distrust of these women, stating, "Exponiendo para lograrlo dos mujeres de quienes aunque se diga ser la una propia de Lorenzo es menester creerla sobre su palabra" (Presenting to that end two women, one of them said to be Lorenzo's wife, while we should believe her own words), in letter from Viceroy Loreto to Francisco Balcarce. Buenos Aires, June 18, 1784, AGN Sala 9, 1-6-2. In the colonial male-oriented logic, a woman was worth half the value of a man: "for two women captives they are bringing they ask three people, one of them a man, who doubles the difference resulting from their number" (por dos cautivas que traen piden tres personas y la una varón, que dobla la diferencia

que resulta por el número), in letter from Viceroy Loreto to Francisco Balcarce. Buenos Aires, August 13, 1784, AGN Sala 9, 1-6-2). In this case again, the viceroy assumed wrongly that captive Bernardo López was Lorenzo Calfilqui's emissary and he did not count him as a captive to be redeemed. When informed that the viceroy refused to exchange the captives he was sending to Buenos Aires for his relatives, cacique Guarán—one of Calfilqui's allies—said angrily that "he had sent the captive recently brought by the two chinas, as well as a female captive that he bought for that purpose, to redeem his wife and son" (se han disgustado mucho, haciéndome presente el Cacique llamado Guaran de Nación Teguelchú, que para el rescate de su mujer e hijo había mandado el cautivo que trajeron últimamente las dos chinas y la cautiva que trae comprada para el mismo efecto), in letter from Francisco Balcarce to Viceroy Loreto. Luján, August 20, 1784, AGN Sala 9, 1-6-2.

42. "Están muy temerosos a bajar porque creen se les ha de hacer algún daño por los cristianos y . . . querían ver cómo les iba a estos segundos emisarios"; "no deja en algún modo de ser fundado el recelo que tienen los caciques para su venida, porque también por nuestra parte he oído se les ha faltado en algunas ocasiones a aquellos términos de la buena fe," in letters from Francisco Balcarce to Viceroy Loreto. Luján, August 11 and 20, 1784, AGN Sala 9, 1-6-2.

43. "Una persona grande," in declaration of Joseph Zampallo, Indian. Buenos Aires, September 7, 1784, AGN Sala 9, 1-7-4.

44. Barr, *Peace Came*, 13.

45. Roulet, *Huincas en tierra*, 200–201. A clear example of this gender diplomacy was the first arrival to the Buenos Aires frontier of cacique Casuel, with one hundred natives. When the pathfinder approached the group to recognize them, Casuel stepped forward with the cacica and two unarmed men, saying that they didn't intend to bring any harm to the Christians but to hunt wild horses. We know nothing about her except that, being very fluent in Spanish, she answered to the questions of Spanish officials; in letters from Francisco Faijô to Governor Juan Joseph de Vértiz, June 10 and 18, 1774, AGN Sala 9, 1-5-6. The presence of a woman in this first contact, together with the absence of weapons, reinforced symbolically the peaceful message that cacique Casuel was delivering.

46. Viceroy Loreto, circular letter to the governor of Córdoba, the commander of arms of Mendoza and the Buenos Aires's commander of frontier, March 7, 1786, AGN Sala 9, 23-2-1.

47. "El gran cacique Calfilqui, poderoso enemigo y dueño de los más vastos campos que conocemos en estas partes"; "ya por el copioso número de sus indios y ya por su distinguido valor y atrevimiento ha sido el terror, el espanto y el azote más cruel de nosotros los cristianos," in testimony of captain Juan Antonio Hernández' merits. Buenos Aires, September 9, 1790, AGN Sala 9, 1-7-5.

48. "A hablar con la señora virreina y dar noticias de dicho cacique," in letter from Viceroy Arredondo to interpreter Blas Pedrosa. Buenos Aires, March 13, 1791, AGN Sala 9, 24-1-8; "haber tenido noticia de que por acá se estaban haciendo prevenciones para irlos a insultar," in letter from Manuel Martínez to Viceroy Arredondo. Ranchos, August 21, 1791, AGN Sala 9, 1-5-1.

49. Letter from Vicente Juan Colomer to Viceroy Arredondo. Ranchos, October 25, 1792, AGN Sala 9, 1-5-1.

50. "Una nieta del cacique Guentenau que ya era reconocida entre ellos por cacica, aunque soltera, por no haber en su nación quién pudiese comprarla en 100 pagas, en que según su rito estaba valuada su mano," Amigorena, "Diario de la expedición," 212. On the bride's price, see note 24.

51. Amigorena informed that, after distributing the captives in particular houses, he retained "a cacica with three daughters and a son" (una cacica con tres hijas y un hijo), in letter from Amigorena to Vértiz. Mendoza, June 23, 1780, AHM Carpeta 55, Documento 4.

52. "La estima singularmente y distingue entre todos los demás," in proceedings from the Cabildo of Mendoza, September 21, 1781 and December 9, 1780, AGN Sala 9, 24-1-1. It is likely that she was not Ignacia's daughter because she is never described as such and because, when she finally married, her husband was Ignacia's brother.

53. Doña Ignacia "ha prometido repetidas veces [solicitar] la amistad, confederación y alianza de todos los de su Nación y [traerlos] a esta frontera, para tratar y establecer una paz segura," in proceedings of the Cabildo of Mendoza, December 9, 1780, in AGN Sala 9, 24-1-1; "la cacica Mujer del Cacique Roco . . . dice que en rehenes quedan las tres hijas de su estimación, que están en mi poder, . . . y me promete ella traerá a esta Ciudad, o al fuerte de San Carlos, a su Marido, y sus tres hermanos que son los caciques que a esta Nación le han quedado, y que hecho el parlamento se sujetarán en nuestra frontera, donde yo los destinase," in letter from Amigorena to Viceroy Vértiz. Mendoza, August 28, 1780, AGN Sala 9, 11-4-5.

54. It is unclear who this other cacica, María Yanqueípi, was. No source mentions that any other indigenous woman traveled to Pehuenche territory with the cacica Ignacia. Did María freely come from there with the cacica and her relatives or is she one of the many female captives already in Mendoza, allowed to participate in the peace talks because of the importance of her lineage? I believe the latter was the case and that she may have been "doña María, Roco's sister," who would later be sent to native territory as Amigorena's emissary to the paramount cacique of the Pehuenches, Ancán Amún. See proceedings from the Cabildo of Mendoza, September 21, 1781, AGN Sala 9, 24-1-1.

55. "Doña Ignacia Guentenau, Doña María Yanqueípi, con sus Hermanos Piampán y Llongopán, su cuñado Antipán, y Peñalef . . . venían a ofrecer una Paz segura con esta ciudad . . . bajo la calidad de haber de quedar sin novedad, como Prisionera o en Rehenes, la Cacica principal, Doña María Josefa, y todas las demás que han estado y están hasta lo presente en esta Ciudad," in proceedings from the cabildo of Mendoza, December 14, 1780, AGN Sala 9, 24-1-1.

56. "El principal objeto de estos infieles es recoger a la cautiva doña María Josepha," in letter from Viceroy Vértiz to Mendoza's *corregidor* (in the Río de la Plata region: regional district magistrate). Buenos Aires, February 9, 1781, AHM Carpeta 46, Documento 32.

57. Acuerdo del Cabildo de Mendoza, April 7, 1781, AGN Sala 9, 24-1-1. Ranquelches are variably recorded as Ranqueles, Ranquelches, Ranquilches, Ranquichules, and/or Rankulches in original sources.

58. Florencia Roulet, "De cautivos a aliados: los 'indios fronterizos' de Mendoza (1780–1806)," *Xama* 12–14 (1999–2001).

59. "Las personas de mayor carácter o estimación entre ellos," in proceedings of the Cabildo of Mendoza, September 21, 1781, AGN Sala 9, 24-1-1.

60. "Perdón por la fuga que hicieron de esta frontera . . . y que me dignase acogerlo otra vez en ella bajo las condiciones que quisiese," in letter from Amigorena to Viceroy Vértiz. Mendoza, August 12, 1782, AHM Carpeta 55, Documento 6.

61. "Respecto a que hoy estos Peguenches son pocos y temen a los indios Guilliches los maten," in letter from Amigorena to Viceroy Vértiz. Mendoza, August 28, 1780, AGN Sala 9, 11-4-5.

62. "Rocco, Antepan, la Ignacia y otros han estado en Santiago de Chile con el señor presidente; allá la puede vuestra merced examinar de cómo le fue," writes the commander of San Carlos to announce her visit to Mendoza, in letter from Esquivel Aldao to Amigorena. San Carlos, August 31, 1784, AHM Carpeta 65, Documento 35.

63. Letter from Amigorena to Viceroy Vértiz. Mendoza August 25, 1787, AHM Carpeta 55, Documento 18.

64. Letter from Esquivel Aldao to Amigorena. San Carlos, September 5, 1787, AHM Carpeta 65, Documento 63.

65. Letter from Esquivel Aldao to Amigorena. San Carlos, September 7, 1793, AHM Carpeta 66, Documento 99; "el Capitanejo Paynechiñé, hijo del Cacique Roco," in letter from Aldao to Amigorena. San Carlos, June 29, 1794, AHM Carpeta 30, Documento 12.

66. "dos Cacicas con un chinillo hijas del cacique Roco"; "para averiguar lo cierto de esta especie no hubo un indio que se atreviese a venir"; "estas cacicas con la confianza de haber estado siete años en mi casa en rehenes, quienes se retiran bien desengañadas de tal noticia," in letter from Amigorena to Rafael de Sobremonte, governor of Córdoba. Mendoza, June 14, 1796, AHM Carpeta 56, Documento 1.

67. Two closely related caciques bore the same name, Antepán (or Antipan): one was Roco's brother, the other Ignacia's brother—also known as Barbas—and María Josefa's husband. It is often hard to distinguish them.

68. "Por sí y a nombre de su anciano padre el cacique Roco," in proceedings of the San Carlos peace talks, July 6, 1799, AHM Carpeta 30, Documento 46.

69. Florencia Roulet, "Guerra y diplomacia en la frontera de Mendoza: la política indígena del comandante José Francisco de Amigorena (1779–1799)," in *Funcionarios, diplomáticos, guerreros: Miradas hacia el otro en las fronteras de pampa y Patagonia (siglos XVIII y XIX)*, ed. Lidia Nacuzzi (Buenos Aires: Sociedad Argentina de Antropología, 2002).

70. The only reference I could find concerning the identity of María Josefa's husband appears in a register of Indian parties arriving to Mendoza for trading purposes in 1802, when she is mentioned as "the widow of cacique Antepán," in letter from Faustino Anzay to the ministers of the royal estate. Mendoza, June 2, 1802, AHM Carpeta 56, Documento 6.

71. "Sus ponchos y lanas y lo demás que trabajan," in letter from Cerro y Zamudio to the Consulate of Buenos Aires. Valle de las Ánimas, August 25, 1803, AGN Sala 9, 39-5-5.

72. "En el tiempo de la sublevación de estas fronteras por las naciones de In-fieles . . . viéndose estrechados los españoles del Rigor de los dichos Indios, que si es cierto que se tomaron el arbitrio . . . que la enunciada doña María Josefa fuese a tierra dentro a reducir a todos los principales caudillos de la nación Peguencha, y con efecto los ha traído a esta Ciudad a efecto de tratar la paz, la que hasta el día se con-serva," in Cerro y Zamudio, examination of Commander Miguel de Telis. Mendoza, August 22, 1804, AGN Sala 9, 39-5-5.

73. Martin Lienhard, "El cautiverio colonial del discurso indígena: los testimo-nios," in *Del discurso colonial al proindigenismo. Ensayos de historia latinoamericana*, ed. José Pinto Rodríguez (Temuco: Universidad de la Frontera, 1998), 10.

74. "A más de ser del linaje más distinguido de los Indios Pehuenches de estas fronteras es viuda de uno de los Caciques que hubo en ellas de más nombre"; "habién-dose formado entonces [la paz] por medio de ella, dura y subsiste hasta ahora por lo mucho que la quieren y respetan todos los demás Indios," in certification from Miguel Teles Meneses. Mendoza, August 25, 1804, AGN Sala 9, 39-5-5.

75. "Se la ofrecía para su felicidad," in letter from Friar Francisco Inalicán to the viceroy. San Rafael, April 9, 1805, AGI Buenos Aires 92. On this treaty, see Roulet, *Huincas en tierra*, 161–71. Agua Caliente was situated four or five leagues from the camp where María Josefa, Paynechiñé, and Caripan lived, on a path that led to San Carlos and Mendoza: the Pehuenches were not surrendering lands but accepting a Spanish enclave in their lands to facilitate trade and military protection (letter from Juan Morel to Sobremonte. San Carlos, April 7, 1805, AGN Sala 9, 30-7-6).

76. Carilef's words: "gloria de nuestra nación," "superior a todo elogio," "digna de todo honor y alabanza," "nos dejas abiertas las puertas de la felicidad." María Jo-sefa says: "Yo fui desde mi tierra a ver al Señor Virrey, es muy bueno, su mujer tam-bién es muy buena, sus hijitos muy buenos, sus consejos me dice que el Rey grande es muy bueno que mucho nos quiere a toda la tierra, he de avisar," in minutes of the conference in the camp of Río Diamante, April 2, 1805, AGN Sala 9, 3-5-2. For a discussion of the three indigenous discourses, see Roulet, "Mujeres, rehenes y secre-tarios," 312–15.

77. "La nueva reducción de naturales," in letter from Teles Meneses to Sobre-monte. San Rafael, December 8, 1806, AGN Sala 9, 11-4-5.

78. "Sus hermanos y paisanos por ser nacidos en las Indias"; "para que trabajasen sus habitantes para subsistir, y . . . para un pueblo para sus paisanos que quisiesen abrazar la religión cristiana," in letter from Friar Francisco Inalicán to Lieutenant Governor Alejo Aguirre. San Carlos, September 28, 1813, AHM Independiente, Car-peta 234, Documento 51.

79. Barr, *Peace Came*, 2.

Conclusion

TO BE CACICA IN COLONIAL TIMES—THE RHETORIC OF "PUREZA"

Mónica Díaz

It sometimes seems that as academics we spend most of our time trying to set the record straight, debating old patterns of thought, and going against traditional historiographical narratives that keep us stagnated. Yet, at times when we look attentively at what scholars are writing about, we can appreciate the changes that have occurred in our disciplines and celebrate important milestones. The publication of this book is definitely one of those moments. The nine chapters included in this first volume dedicated to cacicas in Spanish America expand our knowledge of indigenous women during colonial times in a large geographical area and make sophisticated claims about their role as political agents.

Cacicas first took a special place in the historiography of Spanish America thanks to the pioneering work of Mexican historian Josefina Muriel, who in 1963 published the only manuscript believed to have survived from the Convent of Corpus Christi in Mexico City, the first convent in the Americas to allow native women to become nuns.[1] One of the requirements to admit natives into the convent was that they had to be nobles or *principales* (hereditary nobles), therefore many stated that they were cacicas or daughters of caciques. That same year, Asunción Lavrin wrote her doctoral dissertation on eighteenth-century Mexican convents, devoting one of the chapters to the establishment of Corpus Christi and its subsequent conflicts.[2] Lavrin's scholarship has not only been the foundation for most studies on female conventual culture in Spanish America produced in the last thirty years, with her edited volumes *Latin American Women: Historical Perspectives* (1978) and *Sexuality and Marriage in Colonial Latin America* (1989), she has also been a leading figure in writing about gender and women's history in Spanish America.[3]

The research that I have conducted in the last few years in Mexican archives on indigenous efforts to open additional convents and other spaces for education during the eighteenth century has led me to rethink the methodological framework that I used to approach the materials for my first book.[4] When I first came across a manuscript composed by three anonymous indigenous nuns about several of the women who had lived in the Convent of Corpus Christi in the 1720s, my main objective was to successfully demonstrate that the manuscript was written by the cacicas living in the convent and that the document that Josefina Muriel had published in 1963 was a later version, edited by the priest Joseph Manuel Camino, of the original found in the convent. While this was a groundbreaking finding and I provided an important analysis of sources written by cacicas, there was more to be done. It is necessary to explore the social networks that indigenous women established outside the religious space and appreciate more fully the authors not only as women but also as colonial agents. This would involve moving away from the framework proposed by many of the studies in the subfield of conventual writing and approaching these phenomena as part of the cultural production of natives and their centuries-long struggle to find accommodation in the colonial world. The cacicas living in the three convents for noble native women in Mexico self-identified as pure *indias* (female Indians) in order to take part of one of the most prominent institutions of the colonial world. However, this self-identification was in most cases strategic and rhetorical, and that's something that needs to be problematized further since it has created misconceptions about what it meant to be india and cacica during this time period.

In their introduction, Sara Guengerich and Margarita Ochoa give credit to the scholars who paved the way with their groundbreaking work on indigenous women and *cacicazgos* (office of the cacique, including sometimes its political role, services, and property), which allowed for the kind of scholarship included in this volume. After almost forty years of exceptional scholarship that has brought a gendered perspective into the historical analysis of Latin American sources, we no longer need to justify the publication of a book dedicated to cacicas. However, there are certain persistent narratives, narratives that reinforce unquestioned representations of women and specifically indigenous women that have remained and that this book aims to dispel.

As Guengerich and Ochoa note in the introduction, during the Conference on Latin American History, Mexican Studies Committee Roundtable on gender in Mexican history in January of 2019, Silvia Arrom made reference to the pervasive historiographical narratives that misconstrue women's lives and remain entrenched, notwithstanding the archival work that has been done to demonstrate the contrary.[5] These narratives, among many others, portray women as passive or portray women who engaged in public activities as exceptional. For example, there seems to be a misconception that to study religious women is to study extraordinary women who participated in an elite institution.[6] Most of the historians who have studied the women who come in contact with the spaces created by the Catholic Church do so because they have identified, as I did, that the colonial Church provided certain resources for women that allowed them to participate in colonial society in important ways. Not all women who came in contact with the Church and convents became nuns, and even those who did were not all from the elite and certainly were not all extraordinary. It was precisely because of the pervasiveness of convents in colonial life that many of us have turned to these spaces to find answers about what women were doing during this time. Both native and African women found in religious institutions a set of values and practices that were appealing to them and provided a means for them to challenge and change their circumstances.

While Silvia Arrom's comment at the roundtable was specifically directed to the many versions of the historiographical narrative that has resisted a more nuanced understanding of Latin America's gender dynamics, it is nonetheless important to note in the context of this publication that when writing about cacicas we not only face the challenge of dispelling inaccurate ideas about colonial women, but we are also dealing with notions of ethnicity and what it meant to be *indio* (Indian) in colonial times. I have argued elsewhere that the processes of European colonization inevitably affected the ways in which natives self-identified during the centuries of colonial rule. Soon after the original inhabitants of the American territory were lumped together under the misnomer "indio," they refashioned their identities by blending aspects of their precontact cultures with the new expectations of colonial institutions. Ultimately, "indio" became a legal category, and indigenous peoples learned to use it as such to their advantage. The pervasive historiographical narratives in the case of natives tend to focus on trying to identify the "authentic" characteristics of indios and lamenting the loss of their original culture due to their adaptation of seemingly European traits.[7] Most importantly, we need to keep in mind that many self-identified indios were in fact mestizos or belonged to other *castas* (mixed races). However, they identified as such to have access to certain privileges, but also because they belonged to communities that continued to self-identify as indigenous. Many cacicas in this volume were not strictly indigenous but made the cultural and political choice to identify as native. It is important therefore, to be aware of the fluidity of the identities of these colonial agents instead of privileging binaries.[8]

Historically, our approach to women's history in Latin America has not been so different. There has been a tendency to see colonial women as a homogenized group oppressed by a patriarchal system. In the introduction of the recently published volume, *Women in Colonial Latin America, 1526 to 1806: Texts and Contexts*, the editors review what they consider the latest historiographical trends in the subfield of women's history in colonial Latin America.[9] Nora Jaffary and Jane Mangan map out the developments of the last few years in nuanced ways, making evident that when writing about women and gender in colonial Latin America, the categories of race and ethnicity overlap with other important factors. For example, the topics of family, religion, and labor are featured prominently in the histories of native women. And yet, in their introduction, the authors include a separate section where they point to the limited attention that has been given to colonial indigenous women in scholarship. I would add that we are particularly in need of works that seek to complicate traditional historical narratives and dissipate assumptions about the limited opportunities granted to indigenous women in the colonial world. Even though that was the case for both native and non-native women, we can find indigenous women as agents, as many of our colleagues have already shown in their scholarship.[10] We should not consider those native women who have been inserted back in historical narratives as exceptions but rather work at normalizing these historiographical facts. By offering an intersectional approach to understanding how indigenous women operated within the colonial system, the present volume aims to expand the traditional narratives we have about indigenous women—especially about cacicas—and adds an unprecedented sophistication to them.

Most importantly, what this book shows is that colonial cacicas were not a homogenous group. There were great variants from region to region and from one time period to another. Some cacica titles were attached to property, as in the cases of the cacicas of Teotihuacan (chapter 1), the Otomí cacicas (chapter 2), the cacicas of Chincha (chapter 7), and the royalist cacica of the Titicaca region (chapter 8). Some titles were attached to positions of power and symbolic authority (independent of property and land ownership or in addition to it), as in the cases of the cacicas of eighteenth-century Mexico City (chapter 3), northern Peru (chapter 5), Guatemala (chapter 4), and the northern Andes region (chapter 6). And others were more nuanced cases of agency, as were the peacemaker intermediaries of the Río de la Plata (chapter 9).

The women portrayed in this book are agents of history.[11] Through intersectional readings of lawsuits (civil and criminal), legal codes, published and unpublished chronicles, testaments, and other notarial and military records, the authors of this volume reveal the tensions that occurred between institutional structures and everyday negotiations of power. Even when colonial institutions gradually diminished cacicas' privileges, these women kept engaging with them in creative ways in order to maintain a certain degree of authority. In some cases, the power they acquired was symbolic, in other cases, quite tangible. Perhaps except for the cacicas of Teotihuacan and the royalist cacica from the Titicaca region, native women who identified as cacicas did not hold public office. Yet their political influence was still present in the legal, economic, and religious realms, and they remained important figures who were regarded with authority by their communities and recognized as such by colonial authorities.

The authors of the essays included herein place their attention on the cacicazgo as a colonial phenomenon.[12] As most contributors recognize in their chapters, there was an inevitable evolution in the ways indigenous women wielded authority after the wars of conquest and the establishment of the colonial order, and there were also dramatic changes in the ways that indigenous leadership was carried out during the colonial period. Bradley Benton states in his chapter that indigenous women in colonial times exercised power in ways that responded to their new realities that were different from pre-Hispanic times and also from Spanish notions of patriarchy. The written records produced by indigenous peoples attest to their ability to cross cultural barriers by adopting and strategically using European legal and religious rhetoric and forgoing aspects of their culture in order to achieve their goals. Therefore, cacicas displayed their own sets of unique characteristics, unlike both precontact Spanish and indigenous notions of female leadership.

In writing about caciques in New Spain, James Lockhart notes that with time, Spaniards increasingly generalized the use of the term "cacique" to refer to an important person regardless of nobility.[13] This becomes true for many of the cases studied in the present volume. Cacicas made choices about whom they married and, in many cases, reshaped ethnicity through these marriages. Some noblewomen who would be eligible to inherit the title of cacica through bloodline, married Spaniards; others married natives who did not belong to the nobility, and in both cases these women contested their titles with colonial authorities with different degrees of success. Ultimately, Lockhart's comment points to the changing nature of cacicazgo within the new sociopolitical context. While colonial authorities viewed cacicas in a new light (different from precontact times), cacicas themselves used their titles in ways that responded to the new circumstances; they deployed both colonial legal institutions and native social networks to their advantage. Catherine Komisaruk also notes that indigenous nobles were gradually incorporated in the category of principales, which was a sort of indigenous elite that had not always inherited a title of nobility, which supports Lockhart's assertion. The case of the Tapias of Querétaro (chapter 2) is a good example of this. These were caciques whose authority came from colonial changes and not from lineage; they were civic leaders and religious patrons.

The laws that were instituted in Spanish America fostered a practice through which many principales and nobles argued for the legitimacy of a pure indigenous lineage in order to get the privileges and recognition that the title of cacique entailed, even when their bloodline was not exclusively indigenous. This was possible because, as Peter Villella has convincingly shown, blood purity was a negotiable rather than an intrinsic quality.[14] The native elites borrowed notions of blood purity from Spanish statutes that were used to differentiate Old Christians from Jewish and Moorish peoples on the Iberian Peninsula. This was a striking adaptation and later deformation of a discourse that, as María Elena Martínez demonstrated, upheld the ideas that one's ancestry could establish one's purity of blood and a cultural-religious identity was somehow inherited through blood, becoming a basis for early modern notions of lineage, or what has been perceived as notions of race.

An increase in the numbers of people of mixed ancestry, commonly known as castas, by the end of the sixteenth century ensured that the discourse of indigenous purity would become more urgent and pervasive. Of course, this became important only because the colonial legal system supported this ideological adaptation of the idea of *limpieza* (purity of blood) in the New World. Native elites quickly learned that it was important (and possible) to establish one's casta in order to receive certain rights, as it is exemplified by the case of doña Micaela de Miranda who wanted to be identified as an "india cacique" to avoid paying tribute (chapter 4). Karen Graubart also shows that many times, well into the seventeenth century, successful legal cases through which indigenous women were granted the title of cacicas, or recovered them from a male relative, had to do with an avid use of certain knowledge about indigenous and Spanish elites' histories and conventions. And it also becomes evident with the intricate cases of the cacicas of Chincha (chapter 7) that these litigating women were as active as their male counterparts in their engagements with the colonial legal system.

During the sixteenth century, mestizos, who by law were not allowed to inherit cacicazgos, would many times appeal to their noble lineage to be granted the benefits of the title. This is exemplified by the case of the cacicas of Teotihuacan (chapter 1) who for three generations were successful in their petitions. The system was such that the use of certain rhetorical tactics together with a solid grasp of the new legal structure allowed for the continuation of cacicazgos during colonial times. We can also see this in the case of the cacicas of the north coast of Peru (chapter 5) whose appeal to pre-Hispanic *uso y costumbre* (use and custom, or customary law), together with adaptations of Spanish notions of inheritance and bloodline aided in their cases. The official recognition of the existence of a pre-Hispanic elite was certainly the basis for the extension of special privileges to the caciques and principales. And we can see that even in the seventeenth century, as in the cases of the cacicas from Chincha (chapter 7), indigenous women who married Spaniards were able to plead for their property rights as cacicas when using the correct legal channels and appropriate rhetoric. A discourse of purity and nobility among natives became a strategy that indigenous peoples combined with a European humanistic tradition and employed in a variety of documents, from the narratives produced by Mexican native historians Hernando de Alvarado Tezozomoc and Fernando de Alva Ixtlilxochitl to the simpler petitions that emerged throughout the Americas in which natives demanded the privileges granted by their status as pure and noble Indians within the laws.[15]

The end of the seventeenth century, under the reign of Charles II—who favored an erasure of the cultural distinctiveness that separated native communities from the rest of the colonial population—created new opportunities for native elites. While the Crown's ultimate goal was to culturally Hispanize the indigenous population, the native elite saw this as a chance to improve their social and political situation.[16] A royal decree was issued in 1697 that would benefit the indigenous nobility. The decree, which eventually became included in the Laws of the Indies, stated that the caciques and their descendants should be given all the honors and preeminence that is generally given to the noble *hijodalgos* (or hidalgos) of Castile, both in the secular and the ecclesiastical arenas. It assured that they could participate in any community that required nobility by the statutes, since as gentiles they were nobles and their inferiors paid tribute to them. It also assured that they could keep, as much as possible, their former rights and privileges and be called caciques. As for the rest of the natives, it is stated that "as long as they kept their blood line untainted from any reprobate sect, they should be given the honor enjoyed in Spain by those with purity of blood [*limpios de sangre*]."[17] In the hands of natives, the laws became tools that bolstered their privileged status.

The Bourbon ascension to power at the turn of the eighteenth century brought about changes in the colonial administration that affected all colonial subjects. However, indigenous populations functioned much differently than in the sixteenth century and therefore reacted to certain enlightened policies with rebellions, particularly in the Andean region. As shown in Sara Guengerich's chapter, we see that society was polarized and, while doña Teresa Choquehuanca remained a royalist, many other indigenous peoples supported the numerous rebellions and revolts of this late colonial era, including the people who would later be under her rule as a *cacica y gobernadora* (governing cacica). In contrast, doña Marcela and other cacicas from Bourbon Mexico City dealt with criminal litigations and displayed very different kinds of authority and power. Things couldn't be more different from one place to another. While some isolated indigenous insurrections happened in the north and south of Mexico, in the capital, indigenous peoples negotiated their place in the new Bourbon regime by creating alliances with other members of society. And in places like Guatemala and El Salvador during the eighteenth and beginning of the nineteenth century we also see what Catherine Komisaruk calls the process of *macehualization*, as cacicas' and caciques' status and privileges declined, increasingly so after independence. Indigenous peoples were also agents in modifying and implementing changes inspired by the Enlightenment, such as privileging merit over inherited rank and administrative and economic efficiency. Therefore, indigenous peoples actively adapted the language contained in the laws for their benefit and redefined what it meant to be pure, noble, and cacique. They manipulated ancient knowledge of their genealogies to make a case for the authenticity and legitimacy of their claims and made reference to the laws in place that would benefit those of pure lineage.

As I stated earlier, while previous work has focused on the cacicas who became the first religious women to take the veil as nuns in Mexico during the eighteenth century, little attention has been given to question the rhetorical nature of the discourses surrounding the exclusivity of the religious spaces opened for these women.[18] The traditional historical narrative asserts that all indigenous women who were accepted into these nunneries were noble, yet archival sources that I have located tell a different story. Ultimately, as Peter Villella avidly puts it, "limpieza was determined by courts, judges, and disputation rather than any inherent, 'objective' metrics."[19] Why would we not question the discursive allegations of purity of these and other colonial subjects who were trying to benefit from the ideological adaptation of a Spanish concept? Distance from my earlier work and years of experience conducting research in archives have taught me that a more nuanced understanding of the very complex use of words in these documents would give us a better picture of the sociopolitical complexities of the time. Because ideologically the discourse of purity and nobility was part of the repertoire of tools that the indigenous elite learned to use early on, it continued to be used when petitioning colonial officials for benefits well into the eighteenth century.

Although caciques often appealed to the laws in their petitions as if they were an unchanging body of rules, they were in practice a flexible set of regulations. In this context, the rhetoric of purity became not only a strategy of social mobility but also a strategy that could be reshaped in judicial proceedings toward specific ends. For example, the caciques of Oaxaca who petitioned for the opening of a convent for indigenous women in the city of Antequera (present-day Oaxaca) in 1742, made reference to the laws that granted noble status not only to those who converted quickly to Christianity but also to those who were nobles before they were instructed in the Catholic faith. Through their use of legal rhetoric, caciques drew attention to the fact that ancestry was inherent to the nobility status granted by the Crown. The Recopilación de las Leyes de Indias states that it is only fair that the natives who were caciques and lords of their pueblos before their conversion to the Holy Catholic faith should keep their rights as such, and that they should not fall into a lesser condition because of their conversion.[20] Cacicas employed the discourse and laws regarding *pureza* (purity) to advance their interests in specific circumstances. Further research that questions the seemingly fixed character of this discourse will be welcomed. However, it is important to keep in mind, as the chapters in this volume illustrate, that indigenous women were active in this process, savvy about the laws, and successful at maneuvering the system. From the early records of women called cacicas in the Caribbean to those in the nineteenth century across Spanish America, this book provides multiple portraits of how women and indigenous communities responded to changes in colonial governance and as independence movements emerged. Their participation in the public sphere and their engagement with colonial authorities might have been outstanding, but they were not the only ones doing this. The more cases we bring to the light, the sooner our historiographical narratives about indigenous women will change.

NOTES

1. Josefina Muriel, *Las indias caciques de Corpus Christi*, 2nd ed. (Mexico City: Universidad Autónoma Nacional de México, 1963).

2. Asunción Lavrin, "Religious Life of a Mexican Convent in the XVIII Century" (PhD diss., Harvard University, 1963). Later she published an article on the racial tensions within the convent; see, Asunción Lavrin, "Indian Brides of Christ: Creating New Spaces for Indigenous Women in New Spain," *Mexican Studies/Estudios Mexicanos* 15 (1999). A version of this article recently appeared in her book, *Brides of Christ: Conventual Life in Colonial Mexico* (Stanford: Stanford University Press, 2008).

3. Together with Silvia Marina Arrom, *The Women of Mexico City, 1790–1857* (Stanford: Stanford University Press, 1992); Patricia Seed, *To Love, Honor, and Obey in Colonial Mexico: Conflicts over Marriage Choice, 1574–1821* (Stanford: Stanford University Press, 1988); Ella Dunbar Temple, "El testament inédito de doña Beatriz Clara Coya, hija del Inca Sayri Tupac," *Fénix. Revista de la Biblioteca Nacional del Peru* 6 (1950); Irene Silverblatt, *Moon, Sun, and Witches: Gender Ideologies and Class in Inca and Colonial Peru* (Princeton: Princeton University Press, 1987); and María Rostworowoski de Diez Canseco, *Doña Francisca Pizarro: Una ilustre mestiza, 1534–1598* (Lima: Instituto de Estudios Peruanos, 1989).

4. Mónica Díaz, *Indigenous Writings from the Convent: Negotiating Ethnic Autonomy in Colonial Mexico* (Tucson: University of Arizona Press, 2010).

5. I had the honor to be part of that same roundtable.

6. A surprising assertion to be found in a recent publication; see Jessica Delgado, *Laywomen and the Making of Colonial Catholicism in New Spain, 1630–1790* (Cambridge: Cambridge University Press, 2018), 3.

7. See Mónica Díaz, "*Indio* Identities in Spanish America," in *To Be Indio in Colonial Spanish America*, ed. Mónica Díaz (Albuquerque: University of New Mexico Press, 2017).

8. Because of this notion, I refer to cacicas in this conclusion as "indigenous" because that is how they chose to be identified.

9. Nora Jaffary and Jane Mangan, eds., *Women in Colonial Latin America, 1526–1806: Texts and Contexts* (Indianapolis: Hackett Publishing, 2018).

10. See for example, Karen Graubart, *With our Labor and Sweat: Indigenous Women and the Formation of Colonial Society in Peru, 1550–1700* (Stanford: Stanford University Press, 2007); Susan Kellogg, *Weaving the Past Weaving the Past: A History of Latin America's Indigenous Women from the Prehispanic Period to the Present* (Oxford: Oxford University Press, 2005); Susan Schroeder, Stephanie Wood, and Robert Haskett, eds. *Indian Women of Early Mexico* (Norman: University of Oklahoma University Press, 1997); and Camilla Townsend, *Malitzin's Choices: An Indian Woman in the Conquest of Mexico* (Albuquerque: University of New Mexico Press, 2006).

11. When our notion of agency expands, we can appreciate the large array of possibilities in which indigenous women were involved. Sherry B. Ortner distinguishes between women's "agency of power" and what she calls "agency of intentions," arguing that the latter "is about people having desires that grow out of their own structures of life, including very centrally their own structures of inequality." Sherry B. Ortner, "Specifying Agency: The Comaroffs and Their Critics," *Interventions* 3, no. 1 (2001): 81.

12. Although some authors in this volume also make reference to the existence of female indigenous leadership in precolonial times.

13. James Lockhart, *The Nahuas after the Conquest: A Social and Cultural History of the Indians of Central Mexico, Sixteenth through Eighteenth Centuries* (Stanford: Stanford University Press, 1992), 133.

14. Peter Villella, "'Pure and Noble Indians, Untainted by Inferior Idolatrous Races': Native Elites and the Discourse of Blood Purity in Late Colonial Mexico," *Hispanic American Historical Review* 91, no. 4 (2011): 639.

15. See Fernando de Alva Ixtlilxochitl, *Obras históricas*, ed. Edmundo O'Gorman, 2 vols. (Mexico City: Universidad Nacional Autónoma de México, 1975); and Hernando de Alvarado Tezozomoc, *Crónica Mexicana* (Madrid: Dastin, 2001).

16. See Rodolfo Aguirre Salvador, *El mérito y la estrategia: Clérigos, juristas y médicos en Nueva España* (Mexico City: Plaza y Valdes, 2003); Matthew O'Hara, *A Flock Divided: Race, Religion, and Politics in Mexico, 1749–1857* (Durham, NC: Duke University Press, 2010); and Peter B. Villella, *Indigenous Elites and Creole Identity in Colonial Mexico, 1500–1800* (New York: Cambridge University Press, 2016).

17. This was included in the petition to open a convent for cacicas in Oaxaca. Newberry Library, Ayer Manuscript 1144, fols. 113–15.

18. For more on the topic, see Díaz, *Indigenous Writings*; and Lavrin, *Brides of Christ*, chap. 8.

19. Villella, "Pure and Noble Indians," 636.

20. Recopilación de las Leyes de Indias, Book 6, Title 7, Law 1. For more on the foundation of the convent of Nuestra Señora de los Angeles, see Monica Díaz, "'Es honor de su nación': Legal Rhetoric, Ethnic Alliances and the Opening of an Indigenous Convent in Colonial Oaxaca," *Colonial Latin American Historical Review* 22, no. 2 (August 2013); and Jessica Criales, "Women of Our Nation: Gender, Race, and Christian Identity in the United States and Mexico, 1753–1867" (PhD diss., Rutgers, State University of New Jersey, 2020).

Cacicas in Nicaragua, 1522–1550

*Patrick S. Werner**

Nicaragua was an area north of Castilla de Oro in Central America and was conquered by Spaniards over a two-year period, from 1522 to 1524.[1] At the onset of the conquest, Nicaragua had approximately seven to eight hundred thousand natives in its western region and about three hundred Spaniards. By 1550, the indigenous population had declined to only about forty-two thousand, and Spaniards loyal to the Crown had died during a short civil war ("rebels" were later killed in a battle at Panama City).[2] In spite of its early turbulent history, there is a database of more than ten thousand transcribed pages of colonial documents that supply little-known information about how a Spanish settlement was established and the role of natives, including caciques and cacicas, in the development of colonial society in today's Central America.[3] This database has yet to be fully mined by researchers, and this appendix is a brief introduction into its early colonial cache. How this database, Colección Somoza, came to be deserves telling.

The documents in the Colección were organized by Andrés Vega Bolaños, the Ambassador to Spain during the dictatorship of General Anastasio Somoza

---

*Among his multiple personal and professional accomplishments, Patrick S. Werner was an authority on the history of colonial Nicaragua. Patrick passed away on November 30, 2019. We are grateful to him for organizing this index of caciques and cacicas, alerting us to the Colección Somoza, and the multiple emails and phone conversations we shared leading up to the completion of this volume.

García (r. 1937–56) in Nicaragua. Beginning in the early 1950s, General So-moza commissioned a history of colonial Nicaragua, tapping Ambassador Bolaños, a lawyer and historian, to oversee the project. The result was a col-lection of files transcribed verbatim—including the lack of punctuation as well as the spelling and grammatical styles typical of early-modern Iberian documents—from the Archivo General de Indias (AGI) in Seville, Spain.[4] The transcriptions were organized into ten volumes that spanned the three centuries of Spanish rule in Nicaragua. Undoubtedly not composed of the complete colonial source base available for colonial Nicaragua at the AGI, nonetheless to my knowledge and as of the writing of this appendix introduc-tion, Bolaños's Colección is the only published cache of transcribed colonial documents that includes substantial material dating back to early sixteenth-century Nicaragua. The collection's sources and online availability can serve as a valuable entry point for more extensive research projects on the history of early Nicaragua.

Some of the highlights of the sixteenth-century files in the collection in-clude a total of 869 documents pertaining to royal cedulas, 110 lawsuits, and 130 detailed *relaciones* (reports) to the Crown.[5] The Colección also includes several *residencias*, which were extended trials held at the end of the tenure of royal officials during which anyone could bring a complaint or charge against the official on trial. For this volume on colonial cacicas and for future research-ers of colonial Nicaragua, residencias may serve as rich sources of informa-tion. The trial of the Nicaraguan governor Rodrigo de Contreras (r. 1535–44), taking place in the context of the New Laws of 1542, is a great example of the richness of these sources.

FRAUDULENT DEEDS AND CACICAS IN THE COLECCIÓN SOMOZA

There are at least 105 names of indigenous persons, some of whom are women and caciques. To understand why these persons were named, two unrelated occurrences should be considered: the residencia of Nicaraguan governor Rodrigo de Contreras (r. 1535–44) and the enactment of the New Laws of 1542.

Rodrigo de Contreras was married to the daughter of Pedrarias Davila, a man with close ties to the court of King Charles V (r. 1519–56). As governor, Contreras quickly created a group of loyalists and inspired another group who detested him and wrote numerous letters to the Crown with complaints focused on him and his family. He got into a dispute with Hernán Sánchez de Badajoz, jailed him, and sent him back to Spain in chains. While in a royal jail, Sánchez de Badajoz decided to file a series of criminal complaints against Contreras.[6] The effect was to finally cause the Crown, in the person of Prince Phillip, to appoint a *juez de residencia* (Spanish official charged with administrative inquiry), Diego de Herrera, to oversee and adjudicate the residencia against Contreras and, in the process, end Contreras's governorship.

The other unrelated occurrence was the enactment of the New Laws of 1542. The Crown perceived that the system of autonomous Spaniards with *encomiendas* (royal grants of indigenous tribute) was a bad idea. The Crown ordered that the encomienda system be ended, with all encomiendas reverting back to the Crown, and Crown officials were prohibited from owning encomiendas.[7] The effect was almost instantaneous rebellion and chaos as the economic basis for Spaniards was outlawed.[8] The attempted abolition of the encomienda system also precipitated a rebellion in Peru, where the Spanish viceroy was assassinated and the rebellion led by Gonzalo Pizarro controlled Peru until he was defeated in battle by Licenciado de la Gasca in 1549. In Nicaragua, the reaction of the Contreras family to the New Laws was massive forgery of documents and backdating deeds of encomienda that on their face complied with the New Laws.[9] Thus, a major effort of Herrera's subsuquent residencia of Contreras in 1544 was to look for and discover evidence of fraud and wrongdoing on the part of Contreras.[10]

Acts of possession, especially after 1542 in Nicaragua, are likely fraudulent documents based on valid originals altered to get around the New Laws. The recorded instances of the naming of caciques and cacicas in the transfer of encomienda possession was thus a sort of historical accident. Herrera, for example, recognized backdated encomienda deeds and wrote a detailed legal memorandum outlining just exactly how encomenderos prepared the fraudulent instruments.[11] Herrera used the *interrogatorio* (questionnaire for hearing and recording testimony), the major tool in civil law for discovery.[12] Following his investigation, it became clear to Herrera that Nicaraguan settlers became aware of the pending New Laws and their provision to abolish the encomienda from a contact in Panama.[13] To circumvent the New Laws, Contreras had altered his deeds using his favorite forger, Martin de Membreño, a royal *escribano* (notary), and gave his encomiendas to his young children, naming his wife María de Peñalosa as their *tutora* (guardian). As a result of this fraud, Peñalosa was embroiled in litigation, eventually losing the case, and the sons of Contreras engaged in an uprising against royal officials.

Table 1
Caciques and Cacicas in Early Nicaragua

Date	Document	Caciques (women in boldface)	Ethnicity	Residence
1528	Bobadilla Interview, Cronistas CS, vol. 3, p. 310 et seq.	Chicoyatonal, cacique; Cipat, huehue; Miseboy, cacique	Nahua	Teoca
1528	Bobadilla Interview, Cronistas CS, vol. 3, p. 324 et seq.	Coyevit, huehue; Quiavit, cacique	Nahua	Xoxoyta
1528	Interview by Oviedo, Cronistas CS, vol. 3, p. 461	Agateyte, cacique	Nahua	Tezuatega
1540	Encomienda Title, CS, vol. 14, pp. 170, 172	Cazamate, principal; **Violante en Cristiano, cacica**; Quiavit, indio	Nahua	Tezuatega
1542	Encomienda Title, CS, vol. 11, p. 302	Pedro, cacique; Quialcoa, principal	Nahua	Ayatega
1541	Encomienda Title, CS, vol. 10, p. 567	Pedro, cacique; Quiaguito, cocomal	Nahua	Potega
1540	Criminal Complaint, CS, vol. 9, pp. 528, 534	Taleguale, cacique	Nahua	Suerre?
1540	Encomienda Title, CS, vol. 14, pp. 170, 172	Nipopoyamat, cacique; Moto, cacique; **Una mujer, Ynesta en Cristiano**; Namayo, cacique	Chorotega	Nicoya

Date	Document	Caciques (women in boldface)	Ethnicity	Residence
1543–44	Encomienda Titles, first deed, CS, vol. 13, pp. 326, 327; second deed, CS, vol. 13, p. 338; third deed, CS, vol. 13, p. 467; fourth deed, CS, vol. 13, p. 454	First deed: Anonboymes, cacique; Dionyndoy, cacique; Zindinodo, cacique; Nayyonbue, cacique; Artiery, cacique; Nacatime, cacique; Potrinario, cacique; Zeteso, cacique; Piron, cacique, Urzarayre; second deed: Cancamari, cacique; Mendome, cacique; third deed: Nanbueme, cacique; Nanboy, cacique; Tiputa, mochacho, cacique; Mondoy indio, cacique; fourth deed: Pedro Niambueme, cacique; Sirayo, cacique	Chorotega	Nandayme
1542	Encomienda Title, CS, vol. 11, p. 302	**Franquisquilla(?)**; Gonzalo	Chorotega	Diriá
1542	Encomienda Title, CS, vol. 14, p. 174	Betoy; Nacey; Mandati	Chorotega	Monimbó
1528	Oviedo Interview, Cronistas, CS, vol. 3, p. 385; and Encomienda Title, CS, vol. 14, p. 473.	Pedro, cacique; Juan, cacique; Diego, cacique	Chorotega	Lendirí
1541	Encomienda Title, CS, vol. 14, p. 170	**Mujer Catalina en Cristiano**; Noghi cacique	Chorotega	Chira
1541; 1542	Criminal Complaint, CS, vol. 9, p. 161; and Encomienda Title, CS, vol. 11, p. 303	Tacal, cacique; Encomienda: Coco, Tochil cacique	Chorotega	Xalteva

(*continued*)

Table 1. Caciques and Cacicas in Early Nicaragua (*continued*)

Date	Document	Caciques (women in boldface)	Ethnicity	Residence
1529	Criminal Complaint, CS, vol. 2, pp. 16, 21	**Una mujer Ezelo**	Chorotega	Nandapio Manbach
1537	Royal Cedula, CS, vol. 5, p. 135	**Tagueman and daughter doña Ana**	Maribios	Mazatega
1542	Encomienda Title, CS, vol. 11, pp. 302, 304	Don Alonso, principal; Don Francisco, principal	Maribios	Pozoltega
1540	Criminal Complaint, CS, vol. 9, p. 481	Don Diego, principal; Nyongua, principal; Ozilo, principal; Migisti, principal; Anbao, principal; Quespal, principal; Teguaisaya, principal; Mycana, principal; Bazo, principal; Taleguale, cacique	Maribios	Cindega
1535	Bond Forfeiture, CS, vol. 9, p. 412 et seq.	**Una india Toyo y en Cristiano Juana La Zagala; una india Teresa; una india Juana;** un indio Quismo; un indio Meza; un indio Abaspapa; un indio Domingo; un indio Tamagaz Jandi; un indio Gasparillo; un indio Yndiqui; un indio Anbatoto; un indio Netey; Ozilo, principal de Abangasca y Cindega	Maribios	Cindega y Abangasca
1538	Encomienda Title, CS, vol. 9, p. 114–115	Uzelo, cacique; **Malina, cacica**	Maribios	Pangua
1536	Bond Forfeiture, CS, vol. 9, pp. 422, 442–43	**Soche, cacica(?) de Abangasca-Ygualteca;** Topagua, principal; Diego, principal; **Juana Cuezno, fallecida**	Maribios	Abangasca-Ygualteca

Date	Document	Caciques (women in boldface)	Ethnicity	Residence
1537	Encomienda Title, CS, vol. 14, p. 169	**Juana Yazesno, difunta (possibly Juana Cuezno mentioned above)**; Francisco, cacique; Migisti, cacique; Maza, cacique; Cosca, cacique	Maribios	Yguala
1529	Encomienda History, CS, vol. 2, p. 101	Teyoa, principal; Hueyac, principal; Olin, principal; Matac, principal; Escoloan, principal; Alzaguancone, principal; Agat, principal; Tezatotot, principal	Maribios	Mistega
1541	Encomienda Title, CS, vol. 10, p. 69	Papalot, cacique; **Sochet, cacica(?)**	Guazama	Mistega
1542	Encomienda Title, CS, vol. 14, p. 174	**Socher, principal(?) cacica**; Chizegue, principal	Chondal	Zagualpa
1526	Encomienda Title, CS, vol. 5, p. 368	Guamul, cacique; Macuna, cacique; Amama, cacique; Capena, cacique; Macoci, cacique; Aguay, cacique		Islands in the Gulf of Fonseca
1542	Criminal Complaint, CS, vol. 10, p. 427	**Una mujer, Soche, difunta**; Zisonate, cacique principal; **otra Soche listed as a witness**		Cosiguina
1544	Rodrigo de Contreras Residencia, CS, vol. 9, pp. 1, 425	Montape, cacique; Anbatonto, otro jefe		Island of Mancarron in Lake Nicaragua

Source: The majority of the fraudulent encomiendas are found in volume 14 of the Colección Somoza. For example, Maria de Peñalosa, et al. v. La Corona, CS, vol. 14, p. 124, August 22, 1548. Other citations for criminal complaints and bond forfeitures are found in this table of cacicas and caciques. An extended lawsuit regarding the rightful owner of Nandayme is found in volume 13 of the Colección. All citations in volume 9 of the Colección are regarding the residencia of Contreras.

Little else is known about the caciques and cacicas named in the deeds. Of the fraudulent deeds cited by Herrera, three encomiendas, Nicoya, Chira, and Diria, involved the Chorotega, Pangua (Maribios), and Tezuatega (Nahuas) pueblos. The most numerous ethnic group in western Nicaragua was the Chorotega, numbering approximately three hundred thousand at the time of the conquest.[14] The next largest groups were the Maribios, with about one hundred thirty thousand persons, the Nahuas with about sixty thousand persons, and the Chondales with about thirty thousand persons.

In table 1, I have listed the instances of "caciques" and "cacicas" in the residencia files of the Colección Somoza. All women identified as cacicas—a total of eighteen—in the documents are in boldface type. While it is impossible to know how reliable this information about caciques and cacicas is, future research of the rich sources of the Colección may one day expand our current knowledge.

NOTES

1. Regarding the conquest of Nicaragua, see Jaime Incer, *Viajes, Rutas y Encuentros, 1502–1838,* 2nd ed. (San Jose, Costa Rica: Editorial Libro Libre, 1993); Linda Newson, *Indian Survival In Colonial Nicaragua* (Norman: University of Oklahoma Press, 1987); Patrick S. Werner, *Los reales de minas y la ciudad perdida de Nueva Segovia* (Managua, Nicaragua: Instituto de Cultura, 1996); Patrick S. Werner, *Epoca temprana de Nicaragua* (Managua, Nicaragua: Instituto de Cultura, 2000); Patrick S. Werner, *Etnohistoria de la Nicaragua temprana* (Managua, Nicaragua: Lea Grupo Editorial, 2009). Werner's works are found at www.nicaraguanpathways.com. The documentary history of early colonial Nicaragua is found at Andrés Vega Bolaños, *La Colección Somoza: Documentos para la historia de Nicaragua, 1504–1550,* 17 vols. (Madrid: Imprenta Viuda de Galo Sáez; Imprenta Sagrado Corazón Juan Bravo, 1954–57).

2. Both Newson and Werner dealt with the population decline. Both used quite different methods and came up with the same result: population in 1522 of 826,248 (Newson) or 699,660 (Werner) indigenous; population of natives in 1548, the date of the first organized census and *tasación* (appraisal), 42,000. See Newson, *Indian Survival,* 88; and Werner, *Etnohistoria,* 262. On the Contreras rebellion, the best source is Lic. de la Gasca's letter to the Crown about the Contreras Rebellion, Colección Somoza (hereafter cited as CS), vol. 17, p. 239, September 22, 1550, and the transcripts of the trials of the surviving rebels, Juicio Promovido, found at CS, vol. 17, p. 7, May 2, 1550.

3. A second source of rich information for this early period of Nicaragua is the work of Gonzalo Fernández de Oviedo y Valdés. He visited Nicaragua for two years in the late 1520s and later, as castle keep in Santo Domingo, wrote his *Historia General y natural de las islas y tierra-firme del mar oceano.* His *Historia General* was published in Spain in 1851–55, and portions have been reprinted in Nicaragua in the

series, *Nicaragua en los cronistas de indias: Oviedo,* Colección Cultural 3 (Managua, Nicaragua: Banco de America, 1976).

4. A digitized copy of the Colección Somoza is available on the Enrique Bolaños Foundation webpage, an educational foundation for the history of Nicaragua named for former president Enrique Bolaños (r. 2002–7). The full web address, as of the printing of this volume, is https://www.enriquebolanos.org/coleccion/Colección-Andrés-Vega-Bolaños. As an undergraduate at Michigan State University in the 1960s, I found a copy of the Colección on the third floor of MSU's main library. Thinking it was a panegyric to General Somoza, I never examined the set until 1994, when I purchased a copy. The family of Andrés Vega Bolaños contends that he was allowed to take original, handwritten documents out of the AGI; he transcribed them and later returned them. The history of Vega Bolaños doing research in Seville was related to me by the late Alejandro Bolaños Geyer, distinguished historian of William Walker and brother to former Nicaraguan president Enrique Bolaños Geyer, who also related family history regarding Vega Bolaños's activities in putting together his Colección Somoza.

5. The work of compilation and transcription of documents came to an end when General Somoza was assassinated in León, Nicaragua, in 1956. Ambassador Bolaños was soon recalled and another ambassador appointed—one closely trusted by acting president Luís Somoza, the general's son. One legend persists that Bolaños had compiled documents for another volume that was never published. The family spoke to me about it, but I have yet to track down that volume.

6. See, for example, Sánchez de Badajoz v. Contreras, CS, vol. 7, p. 385, September 30, 1541. See also, Sánchez de Badajoz, CS, vol. 7, p. 409, 3 April 1541 and CS, vol. 8, p. 213, August 22, 1548.

7. See Article 26 of the News Laws of 1542, as transcribed in CS, vol. 7, p. 333, 1542.

8. The provision to abolish the encomienda system provoked opposition among many Crown officials. Its enforcement was a major factor in the political developments that plagued Nicaragua, from sending Contreras to Spain in chains to be tried by the Holy Inquisition (he deftly wiggled out of that brouhaha) to the revolt of Contreras's sons Pedro and Hernando, who murdered Bishop Valdivieso and most or all of the Crown officials opposed to the Contreras brothers in Nicaragua, resulting in a quite widespread revolt that threatened to destroy the colony of Panama.

9. This practice of backdating deeds was used commonly during the Contra War in Nicaragua by families trying to preserve their assets or by persons trying to defraud new purchasers. An essential document was and is the *libro de protocolos* (book of protocols) of each lawyer, who must still periodically turn in his or her libros to the Supreme Court of Nicaragua. The participating lawyer leaves some pages in his libro empty, so that he can go back and fill in the page located between other pages with accurate dates, to appear as if the deed was prepared and executed on its stated date and not when it was actually executed. As for Contreras and other *encomenderos* (encomienda holders) in colonial Nicaragua, further research may consider looking into fraudulent deeds of encomienda, or lawsuits to set aside the deeds, centered around the dates of the New Laws of 1542.

10. Título de Encomienda, CS, vol.14, p. 174, April 15, 1542.

11. See, CS, vol. 11, p. 285, August 16, 1544, written at Leon (Viejo), Nicaragua.

12. For the use of interrogatories, see *Las Siete Partidas*, 3.12, laws 1 and 2, facsimile of the Gregorio López 1556 edition (Madrid: Spanish Cortes, 1985). See also Harold J. Berman, *Law and Revolution: The Formation of the Western Legal Tradition* (Cambridge, MA: Harvard University Press, 1983), 250–52.

13. Maria de Peñalosa et al v. La Corona, CS, vol. 14, p. 124, August 22, 1548, in Valladolid. The deeds were as follows: to his wife Maria de Peñalosa, the plazas of Mistega; to his son Pedro de Contreras, the plazas of Utega, Quizaluaque, Utegazimba, Chilitega, and Opotega; to his son Diego de Contreras, the plazas of Abangasca, Yoteca, Yguala, and Mazacon; to his wife Maria de Peñalosa, the plazas of Tezuatega, Nicoya, and Chira; and to his son Pedro de Contreras, the plazas of Cazaulaque, the two Utegas, and Chandal; and to Vasco de Contreras, the plazas of Monimbo, Cagualpa, Chinagalpa, Motolynes, and Chontales.

14. See Patrick S. Werner, *Ethnohistory of Early Colonial Nicaragua: Demography and Encomiendas of the Indian Communities*, Institute for Mesoamerican Studies, Occasional Paper 4 (Albany: State University of New York, 2000), 121–28.

Bibliography

ARCHIVES AND LIBRARIES

Archivo Arzobispal de Lima, Peru
Archivo del Instituto de Antropología, Otavalo, Ecuador
Archivo Documental de Cajamarca, Peru
Archivo General de Centro América, Guatemala
Archivo General de Indias, Seville, Spain
Archivo General de la Nación, Argentina
Archivo General de la Nación, Mexico
Archivo General de la Nación, Peru
Archivo General de la Nación, Puerto Rico
Archivo General de Simancas, Spain
Archivo General del Estado de Querétaro, Mexico
Archivo Histórico de Límites, Lima, Peru
Archivo Histórico de Mendoza, Argentina
Archivo Histórico Nacional, Spain
Archivo Nacional de Historia, Quito, Ecuador
Archivo Regional del Cuzco, Peru
Archivo Regional de La Libertad, Peru
Archivo y Biblioteca Nacional de Bolivia
Biblioteca Nacional del Perú
Biblioteca Nacional de México

PUBLISHED SOURCES

Acuña, René, ed. *Relaciones geográficas del siglo XVI.* 10 vols. Mexico City: Universidad Nacional Autónoma de México, Instituto de Investigaciones Antropológicas, 1981–88.

Acuña y Silva, Rodrigo. *Tractatus de Confessaris Solicitantibus.* Valladolid: Juan de Rueda, 1620.

Adanaqué, Raúl. *Poder y riqueza: caciques y principales (siglos XVI–XVIII).* Lima: Editorial Quellca, 2014.

Aguirre Salvador, Rodolfo. *El mérito y la estrategia: Clérigos, juristas y médicos en Nueva España.* Mexico City: Plaza y Valdés, 2003.

Alaperrin-Bouyer, Monique. *La educación de las élites indígenas en el Perú colonial.* Lima: Instituto Francés de Estudios Andinos, 2007.

Albiez-Wieck, Sarah. "Contactos exteriores del Estado Tarasco: Influencias desde dentro y fuera de Mesoamerica." PhD diss., Universitat Bonn, 2011. http://hss.ulb .uni-bonn.de/2011/2626/2626.htm.

Altman, Ida. "Failed Experiments: Negotiating Freedom in Early Puerto Rico and Cuba." *Colonial Latin American Review* 29, no. 1 (2020).

———. "The Revolt of Enriquillo and the Historiography of Early Spanish America." *Americas* 63, no. 4 (April 2007): 587–614.

Altman, Ida, Sarah Cline, and Juan Javier Pescador, eds. *The Early History of Greater Mexico*. Upper Saddle River, NJ: Prentice Hall, 2003.

Altuve, Leonardo. *Choquehuanca y su arenga a Bolívar*. Buenos Aires: Planeta, 1991.

Alva Ixtlilxochitl, Fernando de. *Obras históricas*. Edited by Edmundo O'Gorman. 2 vols. Mexico City: Universidad Nacional Autónoma de México, Instituto de Investigaciones Históricas, 1975.

Alvarado Tezozomoc, Hernando de. *Crónica Mexicana*. Madrid: Dastin, 2001.

Amigorena, José Francisco de. "Diario de la expedición que de orden del Exmo. Señor virrey acabo de hacer contra los indios bárbaros peguenches." In *Colección de obras y documentos relativos a la historia del Río de la Plata*, edited by Pedro de Angelis, vol. 4, 203–20. 1760. Reprint, Buenos Aires: Plus Ultra, 1969.

Aram, Bethany. "From the Courts to the Court: History, Literature, and Litigation in the Spanish Atlantic World." *Colonial Latin American Review* 21, no. 3 (December 2012): 343–64.

Ardren, Traci, ed. *Ancient Maya Women*. Walnut Creek, CA: AltaMira Press, 2002.

———. "Women and Gender in the Ancient Maya World." In *Ancient Maya Women*, edited by Traci Ardren, 1–11. Walnut Creek, CA: AltaMira Press, 2002.

Argouse, Aude. "¿Son todos caciques? Curacas, principales e indios urbanos en Cajamarca (siglo XVII)." *Bulletin de l'Institut Français d'Études Andines* 37, no. 1 (October 2008): 163–84.

Ariès, Philippe. 1977. *L'homme devant la mort*. Paris: Seuil, 1977.

Arrom, Silvia Marina. "Gender in Mexican History: How Are We Doing?" Discussion at the Mexican Studies Committee Roundtable, 133rd American Historical Association meeting, Chicago, IL, January 4, 2019.

———. *The Women of Mexico City, 1790–1857*. Stanford: Stanford University Press, 1985.

Barr, Juliana. *Peace Came in the Form of a Woman: Indians and Spaniards in the Texas Borderlands*. Chapel Hill: University of North Carolina Press, 2007.

Beard, Mary. "The Public Voice of Women." In *Women and Power: A Manifesto*. London: Profile Books, 2017.

Behar, Ruth. "Sexual Witchcraft, Colonialism, and Women's Powers: Views from the Mexican Inquisition." In *Sexuality & Marriage in Colonial Latin America*, edited by Asunción Lavrin, 178–206. Lincoln: University of Nebraska Press, 1989.

Béligand, Nadine. "De la forme au contenu. Propriété et parenté indiennes à travers les testaments nahua de la vallée de Toluca à l'époque colonial." In *Des Indes Occidentales à l'Amérique Latine: A Jean-Pierre Berthe*, edited by Alain Musset and Thomas Calvo, 279–308. Paris: ENS/Fontenay-Saint Cloud, 1997.

Bennassar, Bartolomé. "Los inventarios post-mortem y la historia de las mentalidades." In *La documentación notarial y la historia*, edited by Antonio Eiras Roel,
139–46. Santiago: University of Santiago de Compostela, 1984.

Benton, Bradley. *The Lords of Tetzcoco: The Transformation of Indigenous Rule in
Postconquest Central Mexico*. New York: Cambridge University Press, 2017.

Berens, Loann "Cristóbal Vaca de Castro y los dominicos del Perú." *Estudios Latino-
americanos* 36–37 (2016–17): 73–99.

Berman, Harold J. *Law and Revolution: The Formation of the Western Legal Tradition*.
Cambridge, MA: Harvard University Press.

Bertonio, Ludovico. *Vocabulario de la lengua aymara*. 1612. Reprint, La Paz: CERES,
1984.

———. *Vocabulario de la lengua aymara*. Facsimile ed. Leipzig: B. G. Teubner, 1879.

Black, Chad Thomas. *The Limits of Gender Domination: Women, the Law, and Political Crisis in Quito, 1765–1830*. Albuquerque: University of New Mexico Press,
2014.

Boccara, Guillaume. "Colonización Resistencia y etnogénesis en las fronteras Americanas." In *Colonización, resistencia y mestizaje en las Américas, siglos XVI-XX*,
ed. Guillaume Boccara, 47–82. Quito: ediciones Abya-Yala, 2002.

Borah, Woodrow. "El status jurídico de los indios en la Nueva España." *América
Indígena* 45, no. 2 (April–June 1985): 257–76.

———. *Justice by Insurance: The General Indian Court of Colonial Mexico and the
Legal Aides of the Half-Real*. Berkeley: University of California Press, 1983.

Borchart de Moreno, Christina. "La transferencia de la propiedad agraria indígena
en el corregimiento de Quito hasta finales del siglo XVII." *Caravelle* 34 (1980):
5–19.

Brading, D. A. *Church and State in Bourbon Mexico: The Diocese of Michoacán
1749–1810*. New York: Cambridge University Press, 1994.

Bray, Warwick. "Emblems of Power in the Chiefdoms of the New World." In *Circa
1492: Art in the Age of Exploration*, edited by J. A. Levenson, 535–39. Washington:
National Gallery of Art, 1991.

Brian, Amber. "The Alva Ixtlilxochitl Brothers and the Nahua Intellectual Community." In *Texcoco: Prehispanic and Colonial Perspectives*, edited by Jongsoo Lee
and Galen Brokaw, 201–18. Boulder: University Press of Colorado, 2014.

———. *Alva Ixtlilxochitl's Native Archive and the Circulation of Knowledge in Colonial Mexico*. Nashville: Vanderbilt University Press, 2016.

Brian, Amber, Bradley Benton, and Pablo García Loaeza, trans. and eds. *The Native
Conquistador: Alva Ixtlilxochitl's Account of the Conquest of New Spain*. Latin
American Originals 10. University Park: Pennsylvania State University Press, 2015.

Bronner, Fred. "Peruvian Arbitristas under Viceroy Chinchón, 1629–1639." *Scripta
Hierosolymitana* 26 (1974): 34–78.

Bueno, Cosme. *Geografía del Perú virreinal (Siglo XVIII)*, edited by Daniel Varcárcel. Lima: Instituto de Historia de la Universidad de San Marcos, 1951.

Burkhart, Louise M. "Gender in Nahuatl Texts of the Early Colonial Period: Native
'Tradition' and the Dialogue with Christianity." In *Gender in Pre-Hispanic America*,

edited by Cecilia F. Klein, 87–107. Washington, DC: Dumbarton Oaks Research Library and Collection, 2001.

Burns, Kathryn. *Colonial Habits: Convents and the Spiritual Economy of Cuzco, Peru.* Durham, NC: Duke University Press, 1999.

Burns, Robert I., ed. *Las siete partidas.* Translated by Samuel Parsons Scott. University of Pennsylvania Press, 2000.

Butcher, Bernardette. *America Bride of the Sun: 500 Years Latin America and the Low Countries.* Leiden: Flemish Community Administration, 1991.

Cabello Balboa, Miguel. *Miscelánea antártica.* Sevilla: Fundación José Manuel Lara, 2011.

"Cacicazgos de los indios Llangarimas." *Boletín del Archivo Nacional de Historia* 10, no. 16 (1966): 32–67.

Cahill, David. "The Long Conquest: Collaboration by Native Andean Elites in the Colonial System, 1532–1825." In *Technology, Disease and Colonial Conquests, Sixteenth to Eighteenth Centuries,* edited by G. Raudzens. Leiden: Brill, 2003.

Caillavet, Chantal. "Caciques de Otavalo en el siglo XVI: Don Alonso Maldonado y su esposa." *Miscelánea Antropológica* 2 (1982): 38–55.

———. "'Como caçica y señora desta tierra mando . . .': Insignias, funciones y poderes de las soberanas del norte andino (siglos XV–XVI)." *Bulletin de l'Institut Français d'Études Andines* 37, no. 1 (October 2008): 57–80.

———. "Ethnohistoire des communautés Indiennes d'Otavalo, Andes de l'Equateur." PhD diss., University of Bordeaux III, 2009.

———. "Ethnohistoire équatorienne: un testament indien inédit du XVIè siècle," *Caravelle* 41 (1983): 5–23.

———. "Masculin-Féminin: les modalités du pouvoir politique des seigneurs et souveraines ethniques (Andes, XV–XVIe siècle)." In *Les autorités indigènes entre deux mondes,* edited by Bernard Lavallé, 37–102. Paris: Sorbonne Nouvelle, 2004.

Campbell, Leon. "Women and the Great Rebellion in Peru, 1780–1783." *Americas* 42, no. 2 (October 1985): 163–96.

Cañada, Brenda. "Agoniza San Bartolomé Aguas Calientes." *Periódico Correo,* December 21, 2015, https://periodicocorreo.com.mx/agoniza-san-bartolome-aguas -calientes.

Cañeque, Alejandro. *The King's Living Image: The Culture and Politics of Viceregal Power in Colonial Mexico.* New York: Routledge Press, 2002.

Cardale de Schrimpff, Marianne; Herrera, Leonor; Rodríguez, Carlos Armando; Jaramillo, Yolanda. "Rito y Ceremonia en Malagana (Corregimiento de El Bolo, Palmira, Valle del Cauca)," *Boletín de Arqueología* 14, no. 3 (September 1999), https://publicaciones.banrepcultural.org/index.php/fian/article/view/5514.

Cardiel, José. "Diario del viaje y misión al Río del Sauce por fines de marzo de 1748." In *Publicaciones del Instituto de Investigaciones Geográficas de la Facultad de Filosofía y Letras,* series A (Buenos Aires: Instituto de Geografía, 1930), 245–87.

Carey, David, Jr. *Engendering Mayan History: Kaqchikel Women as Agents and Conduits of the Past, 1875–1970*. New York: Routledge, 2006.

Carlos II. *Recopilación de leyes de los reinos de las Indias*. 5th ed. Madrid: Boix, 1841.

Carmack, Robert M. *Rebels of Highland Guatemala: The Quiché-Mayas of Momostenango*. Norman: University of Oklahoma Press, 1995.

Carmack, Robert M., John Early, and Christopher Lutz, eds. *The Historical Demography of Highland Guatemala*. Albany: Institute for Mesoamerican Studies of the State University of New York at Albany, 1982.

Carrasco, Pedro. "Indian-Spanish Marriages in the First Century of the Colony." In *Indian Women of Early Mexico*, edited by Susan Schroeder, Stephanie Wood, and Robert Haskett, 87–103. Norman: University of Oklahoma Press, 1997.

———. "Royal Marriages in Ancient Mexico." In *Explorations in Ethnohistory: Indians of Central Mexico in the Sixteenth Century*, edited by H. R. Harvey and Hanns J. Prem 41–81. Albuquerque: University of New Mexico Press, 1984.

———. *The Tenochca Empire of Ancient Mexico: The Triple Alliance of Tenochtitlán, Tetzcoco, and Tlacopan*. Norman: University of Oklahoma Press, 1999.

Carrasco, Pedro, and Johanna Broda, eds. *Estratificación social en la Mesoamérica prehispánica*. Mexico City: Centro de Investigaciones Superiores, Instituto Nacional de Antropología e Historia, 1976.

Carrasco Pizana, Pedro. *Los otomíes: cultura e historia prehispánica de los pueblos mesoamericanos de habla otomiana*. Toluca: Gobierno del Estado de México, 1950.

Carrera, Magali M. *Imagining Identity in New Spain: Race, Lineage, and the Colonial Body in Portraiture and Casta Paintings*. Austin: University of Texas Press, 2003.

Castañeda de la Paz, María. *Conflictos y alianzas en tiempos de cambio: Azcapotzalco, Tlacopan, Tenochtitlan y Tlatelolco (siglos XII–XVI)*. Mexico City: Universidad Nacional Autónoma de México, Instituto de Investigaciones Antropológicas, 2013.

———. *Verdades y mentiras en torna a don Diego de Mendoza Austria Moctezuma*. Mexico City: Universidad Nacional Autónoma de México, Universidad Intercultural del Estado de Hidalgo, El Colegio Mexiquense, 2017.

Castañeda Delgado, Paulino. "La condición miserable del indio y sus privilegios." *Anuario de Estudios Americanos* 28 (1971): 245–335.

Chamberlain, Robert S. "The Concept of the *Señor Natural* as Revealed by Castilian Law and Administrative Documents." *Hispanic American Historical Review* 19, no. 2 (May 1939): 130–37.

Chance, John K. "The Caciques of Tecali: Class and Ethnic Identity in Late Colonial Mexico." *Hispanic American Historical Review* 76, no. 3 (August 1996): 475–502.

———. "From Lord to Landowner: The Predicament of the Late Colonial Mixtec Cacique." *Ethnohistory* 57, no. 3 (Summer 2010): 445–66.

———. "Marriage Alliances among Colonial Mixtec Elites: The Villagómez Caciques of Acatlan-Petlalcingo." *Ethnohistory* 56, no. 1 (Winter 2009): 91–123

Charlevoix, Pierre François-Xavier de. *Histoire du Paraguay*. Paris: Dessaint & Saillant, 1756.

———. *Histoire du Paraguay*. Paris: Chez Didot, Giffart et Nyon, 1757.

Chocano, Magdalena. "Contrastes y paralelismos provinciales: La autoridad indígena entre Lucanas y Conchuco." In *Élites indígenas en los Andes: Nobles, caciques y cabildantes bajo el yugo colonial*, edited by David Cahill and Blanca Tovías, 111–38. Quito: Abya Yala, 2003.

Christensen, Mark Z. *Nahua and Maya Catholicisms: Texts and Religion in Colonial Central Mexico and Yucatan*. Stanford: Stanford University Press, 2013.

Christensen, Mark Z., and Jonathan G. Truitt, eds. *Native Wills from the Colonial Americas: Dead Giveaways in a New World*. Salt Lake City: University of Utah Press, 2015.

Cieza de León, Pedro de. *Crónica del Perú: primera parte*. Edited by Franklin Pease G. Y. Lima: Pontificia Universidad Católica del Perú, Fondo Editorial, 1984.

———. *Crónica del Perú: tercera parte*. Edited by Francesca Cantù. 1553. Reprint, Lima: Pontificia Universidad Católica del Perú, Fondo Editorial, 1989.

———. *Las guerras civiles del Perú*, vol. 2 of *Obras completas*, edited by Carmelo Sáenz de Santa María. Madrid: Consejo Superior de Investigaciones Científicas, Instituto Gonzalo Fernández de Oviedo, 1984–85.

Cline, Sarah L. *Colonial Culhuacan, 1580–1600: A Social History of an Aztec Town*. Albuquerque: University of New Mexico Press, 1986.

Collantes de Terán de la Hera, María José. "La mujer en el proceso inquisitorial: Hechicería, bigamia y solicitación." *Anuario de Historia del Derecho Español* 77 (2017): 55–87.

Connell, William F. *After Moctezuma: Indigenous Politics and Self-Government in Mexico City, 1524–1730*. Norman: University of Oklahoma Press, 2011.

Cook, Noble David. *La catástrofe demográfica andina: Perú 1520–1620*. Lima: Fondo Editorial, Pontificia Universidad Católica del Perú, 2010.

———. "Population Data for Indian Peru: Sixteenth and Seventeenth Centuries." *Hispanic American Historical Review* 62, no. 1 (February 1982): 73–120.

Cook, Sherburn F., and Woodrow Borah. *Essays in Population History: Mexico and the Caribbean*. Vol. 1. Berkeley: University of California Press, 1971.

Cortés y Larraz, Pedro. *Descripción geográfico-moral de la diócesis de Goathemala*, edited by Julio Martín Blasco and Jesús María García Añoveros. Madrid: Consejo Superior de Investigaciones Científicas, 2001.

Couturier, Edith. "Women and the Family in Eighteenth-Century Mexico: Law and Practice." *Journal of Family History* 10 (September 1985): 294–304.

Crespo, Juan Carlos. "Chincha y el mundo andino en la relación de 1558." *Histórica* 2, no. 2 (December 1978): 185–212.

———. "La relación de Chincha (1558)." *Historia y Cultura* 8 (1974): 91–104.

Criales, Jessica. "Women of our Nation: Gender, Race, and Christian Identity in the United States and Mexico, 1753–1867." PhD diss., Rutgers, State University of New Jersey, 2020.

Crivelli Montero, Eduardo. "Malones, ¿saqueo o estrategia? El objetivo de las invasiones de 1780 y 1783 a la frontera de Buenos Aires." *Todo es Historia* 283 (1994): 6–32.

———. "Pactando con el enemigo: la doble frontera de Buenos Aires con las tribus hostiles en el período colonial." In *Los mundos de abajo y los mundos de arriba*.

Individuo y sociedad en las tierras bajas, en los Andes y más allá, edited by María Susana Cipoletti (Quito: Ed. Abya-Yala, 2004): 313–56.

Cruz Rangel, José Antonio. *Chichimecas, Misioneros, Soldados, y Terratenientes: Estratégias de colonización, control, y poder en Querétaro y la Sierra Gorda, siglos XVI–XVIII*. Mexico City: Archivo General de la Nación, 2003.

Cunill, Caroline. "El indio miserable: Nacimiento de la teoría legal en la América colonial del siglo XVI." *Cuadernos Intercambio* 8, no. 9 (2011): 229–48.

———. "Un mosaico de lenguas: Los intérpretes de la Audiencia de México en el siglo XVI." *Historia Mexicana* 68, no. 1 (2018): 7–48.

Curatola, Marco. "Guano: Una hipótesis sobre el origen de la riqueza del señorío de Chincha." In *Arqueología, antropología e historia en los Andes: Homenaje a María Rostworowski*, edited by Rafel Varón Gabai and Javier Flores Espinoza, 223–39. Lima: Instituto de Estudios Peruanos and Banco Central de Reserva del Perú, 1997.

Cutter, Charles R. *The Legal Culture of Northern New Spain, 1700–1810*. Albuquerque: University of New Mexico Press, 1995.

Danticat, Edwidge. *Anacaona: Golden Flower, Haiti 1490*. New York: Scholastic, 2005.

Davis, Natalie Zemon. *Fiction in the Archives: Pardon Tales and their Tellers in Sixteenth-Century France*. Cambridge: Polity Press, 1987.

Dayton, Cornelia Hughes. *Women before the Bar: Gender, Law & Society in Connecticut, 1639–1789*. Chapel Hill: University of North Carolina Press, 1995.

Del Barco Centenera, Martín. "La Argentina o Conquista del Río de la Plata." In *Colección de obras y documentos relativos a la historia antigua y moderna de las provincias del Río de la Plata*, edited by Pedro de Angelis, 3:17–420 (Buenos Aires: Plus Ultra, 1969).

Del Valle, Maria Eugenia. *Historia de la rebelión de Tupac Catari, 1781–1782*. 3rd ed. La Paz: Biblioteca del Bicentenario de Bolivia, 2017.

Delgado, Jessica. *Laywomen and the Making of Colonial Catholicism in New Spain, 1630–1790*. Cambridge: Cambridge University Press, 2018.

Díaz, Mónica. "'Es honor de su nación': Legal Rhetoric, Ethnic Alliances, and the Opening of an Indigenous Convent in Colonial Oaxaca." *Colonial Latin American Review* 22, no. 2 (August 2013): 235–58.

———. "The Indigenous Nuns of Corpus Christi: Race and Spirituality." In *Religion in New Spain*, edited by Susan Schroeder and Stafford Poole, 179–92. Albuquerque: University of New Mexico Press, 2007.

———. *Indigenous Writings from the Convent: Negotiating Ethnic Autonomy in Colonial Mexico*. Tucson: University of Arizona Press, 2010.

———. "*Indio* Identities in Spanish America." In *To Be Indio in Colonial Spanish America*, edited by Mónica Díaz, 1–28. Albuquerque: University of New Mexico Press, 2017.

Díaz Rementería, Carlos. *El cacique en el virreinato del Peru. Estudio histórico-jurídico*. Sevilla: Facultad de Filosofía y Letras de la Universidad de Sevilla, 1977.

Documentos inéditos para la historia de Querétaro. 8 vols. Querétaro: Universidad Autónoma de Querétaro, 1982–90.

Dueñas, Alcira. *Indians and Mestizos in the 'Lettered City': Reshaping Justice, Social Hierarchy and Political Culture in Colonial Peru*. Boulder: University of Colorado Press, 2010.

Dunbar Temple, Ella. "El testamento inédito de doña Beatriz Clara Coya, hija del Inca Sayri Tupac." *Fénix. Revista de la Biblioteca Nacional del Perú* 6 (1950): 109–22.

Dunn, Alvis E. "A Cry at Daybreak: Death, Disease, and Defense of Community in a Highland Ixil-Mayan Village." *Ethnohistory* 42, no. 4 (November 1996): 595–606.

Dutt, Rajeshwari. *Maya Caciques in Early National Yucatán*. Norman: University of Oklahoma Press, 2017.

Duve, Thomas. "Indigenous Rights in Latin America." In *The Oxford Handbook of Legal History*, edited by Markus D. Dubber and Christopher Tomlins, 817–37. Oxford: Oxford University Press, 2018.

Duve, Tomas and Heikki Pihlajamäki, eds. *New Horizons in Spanish Colonial Law: Contributions to Transnational Early Modern Legal History*. Frankfurt: Max Planck Institute for European Legal History, 2015.

Earle, Rebecca. "Algunos pensamientos sobre 'El indio borracho' en el imaginario criollo." Translated by Iván Martínez Jimenez. *Columbia: Red Revista de Estudios Sociales* 29 (2008): 18–27.

Eire, Carlos M. N. *From Madrid to Purgatory: The Art and Craft of Dying in Sixteenth-Century Spain*. Cambridge: Cambridge University Press, 1995.

Eiss, Paul K. *In the Name of the Pueblo: Place, Community, and the Politics of History in Yucatán*. Durham, NC: Duke University Press, 2010.

Escobari de Querejazú, Laura. *Caciques, yanaconas y extravagantes. Sociedad y educación colonial en Charcas, s. XVI–XVIII*. La Paz: Plural Editores, 2001.

Espejo-Ponce Hunt, Marta and Matthew Restall. "Work, Marriage, and Status: Maya Women of Colonial Yucatan." In *Indian Women of Early Mexico*, edited by Susan Schroeder, Stephanie Wood, and Robert Haskett, 231–52. Norman: University of Oklahoma Press, 1997.

Espinosa, Isidro Félix de. *Crónica de la provincia franciscana de los apóstoles San Pedro y San Pablo de Michoacán*. Mexico City: Editorial Santiago, 1945.

Falkner, Thomas. "Derrotero desde la ciudad de Buenos Aires hasta la de los Césares, que por otro nombre llaman la 'Ciudad encantada.'" In *Colección de obras y documentos relativos a la historia antigua y moderna de las provincias del Río de la Plata*, edited by Pedro de Angelis, 2:563–69. 1760. Reprint Buenos Aires: Plus Ultra, 1969.

———. *A Description of Patagonia and the Adjoining Parts of South America*. 1777. Reprint, Chicago: Armann & Armann, 1935. http://www.rockvillepress.com/TIERRA/TEXTS/FALKNER.HTM#Intro1.

Farriss, Nancy M. *Maya Society under Colonial Rule: The Collective Enterprise of Survival*. Princeton: Princeton University Press, 1984.

Fernández Alonso, Serena. "Un noble canario en el gobierno local indiano: El Marqués de Casa Hermosa en la Intendencia de Puno." In *Coloquio de Historia Canario-Americana* 9. Las Palmas, Spain: Cabildo Insular de Gran Canaria (1990): 717–36.

Fernández Villegas, Oswaldo. "La huaca Narihuala: Un documento para la etnohistoria de la costa norte del Perú, 1000–1200 DC." *Boletín del Instituto Francés de Estudios Andinos* 19, no.1 (1990): 103–27.

Few, Martha. *For All of Humanity: Mesoamerican and Colonial Medicine in Enlightenment Guatemala.* Tucson: University of Arizona Press, 2015.

———. *Women Who Live Evil Lives: Gender, Religion, and the Politics of Power in Colonial Guatemala, 1650–1750.* Austin: University of Texas Press, 2002.

Floyd, Troy S. *The Columbus Dynasty in the Caribbean, 1492–1526.* Albuquerque: University of New Mexico Press, 1973.

Fondo de Inversión Social para el Desarrollo Local. "Alegria." Accessed December 21, 2018. http://www.fisdl.gob.sv/servicios/en-linea/ciudadano/conoce-tu-municipio/usulutan/837.html.

Frank, Ross. *From Settler to Citizen: New Mexican Economic Development and the Creation of Vecino Society, 1750–1820.* Berkeley: University of California Press, 2000.

Fuertes, Phelipe. *Por el Real Convento de Religiosas de Santa Clara de Jesús de la Ciudad de Querétaro, en el pleyto con la Provincia de San Hypólito de esta Ciudad, de el Orden de la Charidad, sobre el cumplimiento y execución de un Legado de Hospital [. . .].* Mexico City: Herederos de la Viuda de Miguel de Rivera, 1725.

Gacto Fernández, Enrique. "Imbecellitas Sexus." *Cuadernos de Historia del Derecho* 20 (2013): 27–66.

Gallagher, Ann Miriam. "The Indian Nuns of Mexico City's *Monasterio* of Corpus Christi, 1724–1821." In *Latin American Women: Historical Perspectives*, edited by Asunción Lavrin, 150–72. Westport, CT: Greenwood, 1978.

Gálvez Peña, Carlos. "'El mejor arbitrio, el sermón.' Discurso religioso y representación política en el Perú del siglo XVII." *Anuario de Estudios Americanos* 71, no. 1 (January–June 2014): 171–94.

Garavaglia, Juan Carlos. "The crisis and transformations of invaded societies: The La Plata Basin (1535–1650)." In *South America*, edited by Frank Salomon and Stuart B. Schwartz, 1–58. Vol. 3 of *The Cambridge History of the Native Peoples of the Americas.* Cambridge: Cambridge University Press, 1999.

Garay, Juan de. "Repartimiento de los indios de esta ciudad [de Buenos Aires] hecho por el general Juan de Garay, año de 1582." In *Colección de obras y documentos relativos a la historia antigua y moderna de las provincias del Río de la Plata*, Pedro de Angelis, 3:474–80. Buenos Aires: Plus Ultra, 1969.

García Pérez, Rafael D. "El regimen tributario en las intendencias novohispanas: La ordenanza para la formación de los autos de visitas, padrones, y matrículas de Revillagigedo II." *Anuario Mexicano de Historia del Derecho* 11–12 (1999–2000): 279–307. http://historico.juridicas.unam.mx/publica/rev/hisder/cont/11/cnt/cnt10.htm.

García Ugarte, Marta Eugenia. *Breve historia de Querétaro.* Mexico City: Colegio de México, 1999.

Garrett, David. "'In Spite of Her Sex': The Cacica and the Politics of the Pueblo in the Late Colonial Cusco." *Americas* 64, no. 4 (April 2008): 547–81.

———. *Shadows of Empire: The Indian Nobility of Cusco, 1750–1824.* New York: Cambridge University Press, 2005.

Gauderman, Kimberly. "The Authority of Gender: Marital Discord and Social Order in Colonial Quito." In *New World Orders: Violence, Sanction, and Authority in the Colonial Americas*, edited by John Smolenski and Thomas J. Humphrey, 71–91. Philadelphia: University of Pennsylvania Press, 2005.

———. *Women's Lives in Colonial Quito: Gender, Law, and Economy in Spanish America*. Austin: University of Texas Press, 2003.

Gerhard, Peter. *A Guide to the Historical Geography of New Spain*. Rev. ed. Norman: University of Oklahoma Press, 1993.

Gibbings, Julie A. "Another Race More Worthy of the Present: History, Race, and Nation in Alta Verapaz, Guatemala, c. 1860s–1940s." PhD diss., University of Wisconsin, Madison, 2012.

Gibson, Charles. "The Aztec Aristocracy in Colonial Mexico." *Comparative Studies in Society and History* 2, no. 2 (1960): 169–96.

———. *The Aztecs under Spanish Rule: A History of the Indians of the Valley of Mexico, 1519–1810*. Stanford: Stanford University Press, 1964.

Gillespie, Jeanne. "In the Shadow of Coatlicue's Smile: Reconstructing Indigenous Female Subjectivity in the Spanish Colonial Record." In *Women's Negotiations and Textual Agency in latin America, 1500–1799*, edited by Mónica Díaz and Rocío Quispe-Agnoli. London: Routledge, 2017.

Gillespie, Susan D. *The Aztec Kings: The Construction of Rulership in Mexica History*. Tucson: University of Arizona Press, 1989.

Glave, Luis Miguel. "Hombres del mar. Caciques de la Costa ecuatoriana en los inicios de la época colonial." *Procesos* 40 (2014): 9–36.

———. "Propiedad de la tierra, agricultura y comercio, 1570–1700: El gran despojo." In *Compendio de historia económica del Perú*, edited by Carlos Contreras, 2:313–446. Lima: Instituto de Estudios Peruanos, Banco Centra del Reserva del Perú, 2009.

———. "*Simiachi*: El traductor o lengua en el distrito de la Audiencia de Lima." In *Las lenguas indígenas en los tribunales de América Latina: Intérpretes, mediación y justicia (siglos XVI–XX)*, edited by Caroline Cunill and Luis Miguel Glave Testino, 121–65. Bogotá: Instituto Colombiano de Antropología e Historia, 2019.

———. *Un curacazgo andino y la sociedad campesina del siglo XVII*. Lima: Insituto de Pastoral Andina, 1989.

Glave, Luis Miguel, and María Isabel Remy. *Estructura agraria y vida rural en una región andina: Ollantaytambo entre los siglos XVI y XIX*. Cusco: Centro de Estudios Rurales Andinos, Bartolomé de Las Casas, 1983.

Gonzalbo Aizpuru, Pilar. *Familia y orden colonial*. Mexico City: El Colegio de México, Centro de Estudios Históricos, 1998.

Gosner, Kevin. *Soldiers of the Virgin: The Moral Economy of a Colonial Maya Rebellion*. Tucson: University of Arizona Press, 1992.

Grandin, Greg. *The Blood of Guatemala: A History of Race and Nation*. Durham, NC: Duke University Press, 2000.

Granados, Luis Fernando. "Cosmopolitan Indians and Mesoamerican Barrios in Bourbon Mexico City: Tribute, Community, Family, and Work in 1800." PhD diss., Georgetown University, 2008.

Graubart, Karen B. "Containing Law within the Walls: The Protection of Customary Law in Santiago del Cercado, Peru." In *Protection and Empire. A Global History*, edited by Lauren Benton, Adam Culow, and Bain Attwood, 29–45. Cambridge: Cambridge University Press, 2017.

———. "Indecent Living: Indigenous Women and the Politics of Representation in Early Colonial Peru." *Colonial Latin American Review* 9, no. 2 (December 2000): 213–35.

———. "Learning from the Qadi: The Jurisdiction of Local Rule in the Early Colonial Andes." *Hispanic American Historical Review* 95, no. 2 (May 2015): 195–228.

———. *With Our Labor and Sweat: Indigenous Women and the Formation of Colonial Society in Peru, 1550–1700*. Stanford: Stanford University Press, 2007.

Guardia, Sara Beatriz. *Mujeres Peruanas. El otro lado de la historia*. Lima: Minerva, 2002.

Guengerich, Sara Vicuña. "Capac Women and the Politics of Marriage in Early Colonial Peru." *Colonial Latin American Review* 24, no. 2 (April 2015): 147–67.

———. "Inca Women Under Spanish Rule: Probanzas and Informaciones of the Colonial Andean Elite." In *Women's Negotiations and Textual Agency in Latin America, 1500–1799*, edited by Mónica Díaz and Rocío Quispe-Agnoli, 106–29. New York: Routledge, 2017.

Guevara Gil, Jorge A. *Diversidad y complejidad legal. Aproximaciones a la Antropología e Historia del Derecho*. Lima: Pontificia Universidad Católica del Perú, Fondo Editorial, 2019.

———. *Propiedad agraria y derecho colonial: los documentos de la hacienda Santotis, Cuzco (1543–1822)*. Lima: Pontificia Universidad Católica del Perú, Fondo Editorial, 1993.

Gunnarsdóttir, Ellen. "The Convent of Santa Clara, The Elite and Social Change in Eighteenth-Century Querétaro." *Journal of Latin American Studies* 33, no. 2 (May 2001): 257–90.

Hampe Martínez, Teodoro. "Notas sobre la encomienda real de Chincha en el siglo XVI (Administración y tributos)." *Revista de Historia de América* 100 (July–December 1985): 119–39.

———. "Relación de los encomenderos y repartimientos del Perú en 1561." *Historia y Cultura* 12 (1979): 75–117.

Haring, Clarence H. *The Spanish Empire in America*. 1947. Reprint, New York: Harcourt, 1975.

Harris, Olivia. "Complementarity and Conflict: An Andean View of Women and Men." In *Sex and Age of Principles of Social Differentiation*, edited by J. La Fontaine, 21–40. London: Academic Press, 1978.

Haskett, Robert. "Activist or Adulteress? The Life and Struggle of Doña Josefa María of Tepoztlan." In *Indian Women of Early Mexico*, edited by Susan Schroeder, Stephanie Wood, and Robert Haskett, 145–63. Norman: University of Oklahoma Press, 1997.

———. *Indigenous Rulers: An Ethnohistory of Town Government in Colonial Cuernavaca*. Albuquerque: University of New Mexico Press, 1991.

———. *Visions of Paradise: Primordial Titles and Mesoamerican History in Cuernavaca*. Norman: University of Oklahoma Press, 2005.

Haslip-Viera, Gabriel. *Crime and Punishment in Late Colonial Mexico City, 1692–1810*. Albuquerque: University of New Mexico Press, 1999.

Hawkins, Timothy P. *José Bustamante and Central American Independence: Colonial Administration in an Age of Imperial Crisis*. Tuscaloosa: University of Alabama Press, 2004.

Henige, David. *In Search of Columbus: The Sources for the First Voyage*. Tucson: University of Arizona Press, 1991.

Herrera, Robinson Antonio. *Natives, Europeans, and Africans in Sixteenth-Century Santiago de Guatemala*. Austin: University of Texas Press, 2003.

Herzog, Tamar. *Defining Nations: Immigrants and Citizens in Early Modern Spain and Spanish America*. New Haven: Yale University Press, 2003.

———. *Frontiers of Possession: Spain and Portugal in Europe and the Americas*. Cambridge, MA: Harvard University Press, 2015.

———. *A Short History of European Law: The Last Two and a Half Millennia*. Cambridge, MA: Harvard University Press, 2018.

Hevia Bolaños, Juan de. *Curia Philipica*. 2 vols. 1797. Reprint, Madrid: Lex Nova. S. A., 1989.

Hicks, Frederic. "Texcoco 1515–1519: The Ixtlilxochitl Affair." In *Chipping Away on Earth: Studies in Prehispanic and Colonial Mexico in Honor of Arthur J. O. Anderson and Charles E. Dibble*, edited by Eloise Quiñones Keber, 235–239. Lancaster, CA: Labyrinthos, 1994.

Hill, Robert M., II. *Colonial Cakchiquels: Highland Maya Adaptation to Spanish Rule, 1600–1700*. Fort Worth, TX: Harcourt Brace Jovanovich, 1992.

———. *The Pirir Papers and Other Colonial Era Cakchiquel-Maya Testamentos*. Vanderbilt University Publications in Anthropology 37. Nashville: Vanderbilt University, 1989.

Horn, Rebecca. *Postconquest Coyoacan: Nahua-Spanish Relations in Central Mexico, 1519–1650*. Stanford: Stanford University Press, 1997.

Hünefeldt, Christine. *Lucha por la tierra y protesta indígena. Las comunidades indígenas del Perú entre colonia y república, 1800–1830*. Bonn: Bonner Amerikanische Studien, 1982.

Incer, Jaime. *Viajes, Rutas y Encuentros, 1502–1838*. 2nd ed. San Jose, Costa Rica: Editorial Libro Libre, 1993.

"Información de los méritos y servicios presentados por don Fernando de Tapia, en la conquista y fundación de Querétaro y provanza del cacicazgo de don Diego de Tapia." *Boletín del Archivo General de la Nación* 5, no. 1 (1939): 34–61.

Jackson, Robert H. *Frontiers of Evangelization: Indians in the Sierra Gorda and Chiquitos Missions*. Norman: University of Oklahoma Press, 2017.

Jacobsen, Nils. *Mirages of Transition: The Peruvian Altiplano, 1780–1930*. Berkeley: University of California Press, 1993.

Jaffary, Nora, and Jane Mangan, eds. *Women in Colonial Latin America, 1526–1806: Texts and Contexts*. Indianapolis: Hackett, 2018.

Jiménez Gómez, Juan Ricardo. *Autos civiles de indios ante el alcalde mayor del pueblo de Querétaro a finales del siglo XVI*. Mexico City: MA Porrúa, 2014.

———. "Estudio introductorio." In *Fundación y evangelización del pueblo de indios de Querétaro y sus sujetos, 1531–1585: Testimonios del cacique don Hernando de Tapia y otros indios españoles en el Pleito Grande, entre el Arzobispado de México y el Obispado de Michoacán*, edited by Juan Ricardo Jiménez Gómez, 11–107. Mexico City: MA Porrúa, 2014.

———, ed. *Fundación y evangelización del pueblo de indios de Querétaro y sus sujetos, 1531–1585: Testimonios del cacique don Hernando de Tapia y otros indios españoles en el Pleito Grande, entre el Arzobispado de México y el Obispado de Michoacán*. Mexico City: MA Porrúa, 2014.

———. *Práctica notarial y judicial de los otomíes: manuscritos coloniales de Querétaro*. Mexico City: MA Porrúa, 2012.

Jiménez Jácome, Myrna Lilí de las Mercedes. "El Convento de Santa Clara de Jesús de Querétaro, mundo de privilegios y restricciones, 1607–1809." PhD diss., Universidad Autónoma de Querétaro, 2012.

Johnson, Lyman L. and Sonya Lipsett-Rivera, eds. *The Faces of Honor: Sex, Shame, and Violence in Colonial Latin America*. Albuquerque: University of New Mexico Press, 1998.

Jones, Kristine L. "Warfare, Reorganization, and Readaptation at the Margins of Spanish Rule: The Southern Margin (1573–1882)." In *Mesoamerica*, edited by Richard E. W. Adams and Murdo J. MacLeod, 138–87. Vol. 2 of *The Cambridge History of the Native Peoples of the Americas*. Cambridge: Cambridge University Press, 1999.

Josserand, J. Kathryn. "Women in Classic Maya Hieroglyphic Texts." In *Ancient Maya Women*, edited by Traci Ardren, 114–51. Walnut Creek, CA: AltaMira Press, 2002.

Julien, Catherine. *Reading Inca History*. Iowa City: University of Iowa Press, 2000.

Jurado, Carolina. "'Descendientes de los primeros': Las probanzas de méritos y servicios de la genealogía cacical. Audiencia de Charcas, 1574–1719." *Revista de Indias* 74, no. 261 (2014): 387–422.

Kagan, Richard. *Lawsuits and Litigants in Castile, 1500–1700*. Chapel Hill: University of North Carolina Press, 1981.

Katzew, Ilona. *Casta Painting: Images of Race in Eighteenth-Century Mexico*. New Haven: Yale University Press, 2004.

Keegan, William F., Corinne L. Hofman, and Reniel Rodríguez Ramos, eds. *The Oxford Handbook of Caribbean Archaeology*. New York: Oxford University Press, 2013.

Keith, Robert G. *Conquest and Agrarian Change: The Emergence of the Hacienda System on the Peruvian Coast*. Harvard Historical Studies 93. Cambridge, MA: Harvard University Press, 1976.

Kellogg, Susan. "From Parallel and Equivalent to Separate but Unequal: Tenochca Mexica Women, 1500–1700." In *Indian Women of Early Mexico*, edited by Susan Schroeder, Stephanie Wood, and Robert Haskett, 123–43. Norman: University of Oklahoma Press, 1997.

————. "Indigenous Testaments of Early-Colonial Mexico City: Testifying to Gender Differences." In *Dead Giveaways: Indigenous Testaments in Colonial Spanish America*, edited by Susan Kellogg and Matthew Restall, 37–57. Salt Lake City: University of Utah, 1998.

————. *Law and the Transformation of Aztec Culture, 1500–1700*. Norman: University of Oklahoma Press, 1995.

————. *Weaving the Past: A History of Latin America's Indigenous Women from the Prehispanic Period to the Present*. New York: Oxford University Press, 2005.

Kellogg, Susan, and Matthew Restall, eds. *Dead Giveaways: Indigenous Testaments of Colonial Mesoamerica and the Andes*. Salt Lake City: University of Utah Press, 1998.

Klein, Cecilia F. "None of the Above: Gender Ambiguity in Nahua Ideology." In *Gender in Pre-Hispanic America*, edited by Cecilia F. Klein, 183–253. Washington, DC: Dumbarton Oaks Research Library and Collection, 2001.

Komisaruk, Catherine. *Labor and Love in Guatemala: The Eve of Independence*. Stanford: Stanford University Press, 2013.

Korth, Eugene H., and Della M. Flusche. "Dowry and Inheritance in Colonial Spanish America: Peninsular Law and Chilean Practice." *Americas* 43, no. 4 (April 1987): 395–410.

Kubler, George. "The Quechua in the Colonial World." In *The Andean Civilizations*, edited by Julian H. Steward, 331–410. Vol. 2 of *Handbook of South American Indians*. (New York: Cooper Square, 1963).

Kuethe, Allan, and Kenneth Andrien. *The Spanish Atlantic World in the Eighteenth Century: War and the Bourbon Reforms, 1713–1796*. Cambridge: Cambridge University Press, 2014.

La Bandera, Damián de. "Relación general de la disposición y calidad de la provincial de Guamanga, llamada San Joan de la Frontera, y de la vivienda y costumbres de los naturales de ella, año de 1557." In *Relaciones geográficas de Indias: Perú*, edited by Marcos Jimenez de la Espada, 176–80. (Madrid: Biblioteca de Autores Españoles 1965).

La Peña Montenegro, Alonso de. *Itinerario para Parochos de Indios*. Amberes: Casa de Juan Bautista Verdussen, 1726.

La Puente Luna, José Carlos de. *Andean Cosmopolitans: Seeking Justice and Reward at the Spanish Royal Court*. Austin: University of Texas Press, 2018.

————. *Los curacas hechiceros de Jauja: Batallas mágicas y legales en el Perú colonial*. Lima: Fondo Editorial de la Pontificia Universidad Católica del Perú, 2007.

————. "The Many Tongues of the King: Indigenous Language Interpreters and the Making of the Spanish Empire." *Colonial Latin American Review* 23, no. 2 (2014): 143–70.

————. "That Which Belongs to All: Khipus, Community, and Indigenous Legal Activism in the Early Colonial Andes." *Americas* 72, no. 1 (January 2015): 19–54.

La Puente Luna, José Carlos de, and Renzo Honores. "Guardianes de la real justicia: Alcaldes de indios, costumbre y justicia local en Huarochirí colonial." *Histórica* 40, no. 2 (December 2016): 11–47.

La Rea, Alonso de. *Crónica de la orden de N. Seráfico P. S. Francisco, provincia de S. Pedro y S. Pablo de Mechoacán en la Nueva España.* Zamora, Michoacán: El Colegio de Michoacán, 1996.

La Soudière, Martin de. "Les testaments et actes de dernière volonté à la fin du Moyen Age." *Ethnologie Française* 5 (1975): 57–80.

Landázuri, Cristóbal. *Los curacazgos pastos prehispánicos: agricultura y comercio, siglo XVI.* Quito: Instituto Otavaleño de Antropología, Banco Central del Ecuador, 1995.

Larson, Brooke, Olivia Harris, and Enrique Tandeter. *Ethnicity, Markets, and Migration in the Andes: At the Crossroads of History and Anthropology.* Durham, NC: Duke University Press, 1995.

Las Casas, Bartolomé de. "Cristóbal Colón: Los cuatro viajes del almirante y su testamento." Biblioteca Virtual Universal. Accessed March 10, 2020. https://www.biblioteca.org.ar/libros/131757.pdf.

Lastra, Yolanda. *Los otomíes: su lengua y su historia.* Mexico City: Universidad Nacional Autonoma de México, 2006.

Lavallé, Bernard. "Divorcio y nulidad de matrimonio en Lima (1650–1700): la desavenencia conyugal como indicador social." *Revista Andina* 4, no. 2 (December 1986): 427–64.

Lavrin, Asunción. *Brides of Christ: Conventual Life in Colonial Mexico.* Stanford: Stanford University Press, 2008.

———. "El convento de Santa Clara de Querétaro: La administración de sus propiedades en el siglo XVII." *Historia Mexicana* 25, no. 1 (1975): 76–117.

———. "Indian Brides of Christ: Creating New Spaces for Indigenous Women in New Spain." *Mexican Studies/Estudios Mexicanos* 15 (1999): 225–60.

———, ed. *Latin American Women: Historical Perspectives.* Westport: Greenwood, 1978.

———. "Religious Life of a Mexican Convent in the XVIII Century." PhD diss., Harvard University, 1963.

———, ed. *Sexuality & Marriage in Colonial Latin America.* Lincoln: University of Nebraska Press, 1989.

———. "Sexuality in Colonial Mexico: A Church Dilemma." In *Sexuality & Marriage in Colonial Latin America*, edited by Asunción Lavrin, 47–95. Lincoln: University of Nebraska Press, 1989.

Lavrin, Asunción, and Edith Couturier. "Dowries and Wills: A View of Women's Socioeconomic Role in Colonial Guadalajara and Puebla, 1640–1790." *Hispanic American Historical Review* 59, no. 2 (May 1979): 280–304.

Leavitt-Alcántara, Brianna. *Alone at the Altar: Single Women and Devotion in Guatemala, 1670–1870.* Stanford: Stanford University Press, 2018.

Leddy Phelan, John. *The Kingdom of Quito in the Seventeenth Century.* Madison: University of Wisconsin Press, 1967.

Leibson, Dana and Mundy Barbara. "Portrait of an Indian Lady. Daughter of a Cacique, 1757." In *Vistas: Visual Culture in Spanish America.* Accessed December 14, 2019. https://www.smith.edu/vistas/.

Levaggi, Abelardo. *Paz en la frontera. Historia de las relaciones diplomática con las comunidades indígenas en la Argentina (siglos XVI–XIX)*. Buenos Aires: Universidad del Museo Social Argentino, 2000.

Levillier, Roberto. *Don Francisco de Toledo, Supremo organizador del Perú: Su vida, su obra (1515–1582)*. Madrid: Espasa Calpe, 1955.

Lienhard, Martin. "El cautiverio colonial del discurso indígena: los testimonios." In *Del discurso colonial al proindigenismo. Ensayos de historia latinoamericana*, edited by José Pinto Rodríguez, 9–28. Temuco: Universidad de la Frontera, 1998.

Lipsett-Rivera, Sonya. *The Origins of Macho: Men and Masculinity in Colonial Mexico*. Albuquerque: University of New Mexico Press, 2019.

———. "A Slap in the Face of Honor: Social Transgression and Women in Late-Colonial Mexico." In *Faces of Honor: Sex, Shame, and Violence in Colonial Latin America*, edited by Lyman L. Johnson and Sonya Lipsett-Rivera, 179–200. Albuquerque: University of New Mexico Press, 1998.

Lira González, Andrés. *Comunidades indígenas frente a la ciudad de México: Tenochtitlan y Tlatelolco, sus pueblos y barrios, 1812–1919*. Mexico City: El Colegio de México, 1983.

Lizárraga, Reginaldo de. *Descripción del Perú, Tucumán, Río de La Plata y Chile*. Madrid: Historia 16, 1986.

Lockhart, James. "Double Mistaken Identity: Some Nahua Concepts in Postconquest Guise." In *Of Things of the Indies: Essays Old and New in Early Latin American History*, 98–119. Stanford: Stanford University Press, 1999.

———. *The Nahuas after the Conquest: A Social and Cultural History of the Indians of Central Mexico, Sixteenth Through Eighteenth Centuries*. Stanford: Stanford University Press, 1992.

———. *Spanish Peru, 1532–1560: A Social History*. Madison: University of Wisconsin Press, 1994.

Lockhart, James, and Stuart Schwartz. *Early Latin America: A History of Colonial Spanish America and Brazil*. New York: Cambridge University Press, 1983.

Lohmann Villena, Guillermo. *Los regidores perpetuos del cabildo de Lima (1535–1821): Crónica y estudio de un grupo de gestión*. 2 vols. Seville: Excma. Diputación Provincial de Sevilla, 1983.

López, Gregorio. *Las Siete Partidas*. 1556. Facsimile. Madrid: Spanish Cortes, 1985.

López Medel, Tomás. "Tratado de los tres elementos." *Cespedesia* 43–44, no. 9 (1982).

López-Portillo, José-Juan. *"Another Jerusalem": Political Legitimacy and Courtly Government in the Kingdom of New Spain (1535–1568)*. Boston: Brill, 2017.

López Sarrelangue, Delfina Esmeralda. *La nobleza indígena de Pátzcuaro en la época virreinal*. Mexico: Universidad Nacional Autónoma de México, Instituto de Investigaciones Históricas, 1965.

Loreto López, Rosalva, ed. *Casas, viviendas y hogares en la historia de México*. Mexico City: Centro de Estudios Históricos, El Colegio de México, 2001.

Lovell, W. George. *Conquest and Survival in Colonial Guatemala: A Historical Geography of the Cuchumatán Highlands, 1500–1821*. 4th ed. Montreal: McGill-Queen's University Press, 2015.

Lozano Armendares, Teresa. *No codiciarás la mujer ajena: El adulterio en las comunidades domésticas novohispanas, ciudad de México, siglo XVIII.* Mexico City: Universidad Nacional Autónoma de México, 2005.

Lutz, Christopher H. *Santiago de Guatemala, 1541–1773: City, Caste, and the Colonial Experience.* Norman: University of Oklahoma Press, 1994.

Lutz, Christopher H., and Karen Dakin, eds. *Nuestro pesar, nuestra aflicción: Tunetuliniliz, tucucuca. Memorias en lengua náhuatl enviadas a Felipe II por indígenas del Valle de Guatemala hacia 1572.* Mexico City: Universidad Nacional Autónoma de México and Centro de Investigaciones Regionales de Mesoamérica, 1996.

MacLachlan, Colin M. *Criminal Justice in Eighteenth-Century Mexico: A Study of the Tribunal of the Acordada.* Berkeley: University of California Press, 1974.

MacLeod, Murdo J. *Spanish Central America: A Socioeconomic History, 1520–1720.* Berkeley: University of California Press, 1973.

Mangan, Jane. *Trading Roles: Gender, Ethnicity, and the Urban Economy in Colonial Potosí.* Durham, NC: Duke University Press, 2005.

Marcus, Joyce. *Emblem and State in the Classic Maya Lowlands.* Washington DC: Dumbarton Oaks, 1976.

Martín, Luis. *Daughters of the Conquistadors: Women of the Viceroyalty of Peru.* University Park: Southern Methodist University Press, 1989.

Martínez, María Elena. *Genealogical Fictions: Limpieza de Sangre, Religion, and Gender in Colonial Mexico.* Stanford: Stanford University Press, 2011.

Martínez Peláez, Severo. *La patria del criollo: Ensayo de interpretación de la realidad colonial guatemalteca.* Guatemala City: Universidad de San Carlos de Guatemala, 1970.

———. *Motines de indios: La violencia colonial en Centroamérica y Chiapas.* Guatemala City: F&G Editores, 2011.

Matthew, Laura. *Memories of Conquest: Becoming Mexicano in Colonial Guatemala.* Chapel Hill: University of North Carolina Press, 2012.

Maura, Juan Francisco. *Carta de Luis Ramírez a su padre desde el Brasil (1528): orígenes de lo 'real maravilloso' en el Cono Sur.* Valencia: Lemir, 2007. http://parnaseo.uv.es/Lemir/Textos/Ramirez.pdf.

McCreery, David. "Atanasio Tzul, Lucas Aguilar, and the Indian Kingdom of Totonicapán." In *The Human Tradition in Latin America: The Nineteenth Century,* edited by Judith Ewell and William H. Beezley, 39–58. Wilmington, DE: Scholarly Resources, 1989.

Medina, Balthasar de. *Chrónica de la S. Provincia de S. Diego de México de Religiosos Descalços de N. S. P. S. Francisco en la Nueva España.* Mexico City: Juan de Ribera, 1682.

Meléndez, Juan de. *Tesoros verdaderos de las Yndias en la historia de la gran provincia de San Juan Bautista del Perú de el Orden de Predicadores.* 2 vols. Rome: Imprenta de Nicolás Angel Tinassio, 1681.

Melton-Villanueva, Miriam. "Cacicas, Escribanos, and Landholders: Indigenous Women's Late Colonial Mexican Texts, 1703–1832." *Ethnohistory* 65, no. 2 (April 2018): 297–322.

Melvin, Karen. *Building Colonial Cities of God: Mendicant Orders and Urban Culture in New Spain*. Stanford: Stanford University Press, 2012.

Mendiola, Daniel. "The Rise of the Mosquito Kingdom in Central America's Caribbean Borderlands: Sources, Questions, and Enduring Myths." *History Compass* 16, no. 1 (December 2017): 1–10.

Menegus Bornemann, Margarita. *Del señorío a la república de indios: El caso de Toluca: 1500–1600*. Madrid: Ministerio de Agricultura, Pesca, y Alimentación, 1991.

———. "El cacicazgo en la Nueva España." In *El cacicazgo en la Nueva España y Filipinas*, edited by Margarita Menegus Bornemann, 13–69 (Mexico City: Plaza y Valdés, 2005).

Menegus Bornemann, Margarita, and Rodolfo Aguirre Salvador, eds. *El cacicazgo en Nueva España y Filipinas*. Mexico City: Universidad Nacional Autónoma de México, Centro de Estudios Sobre la Universidad, Plaza y Valdés, 2005.

———. *Los indios, el sacerdocio y la Universidad en Nueva España, siglos XVI–XVIII*. Mexico City: Universidad Nacional Autónoma de México, Centro de Estudios Sobre la Universidad, Playa y Valdés, 2006.

Mirow, M. C. *Latin American Law: A History of Private Law and Institutions in Spanish America*. Austin: University of Texas Press, 2004.

Molloy, John P. and William L. Rathje, "Sexploitation among the Late Classic Maya." In *Mesoamerican Archaeology: New Approaches*, edited by Norman Hammond, 431–44. Austin: University of Texas Press, 1974.

Moreno-Cebrian, Alfredo. "El Marqués de Casa Hermosa, corregidor de Huaylas." *Anuario de Estudios Atlánticos* 24 (1978): 81–120.

Morrone, Ariel. "Mujeres cacicales en el tablero colonial. Familia, parentesco y poder étnico en el lago Titicaca, 1580–1750." *Andes Antropología e Historia* 1, no. 29 (2018): 1–31.

Moscoso, Francisco. *Caguas en la conquista española del siglo 16*. Rev. ed. Río Piedras: Publicaciones Gaviota, 2016.

Mostajo, Francisco. "Los Chuquihuancas hasta la época de Tupac Amaru." *Revista de la Universidad de Arequipa* 25, no. 38 (1953).

Mumford, Jeremy Ravi. "Aristocracy in the Auction Block. Race, Lords, and the Perpetuity Controversy of Sixteenth-Century Peru." In *Imperial Subjects: Race and Identity in Colonial Latin America*, edited by Matthew O'Hara and Andrew Fisher, 39–60. Durham, NC: Duke University Press, 2009.

———. *Vertical Empire: The General Resettlement of Indians in the Colonial Andes*. Durham, NC: Duke University Press, 2012.

Munch, Guido. *El cacicazgo de San Juan Teotihuacan durante la colonia, 1521–1821*. Mexico City: Instituto Nacional de Antropología e Historia, Centro de Investigaciones Superiores, 1976.

Mundy, Barbara E. *The Death of Aztec Tenochtitlan, the Life of Mexico City*. Austin: University of Texas Press, 2015.

Muriel, Josefina. *Las indias caciques de Corpus Christi*. 2nd ed. Mexico City: Unviersidad Nacional Autónoma de México, 2001.

———. *Los recogimientos de mujeres: respuesta a una problemática social novohispana.* Mexico City: Universidad Nacional Autónoma de México, 1974.

Murra, John V. *Formaciones económicas y políticas del mundo andino.* Lima: Instituto de Estudios Peruanos, 1975.

———. "Nueva información sobre las poblaciones yana." In *Formaciones económicas y políticas del mundo andino.* Lima: Instituto de Estudios Peruanos, 1975.

———. "Social Structural and Economic Themes in Andean Ethnohistory." *Anthropological Quarterly* 34, no. 2 (April 1961): 47–59.

Nacuzzi, Lidia. *Identidades impuestas. Tehuelches, aucas y pampas en el norte de la Patagonia.* Buenos Aires: Sociedad Argentina de Antropología, 1998.

Nader, Helen. *Power and Gender in Renaissance Spain: Eight Women of the Mendoza Family: 1450–1650.* Urbana, IL: University of Illinois Press, 2004.

———. *Liberty in Absolutist Spain: The Sale of Habsburg Towns, 1516–1700.* Baltimore: Johns Hopkins University Press, 1993.

Navarrete, Francisco Antonio. *Relación peregrina de la agua corriente que [. . .] goza la muy noble, leal, y florida ciudad de Santiago de Querétaro.* Mexico City: José Bernardo de Hogal, 1739. http://www.cervantesvirtual.com/nd/ark:/59851/bmc41780.

Nazzari, Muriel. *Disappearance of the Dowry: Women, Families, and Social Change in São Paulo, Brazil, 1600–1900.* Stanford: Stanford University Press, 1991.

Netherly, Patricia. "Local Level Lords on the North Coast of Perú." PhD diss., Cornell University, 1977.

Newson, Linda. *The Cost of Conquest: Indian Decline under Spanish Rule.* Boulder: Westview Press, 1986.

———. *Indian Survival in Colonial Nicaragua.* Norman: University of Oklahoma Press, 1987.

Niles, Susan A. *The Shape of Inca History: Narrative and Archaeology in an Andean Empire.* Iowa: University of Iowa Press, 1999.

Núñez Cabeza de Vaca, Álvar. *Relación de los naufragios y comentarios.* 2 vols. Madrid: Librería General de Victoriano Suárez, 1906. http://www.cervantesvirtual .com/obra/relacion-de-los-naufragios-y-comentarios-de-alvar-nunez-cabeza-de -vaca-tomo-1-788658/.

Obara-Saeki, Tadashi, and Juan Pedro Viqueira Alban. *El arte de contar tributarios. Provincia de Chiapas, 1560–1821.* Mexico City: El Colegio de México, 2017.

Oberem, Udo. "Diego de Ortegóns Beischreibung der 'Gobernación de los Quijos, Zumaco y la Canela.' Ein Ethnographischer Bericht aus dem Jahre 1577." *Zeitschrift für Ethnologie* 83, 1958.

———. "Testamentos de doña Francisca Sina Sigchi y Don Juan Sancho Hacho de Velasco." *Boletín del Archivo Nacional de Historia* 16 (1966): 13–21.

———. "Don Sancho Hacho, ein 'cacique mayor' des 16 Jahrhunderts." *Jahrbuch für Geschichte von Staat, Wirtschaft und Gesellschaft Lateinamerikas* 4, no. 1 (1967): 199–225.

Ochoa, Margarita R. "Illicit Relations in a Multiethnic City: Emotions, Fidelity, and Economic Obligations in Colonial Mexico." In *Courtship, Marriage and Marriage Breakdown: Approaches from the History of Emotion*, edited by Katie Barclay, Jeffrey Meek, and Andrea Thomson, 48–65. New York: Routledge, 2019.

O'Hara, Matthew. *A Flock Divided: Race, Religion, and Politics in Mexico, 1749–1857.* Durham, NC: Duke University Press, 2010.

Oliver, José. *Caciques and Cemí Idols: The Web Spun by Taíno Rulers between Hispaniola and Puerto Rico.* Tuscaloosa: University of Alabama Press, 2009.

Ondegardo, Polo. "Informe del licenciado Polo Ondegardo al licenciado Briviesca de Muñatones sobre la perpetuidad de las encomiendas en el Perú." 1561. Reprint in *Pensamiento colonial crítico. Textos y actos de Polo Ondegardo*, edited by Gonzalo Lamana Ferrario, 139–204. Lima: Instituto Francés de Estudios Andinos, Centro Bartolomé de Las Casas, 2002.

O'Phelan Scarlett. *Kurakas sin sucesiones: Del cacique al alcalde de indios, Perú y Bolivia, 1750–1835.* Cusco: Centro de Estudios Bartolomé de las Casas, 1997.

Ortner, Sherry. "Specifying Agency: The Comaroffs and Their Critics." *Interventions* 3, no. 1 (2001): 76–84.

Osowski, Edward W. *Indigenous Miracles: Nahua Authority in Colonial Mexico.* Tucson: University of Arizona Press, 2010.

O'Toole, Rachel. "As Historical Subjects: The African Diaspora in Colonial Latin American History." *History Compass* 11, no. 12 (December 2013): 1094–1110.

Oudijk, Michel R., and Matthew Restall. "Mesoamerican Conquistadors in the Sixteenth Century." In *Indian Conquistadors: Indigenous Allies in the Conquest of Mesoamerica*, edited by Laura E. Matthew, 28–63. Norman: University of Oklahoma Press, 2007.

Oviedo y Valdés, Gonzalo Fernández. *Corónica de las Yndias y la conquista del Peru.* Salamanca: Juan de Junta, 1547.

———. *Historia general y natural de las islas y tierra-firme del mar océano.* Madrid: Impressa de la Real academia de la historia, 1851–55.

———. *Nicaragua en los Cronistas de Indias: Oviedo.* Colección Cultural 3. Managua, Nicaragua: Banco de America, 1976.

Owensby, Brian. *Empire of Law and Indian Justice in Colonial Mexico.* Stanford: Stanford University Press, 2008.

Paredes Martínez, Carlos S. "La nobleza tarasca: poder político y conflictos en el Michoacán colonial." *Anuario de Estudios Americanos* 65, no. 1 (2008): 101–17.

Pastor, Rodolfo. *Campesinos y reformas: La Mixteca 1700–1856.* Mexico City: El Colegio de México, 1987.

Pease G. Y., Franklin. *Curacas, reciprocidad y riqueza.* Lima: Pontificia Universidad Católica del Perú, Fondo Editorial, 1992.

———. *Inka y Kuraka: Relaciones de poder y representación histórica.* Working papers 8. College Park, MD: University of Maryland at College Park, 1990.

Penyak, Lee M. "Safe Harbors and Compulsory Custody: Casas de Depósito in Mexico, 1750–1865." *Hispanic American Historical Review* 79, no. 1 (February 1999): 83–99.

Pérez Fernández, O. P. Isacio. *Bartolomé de Las Casas en el Perú. El espíritu lascasiano de la primera evangelización del imperio incaico (1531–1573).* Cusco: Centro de Estudios Rurales Andinos Bartolomé de Las Casas, 1986.

Pérez Miguel, Liliana. *Mujeres ricas y libres: Mujer y poder: Inés Muñoz y las enco-menderas en el Perú -s. XVI.* Sevilla: Centro Superior de Investigaciones Científi-cas, Universidad de Sevilla y Diputación de Sevilla, 2020.

Pérez-Rocha, Emma, and Rafael Tena. "Estudio preliminar." In *La nobleza indígena de México después de la conquista,* edited by Emma Pérez-Rocha and Rafael Tena, 11–72. Mexico: Instituto Nacional de Antropología e Historia, 2000.

———. *La nobleza indígena del centro de México después de la conquista.* Mexico City: Instituto Nacional de Antropología e Historia, 2000.

Perrot, Michelle. "Faire l'histoire des femmes: bilan d'une expérience." In *Masculin—Féminin: questions pour les sciences de l'homme,* edited by Jacqueline Laufer, Catherine Marry, and Margarat Maruani, 229–44. Paris: Presses Universitaires de France, 2001.

———. *Les femmes ou les silences de l'Histoire.* Paris: Flammarion, 1998.

———. "L'histoire ouverte." *Critique* 843–44, no. 8 (2017): 611–12.

Pescador, Juan Javier. *De bautizados a fieles difuntos: Familia y mentalidades en una parroquia urbana, Santa Catarina de México, 1568–1820.* Mexico City: Colegio de México, Centro de Estudios Demográficos y de Desarrollo Urbano, 1992.

Phillips, William D., Jr. "Testaments in the Spanish world in the Early Modern pe-riod." In *Historia del derecho privado,* edited by M. J. Peláez, 2965–80. Barcelona: Promociones Publicaciones Universitarias, 1989.

Pizzigoni, Caterina, ed. and trans. *Testaments of Toluca.* Stanford: Stanford Univer-sity Press, 2006.

Platt, Tristan, Therese Bouysee-Cassagne, and Harris Olivia, eds. *Qaraqara-Charca. Mallku, Inca y Rey en la provincia de Charcas (siglos XVI–XVII). Historia antrop-ológica de una confederación Aymara.* La Paz: Plural, 2006.

Pollack, Aaron. *Levantamiento K'iche' en Totonicapán, 1820: Los lugares de las políticas subalternas.* Guatemala City: Avansco, 2008.

Porras Barrenechea, Raúl, ed. *Una relación inédita de la conquista: la crónica de Diego de Trujillo.* Lima: Universidad Nacional Mayor de San Marcos, 1970.

Powell, Philip Wayne. "North America's First Frontier, 1546–1603." In *Essays on Frontiers in World History,* edited by George Wolfskill and Stanley Palmer, 11–31. College Station, TX: Texas A&M University Press, 1983.

Powers, Karen Vieira. "A Battle of Wills: Inventing Chiefly Legitimacy in the Colo-nial North Andes." In *Dead Giveaways. Indigenous Testaments of Colonial Meso-america and the Andes,* edited by Susan Kellogg and Matthew Restall, 183–214. Salt Lake City: University of Utah Press, 1998.

———. *Women in the Crucible of Conquest: The Gendered Genesis of Spanish Ameri-can Society, 1500–1600.* Albuquerque: University of New Mexico Press, 2005.

Premo, Bianca. *The Enlightenment on Trial: Ordinary Litigants and Colonialism in the Spanish Empire.* New York: Oxford University Press, 2017.

———. "From the Pockets of Women: The Gendering of the Mita, Migration and Tribute in Colonial Chucuito, Peru." *Americas* 57, no.1 (July 2000): 63–93.

———. "On Currents and Comparisons: Gender and the Atlantic 'Turn' in Spanish America." *History Compass* 8, no. 3 (March 2010): 223–37.

Presta, Ana María. "Detrás de la mejor dote, una encomienda. Hijas y viudas de la primera generación de encomenderos en el mercado matrimonial de Charcas, 1534–48." *Revista Andes* 8 (1997): 27–46.

———. "Doña Isabel Sisa: A Sixteenth-Century Indian Woman Resisting Gender Inequalities." In *The Human Tradition in Colonial Latin America*, edited by Kenneth J. Andrien, 35–50. Wilmington, DE: Scholarly Resources, 2002.

———. "Portraits of Four Women: Traditional Female Roles and Transgressions in Colonial Elite Families in Charcas, 1550–1600." *Colonial Latin American Review* 9, no. 2 (December 2000): 237–62.

Puertas, Elizabeth. "La mujer frente al poder en la sociedad colonial peruana (siglos XVI–XVIII)." In *La mujer en la historia del Perú (siglos XV al XX)*, edited by Carmen Meza and Teodoro Hampe, 147–88. Lima: Fondo Editorial del Congreso, 2007.

Ramírez, Susan E. "The 'Dueño de Indios': Thoughts on the Consequences of the Shifting Bases of Power of the 'Curaca de los Viejos Antiguos' under the Spanish in Sixteenth-Century Peru." *Hispanic American Historical Review* 67, no. 4 (November 1987): 575–610.

———. "Historia y memoria: la construcción de las tradiciones dinásticas andinas." *Revista de Indias* 66, no. 236 (2006): 13–56.

———. *Provincial Patriarchs: Land Tenure and the Economics of Power in Colonial Peru*. Albuquerque: University of New Mexico Press, 1986.

———. "Rich Man, Poor Man, Beggar Man, or Chief." In *Dead Giveaways: Indigenous Testaments in Colonial Spanish America*, edited by Susan Kellogg and Matthew Restall, 215–48. Salt Lake City: University of Utah, 1998.

———. *To Feed and Be Fed: The Cosmological Bases of Authority and Identity in the Andes*. Stanford: Stanford University Press, 2005.

———. *The World Upside Down: Cross-Cultural Contact and Conflict in Sixteenth-Century Peru*. Stanford: Stanford University Press, 1998.

Ramírez Montes, Guillerma. *Niñas, doncellas, vírgenes eternas: Santa Clara de Querétaro (1607–1864)*. Mexico City: Universidad Nacional Autónoma de México, 2005.

Ramos, Gabriela. "El rastro de la discriminación. Litigios y probanzas de caciques en el Perú colonial temprano." *Fronteras de la Historia* 21, no.1 (June 2016): 64–88.

Ramos, Gabriela, and Yanna Yannakakis, eds. *Indigenous Intellectuals: Knowledge, Power, and Colonial Culture in Mexico and the Andes*. Durham, NC: Duke University Press, 2014.

Ramos de Cárdenas, Francisco. "Relación de Querétaro." In *Michoacán*, 215–45. Vol. 9 of *Relaciones geográficas del siglo XVI*, edited by René Acuña. Mexico City: Universidad Nacional Autónoma de México, Instituto de Investigaciones Antropológicas, 1987.

Ramos Zambrano, Augusto. *J. D. Choquehuanca. El cantor de Bolívar. Los Chukiwanka y sus testamentos*, edited by Jessica Bendezú and Margarita Salazar. Lima: A. F. A. Editores, 2012.

———. "Los Choquehuanca de Azángaro en el proceso de la Independencia nacional." In *Pueblos, provincias y regiones en la historia del Perú*, edited by Jessica Bendezú and Margarita Salazar, 617–39. Lima: Academia Nacional de la Historia, 2006.

Real Academia Española. *Diccionario de la Lengua Española*. 23rd ed. Madrid: Real Academia Española, 2014. https://dle.rae.es/.

"Real Cédula que se considere a los descendientes de caciques como nobles en su raza." In *Colección de documentos para la historia de la formación social de Hispanoamérica (1493–1810)*, edited by Richard Konetzke, 2:66–69. Madrid: Consejo Superior de Investigaciones Científicas, 1953.

Reeves, René. *Ladinos with Ladinos, Indians with Indians: Land, Labor, and Regional Ethnic Conflict in the Making of Guatemala*. Stanford: Stanford University Press, 2006.

Restall, Matthew. *Life and Death in a Maya Community: The Ixil Testaments of the 1760s*. Lancaster: Labyrinthos, 1995.

———. *The Maya World: Yucatec Culture and Society, 1550–1850*. Stanford: Stanford University Press, 1999.

———. "The People of the Patio: Ethnohistorical Evidence of Yucatec Maya Royal Courts." In *Data and Case Studies*, edited by Takeshi Inomata and Stephen D. Houston, 335–90. Vol. 2 of *Royal Courts of the Ancient Maya*. Boulder: Westview Press, 2001.

Restall, Matthew, and Kris Lane. *Latin America in Colonial Times*. 2nd ed. New York: Cambridge University Press, 2018.

Restall, Matthew, Lisa Sousa, and Kevin Terraciano, eds. *Mesoamerican Voices: Native-Language Writings from Colonial Mexico, Oaxaca, Yucatan, and Guatemala*. Cambridge: Cambridge University Press, 2005.

Reyes García, Luis. *Cómo te confundes? Acaso no somos conquistadores?: Anales de Juan Bautista*. Mexico City: Centro de Investigaciones y Estudios Superiores en Antropología Social, 2001.

Rodríguez Demorizi, Emilio. *Los dominicos y las encomiendas de indios de la Isla Española*. Santo Domingo: Editora del Caribe, 1971.

Rostworowski de Diez Canseco, María. *Costa peruana prehispánica*. Lima: Instituto de Estudios Peruanos, 1989.

———. *Curacas y sucesiones. Costa norte*. Lima: Minerva, 1961.

———. *Doña Francisca Pizarro: Una ilustre mestiza, 1534–1598*. Lima: Instituto de Estudios Peruanos, 1989.

———. *Estructuras andinas del poder: Ideología religiosa y política*. Lima: Instituto de Estudios Peruanos, 2007.

———. *Etnia y sociedad. Costa peruana prehispánica*. Lima: Instituto de Estudios Peruanos, 1977.

———. "La estratificación social y el Hatun Curaca en el mundo andino." *Histórica* 1, no. 2 (1977): 249–86.

———. "La mujer en el Perú prehispánico." *Instituto de Estudios Peruanos Documento de Trabajo* 72 (1995).

———. "Los curacas costeños." *Histórica* 23, no. 2 (1999): 283–311.

———. *Recursos naturales renovables y pesca, siglos XVI y XVII. Curacas y sucesiones, costa norte.* Lima: Instituto de Estudios Peruanos, 2005.

———. *Señoríos indígenas de Lima y Canta.* Lima: Instituto de Estudios Peruanos, 1978.

———. "Succession, Coöptation to Kingship, and Royal Incest Among the Inca." *Southwestern Journal of Anthropology* 16, no. 4 (1960): 417–27.

Roulet, Florencia. "De cautivos a aliados: los 'indios fronterizos' de Mendoza (1780–1806)." *Xama* 12–14 (1999–2001): 199–239.

———. "Embajadoras y hechiceras indígenas. El poder de las mujeres en la frontera sur." *Todo es Historia* 489 (April 2008): 6–24.

———. "Guerra y diplomacia en la frontera de Mendoza: la política indígena del comandante José Francisco de Amigorena (1779–1799)." In *Funcionarios, diplomáticos, guerreros: Miradas hacia el otro en las fronteras de Pampa y Patagonia (siglos XVIII y XIX)*, edited by Lidia Nacuzzi, 65–118. Buenos Aires: Sociedad Argentina de Antropología, 2002.

———. *Huincas en tierra de indios. Mediaciones e identidades en los relatos de viajeros tardocoloniales.* Buenos Aires: Eudeba, 2016.

———. "Mujeres, rehenes y secretarios: Mediadores indígenas en la frontera sur del Río de la Plata durante el período hispánico." *Colonial Latin American Review* 18, no. 3 (December 2009): 303–37.

———. "Violencia indígena en el Río de la Plata durante el período colonial temprano: un intento de explicación." *Nuevo Mundo Mundos Nuevos*, online (2018). https://doi.org/10.4000/nuevomundo.72018.

Rubio Semper, Agustín. "Piedad, honras fúnebres y legados piadosos en Aragón (Calatayud) en la Baja Edad Media." In *Muerte, religiosidad y cutura popular: siglos XIII-XVIII*, edited by Eliseo Serrano Martín, 241–77 (Zaragoza: Instituto Fernando El Católico, 1994).

Ruiz, Teofilo. *From Heaven to Earth: The Reordering of Castilian Society, 1150–1350.* Princeton: Princeton University Press, 2004.

———. *Spanish Society, 1400–1600.* Harlow, England: Pearson Education, 2001.

Ruiz de Arce, Juan. "Advertencias de Juan Ruiz de Arce a sus subcesores." In *Tres Testigos de La Conquista Del Perú: Hernando Pizarro, Juan Ruiz de Arce y Diego de Trujillo*, 3rd ed., edited by Conde Miguel Muñoz de San Pedro Canilleros, 67–115. 1545. Reprint, Madrid: Espasa Calpe, 1964.

Saitō, Akira, and Claudia Rosas Lauro. *Reducciones: La concentración forzada de las poblaciones indígenas en el Virreinato del Perú.* Lima: Pontificia Universidad Católica del Perú and National Museum of Ethnology, 2017.

Sala i Vila, Nuria. "Indígena y abogado: el caso de José Domingo Choquehuanca de Azángaro." *Histórica* 42, no. 2 (2018): 43–88.

———. *Y se armó el tole tole. Tributo indígena y movimientos sociales en el virreinato del Perú, 1790–1814.* Arequipa: Instituto de Estudios Regionales José María Arguedas, 1996.

Salerno, Natalia. "Cautivas indígenas. Abusos, violencia y malos tratos en el Buenos Aires colonial." In *Devastación: Violencia civilizada contra los indios de las llanuras del Plata y Sur de Chile (siglos XVI a XIX)*, compiled by Sebastián Alioto, Juan F. Jiménez, and Daniel Villar, 237–57. Buenos Aires: Prohistoria: 2018.

Salles-Reese, Verónica. *From Viracocha to the Virgin of Copacabana*. Austin: University of Texas Press, 2010.

Salles, Estela Cristina, and Héctor Omar Noejovich. "La herencia femenina andina prehispánica y su transformación en el mundo colonial." *Bulletin de l'Institut Français d'Études Andines* 35, no. 1 (April 2006): 37–53.

Salinas, María Laura and Julio Folkenand. *Cartas Anuas de la Provincia Jesuítica del Paraguay: 1714–1720, 1720–1730, 1730–1735, 1735–1743, 1750–1756, 1756–1762*. Asunción, Paraguay: Centro de Estudios Antropológicos de la Universidad Católica, 2016.

Salomon, Frank. "Indian Women of Early Colonial Quito as Seen through Their Testaments." *Americas* 44, no. 3 (1988): 325–41.

———. "Indian Women of Early Colonial Quito as Seen through Their Testaments." *Americas* 44, no. 3 (1988): 325–41.

———. *Native Lords of Quito in the Age of the Incas: The Political Economy of North-Andean Chiefdoms*. New York: Cambridge University Press, 1986.

———. "Shamanism and Politics in Late-Colonial Ecuador." *American Ethnologist* 10, no. 3 (1983): 413–28.

Sánchez Labrador, Joseph. *Los Indios Pampas, Puelches, Patagones*. Buenos Aires: Viau y Zona, 1936.

Santa Cruz Pachacuti Salcamaygua, Joan de. *Relación de las antiguedades deste reyno del Piru: Estudio ethnohistórico y linguístico*. Edited by Pierre Duviols and César Itier. Lima: Institut Français d'Etudes Andines y Centro de Estudios Regionales Andinos Bartolomé de las Casas, 1993.

Santillán, Hernando de. "Relación del orígen, descendencia, política y gobierno de los Incas." In *Crónicas peruanas de interés indígena*, edited by E. Barba, 97–149. Vol. 209 of *Biblioteca de autores españoles*. Madrid: Atlas, 1968.

Santillana, Julián Idilio. "La Centinela: Un asentamiento Inka-Chincha. Rasgos arquitectónicos estatales y locales." *Arqueología y Sociedad* 10 (1984): 13–32.

Sarabia Viejo, Maria Justina. *Francisco de Toledo: Disposiciones gubernativas para el virreinato del Perú*. 2 vols. Sevilla: Escuela de Estudios Hispano-Americanos de Sevilla, 1986.

Schmidl, Ulrich. *Viaje al Río de la Plata, 1534–1554*. 1567. Reprint, Buenos Aires: Cabaut y Cía., 1903.

Schröder, Jan "Legal Scholarship: The Theory of Sources and Methods of Law." In *The Oxford Handbook of European Legal History*, edited by Heikki Pihlajamäki, Markus D. Dubber, and Mark Godfrey, 551–65. Oxford: Oxford University Press, 2018.

Schroeder, Susan. "The Noblewomen of Chalco." *Estudios de Cultura Nahuatl* 22 (1992): 45–86.

Schroeder, Susan, Stephanie Wood, and Robert Haskett, eds. *Indian Women of Early Mexico*. Norman: University of Oklahoma Press, 1997.

Schwaller, John Frederick. "The Brothers Fernando de Alva Ixtlilxochitl and Bartolomé de Alva: Two 'Native' Intellectuals of Seventeenth-Century Mexico." In

Indigenous Intellectuals: Knowledge, Power, and Colonial Culture in Mexico and the Andes, edited by Gabriela Ramos and Yanna Yannakakis, 39–59. Durham, NC: Duke University Press, 2014.

Schwaller, Robert C. *Géneros de Gente in Early Colonial Mexico: Defining Racial Difference*. Norman: University of Oklahoma Press, 2016.

Seed, Patricia. "Marriage Promises and the Value of a Woman's Testimony in Colonial Mexico." *Signs* 13, no. 2 (Winter 1988): 253–76.

———. *To Love, Honor, and Obey in Colonial Mexico: Conflicts over Marriage Choice, 1574–1821*. Stanford: Stanford University Press, 1988.

Seijas, Tatiana. *Asian Slaves in Colonial Mexico: From Chinos to Indians*. New York: Cambridge University Press, 2014.

Sell, Barry D., Louise M. Burkhart, and Elizabeth R. Wright, eds. *Spanish Golden Age Drama in Mexican Translation*. Vol. 3 of *Nahuatl Theater*. Norman: University of Oklahoma Press, 2008.

Sellers-García, Sylvia. *Distance and Documents at the Spanish Empire's Periphery*. Stanford: Stanford University Press, 2014.

Septién y Septién, Manuel. *Obras de Manuel Septién y Septién*. 5 vols. Santiago de Querétaro: Gobierno del Estado de Querétaro, 1999.

Sheptak, Russell N. "Moving Masca: Persistent Indigenous Communities in Spanish Colonial Honduras." In *Indigenous Persistence in the Colonized Americas: Material and Documentary Perspectives on Entanglement*, edited by Heather Law Pezzarossi and Russell N. Sheptak, 19–38. Albuquerque: University of New Mexico Press, 2019.

Sherman, William. *Forced Native Labor in Sixteenth-Century Central America*. Lincoln: University of Nebraska Press, 1979.

Silverblatt, Irene. *Moon, Sun, and Witches: Gender Ideologies and Class in Inca and Colonial Peru*. Princeton: Princeton University Press, 1987.

Sinclair, Thomson. *We Alone Will Rule: Native Andean Politics in the Age of Insurgency*. Madison: University of Wisconsin Press, 2002.

Smith, Michael E., Abhishek Chatterjee, Angela C. Huster, Sierra Stewart, and Marion Forest. "Apartment Compounds, Households, and Population in the Ancient City of Teotihuacan, Mexico." *Ancient Mesoamerica* 30 (2019): 399–418.

Socolow, Susan Migden. *The Women of Colonial Latin America*. 2nd ed. New York: Cambridge University Press, 2015.

Solórzano y Pereira, Juan de. *Política Indiana*. 2 vols. Madrid: Fundación Antonio de Castro, 1996.

Somohano Martínez, Lourdes. *La versión histórica de la conquista y la organización política del pueblo de indios de Querétaro*. Querétaro, Mexico: Instituto Tecnológico y de Estudios Superiores de Monterrey-Querétaro, 2003.

Sousa, Lisa. *The Woman Who Turned into a Jaguar and Other Narratives of Native Women in Archives of Colonial Mexico*. Stanford: Stanford University Press, 2017.

Sousa, Lisa, and Kevin Terraciano. "The 'Original Conquest' of Oaxaca: Nahua and Mixtec Accounts of the Spanish Conquest." *Ethnohistory* 50, no. 2 (Spring 2003): 349–400.

Spalding, Karen. "Kurakas and Commerce: A Chapter in the Evolution of Andean Society." *Hispanic American Historical Review* 53, no. 4 (November 1973): 581–99.

———. *Huarochirí: An Andean Society Under Inca and Spanish Rule.* Stanford: Stanford University Press, 1984.

———. "Social Climbers: Changing Patterns of Mobility Among the Indians of Colonial Peru." *Hispanic American Historical Review* 50, no. 4 (November 1970): 645–64.

Spores, Ronald. "Mixteca *Cacicas*: Status, Wealth, and the Political Accommodation of Native Elite Women in Early Colonial Oaxaca." In *Indian Women of Early Mexico*, edited by Susan Schroeder, Stephanie Wood, and Robert Haskett, 185–97. Norman: University of Oklahoma Press, 1997.

———. *The Mixtec Kings and their People.* Norman: University of Oklahoma Press, 1967.

Stanish, Charles. *Ancient Titicaca: The Evolution of Complex Society in Southern Peru and Northern Bolivia.* Berkeley: University of California Press, 2003.

Stavig, Ward and Ella Schmidt. *The Tupac Amaru and Catarista Rebellions: An Anthology of Sources.* Indianapolis: Hackett, 2008.

Stern, Steve. *Peru's Indian Peoples and the Challenge of Spanish Conquest: Huamanga to 1640.* Madison: University of Wisconsin Press, 1982.

Super, John C. *La vida en Querétaro durante la colonia, 1531–1810.* Mexico City: Fondo de Cultura Economica, 1983.

———. "Querétaro: Society and Economy in Early Provincial Mexico, 1590–1630." PhD diss., University of California, Los Angeles, 1973.

Szeminzki, Jan. *La Utopía tupamarista.* 2nd ed. Lima: Pontificia Universidad Católica del Peru, 1993.

Tanodi, Aurelio, trans. and comp. *Documentos de la real hacienda de Puerto Rico.* Vol. 1, *1510–1519.* San Juan: Universidad de Puerto Rico, 1971.

Taylor, William B. *Drinking, Homicide, and Rebellion in Colonial Mexican Villages.* Stanford: Stanford University Press, 1979.

Tedlock, Barbara. *Time and the Highland Maya.* Rev. ed. Albuquerque: University of New Mexico Press, 1992.

Terraciano, Kevin. "Crime and Culture in Colonial Mexico: The Case of the Mixtec Murder Note." *Ethnohistory* 45, no. 4 (Fall 1998): 709–45.

———. *The Mixtecs of Colonial Oaxaca: Ñudzahui History, Sixteenth through Eighteenth Centuries.* Stanford: Stanford University Press, 2001.

Tieffemberg, Silvia. *Argentina. Historia del descubrimiento y conquista del Río de la Plata de Ruy Díaz de Guzmán.* Buenos Aires: editorial de la Facultad de Filosofía y Letras, 2012. http://publicaciones.filo.uba.ar/sites/publicaciones.filo.uba.ar/files/Argentina. Historia del Descubrimiento y Conquista del Río de la Plata de Ruy Díaz de Guzmán_interactivo.pdf.

Torquemada, Juan de. *Monarquía indiana: De los veinte y un libros rituales y monarquía indiana [. . .].* 3rd ed. Vol. 6. Mexico City: Universidad Nacional Autónoma de México, Instituto de Investigaciones Históricas, 1978.

Torre Revello. *El libro, la imprenta y el periodismo.* Mexico City: Universidad Nacional Autónoma de México, 1940.

Townsend, Camilla. *Malintzin's Choices: An Indian Woman in the Conquest of Mexico.* Albuquerque: University of New Mexico Press, 2006.

——. "Polygyny and the Divided Altepetl: The Tetzcocan Key to Pre-conquest Nahua Politics." In *Texcoco: Prehispanic and Colonial Perspectives,* edited by Jongsoo Lee and Galen Brokaw, 93–116. Boulder: University Press of Colorado, 2014.

Trouillot, Michel-Rolph. *Silencing the Past. Power and the Production of History.* Boston: Beacon Press, 1995.

Trujillo, Diego de. *Una relación inédita de la conquista: la crónica de Diego de Trujillo,* edited by Raúl Porras Barrenechea. Lima: Universidad Nacional Mayor de San Marcos, 1970.

Truitt, Jonathan. *Sustaining the Divine in Mexico Tenochtitlan: Nahuas and Catholicism, 1523–1700.* Norman: University of Oklahoma Press, 2018.

Turpo, Fortunato. *El templo de oro y los Choquehuanca.* Azángaro, Peru: Bicentenario de la Independencia, 1945.

Tutino, John. *Making a New World: Founding Capitalism in the Bajío and Spanish North America.* Durham, NC: Duke University Press, 2011.

Twinam, Ann. "Pedro de Ayarza: The Purchase of Whiteness." In *The Human Tradition in Colonial Latin America,* 2nd ed., edited by Kenneth J. Andrien, 215–37. Lanham: Rowman & Littlefield, 2013.

——. *Public Lives, Private Secrets: Gender, Honor, Sexuality, and Illegitimacy in Colonial Spanish America.* Stanford: Stanford University Press, 1999.

——. *Purchasing Whiteness: Pardos, Mulattos, and the Quest for Social Mobility in the Spanish Indies.* Stanford: Stanford University Press, 2015.

Uceda Castillo, Santiago, curator. "Le Pérou avant les Incas." Exhibition, Musée du quai Branly-Jacques Chirac, Paris, 2017–18.

Uribe-Uran, Victor M. *Fatal Love: Spousal Killers, Law, and Punishment in the Late Colonial Spanish Atlantic.* Stanford: Stanford University Press, 2015.

Van Caenegem, R. C. "History of European Civil Procedure." In *Civil Procedure: International Encyclopedia of Comparative Law,* edited by Mauro Capelletti, 2–79. New York: Oceana Publications, 1972.

Varón Gabai, Rafael. *Curacas y encomenderos: acomodamiento nativo en Huaraz, siglos XVI y XVII.* Lima: P. L. Villanueva, 1980.

——. *La ilusión del poder. Apogeo y decadencia de los Pizarro en la conquista del Perú.* Lima: Instituto de Estudios Peruanos, Instituto Francés de Estudios Andinos, 1997.

Vega Bolaños, Andrés, *Colección Somoza: Documentos para la historia de Nicaragua, 1504–1550.* 17 vols. Madrid: Imprenta Viuda de Galo Sáez; Imprenta Sagrado Corazón Juan Bravo, 1954–57.

Velasco Murillo, Dana. "The Eighty-Year's War of Indigenous Attrition." Paper presented at the 63rd Annual Meeting of the American Society for Ethnohistory, Winnipeg, MB, October 12, 2017).

———. "Laboring Above Ground: Indigenous Women in New Spain's Silver Mining District, Zacatecas, Mexico, 1620–1770." *Hispanic American Historical Review* 93, no. 1 (February 2013): 3–32.

Vértiz, Juan José de. "Memorias." *Revista del Archivo General de Buenos Aires* 3 (1871): 411–29.

Villadiego Vascuñana y Montoy, Alonso de. *Instrucción política y práctica judicial: conforme al estilo de los consejos, audiencias y tribunales de corte.* Madrid: Oficina de Antonio Morin, 1766.

Villamarín, Juan. "Chiefdoms: The Prevalence and Persistence of 'señoríos naturales,' 1400 to European Conquest." In *South America,* edited by Frank Salomon and Stuart Schwartz, 577–667. Vol. 3 of *The Cambridge History of the Native Peoples of the Americas.* Cambridge: Cambridge University Press, 1999.

———. "Kinship and Inheritance among the Sabana de Bogota Chibcha at the time of Spanish Conquest." *Ethnology* 14, no. 2 (1975): 173–79.

Villella, Peter B. *Indigenous Elites and Creole Identity in Colonial Mexico, 1500–1800.* New York: Cambridge University Press, 2016.

———. "'Pure and Noble Indians Untainted by Inferior or Idolatrous Races': Native Elites and the Discourse of Blood Purity in Late Colonial Mexico." *Hispanic American Historical Review* 91, no.4 (2011): 633–63.

Von Germeten, Nicole. *Profit and Passion: Transactional Sex in Colonial Mexico.* Oakland: University of California Press, 2018.

Von Wobeser, Gisela. "La función social y económica de las capellanías de misas en la Nueva España del siglo XVIII." *Estudios de Historia Novohispana* 16 (1996): 119–38.

Wachtel, Nathan. *The Vision of the Vanquished: The Spanish Conquest of Peru Through Indian Eyes, 1530–1570.* Hassocks, Sussex : Harvester Press, 1977.

Wagley, Charles. *The Social and Religious Life of a Guatemalan Village.* Menasha, WI: American Anthropological Association, 1949.

Walker, Charles. *Smoldering Ashes: Cuzco and the Creation of Republican Peru, 1780–1840.* Durham, NC: Duke University Press, 1999.

———. *The Tupac Amaru Rebellion.* Cambridge, MA: Harvard, 2014.

Wasserstrom, Robert. *Class and Society in Central Chiapas.* Berkeley: University of California Press, 1983.

Weber, David J. *Bárbaros. Spaniards and their Savages in the Age of Enlightenment.* New Haven: Yale University Press, 2005.

Werner, Patrick S. *Epoca temprana de León Viejo: Una historia de la primera capital de Nicaragua.* Managua, Nicaragua: Instituto de Cultura, 2000.

———, ed. *Ethnohistory of Early Colonial Nicaragua: Demography and Encomiendas of the Indian Communities.* Institute for Mesoamerican Studies, Occasional Paper 4. Albany: State University of New York, 2000. https://www.albany.edu/ims/Publications/Occasional Publications/4_IMS_OcPub4_Final.pdf.

———. *Etnohistoria de la Nicaragua temprana.* Managua, Nicaragua: Lea Grupo Editorial, 2009.

———. *Los Reales De Minas Y la Ciudad Perdida de Nueva Segovia.* Managua, Nicaragua: Instituto de Cultura, 1996.

White, Richard. *The Middle Ground: Indians, Empires, and Republics in the Great Lakes Region, 1650–1815*. New York: Cambridge University Press, 1991.

Wightman, Ann W. *Indigenous Migration and Social Change: The Forasteros of Cuzco, 1570–1720*. Durham, NC: Duke University Press, 1990.

Wilson, Samuel M. *Hispaniola: Caribbean Chiefdoms in the Age of Columbus*. Tuscaloosa: University of Alabama Press, 1990.

Wood, Stephanie. "Matters of Life and Death: Nahuatl Testaments of Rural Women, 1589–1801." In *Indian Women of Early Mexico*, edited by Susan Schroeder, Stephanie Wood, and Robert Haskett, 165–82. Norman: University of Oklahoma Press, 1997.

Woodward, Ralph Lee, Jr. "Changes in the Nineteenth-Century Guatemalan State and Its Indian Policies." In *Guatemalan Indians and the State: 1540–1988*, edited by Carol A. Smith, 52–71. Austin: University of Texas Press, 1994.

Wortman, Miles. *Government and Society in Central America, 1680–1840*. New York: Columbia University Press, 1982.

Wright Carr, David Charles. *La conquista del Bajío y los orígenes de San Miguel de Allende*. Mexico City: Fondo de Cultura Económica, 1998.

———. *Conquistadores otomíes en la Guerra Chichimeca*. Querétaro, Mexico: Gobierno del Estado de Querétaro, 1988.

———, ed. *Querétaro en el siglo XVI: Fuentes documentales primarias*. Querétaro, Mexico: Gobierno del Estado de Querétaro, 1989.

Wu, Celia. "The Population of the City of Querétaro in 1791." *Journal of Latin American Studies* 16, no. 2 (November 1984): 277–307.

Yannakakis, Yanna. *The Art of Being In-between: Native Intermediaries, Indian Identity, and Local Rule in Colonial Oaxaca*. Durham, NC: Duke University Press, 2008.

———. "Hablar para distintos públicos: testigos zapotecos y resistencia a la reforma parroquial en Oaxaca en el siglo XVIII." *Historia Mexicana* 55, no. 3 (January–March 2006): 833–93.

———. "Indigenous People and Legal Culture in Spanish America." *History Compass* 11, no. 11 (November 2013): 931–47.

———. "Witnesses, Spatial Practices, and Land Dispute in Colonial Oaxaca." *Americas* 65, no. 2 (October 2008):161–92.

Zantwijk, Rudoph van. *The Aztec Arrangement: The Social History of Pre-Spanish Mexico*. Norman: University of Oklahoma Press, 1985.

Zavala, José Manuel. *Les Indiens Mapuche du Chili. Dynamiques inter-ethniques et stratégies de résistance, XVIIIe siècle*. Paris: L'Harmattan, 2000.

Zelaá e Hidalgo, Joseph María and Carlos de Sigüenza y Góngora. *Glorias de Querétaro, en la fundación y admirables progresos de la muy 1. y venerable congregación eclesiástica de presbíteros seculares de María Santísitma de Guadalupe de México*. Mexico City: Oficina de D. Mariano Joseph de Zúñiga y Ontiveros, 1803.

Zevallos Quiñones, Jorge. *Los cacicazgos de Lambayeque*. Trujillo, Peru: Gráfica Cuatro, 1989.

Zizur, Pablo. "Diario que yo don Pablo Zizur Primer Piloto de la Real Armada boi á hacer desde la ciudad de Buenos Aires hasta los establecimientos nuestros en la

Costa Patagónica; por comisión del Excelentísimo Señor Virrey; a fin de conducir varios indios y indias para entregar al cacique Lorenzo, tratar con éste y sus
aliados las pases, y inspeccionar la campaña." *Revista del Archivo General de la
Nación* 3, no. 3 (1973): 67–116.

Zubillaga, Félix, ed. *Monumenta Mexicana.* 8 vols. Rome: Institutum Historicum
Societate Iesu, 1956–91.

Zuidema, R. Tom. *La civilisation Inca au Cuzco.* Paris: Presses Universitaires de
France, 1986.

Zuloaga, Marina. *La conquista negociada: Guarangas, autoridades locales e imperio
en Huaylas, Perú (1532–1610).* Lima: Instituto de Estudios Peruanos-Instituto
Francés de Estudios Andinos, 2012.

Contributors

Ida Altman (Ph.D., Johns Hopkins University, 1982) is Professor Emerita of History, University of Florida. She is the author, coauthor, or editor of books and articles on the early modern Spanish empire, including the history of early Mexico, the Caribbean, and the Atlantic world. She is the author of *Emigrants and Society: Extremadura and Spanish America in the Sixteenth Century* (1989); *Transatlantic Ties in the Spanish Empire* (2000); *The Early History of Greater Mexico* (2003), coauthored with Sarah Cline and Juan Javier Pescador; *The War for Mexico's West: Spaniards and Indians in New Galicia, 1524–1550* (2010); and *Contesting Conquest: Indigenous Perspectives on the Spanish Occupation of Nueva Galicia, 1524–1550* (2017); and is coeditor, with David Wheat, of *The Spanish Caribbean and the Atlantic World in the Long Sixteenth Century* (2019). She twice received fellowships from the National Endowment for the Humanities, and her book *Emigrants and Society* is a cowinner of the Bolton-Johnson Prize from the Conference on Latin American History.

Bradley Benton is Associate Professor of History at North Dakota State University. He is the author of *The Lords of Tetzcoco: The Transformation of Indigenous Rule in Postconquest Central Mexico* (2017). He is also coeditor and cotranslator of *The Native Conquistador: Alva Ixtlilxochitl's Account of the Conquest of Mexico* (2015) and *History of the Chichimeca Nation: Don Fernando de Alva Ixtlilxochitl's Seventeenth-Century Chronicle of Ancient Mexico* (2019). He is a member of the editorial board of the journal *Ethnohistory* and a contributing editor of the Library of Congress's *Handbook of Latin American Studies.*

Chantal Caillavet, who was educated at the École Normale Supérieure at Fontenay (Paris), holds an *agrégation* and received a doctorate from the University of Bordeaux for her thesis "Ethnohistoire des communautés indiennes d'Otavalo, Andes de l'Équateur" (2009). For many years she was with the National Centre of Scientific Research in Paris, where she worked as an ethnohistorian specializing in the northern Andes during the pre-Hispanic and contact periods. Her other main research interest is cultural history, pursued through studies of Spanish and Latin American interactions. She is the author of *Etnias del Norte: Etnohistoria e Historia de Ecuador* (2000) and is coauthor and joint editor, with Susan E. Ramírez, of *Dinámicas del poder: Historia y actualidad de la autoridad andina* (2008), a monographic issue of the *Bulletin de l'Institut Français d'Études Andines*. She has published numerous articles in French, Spanish, and English.

Mónica Díaz is Associate Professor of Hispanic Studies and History at the University of Kentucky. She is the author of *Indigenous Writings from the Convent: Negotiating Ethnic Autonomy in Colonial Mexico* (2010), the coeditor, with Rocío Quispe-Agnoli, of *Women's Negotiations and Textual Agency in Latin America, 1500–1799* (2017), and the editor of *To Be Indio in Colonial Spanish America* (2017). She has published numerous articles and book chapters on the natives of colonial Mexico, gender, and religion. Her research has been funded by grants from the National Endowment for the Humanities, the Ministry for Cultural Cooperation between Spain and the United States, the Newberry Library, the Lilly Library, and the Fulbright-García Robles scholarship program.

Karen B. Graubart is Associate Professor of History, Gender Studies, and Romance Literatures and Languages at the University of Notre Dame. She is the author of *With Our Labor and Sweat: Indigenous Women and the Formation of Colonial Society in Peru, 1550–1700* (2007) as well as articles in *Hispanic American Historical Review, Slavery and Abolition, Colonial Latin American Review,* and other journals. Her work has been supported by the National Endowment for the Humanities, the American Council of Learned Societies, the John Carter Brown Library, Fulbright, and other institutions. She is currently completing a new monograph on the transatlantic meaning of "republic" in the early modern Iberian world, as well as work on enslaved men and women's lives and mentalities.

Sara Vicuña Guengerich is Associate Professor of Spanish at Texas Tech University. She specializes in the literature and history of the colonial Andes. She has published numerous articles and chapters devoted to the analysis of colonial subaltern subjects (women, Indians, and Blacks) in colonial manuscripts in the context of the Spanish conquest and colonization of Peru and its connections to the early modern Atlantic world. Her research has received funding from such institutions as the John Carter Brown Library and the Newberry Library. Her current book project, "Daughters of the Inca Conquest: Inca Women under Spanish Rule," explores the role of indigenous noblewomen in the delineation of a neo-Inca identity, key to preserving this group's cohesiveness during the colonial period.

Renzo Honores teaches law at the Universidad Peruana de Ciencias Aplicadas in Lima and is also a researcher at the Instituto Internacional de Derecho y Sociedad. His main field of study is the history of the legal profession and litigation in the Habsburg Andes. Currently he is finishing a book manuscript on litigation and legal culture in the city of Lima, tentatively titled "Legal Polyphony in the Colonial Andes: Professionals, Litigants, and the Legal Culture in the City of Lima, 1538–1640."

Catherine Komisaruk is Associate Professor of History at the University of Texas in San Antonio. She is the author of *Labor and Love in Guatemala: The Eve of Independence* (2013), and her articles have appeared in the journals *Biography*, *Labor*, and *Hispanic American Historical Review*. Currently she is writing a book about indigenous families, migration, and activism in colonial Guatemala and Mexico.

Margarita R. Ochoa is Associate Professor of History at Loyola Marymount University in Los Angeles, California. Her research focuses on the indigenous peoples of colonial Mexico and the intersections of gender, identity, and law. She is currently writing a book that explores the constructs of native families in the late colonial and early national periods of Mexico City. She is coeditor of *City Indians in Spain's American Empire* (2012) and author of several articles and chapters on natives in colonial Latin America, gender, and the history of emotions.

Liliana Pérez Miguel teaches history at the Pontificia Universidad Católica del Perú in Lima. She received a PhD in history from the University of Burgos, Spain. Her dissertation on the *encomenderas* in viceregal Peru was awarded the Nuestra América 2018 prize for best monograph and will be published as *Mujeres ricas y libres: Encomenderas en el Perú (1532–1600)* in 2020. Her research focuses on women's history as well as *encomiendas* and religious institutions in the Peruvian viceroyalty and in Atlantic history. She has received several research grants from renowned institutions, including the John Carter Brown Library, the Huntington Library, and the Spanish Agency for International Cooperation (Spanish Ministry of Foreign Affairs).

Florencia Roulet is an Argentinian scholar living in Switzerland. She holds a Bachelor in History from University of Buenos Aires, a master's in international relations from the Graduate Institute, Geneva, and a PhD in Anthropology from the University of Buenos Aires. She works in the fields of ethnohistory and human rights of indigenous peoples. In the past two decades, she has conducted research on the diplomatic relations between the Spanish colonial state and indigenous peoples of the pampas and northern Patagonia, focusing on indigenous go-betweens, ethnic identities, native diplomatic protocols, interethnic forms of violence, and the role of indigenous women in native politics. She is a member of TEFROS (Taller de Etnohistoria de la Frontera Sur), Periplos (Programa de Estudios de las Relaciones Interétnicas y los Pueblos Originarios de las Fronteras), and l'Association Suisse des Américanistes and is an associate researcher with the Centre de Recherche sur l'Amérique Espagnole Coloniale (CRAEC) de l'Université Sorbonne-Nouvelle, Paris 3.

Peter B. Villella is Associate Professor of History at the United States Air Force Academy. His research centers on the political, legal, and intellectual activities of indigenous leaders in New Spain. He is the author of *Indigenous Elites and Creole Identity in Colonial Mexico* (2016) and coeditor and translator of Fernando de Alva Ixtlilxochitl's *History of the Chichimeca Nation* (2019). He has been a fellow with the National Humanities Center and the American Council of Learned Societies. Currently, he is Executive Director of the American Society for Ethnohistory and a contributing editor of the Library of Congress's *Handbook of Latin American Studies*.

Patrick S. Werner (d. 2019) was retired as Professor at Keiser University and served as the Appointed Director of Archaeology by HKND of the Nicaraguan Gran Canal. He authored several monographs on the colonial history of Nicaragua, including *Los Reales de Minas y la Ciudad Perdida de Nueva Segovia* (1996), *Época Temprana de León Viejo, La Primera Capital de Nicaragua* (2000), *Ethnohistory of Early Colonial Nicaragua* (2000), and *Etnohistoria de la Nicaragua Temprana* (2009).

Index

References to illustrations appear in italic type.

Acuña y Silva, Rodrigo, 203, 213n69
Adrean y Salas, Antonio, 92–96, 100–102, 103–4, 110n51
adultery, 93, 94–95, 96–97, 178–79
Agara, Carolina de, 4
alcohol. *See* drinking and drunkenness
Altman, Ida, 11, 24, 32; prologue, 1–8
Alva, Bartolomé de, 55
Alva Ixtlilxochitl, Fernando de, 55, 60n9, 275
Alvarado Tezozomoc, Hernando de, 275
Alva y Cortés, Josefa Antonia de, 56–58
Amaru, José Gabriel Tupac. *See* Tupac Amaru II (José Gabriel Condorcanqui)
Amigorena, José Francisco de, 246, 255, 256
Anacaona, 3, 6, 11; in fiction, 7n5
Ancán Amún, 246, 254
Ango, Beatriz, 188n60
Ango, Luis, 177
Ango, Otavalango. *See* Otavalango Ango
Ango Quilago, Ana, 178–79
Anrrafernango Puento Maldonado, Alonso, 175
Antepán (died 1803), 255–56, 267n67
Antepán (died 1802), 256, 267n67
Apaza, Gregoria, 224, 225
Apaza, Julián. *See* Tupac Katari
Araucanians, 242–43
archaeology, 6, 11, 12, 166
Arias, José de, 91, 93, 101
Arredondo, Nicolás de, 251

Atotoztli, 45
Aucas, 241, 247, 262n21
Avendaño, Miguel de, 152
Ayabibix, Catalina de, 4
Aymara regions, 21, 22, 31, 33, 233n2
Ayra, Francisca, 157–59
Ayra, Francisco, 157, 159
Ayra, Pedro, 157, 159
Ayra, Santiago, 158
Aztec Triple Alliance, 46, 53, 60n6

Barrionuevo, Feliciana and María de, 155
bastardy and "illegitimate" children, 158, 159, 174, 176
Bastidas, Micaela, 225, 237n49, 238n72
Bautista Curicaya, Juan, 157
blood purity. *See* limpieza de sangre
Bolaños, Ambassador. *See* Vega Bolaños, Andrés
Bourbon Reforms, 13–14, 29, 221, 223
Bravo, Juan, 4

Cabello de Balboa, Miguel, 145
"cacica": word, 4, 31–32; from tlatoani to cacica, 53, 58
cacica nuns, 9, 23, 31, 63, 64, 77, 78, 269, 270; historiography, 15, 27, 104–5; portraits, 9, 31
"cacica principal" (title), 155, 158
cacicas, diplomacy by. *See* diplomacy by cacicas
"cacica y gobernadora" (title), 215, 226, 231, 232, 276

327

Printed in the USA
CPSIA information can be obtained
at www.ICGtesting.com
CBHW030212140924
14499CB00004B/525